WILLIAM AND LUCY
THE OTHER ROSSETTIS

WILLIAM AND LUCY

THE OTHER ROSSETTIS

Angela Thirlwell

Yale University Press   New Haven & London

Copyright © 2003 by Angela Thirlwell

Library of Congress Cataloging-in-Publication Data
Thirlwell, Angela.
    The other Rossettis : a joint biography of William Michael Rossetti
and Lucy Madox Brown Rossetti / by Angela Thirlwell.
            p. cm.
Includes bibliographical references and index.
    ISBN 0-300-10200-3 (perm. paper)
    1. Rossetti, William Michael, 1829-1919. 2. Rossetti, Lucy Madox
Brown, 1843-1894. 3. Artist couples--England--Biography. 4.
Authors--England--Biography. 5. Pre-Raphaelite Brotherhood. 6.
Aesthetics, British--19th century. I. Title: Joint biography of William
Michael Rossetti and Lucy Madox Brown Rossetti. II. Title.
    NX543.Z9R6737 2003
    700'.92'241--dc21

                                        20030109

Typeset in Bembo; typesetting and design by Kate Gallimore
Printed in China

Quotation from 'The Love Song of J. Alfred Prufrock' from *Collected Poems 1909–1962* by T.S. Eliot, by kind permission of Faber and Faber Ltd.

Illustration on page ii: William Michael Rossetti (aged 11), *Viola*, signed and dated on verso, January 1841. Pen, ink and watercolour, 75 × 50 mm. Private collection.
Illustrations on pages vi and viii/ix by Cliff Guttridge.

For John, Zoë and Adam

William and Lucy's London.

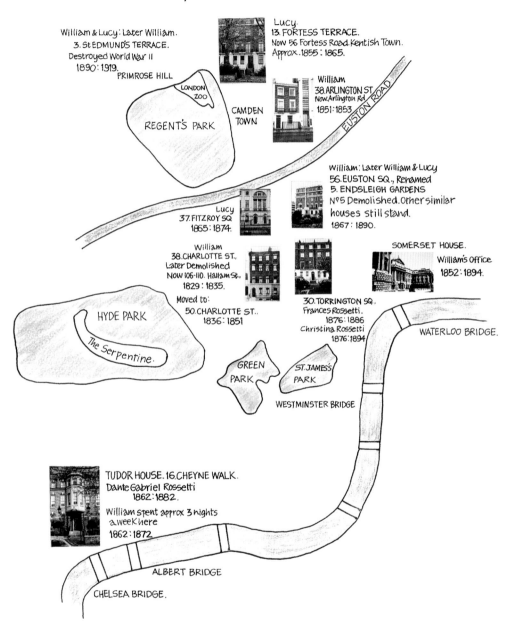

William & Lucy: Later William.
3. St EDMUND'S TERRACE.
Destroyed World War II
1890 : 1919.
PRIMROSE HILL

LONDON ZOO

REGENT'S PARK

CAMDEN TOWN

Lucy.
13. FORTESS TERRACE.
Now 56 Fortess Road. Kentish Town.
Approx. 1855 : 1865.

William
38. ARLINGTON ST.
Now. Arlington Rd.
1851 : 1853

EUSTON ROAD

William: Later William & Lucy
56. EUSTON SQ., Renamed
5. ENDSLEIGH GARDENS
No 5 Demolished. Other similar
houses still stand.
1867 : 1890.

Lucy
37. FITZROY SQ
1865 : 1874.

William
38. CHARLOTTE ST.,
Later Demolished
Now 106-110. Hallam St.,
1829 : 1835.

Moved to:
50. CHARLOTTE ST..
1836 : 1851

HYDE PARK

The Serpentine.

30. TORRINGTON SQ.,
Frances Rossetti.
1876 : 1886
Christina Rossetti
1876 : 1894

SOMERSET HOUSE.
William's Office
1852 : 1894.

WATERLOO BRIDGE.

GREEN PARK

ST. JAMES'S PARK

WESTMINSTER BRIDGE

TUDOR HOUSE. 16. CHEYNE WALK.
Dante Gabriel Rossetti
1862 : 1882.

William spent approx 3 nights
a week here
1862 : 1872.

ALBERT BRIDGE

CHELSEA BRIDGE.

CONTENTS

ROSSETTI

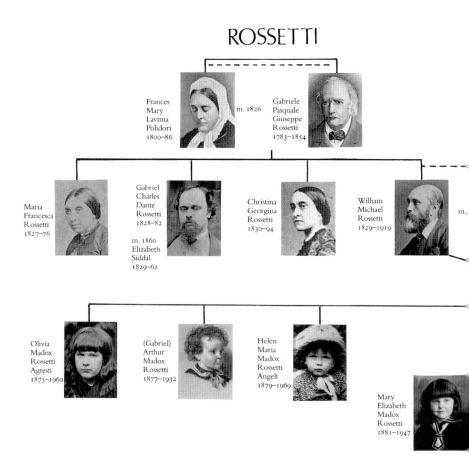

Frances Mary Lavinia Polidori 1800–86

m. 1826

Gabriele Pasquale Giuseppe Rossetti 1783–1854

Maria Francesca Rossetti 1827–76

Gabriel Charles Dante Rossetti 1828–82

m. 1860 Elizabeth Siddal 1829–62

Christina Georgina Rossetti 1830–94

William Michael Rossetti 1829–1919

m.

Olivia Madox Rossetti Agresti 1875–1960

(Gabriel) Arthur Madox Rossetti 1877–1932

Helen Maria Madox Rossetti Angeli 1879–1969

Mary Elizabeth Madox Rossetti 1881–1947

BROWN

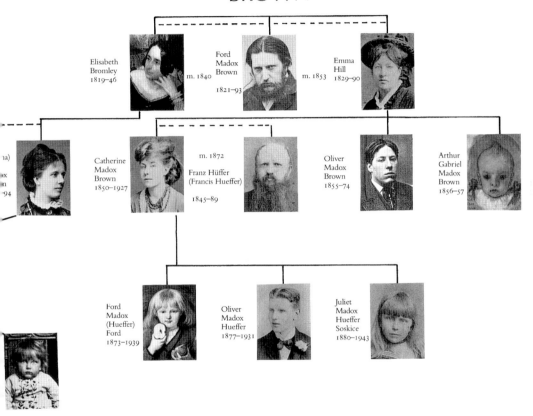

Elisabeth Bromley 1819–46 — m. 1840 — Ford Madox Brown 1821–93 — m. 1853 — Emma Hill 1829–90

(na) ...ex ...n ...94

Catherine Madox Brown 1850–1927 — m. 1872 — Franz Hüffer (Francis Hueffer) 1845–89

Oliver Madox Brown 1855–74

Arthur Gabriel Madox Brown 1856–57

Ford Madox (Hueffer) Ford 1873–1939

Oliver Madox Hueffer 1877–1931

Juliet Madox Hueffer Soskice 1880–1943

ACKNOWLEDGEMENTS

William Michael Rossetti had a gift for friendship. So did Lucy, although she knew she could make enemies. Researching their lives has given me many new friends across the world. First, I would like to thank today's generation of Rossetti and Madox Brown descendants and family members in England and in Italy who have offered me unfailing access to their collections of visual and literary material. Chief among these has been Mary Rossetti Rutterford to whom I am particularly grateful for her unique expertise and constant encouragement throughout the project. I have also had enormous help and kindness from the late Roderic O'Conor, Turlough and Nell O'Conor, Dr Rory O'Conor, Susan Plowden, Charles and Angela Rossetti, Cicely Rossetti, Geoffrey Rossetti, the late Joan Rossetti, Nick Rossetti, and the Hon. Oliver Soskice. I offer special thanks to Helen and Luigi Guglielmini, and Edward Dennis.

In Canada, the late Dick Fredeman gave me unstinting help and the run of his miraculous private collection of Pre-Raphaelite material, while his wife Betty was constantly hospitable. In Italy, Rodolfo and Valerie Falchi made research into Lucy's time at San Remo continually exciting. They also identified her grave. In England, Sue Bradbury of the Folio Society initiated my first publication on William Michael Rossetti and always encouraged me. Virginia Surtees offered me the benefit of her unsurpassed knowledge of Dante Gabriel Rossetti's works. In addition, I would like to thank the following scholars, collectors and friends who have helped me in many different ways: Victor Adams, Claire Alexander, John Allitt, Gary Attlesey, Professor John Batchelor, Georgina Battiscombe, Mary Bennett, Paul and Suzanne Bergne, Judith Bronkhurst, Georgie, Lady Colin Campbell, Robert Cannon, Michael Cayley, John Christian, David Clifford, Genene Collins, Elena Colombo, John Constable, Colin Cruise, Maria Ricci Curlo, Betty Daughton, Kate Denby, Marie Eller, Valerie Fehlbaum, the Lady Gibson, Alfred Goldman, Paul Goldman, Lavinia Greacen, Jonathon Greene, Antony H. Harrison, Anne Harvey, Laurie Harwood, Michelle Hawley, Michael Hickox, Carola Hicks, Elsa Honig Fine, Simon Humphries, Barry Johnson, Elaine Kaye, Father Ian Ker, Lorraine Janzen Kooistra, Professor Niki Lacey, David Lanch, Mark Samuels Lasner, Deborah Lavin, Edith Leathart, Dr Gilbert Leathart, Julie L'Enfant, Rupert Maas, Katharine Macdonald, Peter Mandler, Jan Marsh, Phyllis Marshall, Tim McGee, Ernest Mehew, Jonathan Miles, Sir Geoffroy Millais, Julian Moore, Alicia Moss, Geoffrey Munn, Nita Murray-Smith, Peter

Nunn, Patricia O'Connor, Professor Leonée Ormond and Richard Ormond, Richard Owen, Professor Roger Peattie, Stephen Ponder, Patricia Potts, Christabel Powell, Peter Prosser, David Rintoul, Len Roberts, Andrea Rose, Professor Max Saunders, Dottoressa Elvira Serafini, Julian Shales, Francis Sharp, Gloria Simmons, Sue Soudah, Professor Allen Staley, Andrew Stauffer, Meg Tasker, Julian Treuherz, Edward Wakeling, Caroline White, Christopher Whittick, Stephen Wildman, Christopher Wood, Tom Wood, Robert Wright and Giulia Zoccai.

For invaluable, specialist advice on Lucy's tuberculosis I thank Dr Elspeth Macdonald, Dr Douglas Puccini and Dr I.P. Williams.

Of the many libraries and public collections which have shown me continued courtesy and professional knowledge, I would like to thank first George Brandak and staff at the University of British Columbia Library, Rare Books and Special Collections. Also Colin Harris, Modern Papers, Department of Western Manuscripts at the Bodleian Library, Oxford, and Sally Brown, Manuscripts, at the British Library and all staff at the British Library. In addition, my thanks go to Arizona State University; Balliol College Library, Oxford; the Bancroft Library at Berkeley, University of California; the Biblioteca Bicknell at Bordighera; Tessa Sidey at Birmingham Museum and Art Gallery; Ian Jenkins, Greek and Roman Antiquities at the British Museum; Donato Esposito, Prints and Drawings at the British Museum; British Library Newspaper Library at Colindale; Eric L. Pumroy, Special Collections at Bryn Mawr College; Peter Martland, Cambridge University Library; Chelsea Local Studies Centre; Jeremy Rex-Parkes at Christie's Archives; City University Library; Bernard Crystal, Columbia University, Rare Book and Manuscript Library; Frederick Bauman at the Library of Congress, Washington; the Book and Witt Libraries at the Courtauld Institute of Art; Rare and Manuscript Collections at Cornell University; Kraig Binkowski at the Delaware Art Museum Library; Trinity College Library, Dublin; National Library of Scotland, Edinburgh; the Fawcett Library; Department of Manuscripts and Printed Books at the Fitzwilliam Museum, Cambridge; Miriam Stewart at the Fogg Art Museum, Harvard University; Folger Shakespeare Library, Washington; Paola Forneris at the Biblioteca Civica, San Remo; the Getty Center for the History of Art and the Humanities; Glasgow University Library, Special Collections; Harry Ransom Humanities Research Center, University of Texas at Austin; House of Lords Record Office; Miriam Stewart, Fogg Art Museum, Harvard University; Huntington Library, California; the Brotherton Library, University of Leeds; the London Library; the London Metropolitan Archives; Manchester Archives Service; Peter McNiven at the John Rylands Library, University of Manchester; Manchester Town Hall; Rare Books and Special Collections at the University of Minnesota Library; Antonia Leak, Heinz Archive Library at the National Portrait Gallery and Tim Morton at the National Portrait

Gallery; the New York Public Library; Rodney Phillips at the Berg Collection at the NYPL; Stephen Wagner at the Pforzheimer Library, NYPL; Isabelle Pébay at the Musée national du château de Pau; the Pierpont Morgan Library; Margaret Sherry Rich at Rare Books and Special Collections, Princeton University Library; Mike Bott at Reading University Library; Dr David Sutton at the Watch Project, Reading University; the National Art Library at the Victoria and Albert Museum; Monty Smith and Tracy Clement at Wightwick Manor, National Trust; Westminster Reference Library; Yale Center for British Art and Yale University Beinecke Rare Book and Manuscript Library.

My thanks also to Bonham's Book Department, Harriet Drummond of British Drawings and Watercolours at Christie's, Phillip's Book Department and Sotheby's Book Department. If I have inadvertently omitted to mention individuals or collections, I hope they will forgive me.

I am indebted to the following web sites: Jerome McGann's Rossetti Archive at www.jefferson.village.virginia.edu/rossetti/index.html; The Pre-Raphaelite Critic at www.engl.duq.edu/servus/PR_Critic, and John J. McCusker, 'Comparing the purchasing power of money in Great Britain from 1264 to any other year including the present', Economic History Services at http://www.eh.net/hmit/ppowerbp/

I should like to thank the Paul Mellon Centre for awarding me two research travel grants in 1998 and 2000, which enabled me to visit important manuscript libraries in Canada and the USA. At the end of the project, the Marc Fitch Fund gave me a major grant towards photographic expenses for which I am extremely grateful. The Authors' Foundation kindly made me an award towards transcribing costs.

Special thanks to Beth Emanuel for transcribing William Michael Rossetti's diaries, as well as some hundreds of his many thousands of letters; to Linda Matlin for transcribing Lucy's letters to William; and to Richard Packard for his dextrous eye surgery.

Many thanks to John Nicoll, my editor at Yale University Press for his support, also to Jacob Lehman, to Kate Gallimore, to Douglas Matthews for the index, and to my agent Giles Gordon for believing in the project from the start. I should also like to thank Cliff Guttridge for endless patience with artwork and photography. My thanks to R. White Cabinets of Dorset for my filing system and to Andrew Lownie whose Biographers' Club provided regular infusions of stimulating talk about the art of biography.

Above all, I want to thank my family who have lived with William and Lucy as well as me over the past seven years. To John, Zoë and Adam Thirlwell goes my love and gratitude for their constant support, re-readings and advice.

INTRODUCTION

As promoter, transcriber, writer and editor, William Michael Rossetti invented our view of the Pre-Raphaelite Brotherhood. And yet he is the least understood of all the Pre-Raphaelites. This biography is a dual portrait of an eminent Victorian and his artist wife, Lucy Madox Brown, who was also intimately connected with the Pre-Raphaelite circle.

Two atypical Victorians, William, art critic and author, and Lucy, painter and writer, married in 1874 – unusually for their times but faithful to their unbelief – in a register office. Their lives thus spliced together were not neatly co-ordinated. Born in 1829, William did not die until 1919, in his ninetieth year. Lucy was born in 1843, nearly fourteen years after William, but died when she was fifty in 1894, leaving William with twenty-five years to live.

That amounts to almost 140 years of lived experience. Rather than attempting to convey this long raft of years in the conventional format of a linear, chronological biography, I have chosen a 'spots of experience' structure. The reader enters a portrait gallery displaying most of the known likenesses of Lucy and William, in order to give an initial overview of each life story. The subsequent chapters focus on particular areas of activity in their lives, either individually – such as Artist (Lucy), Man of Letters (William), or jointly – Radicals, Marriage, The Patient. The demarcations are fluid. Inevitably, Lucy impacts on the 'William' chapters, and William walks in to the 'Lucy' chapters. Underlying this arrangement is the natural thrust of chronology.

The structure of thematic chapters is intended to build up an impression of both lives, by increments, rather than subscribing to the biographic fallacy that a Life, or in this case, two Lives, with all their fragmentary atoms of experience, can be artificially re-created as a fiction-like narrative, with significant structure, major turning-points and recurring patterns.

Coming from the future, as biography does, to re-examine the past, it cannot reanimate dead subjects exactly as they once lived. I can only re-imagine William and Lucy and present a version. My version. A selective version.

Like Lytton Strachey's biographer's bucket. In his luminescent marine image, the biographer, the explorer of the past, 'will row out over that great ocean of material, and lower down into it, here and there, a little bucket, which will bring up to the light of day some characteristic specimen, from those far depths, to be examined with a careful curiosity.' Or, like a geologist drilling down through the layers of the earth's crust at certain local points, a biographer may sink probes into the accumulated strata of lives, and bring up samples for analysis, whose results may prove both specific and universal.

Those who sift the evidence can interpret the findings of biographic investigation in a myriad different ways. There are as many views of a life as there are biographers to write it, just as there are as many facets of a face as there are artists to paint it. Biography, like translation, can never be definitive. But it can be the first. And this is the first biography of either William or Lucy.

It is an irony that, as the facilitator of the Pre-Raphaelite and Rossetti family myths, William Michael Rossetti was responsible for downplaying his own reputation and, by association, Lucy's. He had been a key player in the Pre-Raphaelite Brotherhood, its advocate, secretary, myth-maker and historian. 'In any other family he would have been famous in his own right', the *New York Bookman* said when he died. William E. Fredeman, pioneer of modern Pre-Raphaelite studies, estimated that of all the more flamboyantly glamorous figures associated with the Brotherhood, William 'was almost the only man of action, and without him there would have been no Brotherhood, no *Germ*, no *PRB Journal*, and no movement to leave its mark on the history of English art'. As Roger Fry did later for Bloomsbury, in his writings William gave identity to the loosely unstructured Pre-Raphaelite movement. In tandem with his full-time career as Assistant Secretary to the Board of Inland Revenue, remarkably he became a prolific and influential critic of Victorian art and literature, and a cultural barometer, an innovator and arbiter of contemporary taste.

In her relatively short artistic career, Lucy Madox Brown painted pictures of high intellectual ambition and genuine accomplishment. Although art was her real *métier*, she wrote a biography of Mary Shelley, considered in detail here for the first time. Examining the trauma of her decade-long struggle with tuberculosis illuminates her personality, the experience of a Victorian patient, and the effects of chronic illness on a marriage.

Lucy and William's relationship provides a fresh perspective on nineteenth-century marriage and challenges our notions of how Victorians behaved in private. They were an unusual couple, sexually frank, avowedly agnostic, politically radical and committedly feminist. Hundreds of unpublished surviving letters between them preserve their distinctive voices and characteristic speech rhythms – William erudite, self-mocking and expressive, Lucy playful, breathless, anxious and questing. The brisk pace of the Victorian postal service allowed interactive correspondence between the partners, sometimes twice a day, leaving a beguiling impression of authentic conversation. Many contemporaries thought Lucy a brilliant conversationalist and her voice may be heard here for the first time. Wherever possible, I have used their own voices and the voices of their contemporaries to speak for the personalities of William and Lucy, in the tone and vocabulary of their times.

Lucy's wit and vivacity is also evident from many contemporary diaries – not just William's, which he kept assiduously for over half a century. A unique record of a life, William made a conscious decision not to destroy his diaries and was quizzical when he heard that a fellow-critic, Frederic George Stephens, had burnt his. By contrast, William conserved, annotated and archived letters, documents, press cuttings and every ephemera, labelled and listed his pictures, books and furniture. As a writer of biography himself, he lobbed into the future the raw material for his own and Lucy's.

Researching the lives of Lucy and William, even in the over-trawled archives of Pre-Raphaelite studies, has revealed striking new visual material, notably an *oeuvre* of drawings by William, some previously invisible work by Lucy, unseen portraits by Ford Madox Brown, William Bell Scott, Arthur Hughes and John Everett Millais, as well as vivid contemporary photographs. The mainsprings of William and Lucy's lives were literature and art, and the intersections between cultural life and private emotions. These re-discovered 'other Rossettis' were both of their times and ahead of them, Victorians with a modern dimension.

William and Lucy

A Certain Tremor

February 1887 had been unseasonably capricious on the Italian Riviera. A wintry dawn had not yet lit the modest *pensione* room where Lucy's canvases, paints, palettes and drawing materials were stacked in a corner and a copy of William's just published edition of Dante Gabriel Rossetti's *Collected Works* lay open on the bureau. Without warning, an ominous subterranean engine rumbled deep beneath the earth's surface and wrenched Lucy and William from sleep. All at once their bed 'heaved up and down under us' like 'the rolling of a ship from side to side.'[1] Jars and jugs, ewer and wash-basin crashed together in the bedroom. Eerily not a single drop of water spilt. In spite of the chronic state of her lungs, Lucy immediately jumped out of bed, galvanized by passionate maternal instincts, and rushed into the next room to wake eleven-year-old Olivia, while William roused Arthur who was nearly ten.

Although the earthquake tipped one man right out of bed, incredibly no one was injured at the Hôtel-Pension Anglo-Américaine. William and Lucy both felt an aftershock and many hotel guests reported a series of minor successive quakes. Everyone came down to breakfast as usual to compare experiences of the early hours and confer with Signor Milano, the hotel proprietor. At first the building appeared to be stable but nevertheless the owner advised immediate evacuation. So all the guests including Lucy, William, Olive and Arty decamped to the garden. Many of the foreigners were delicate, suffering like Lucy from a range of asthmatic, bronchial and unspoken tubercular conditions. San Remo in February seemed an exotic, flowery hothouse, a safe haven to northern Europeans. It especially appeared so from a distance. When Christina Rossetti – who had never visited San Remo – wrote to her brother and sister-in-law from smoky London, she imagined it as an 'earthly-paradise'.[2]

But even in dazzling sunshine the wind could cut through shrinking flesh. William Michael Rossetti had arrived in late January to join Lucy who, on the insistent advice of Dr Wilson Fox, had been staying on the Ligurian Riviera since 16 November with their two eldest children. 'The weather was at first most brilliant, and, so long as the sun was above the horizon, scarcely

5

to be distinguished from an English June or July', he enthused, although he noticed an ominous and 'substantial sub-stratum of cold, and also of wind. These three days past the weather is spoiled – raining, dull, and once snowy: but I suppose it may mend again. The earlier the better.'[3]

Then suddenly, the morning after the *terremoto* dawned tranquil, lucent and unnaturally still. Witnesses noticed extremely high atmospheric pressure, the sun veiled in light mist and a quiescent sea subsiding by up to 30 centimetres. William observed: 'Nature seemed to have lulled herself into a dreamless sleep after the one spasmodic effort, and there was scarcely a breath of air stirring.'[4] The hotel garden became a Victorian extra-mural drawing-room with ladies sitting out, reading or knitting, men strolling among them smoking and chatting. The English invalids had brought both their manners and their phlegm to the Italian resort, only a little less fashionable than Cannes and Nice. 'If an earthquake were to engulf England tomorrow', commented one social observer dryly, 'the English would manage to meet and dine somewhere among the rubbish, just to celebrate the event.'[5]

As further damage to property was feared that evening, everyone slept outside in spherical white tents, so that gardens and public spaces looked like medieval jousting yards lit up by fires for light and warmth. This experience thoroughly unnerved Lucy who, because of her consumptive tendency, was terrified of night air. She usually only ventured out of doors for an hour or so either side of noon. On this post-earthquake night she fretted additionally about young Arty who had caught a feverish cold. Most of the population of San Remo also camped out, crowding onto the promenade and the beach. By chance, no one in the town died or was injured in the earthquake. Much property was pronounced unsafe, though hardly dangerous enough, in William's opinion, to justify the later opportunist rebuilding programme that vulgarized the authentic, medieval charm of the old town.

However, a few miles away in the hills behind San Remo, the village of Baiardo was completely devastated. 'In the earliest morning of that Ash Wednesday the villagers had thronged the church to receive the ashes' when 'the church crashed down upon them', killing about two hundred people (fig. 1).[6]

In the whole province of Porto Maurizio (now Imperia) over 600 people died and hundreds were injured. Only a few hours after Bacchanalian sounds of revelry and *carnevale* had faded away, the town of Diano Marina was devastated at the epicentre of an area affected from Genoa to Nice. The first violent seismic shifts, accompanied by rumbling thunder, registered Grade 9 or 'Disastrosa' on the Italian 'Mercalli' earthquake scale. Bells tolled, people tumbled to the ground, houses collapsed as the jolts and tremors continued. 'Sand bounced on the sea shore as if on a vibrating metal sheet.' Cries and moans were heard from the debris. 'Some had found immediate burial in their own beds, others fled or rushed from their dwellings' only to be

1. The church at Baiardo after the earthquake, 1887. From *Sanremo com'era* (Sanremo: Famia Sanremasca, 1974).

crushed by falling walls in the narrow, ancient streets. At least three further tremors occurred up till 9 a.m. and no one could predict whether or when worse might follow.[7]

Fears and statistics like these immediately panicked Lucy into abandoning San Remo, although the town had escaped relatively lightly from the earthquake and had done her so much good over the past few months. The Ligurian sunlight had stirred Lucy's creativity which over the past decade she had redirected into fierce maternity of her five children. Painting again, she sent her pictures for critical comment to her father Ford Madox Brown, together with boxes of citrus and blooms from the south. 'Your flowers & your oranges & your pictures seemed quite startling', he wrote from wintry Manchester, 'with your blue skies contrasted with our grey shadows here. That of the young Italian lady [Signorina Carsini, the children's Italian teacher[8]] is nice in sentiment & quality. If you worked regularly I think you would regain your old colour & skill, but the landskapes [*sic*] are rather cruder colour than pleasant', although he accepted she was responding to Italy's vibrant tones and shades.[9]

William tried to dissuade her from leaving San Remo but at the earliest opportunity they set off for Dijon where they had to separate. He returned to his desk at the Board of Inland Revenue in London. Lucy remained with Olive and Arty at the Hôtel de la Cloche, favoured by many other refugees driven inland by the earthquake that had been felt all along the Riviera. She breathlessly justified her decision to decamp. 'A General who had lived in a country where there were 40 shocks a year said it was nothing to this earthquake.'[10] 'A great many English have come for a day or two from the scene of the Earthquake unable to remain after all, today some people came from Cannes where they said it was really felt very slightly and yet it had such an effect upon their nerves that it was impossible to stay longer than this.'[11]

After an anxious exchange of telegrams with William, his sister Christina Rossetti voiced her own fears, which echoed Lucy's. 'What an awful awestriking experience an earthquake must be…I cannot help wishing that you and yours may already be on the homeward road. Of course, no more shocks may ensue', she conceded, 'but who can feel even ordinarily secure at San Remo after what has happened?'[12] Always paradoxically closer from a distance, Christina empathized with Lucy and underlined the bonds of sisterhood. 'My dear Lucy, So *I* was in your kind thoughts at such a moment! I hope never to forget it with sisterly love and gratitude. I fully agree with you that it is impossible to pass through so awful an experience without deep impressions: the suspense…sent me to prayer…What alarming prognostics till the end of this year are published about earthquakes on the Riviera.'[13] In spite of her terrors, the earthquake had not sent Lucy to prayer, as she told her father, 'One singular thing which struck William & myself was that no one in our hotel ventured to pray or speak of God.' Lucy observed that people only began to refer to God's protection four days later when the threat of further earth movements had subsided.[14]

Eventually, the Hôtel-Pension Anglo-Américaine, a short walk from San Remo's original nineteenth-century railway station, was demolished and never rebuilt. No trace of it now remains on a street once called the Corso Ponente.[15] William reported press comment at the time, which circulated the theory that earthquake survivors can never entirely forget their experiences: 'A certain tremor continues lurking in the nerves'.[16] Five years later when staying at the more sedate spa town of Malvern Wells, which registered a smaller quake, Lucy noticed to her horror the windows shuddering without a breath of wind. She stayed awake all night, waiting for earthquakes.[17]

I

Portraits

Images of William and Lucy Rossetti hang in a virtual nineteenth-century portrait gallery, their faces filtered and fixed through an artist's gaze or a photographer's lens. Art was at the centre of both their lives. A late Pre-Raphaelite artist, Lucy was the daughter of painter Ford Madox Brown. William, the art critic and author, was brother to Dante Gabriel Rossetti. Portraits left to posterity, either by intention or by chance, provide unique access into Lucy and William's stories, self-images and fantasies. A face on canvas or on the photographer's plate is of course an artful and an artificial construction, doubly arranged, both by its owner and its interpreter. Yet we endlessly scan portraits to glean something significant about the character behind the face and about the past itself.

In considering two lives that were both so concerned, in their differing ways, with visual messages, portraits of Lucy and William are not merely fascinating in themselves but also fulfil a special biographical function. Fine art portraits entail a temporal, talking relationship between artist and sitter which may result in more leisured insights into personality, different from swifter photographic likenesses. Pencil, brush and lens are all instruments of assessment. Photography was a rapidly developing new medium in William and Lucy's era and over his long lifetime (1829–1919), William at least learnt how to manipulate it. Portraits of him range from a little boy of nine to an old man in his eighties.

Set side by side, two portraits of William, one in childhood, one in old age, are emblematic of his passage through life (figs 2 and 3). As a child William is subsidiary (physically smaller or placed at a lower level) in relation to his elder brother, Dante Gabriel Rossetti. Unlike Gabriel who faces the viewer head-on, William's diffident gaze is slightly diverted. He has no control over the artful composition of Pistrucci,[1] a practitioner of traditional watercolours. By contrast, in his eighties, William is totally in command of the new art of photography. Assured, at the centre of the picture, against a backdrop of books indicating his life's work, William is no longer diminished. The sole surviving Rossetti, he examines the camera as rigorously as the lens inquires of him.

2. Dante Gabriel Rossetti and William Michael Rossetti as children. From a watercolour by Filippo Pistrucci, published in William Michael Rossetti, *Gabriele Rossetti: A Versified Autobiography*, 1901.

3. Photograph of William Michael Rossetti at eighty, in front of his books, 22 June 1910. Private collection.

Though both are touched with mortality, the juxtaposition recalls Susan Sontag's insight that the sitter is somehow more in command of his or her image in a photograph than in an artist's picture, 'it is in the nature of a photograph that it can never entirely transcend its subject, as a painting can.'[2] Many portraits of William in maturity survive – drawn, painted and photographed; far fewer of Lucy Madox Brown Rossetti who, with her intense self-consciousness, dreaded the camera. Yet her father, Ford Madox Brown, managed to describe her face repeatedly in its many shifting phases of childhood.

On 5 December 1847, Brown noted in his diary, 'It is today 18 months since the death of my poor wife. These are thoughts I must banish, it unnerves me. I have dedicated the day to my child and the memory of her mother.' In tribute to his dead wife he drew a delicate sketch of their 'beautiful babe', with her soft hair tumbling to her shoulders (fig. 4).

The adult Lucy usually evaded the camera or the artist's brush but occasionally her father or her brother-in-law, Dante Gabriel Rossetti, were allowed to portray her, and once or twice her half-sister, Cathy, notated her face. Images of William tacitly speak of a far greater natural physical confidence than Lucy possessed. Ease with his body increased with maturity; exacerbated by illness, her self-image dived into parallel decline.

William published a rare pencil portrait of himself by Dante Gabriel Rossetti in his biography of his brother in 1895 (fig. 5).[3] Few portraits of William by Gabriel survive. This early half-length portrait in profile is variously dated 1846, 1847 or 1848.[4] Whichever is accurate, it shows William still in his teens. On 6 February 1845 aged fifteen, his education at King's College School brusquely terminated, he began full-time employment as a clerk at the Excise Office in Old Broad Street. Family finances dictated this decision, as there was little expectation that his elder brother, the multi-talented Gabriel should find a mundane job. William's young face is casual, sensitive. The clothes are not expensive but are studied, the beginning of a lifelong trend.

Even though New Year's Day 1853 was a Saturday, William would have spent that morning at the office. Joining friends later he instantly fell asleep, to be impaled by his brother's mocking pen (fig. 6). Writing gleefully to his ex-Pre-Raphaelite Brother, sculptor Thomas Woolner, Gabriel inserted a sketch of William slumped in exhaustion 'while I write, in one of his usual anti-anatomical actions. The candle has just been gulped into its socket, and I wake him unrelentingly to ask him if there is another in the room. He says "no" with benevolent self-possession, and falls asleep again.'[5]

Gabriel drew William again, on 12 April 1853, the day those who remained from the original seven Pre-Raphaelite Brothers met to draw each other's portraits, as presents for Woolner who had sailed to Australia the previous year (fig. 7). Gabriel signed, dated and inscribed his picture of William – 'to Thomas Woolner/Edward Bateman/Bernhard Smith'.[6] On this very same day, in the same series of portraits for Woolner, William drew an exquisitely delicate profile head of Millais (see fig. 55).

4. Ford Madox Brown, *Lucy at Four Years, Four Months*, 1847. Pencil, 135 × 163 mm. Signed with monogram, dated Dec 5/47, inscribed at a later date to Lucy's half-sister, Cathy Madox Brown Hueffer. National Museums, Liverpool (the Walker).

6. Dante Gabriel Rossetti, *William Michael Rossetti Asleep*, Saturday, 1 January 1853. Published in Amy Woolner, *Thomas Woolner*, 1917.

5. Dante Gabriel Rossetti, *William Michael Rossetti*, 1846/7/8. Pencil, 254 × 203 mm. Published in *DGRFLM*, II, 1895. Surtees 452, pl. 416.

7. Dante Gabriel Rossetti, *William Michael Rossetti*, 12 April 1853. Pencil, 255 × 185 mm. By courtesy of the National Portrait Gallery, London.

8. John Everett Millais, *William Michael Rossetti*, October 1852. Pen and ink, 172.5 × 105 mm. Private collection.

9. Arthur Hughes, *William Michael Rossetti*, 1854. Pen and ink, 172.5 × 107.5 mm. Private collection.

At twenty-three, William's high forehead was already accentuated by his receding hairline. 'Between you and me, I have long thought that the fact of his early misfortune of *baldness* may have rather affected his innermost feelings. He was a very good-looking man and he had almost as much feeling for beauty in man and woman as his brother had, and tho' he did not speak about it, he cannot have liked losing all his hair at 19 or 20', wrote his daughter, Helen Rossetti Angeli.[7] The eyes, which are the main feature of most of William's portraits, here are large and expressive, the nose nearly aquiline (with a slight bump at the end) but the mouth is set in a disconsolate *moue*. Bureaucratic days at the office are taking their toll. The mood of the drawing is sombre, brooding, and pensive. His brother's soft grey pencil captures a subtle sense of inner disappointment.

But throughout his life, up to extreme old age, portraits testify that William had charisma and sensitivity. Two hitherto unpublished drawings by John Everett Millais (fig. 8) and Arthur Hughes (fig. 9) reveal that both artists saw these qualities, although very differently, in direct outcome of their own contrasting world views. Millais's more superficial portrait, dated October 1852, evokes a smooth man of the world in suave, confident pen-and-wash strokes. Half a century later William told Frederic George Stephens, 'I don't think it very successful, either as a likeness or otherwise'.[8] Arthur Hughes's more intimate portrait of 1854 perceives a wholly different persona. In his delicate drawing of William's head, Hughes conveys a fineness of character, a distinction of sensibility. These two portraits show two contradictory personalities; placed adjacent to one another they suggest outer and inner man. Millais shows worldly William, man about town, doing, coping, and above all, earning. Arthur Hughes penetrates deeper into William's interior soul. The contrast between these two portraits implies a developing dichotomy in William's own personality; counterpoising them provides a route into his inner dialogue with himself. They hint at the dilemma of T.S. Eliot's Prufrockian man – '(They will say: "How his hair is growing thin!")' – an ironic comedy of reticence (fig. 10).

Coming straight from the office, his city clothes made a humorous contrast with the casual, bohemian garb affected by the other Pre-Raphaelite Brothers. His top hat is at the ready to cover the

> …bald spot in the middle of my hair…
> My morning coat, my collar mounting firmly to the chin,
> My necktie rich and modest, but asserted by a simple pin –[9]

Madox Brown painted William aged twenty-seven (fig.11), in exactly this costume, asserting a neat mulberry necktie fixed with a simple but distinctive black and white onyx pin – for mourning. This kind of pin might have opened or contained a lock of hair. A snake coils round, head down, emblematic of eternal remembrance. By this date the only major loss William had suffered

10. Dante Gabriel Rossetti, caricature of the two brothers, *c.* 1853. Pen and ink, 171 × 197 mm. Surtees 594. Fredeman Family Collection.

11. Ford Madox Brown, *William Michael Rossetti by Gaslight*, 1856/7. Oil on panel, 17 × 16.5 cm. Inscribed 'To FMLR' by FMB. Wightwick Manor, National Trust.

was the death on 26 April 1854 of his father, Gabriele Rossetti, to whom he was never as naturally devoted as to his beloved mother, Frances Mary Lavinia Rossetti. One night at the theatre in Paris in August 1867, to his distress, he lost but later recovered the 'Napoleonic breast pin', which his father had given him years before.[10] It is probably the one in Madox Brown's picture and recurs in William's portraits from this date onwards. Fixed not merely with a pin but strongly handled in oils, Brown delivers William with charge and intensity, a mustachioed mid-Victorian, dramatically lit and shadowed in front of contemporary, bordered wallpaper.

Painting by gaslight, Brown began the picture at 8 o'clock in the evening on 8 November 1856 and worked with concentration until midnight. (It was finally completed a few months later in March 1857.) Knowing such precise detail about the conception of the portrait brings that located moment closer, helps us participate in the relationship between sitter and artist. Brown suggests that William's head has a monumental quality. His eyes are warm and hazel but they avert our gaze. The artist conveys his subject's modesty and other-worldliness, as well as his approachability.

When Pauline, Lady Trevelyan, met William at about this time she thought him so 'beautiful' that she wrote to tell William Bell Scott. Scott agreed. 'He *is* beautiful and one of the best informed and balanced minds I have had the luck to know…I absolutely love him although should not think of telling him so.'[11] Madox Brown's portrait shows William as a man of deep feeling and physical appeal, during the buoyant years between 1855 and 1860 when he was in love with and engaged to Henrietta Rintoul, daughter of R.S. Rintoul, founder-editor of the *Spectator*. William had become the paper's art editor in October 1850, aged twenty-one.

Slipped inside one of the acid-free archive boxes in Special Collections at the University of British Columbia are two amusing but acutely observant sketches of William by his younger sister Christina.[12] Many years later William noted that the smaller one was 'By Christina – The pencil sketch must be meant for me – perhaps done in Normandy in /61'. On squared exercise or graph paper, beneath a jaunty peaked cap, it shows a small, beaky profile looking left, a deeply defined eye socket, exuberant side-whiskers and beard (fig. 12). Faintly untidy and slightly absurd, the likeness has all the marks of an eccentric, mid-Victorian English tourist abroad, reminiscent of Edward Lear's cartoon figures. If William's remembered dating of the sketch is correct, he was only in his early thirties – but it could be of a man double that age.

The second sketch signed with Christina's initials is also on squared paper (fig. 13). This one is more extensive but just as spontaneous. Perched on a bench seat, Christina may have drawn William as they jolted along in a carriage or by train. In his hand is the slim, flip-over travel diary he wrote up habitually every day. Christina has shown William again wearing his cap but she has added his pipe, greatcoat and umbrella, essential accoutrements for an Englishman abroad – and at home – as William himself observed ironically:

> 'Yes,' answered one who met a travelling friend;
> 'I had forgotten that in England you
> Must carry your umbrella every day.
> An Englishman's a centaur of his sort,
> Man cross-bred with umbrella.'[13]

12 and 13. Christina Rossetti, *William Michael Rossetti*, c. 1861. Pencil on squared paper, 140 × 70 mm. University of British Columbia Library, Rare Books and Special Collections, Angeli-Dennis Collection, 10-3.

If these intuitive, comic sketches are souvenirs of Christina's Normandy excursion (one of the only two occasions when she left the British Isles – on both occasions with William and their mother) they may be dated to the weeks 10 June to 13 July 1861, when William was thirty-one. Since April, he had been planning their trip to Coutances, Bayeux, Mont-St-Michel, Paris and Jersey, although with some misgivings, as he told William Bell Scott, 'that, when it comes to the point, my mother, and Christina…will prefer not going'.[14] However, conscious that William was mourning his broken engagement to Henrietta Rintoul six months earlier, Frances and Christina were determined to offer practical, unspoken support. So the travel companions set off from home at 6 a.m. on Monday, 10 June. Although Christina self-mockingly told her friend Amelia Heimann that this was an 'unexampled' break from her usual routine, she enthusiastically recommended the experience. 'I cannot tell you how health-promoting and enjoyable was our Paris and Normandy expedition'.[15]

Christina Rossetti's humorous sketches are in complete contrast with the moody art photographs taken by Julia Margaret Cameron on the lawn at Little Holland House, four years later in 1865 (fig. 14).[16] Cameron theoretically shared with William a 'warts and all' approach to photography which he applied to biography. 'As to spots, they must, I think remain. I could have them touched out,' she wrote, 'but I am, I think, the only photographer who always issues untouched photographs and artists, for this reason, among others, value my photographs. So Mr Watts and Mr Rossetti, and Mr du Maurier write me above all others.'[17] But Cameron's studied technical carelessness disguised her supremely romantic contrivances.

William wears a magisterial, velvet robe, with a splash of satin foulard escaping from the neckline. Julia Margaret Cameron counterpoints artifice with nature, artfully playing with contrasting textures of velvet, skin and whiskers. William's sultry gaze is fixed on the middle distance. His face is dominated by fine, Italian eyes beneath dark brows and by a handsome Victorian beard, indicating actual or wished-for bohemianism. Concealing his unromantic baldness is an artist's beret that perfectly balances the portrait. Julia Margaret Cameron probably chose every detail of William's costume for this sitting. Taking a series of studies and asking him to hold the pose for as long as two minutes' exposure, photographer conspired with sitter to achieve a highly theatrical, sleekly finished image. The stare is soulful, dreamy, but also poised and assured, showing William in his prime at thirty-six, recovered from the débâcle with Henrietta Rintoul.

For his part, William admired Cameron's working methods, explicitly rejecting precise focus, and her subtle achievement in making photographic portraits that rivalled fine art: 'To Mrs Cameron a photographed face is a flash of vitality as well as of light...The power of a strong head, the intellect of a thoughtful one, the harmonious suavity of beauty...all these are given to perfection by her method.'[18]

The extreme artificiality of this image heightens the glamour often attached to old photographs but at the same time averts sentimentality. In her book *On Photography* Susan Sontag writes: 'All photographs are *memento mori*. To take a photograph is to participate in another person's (or thing's) mortality, vulnerability, mutability. Precisely by slicing out this moment and freezing it, all photographs testify to time's relentless melt.'[19] Cameron's unique working method, establishing an almost symbiotic empathy with her subjects, achieved here an indelible image of William, and she knew it, 'I have never had more remarkable success with any Photograph' she wrote to him on 23 January 1866.[20]

14. Julia Margaret Cameron, photograph of William Michael Rossetti, 1865. WMR has inscribed on the back: 'The hand with umbrella is Browning's'; Julia Margaret Cameron sometimes used an umbrella to help angle her dramatic lighting effects. Private collection.

In January 1866, Madox Brown's eldest daughter Lucy was twenty-two years old. William had known her since she was a little girl of six, although she had not been until recently a permanent member of Brown's household. She visited him in Finchley and Kentish Town during school holidays but was educated at her aunt's school in Gravesend, Kent. After the death of her mother, Elisabeth, from consumption, Lucy became a symbol to Brown of everything that he had lost with Elisabeth. So he repeatedly drew and painted Lucy from babyhood onwards.

This first surviving picture of Lucy shows her aged about three months, in an enveloping bonnet edged with lace, tied with flamboyant bows (fig. 15). Her father relished the massive absurdities of babyhood, expressed in free, broad brushstrokes. Her eyes are clear and penetrating, the mouth determined. Although unformed, the face gives some indication of a character in creation. Daughter fixes father with an unwavering gaze, an interactive relationship that was to become an enduring feature of Lucy's adult emotional life.

A few months later in Paris, Madox Brown began *Out of Town*, one of his most touching studies of a mother and child (fig. 16). Brown's first wife, Elisabeth Bromley, and daughter Lucy were the initial models for this picture in 1843–4. After Elisabeth's death, Brown put it aside but eventually finished it in 1858 from different models. Elisabeth wears a fashionable deep purple dress with a lace collar and sleeves. Beneath her streamered straw hat, her hair falls in blond ringlets. In reality, Elisabeth's hair was dark and sleek. Here she has eyes only for her child whom she clasps as if she will never let her go. By contrast the baby in her long white robe and piecrust bonnet looks outwards to the world, one hand clenched in a small fist, the other splayed out in childish resolution. The upright stance of the child straining to stand free, indicates Lucy's early independence of spirit.

Elisabeth, however, died when Lucy was nearly three. It was Lucy's first bereavement. 'My Mother['s] loss was often felt by me with bitter tears; tho never could a father have been kinder'.[21]

Madox Brown also painted his wife and daughter in Rome in 1845, in two matching oval pictures (fig. 17). Elisabeth is tragically consumptive, wistful and delicate. An unusual circular cameo at her throat depicting an archetypal mother and child underlines her ethereal grasp on maternity. In complete contrast, two-year-old Lucy has a clear sense of herself, perched imperiously in an armchair, one arm casually thrown back, the other clasping a small gilt basket. Wearing a short unstructured dress, tied at the waist with a crimson sash, her damp brown hair is hastily brushed across her forehead.

After the death of his wife, Elisabeth, in Paris on 5 June 1846, Ford Madox Brown returned to England with his infant daughter. Desperately trying to establish an artistic career in London, he placed Lucy with his sister-in-law by

15. Ford Madox Brown, *Lucy Madox Brown in Infancy*, c. 1843. Oil, 29 × 25 cm. Private collection.

16. Ford Madox Brown, *Out of Town*, begun 1843–4, completed 1858. Oil on canvas, 23.2 × 14.4 cm. © Manchester Art Gallery.

17. Ford Madox Brown, *Elisabeth Madox Brown, née Bromley and Lucy Madox Brown*, 1845–6. Oil on canvas, each oval 29.2 × 21.6 cm, painted on the same canvas. Private collection.

marriage, Helen Bromley and her young family in Meopham, Kent and visited his daughter when he could, trying especially to be with her on birthdays and at Christmas. He rose before dawn, caught the train from Bishops Gate station to Gravesend, or sometimes the steam packet that left on the hour. Occasionally he took Lucy on short holidays, painting and drawing as distraction, always feeling the pull of his child, worried when she had a cold or 'ear ake'[22] or 'the Hooping cough'.[23] 'I have parted from Lucy O! God! ought not that thought to make me strive & struggle agains[t] indolence. O! the hell of poverty!!!'[24] 'Tomorrow I shall have a days rest & see Lucy bless her'... 'Went to Gravesend to see Lucy dear.'[25]

With Lucy as his model, he began his lifelong series of perceptive, realistic child studies, which show genuine insight into both the mischief and the pathos of infancy. Madox Brown was only in his early twenties when he started recording the phases of childhood, still close enough to his own to engage with his daughter's. 'Made a little study of Lucy in sunshine.'[26] At every turn of her head, Lucy reminded him of his dead wife whose grave he visited on the 5th of each month, in the early days of bereavement at least. 'Got up at 8 went out by 9 to Highgate Cemetery had some standard roses planted on my poor Wife's grave, too high, ordered lower ones to be put'.[27]

By the time Lucy was five-and-a-half, there was a new woman in her father's life. Emma Hill made her first appearance in Ford Madox Brown's diary, as 'a girl as loves me', just as the year turned from 1848 into 1849.[28] By the spring, Brown was in love with Emma. One arresting likeness of Lucy dates from this time (fig. 18). She engages the viewer with her now familiar, unflinching gaze. The eyes that had earlier been blue are now hazel or grey. Drooping from a simple dark neckline is a single red rosebud, hinting that Brown's little daughter is a rose herself, but a rose with thorns. This concentrated small portrait is painted on a sombre background. The arrival of Emma meant Lucy was no longer in the sunshine.

Although there are a number of representations of Lucy in childhood (fig. 19), it is frustratingly difficult to build up any visual image of Lucy in the crucial years of her teens and twenties. As Lucy grew past adolescence, the most vivid picture of her is in words, documented by Laura Hain Friswell, another girl of the period. Lucy and her half-sister, Cathy Madox Brown, were scions of bohemianism with impeccable artistic connections and credentials. In the late 1860s and early 1870s both young women were training to be artists in their father's studio, exhibiting pictures in London galleries such as the Dudley and the Royal Academy and attracting genuine praise. They interpreted fashion in the modish, aesthetic conventions of unconventionality, and their effect on other young women could be clearly intimidating:

> They were always dressed in what was then considered the height of artistic and aesthetic fashion. It consisted in wearing soft, limp, full dresses with

18. (above) Ford Madox Brown, *Lucy as a child, with a rose, c.* 1849. Oil on cardboard, 15.9 cm diameter. Private collection.

19. (left) Ford Madox Brown, *Lucy as a child, with bunches, c.* 1850. Charcoal, 430 × 320 mm. Wightwick Manor, National Trust.

short waists or none at all. The material was generally cashmere or what is now called nun's veiling; the favourite colours dull brick red, peacock blue, sage green and cinnamon brown. The dresses were often cut slightly square at the throat and had very full sleeves; jewellery of the barbaric kind was worn with them, and the whole effect was Rossettian and Burne-Jonesian in the extreme.

They were the epitome of Pre-Raphaelite femininity. Like models today, they were suspected of eating disorders and although Madox Brown was aware his daughters must eat, Hain Friswell hinted that they were close to anorexia,

> not quite so consumptive and willowy-looking as Burne-Jones made his figures – no human being could be so and live; but their hair, colour, and pose were all very like a Burne-Jones picture, and I wondered how they did it. Was it, I asked myself, [by] eating very little and drinking vinegar? Did they breakfast on redcurrant jelly and a glass of champagne, as I had heard of Swinburne doing, and dine off the wing of a lark, as another genius was supposed to do?

Lucy and Cathy didn't just paint pictures. They also presented themselves as pictures. In the London social scene, they achieved minor celebrity status, heightened by sexual allure and standoffish poise. Laura Hain Friswell wickedly described their body politics, noting the unspoken

> something in the superior way that very slim, willowy people look at big ones that makes the latter ashamed of their size... The Misses Madox Brown and their friends looked tall from their slimness, and Miss Duffus Hardy and I used to squeeze ourselves into as small a space as we could and sit and admire them though they never spoke to us that I can remember.[29]

Laura Hain Friswell accurately conveyed the power of Lucy and Cathy's physical appeal – and the bitterness their appeal caused. The much older artist-poet William Bell Scott (b. 1811) snidely condemned the Madox Brown women for wearing make-up. But they enjoyed the power it gave them and had little interest in his old-fashioned opinions. They were the 'It' girls of their circle. The *Saturday Review* of 14 March 1868 carried a much discussed article on 'The Girl of the Period' who enjoyed 'slang, bold talk, and fastness'. An antidote to 'the angel in the house', this new kind of woman was addicted to fashion, cosmetics and flirting.

In addition, Lucy and her sister claimed a special freedom from conventional, Victorian, middle-class restraints on ordinary girls – this was the acceptable eccentric autonomy allowed to the woman artist. Nathaniel Hawthorne's New England artist Hilda had to travel to Rome to claim this artistic liberty for herself. 'The customs of artist-life bestow such liberty upon the sex, which is elsewhere restricted within so much narrower limits; and it is perhaps an indication that, whenever we admit women to a wider scope of pursuits and professions, we must also remove the shackles of our present conventional rules, which would then become an insufferable restraint on either maid or wife', observed the American novelist.[30] In the 1860s, just after the huge popular success in England of Hawthorne's *Marble Faun*, Lucy asserted a similar independence in London.

None of these factors intimidated William Michael Rossetti. For several years before 1873 he had become increasingly attracted to Lucy. Although separated by almost fourteen years, William and Lucy had been part of each other's lives since 1850 when Lucy was only six. 'It was I think at Madox Brown's house-warming (at his studio in Clipstone Street, Portland Place) in January 1850, that I first met my future wife, a quiet candid-looking little girl, aged less than seven, modestly self-possessed'.[31] Later, Lucy played a walk-on part in the Rossetti family scenario. In her early teens she boarded at the Rossetti family home, then at 45 Upper Albany Street, for private tutoring from William's mother, and his elder sister, Maria. The serious young man who was courting Henrietta Rintoul brushed past Lucy as she ran up the narrow stairs to be on time for lessons.

In 1873 Madox Brown plotted quietly that Lucy, who was nearly thirty and had been unwell, should join a party to Italy together with that curious *ménage à trois*, William Bell Scott, his wife, Letitia, and his permanent companion Alice Boyd. William Michael Rossetti completed the group.

A single albumen print by L. Suscipj is a record of Lucy's happiness on the Italian trip (fig. 20).[32] Her giddy cousin Lizzie Cooper protested the photo did not flatter darling Lucy who was fifty times prettier than that![33] Her dark, semi-transparent, striped silk dress edged with lace, slipping slightly from narrow shoulders, had been chosen with regard to sexual allure as well as aesthetics. A large brooch at her throat and two necklaces of decidedly barbaric dimensions decorate her corsage. Lucy did not engage directly with the camera. She disliked being photographed, but at this significant point in her emotional life, she felt assured enough to allow it. By the time they reached home, Lucy and William were an engaged couple.

They returned to Rome on their honeymoon the following April and perhaps to the same studio photographer. At least one picture survives from this sitting (fig. 21).[34] This time they are together in natural interaction. Lucy's hair is dressed with a creamy-white or perhaps a pale pink rose. A few tendrils still escape on to her forehead. The dark dress is extravagantly frilled along a deep v-neck and tightly buttoned to her slender waist, where another rose is fastened. She holds a fan. More importantly, her hand meets his and his other arm enfolds her in a protective embrace, speaking physical intimacy. Lucy wears a necklace of either ancient Sassanian dome and cylinder seals or monumental coral beads. Both could have been bought in Rome. They are an unconven-

20. Lucy in Rome, 1873. Cathy Hueffer's photograph album, STH/BH/2/3-6. The Stow Hill Collection, HLRO, and the Hon. Oliver Soskice.

21. Mr and Mrs William Rossetti, honeymoon photograph, Rome 1874. Published in Mary Sandars, *Christina Rossetti*, 1930. (See also enlarged view on p. 4).

tional couple, Lucy at thirty in her individual, romanticized version of Victorian fashion and William in his jaunty fez or smoking cap. His beard is as prolific as it was in Julia Margaret Cameron's shot nearly a decade earlier. In spite of his facial hair, he looks younger than forty-four. But there is a suggestion of a shadow around Lucy's eyes, a reminder that her health was causing concern even on her honeymoon.

As his wedding present to Lucy, her brother-in-law Gabriel offered to paint her portrait (fig. 22). In fact, he worked on it after Lucy's return from her honeymoon during the summer of 1874, partly at Kelmscott in June and partly in London in August. What he did not know for certain, but suspected, was that Lucy was in the early weeks of her first pregnancy. In subtle tones of coloured chalks on pale green paper, this portrait is the most beautiful surviving evocation of Lucy's physical presence. It manages to capture both her vulnerability and her strength. The artist conflates these qualities and conveys an integrated, if idealized personality. Lucy holds a steady gaze but seems to stare past us, indicating what her husband called her 'elevated tone of thought, loyal to the high things in life and in art and literature'.[35]

Her auburn brown hair is dressed with the simplest of pale pink English roses. Coincidentally, this echoes Brown's portrait of Lucy as a child with a

22. Dante Gabriel Rossetti, *Lucy Madox Brown Rossetti*, 1874. Coloured chalks on pale green paper, 517 × 390 mm. Surtees 454, pl. 417. Private collection.

rose. The lower part of the face is the least like Lucy, much more like Gabriel's model and lover Janey Morris, but the artist makes Lucy's face softer than Janey's dramatic sexuality. Lucy's unusual jewellery – a necklace either of chalcedony or blue-stained ivory beads, and an electrotyped medallion of an ancient coin or perhaps a gorgon's head at the focus of her stiffly frilled collar – testify to her aesthetic taste and sense of personal identity. Some people thought the portrait too much like Rossetti's usual templates of female beauty to be a true likeness of Lucy, but her husband considered it authentic. Twenty years later, for complex reasons, this portrait was the only item Lucy left to William under the terms of her will.

Lucy gave Gabriel one of her final sittings for the portrait on Sunday, 9 August 1874. On Friday, 14 August, Lucy miscarried. It was her honeymoon baby. The following day William explained to his mother Frances Rossetti that

> ever since the close of June or beginning of July she and I had some reason to think she was pregnant: but from motives which one woman will readily understand of another, she was reticent on the subject - hinted of it to no one save Cathy. Tho' she suffered some discomforts, everything seemed to proceed regularly and harmlessly till Tuesday, when I fear she walked more than was good for her: Wednesday and Thursday were not much amiss, but Friday morning very early produced a miscarriage, the process of which is still going on.

As Lucy's own Doctor Marshall was away in Switzerland, William called round on Jenner, doctor to royalty, who recommended a local *accoucheur*, Mr Gill of 43 Woburn Place, who would attend Lucy not only through pregnancies but also for years to come. Lucy suffered much pain, he told his mother, so he thought 'as little said on the subject as convenient without needless secretiveness' might be best. [36]

The event sadly recalled the fact that Lucy's mother, Elisabeth, had lost her first child, a son at just five days old. Nor was it made easier for Lucy by the fact that Cathy had successfully given birth to her first child (the future novelist Ford Madox Ford) at the end of the previous year, on 17 December 1873. The delicacy apparent in Gabriel's portrait makes it no surprise that Lucy failed to recover quickly from her miscarriage. A little less than a year later, Lucy safely delivered her first child, a daughter, Olivia Frances Madox Rossetti, on 20 September 1875.

Madox Brown, who had recorded his daughter's face since babyhood, made a rare portrait of her as an adult, in a study of her new maternity into which she was to pour all her frustrated artistic ambitions (fig. 23).

The portrait is intimate and archetypal at the same time. Brown's palette of green and ochre tones suggests an autumnal date and setting, to mark Olivia's

23. Ford Madox
Brown, *Lucy and
Olivia*, 1876.
Coloured chalks,
1016 × 864 mm.
Private collection.

first birthday in September 1876. In a fluid, aesthetic gown of deep charcoal
with a cream lace fichu at the neck, Lucy is completely unadorned, without
any flowers or jewellery. Her auburn hair is plaited and coiled on top of her
head and at the nape of her neck. Her nose is pressed to her infant's brighter
auburn head, inhaling its scent.

Olivia is a plump personality already. While her mother is lost in thought,
gazing beyond the limits of the picture, Olivia critically examines her grandfather, the artist. In one of Brown's characteristic observations of childhood,
Olivia has kicked off one soft shoe and grips it in her left fist. Its coral note
provides the central flash of colour in the picture. With her other hand she
offers a marigold to her grandfather and the spectator. A bronze aura behind
the baby makes semi-abstract reference to a halo. The baby exerts the central
physical and symbolic force in the picture so she seems to diminish her pallid
mother. The artist implies that maternity has drained something away from
Lucy – the vitality of youth – or a sense of personal identity.

A physiological reason may explain Lucy's apparent lack of energy. If the
picture was painted to mark Olivia's first birthday in September 1876, then
Lucy would have been four months pregnant with her second child, Gabriel

Arthur Madox Rossetti who was born in the frosty small hours of 28 February 1877. William recorded the event in his diary with poetic precision and rueful humour:

> 4.16 a.m. Lucy gave birth to a son: this is the anniversary of my father's birth wh. must have occurred, I believe, in 1783. Nothing particularly bad happened till about 1. a.m: at 3.15 I had to go round for the Surgeon, Gill, in a most brilliant frosty moonlight. He accompanied me back, arriving by 3.45, & in another half hour all was over. Lucy has gone on extremely well ever since, & the baby, tho' grotesque enough in aspect, seems to be sound & hearty.[37]

William felt the portrait with Olivia made Lucy look mundane. It leached her of her special qualities. Presenting her in an ordinary, domestic role and setting made her look '*too* ordinary, and approaching the commonplace'.[38] Embracing her child, Lucy is both completed as a human being and yet rather less than the independent young artist she had been in her twenties. It is a picture that looks both back and forward. The grandfather artist celebrates his stake into the future.

Madox Brown asked Lucy and two of her children to pose for him in 1881/2 when he was designing the fifth of his great murals for the Manchester Town Hall series. Showing *William Crabtree Watching the Transit of Venus, A.D. 1639*, its intellectual, historical subject and political subtext appealed to Lucy. The man Christina Rossetti loved but did not marry, Charles Bagot Cayley, scholar and translator of Dante, posed for the working-class amateur astronomer transfixed by the image of the planet through his telescope. Lucy as Mrs Crabtree clasping her excited and wondering children, probably Arthur and her second daughter Helen, make a resonant and dramatic grouping (fig. 24).

Only one other authenticated image of Lucy survives: another very small studio photograph, unattributed and undated, probably taken for a *carte-de-visite* (fig. 25). Holding a long-stemmed rose in one hand, Lucy rests the other on the back of a rustic chair while artfully arranged twigs sprinkle the foreground. Her dress is conventional, a fairly full Victorian crinoline, which would have floated as she moved, unlike the earlier aesthetic, Pre-Raphaelite Lucy. The style of bonnet and deep pointed shawl date the costume to the early 1860s. Lucy's face looks older than this date would suggest but it was not unusual for Victorian women to choose to be photographed in dresses ten or more years old.

For once Lucy faces the camera almost head on, only angled by an infinitesimal turn of the chin. She seems uncomfortable, constrained under dozens of layers of petticoats and undergarments, corsets, bodices, and hooped cages that gave Victorian women their characteristic sloping shoulders and tiny

24. Ford Madox Brown, *Crabtree Watching the Transit of Venus, A.D. 1639*, 1881–3. Gambier-Parry process of spirit fresco, detail from one of the twelve murals, each 146.1 × 313.1 cm, painted for Manchester Town Hall. © Manchester Art Gallery/ Manchester Town Hall.

25. Studio photograph of Lucy. Private collection.

waists, ideal for setting off the drape of a shawl. This is neither artist, nor bohemian, nor young wife. Apparently gripped by personal paralysis and internal tension, Lucy accepts for once the conventions of her status, class and the medium.

Unlike Lucy, William was almost insouciantly casual in front of the camera. Lewis Carroll took a famous set of photographs of the Rossetti family on 7 October 1863. It was a convivial occasion as the photographer remarked in his diary. 'Mr William Rossetti is the one who writes in the *Monthly Register*. Both the sisters seem clever, and are very pleasant to converse with'. He returned the next day to dine with the Rossetti brothers, together with the Pre-Raphaelite sculptor Alexander Munro and artist Arthur Hughes.[39]

The albumen print photographs Carroll took in Gabriel's garden at Tudor House, Cheyne Walk, are carefully composed showing the family in various groupings at the foot of a flight of steps. In the one shown here (fig. 26), the two brothers flank their mother and at the lowest point, a diminutive Christina who is half-smiling towards William on the outside edge of the composition. William with his domed, bald cranium is taller and leaner than his brother, Gabriel, who occupies more central, dramatic space in the picture. William's unbuttoned dark frock-coat reveals a waistcoat and watch-chain. Elegantly bent, his left knee inclines with familiarity against his mother. He has tucked his left hand nonchalantly into a trouser pocket. Exploiting the garden setting

26. Charles
Lutwidge
Dodgson (Lewis
Carroll),
photograph of the
Rossetti family, 7
October 1863. By
courtesy of the
National Portrait
Gallery, London.

with autumn leaves scattered across the foreground, Lewis Carroll suggests the natural although quite disparate bonds existing between all four.

An alternative 'family' group photograph was also taken in the garden at Cheyne Walk in 1863 by William Downey (fig. 27). The Rossetti brothers, wearing the same formal clothes as in Lewis Carroll's picture, pose either side of a slender flowering tree. Against its trunk, in comic reversal of Mrs

27. William Downey, photograph of
Dante Gabriel Rossetti, William
Michael Rossetti, Algernon Charles
Swinburne and Fanny Cornforth, *c.*
1863. By courtesy of the National
Portrait Gallery, London.

Rossetti's severe maternity in the previous photograph, lolls Fanny Cornforth, Gabriel's mistress, model and housekeeper. Her weight threatens to uproot the delicate tree against which Gabriel places a witty, supporting hand. Almost absurdly diminished in a low garden chair at Fanny's skirts, bright-eyed and elfin sits the poet Algernon Charles Swinburne. Like Christina in the previous picture, he occupies the lowest spatial position. The various relationships between the four figures are much more ambiguous and intriguing than in Lewis Carroll's family photograph. Yet there are siblings here, a mother figure, a child figure and an undercurrent of sexuality.

Sixty years later Max Beerbohm told Sydney Cockerell how ravishing he found this 'wondrous' little photograph:

> Miss Cornforth is incredible. Credo accordingly – and indeed am but confirmed in a belief I already had – that she must have been just like that…William Michael is decidedly the most distinguished in aspect of the figures in that group of four. You and I were arguing, in Nicholson's studio, that William Michael had been under-rated because he happened to be the one (superficially) dull man in a bevy of brilliant ones. Perhaps a time will come when he will be *over*-rated, as having been the one sane man among lunatics! – for there was, wasn't there? a silver thread of lunacy in the rich golden fabric of 16 Cheyne Walk.[40]

In 1864, a year after the Downey and Carroll photographs, the Rossetti brothers met Alphonse Legros, a French painter brought to England by James Abbott McNeill Whistler who plucked him from penury and told him 'in London (never mind the fogs!) gold sovereigns would come to him and restore his health.' William considered Legros's large picture *Ex Voto* 'most masterly in character, and profound in feeling' when he saw it in the Paris Salon in 1861.[41] Legros became part of the London artistic circle including Whistler, George Frederic Watts and Edward Poynter. Gabriel promoted his works among potential buyers. During 1864-5 Legros painted an oil portrait of William, who chose it as the opening plate to his autobiography in 1906 (fig. 28).[42] He explained in his diary, on 17 March 1906, 'I am not enamoured of the frequent practice of representing an old man as being old & semi-decrepit: he was once young & middle-aged.'

It is a curiously stylized but powerful portrait. It does not suggest the Frenchness of the artist nor the Italian origins of the sitter but has a mesmeric, almost sinister quality more reminiscent of an iconic character from nineteenth-century Russian history. Testifying to strength of character, it is flat and opaque and fails to explore the complexities of that character. William's bald pate is exaggeratedly egg-shaped, in startling contrast to his fashionable mane of beard. Today the picture has darkened, which intensifies its sinister effect. The friendship between Legros and the Rossettis flourished for a few years

28. Alphonse Legros, *William Michael Rossetti, c.* 1864. Oil, 45.7 × 30.5 cm. Private collection.

29. John Lucas Tupper, *William Michael Rossetti*, 1869. Plaster medallion, 45.7 cm diameter. Private collection.

until they lost touch, although William always retained a 'high estimate of his art, and my entire goodwill towards himself'.[43]

A far more successful portrait of William dates from five years later in 1869. It is a plaster medallion head by the minor Pre-Raphaelite figure John Lucas Tupper (fig. 29). Tupper had many talents but worldly success completely eluded him. In the early days of the Pre-Raphaelite movement, he had been an effervescent composer of doggerel verse:

> And somewhat quickly they arose –
> He could distinguish Gabriel's nose
> From William's mouth in sweet repose,
> Whose measured murmurs now began;
> While John L. Tupper, half in doze,
> Was crooning as he only can.[44]

By 1863 Tupper had become a schoolmaster of 'geometrical or scientific drawing' at Rugby School where William visited him on his way to Penkill Castle in July 1867, when he noticed Tupper's complete lack of enthusiasm for his classes – and they for him. They discussed a holiday in Italy together and a projected portrait of William. Eventually, he sat to Tupper at Rugby in March 1869 just before they travelled to Rome.

The portrait head, which shows William facing left in profile, is both sensitive and severe, combining Greek and Roman elements. The features are

30. (right)
William Bell
Scott, *William
Michael Rossetti*,
1869. Oil, 47 × 33
cm. Private
collection.

(Far right) William
as Prospero by
Lucy, 1872, detail
of fig. 87.

finely sculpted, the nose straight and Roman with a little bend at the end. Closely observed and a testament to friendship, Tupper finds nobility in his sitter and accurately senses how repression keeps temperament in check. Textural contrasts are highlighted – smoothness of brow, cheek and neck off-set the elegant profusion of facial hair. Tupper joked to Holman Hunt that the medallion head of William treated a 'mystic subject'. The sculptor reported that William, one of the most thoughtful connoisseurs of Victorian sculpture, considered it 'a good work of portrait-sculpture...a likeness rapturously lauded by the mamma and daughters, and known at once by strangers, so I suppose it is mystically objectionable'.[45] Tupper's habitual lack of success ensured that the medallion failed to please the hanging committee at the Royal Academy. Today it remains as fresh and impressive as the day it was completed.

A gauche portrait of William by Bell Scott, also dating from 1869, is far less successful (fig. 30).[46] William is sitting reading in an armchair. At his elbow is a small side table and several works of art are stacked casually above a stone fireplace. William is literally in a brown study, absorbed in reading some lecture notes. Their title is quite legible, *Half-Hour lectures to students in Art on the History and Practice of the Fine and Ornamental Arts* – written by the artist William Bell Scott, first published in 1861, with a second edition in 1867. It was entirely characteristic of Scott's personal vanity that he chose to depict William reading one of his own works. The artist's initials 'W.B.S.' run vertically down the back left-hand leg of the table in the front right foreground.[47]

Photographs and portraits send covert reports down the generations about family dynamics. Lucy lost conventional family life when she was less than three years old but exchanged it for an extended surrogate family with her Bromley cousins at Melliker Farm in Kent. Her quest for family may be seen in the patterns of her life, in the subjects she chose to paint, and in her choice of family members as models for her pictures.

One of her most complex treatments of the family theme is to be found in an ambitious picture, her first oil painting, *Ferdinand and Miranda Playing Chess*, 1872 (see fig 87). Based on a dramatic scene from *The Tempest*, the central character is Miranda, like Lucy a motherless girl. Miranda had Prospero, a magician, for a father; Lucy had an artist for a father, another sort of magician. Miranda had grown up on a magical island, Lucy in a child's heaven at Aunt Helen's country farmhouse.

In *The Tempest*, jealous Antonio had deprived his brother Prospero of his rightful dukedom. The scene Lucy chose to paint focused on the restoration of family bonds. In a second tempest, Prospero brought to the island not only his evil brother but also Alonso, King of Naples, and his eligible son Prince Ferdinand, whom his father believed drowned. Lucy's picture shows paternity restored, an archetypal theme recalling the Prodigal Son or Cordelia restored to Lear. Prospero on the extreme right of the picture indicates to Alonso the healing sight of their two adult children playing chess. Miranda has found a lover and, in a dramatic irony, Lucy's future husband, William Michael Rossetti, modelled for the figure of Prospero (see left). Her father, Ford Madox Brown, posed for King Alonso.

Thus father and lover merge and combine – in life as in the picture. The human family in Shakespeare's play and Lucy's picture is seen reunited and extended. Prospero is unmistakably a portrait of William. Here, far from making him a figure of fun, William's bald, shining head symbolizes wisdom. He is a man of obvious maturity, almost of the same generation as Lucy's father. Semi-orphaned as a child, all her life Lucy fed off her relationship with her father. Father/lover, lover/father – this picture exposes some aspects of Lucy's questing psyche. Family dynamics are further complicated by the fact that Miranda and Ferdinand the young lovers, subliminally proxies for Lucy and William, are modelled by Lucy's half-siblings, Catherine and Oliver Madox Brown.

Two years later on 31 March 1874 William and Lucy were united in marriage. In the honeymoon photograph taken in Rome (see fig. 21), the romantic young lovers of Miranda and Ferdinand are replaced with a mature William and Lucy. In *The Tempest*, Miranda is easily defeating Ferdinand at chess, symbolically in the superior position in Lucy's composition. However, in the honeymoon photograph the relative dominance between the sexes has been reversed with the man now placed higher in the composition, dominant and assertive above his wife.

31. Ford Madox Brown, *William Michael Rossetti*, 1 January 1882. Pencil, 152 × 127 mm. Private collection.

On New Year's Day 1882 William, aged fifty-three, had been married for seven years and was the father of five children, when Madox Brown made a pencil portrait of him (fig. 31). It is an intimate, eccentric study. With his interest in unusual headgear, he now sports a turned back knitted cap, pulled down low over his ears. Unlike Lucy, he has no inhibitions about engaging with the spectator.

William continued to face up to photographers throughout the 1890s. After Lucy's death from consumption in April 1894, he became increasingly alarmed when his second daughter Helen exhibited similar symptoms. He took her away to the mountains of Switzerland where they both made different kinds of recoveries. A photograph of father and daughter was taken in Davos-Platz where they stayed from January till June 1896 (fig. 32),[48] the standard winter period advised for consumptives.

On Christmas Eve 1896 William and Helen set off again, this time for Australia, embarking on the steamship *Nineveh*. They reached Melbourne on 5 February 1897 where the port authorities discovered smallpox on board. Even Captain Allan, 'a bluff and genial Hercules',[49] was infected. William and Helen were allowed to go on to Sydney where they were quarantined for three weeks at the Heads in Sydney Harbour. Today the long, low series of bungalows, divided rigorously in those days according to which class of accommodation passengers had bought, is preserved as an evocative Quarantine Museum.[50] William appreciated the glorious views but suffered from intense heat in his formal London clothes. In the event neither William nor Helen contracted the disease, probably thanks to Lucy who had continually insisted on revaccination during the years of their marriage.

On release from quarantine, William and Helen stayed in North Sydney with the son of old friends, the Allports, from 6 to 20 March 1897. During this fortnight William, a robust sixty-seven year old, sat for a portrait photograph at the Falk Studios in the Royal Arcade, 496 George Street, Sydney (fig. 33).

Henry Walter Barnett, an innovative photographer, owned the Falk Studios. He had a reputation for photographing all major celebrities who visited Sydney, especially stage stars. His starriest sitter was Sarah Bernhardt in 1891 who thanked him 'a thousand times for the adorable photographs.' He introduced a new technique, using 'dramatic sidelights, emphasizing bone-structure and skin texture, allowing his sitters' individual personalities to shine through'. It was a photographic version of chiaroscuro, influenced by the work of Julia Margaret Cameron and Nadar, which emphasized the sculptural qualities of the human head. Barnett, like Cameron, scorned retouching, particularly in his studies of male subjects, a policy William approved. When

32. Photograph of William Michael Rossetti with his daughter Helen in Davos-Platz, Switzerland, 1896. William Michael Rossetti Collection, Department of Rare Books and Special Collections, Princeton University Library.

33. Photograph of William Michael Rossetti in Australia, 1897. The Falk Studios, Sydney. Private collection.

William sat for his portrait photograph in the 'handsome, commodious and elegantly furnished' Falk Studios, Barnett was away on a trip to England. It is likely that his 'chief operator', Edward E. Gray, also a fine portraitist trained in Barnett's principles, took William's picture.[51]

William looks sunburnt and relaxed, although heavily dressed in waistcoat, jacket and overcoat. Even in the Australian climate, William's attention to dress was punctilious. His snake-headed tie-pin secures a polka-dotted cravat and a long-linked watch-chain lies across his stomach. He has tucked a silk hand-kerchief into his breast pocket. The fine picture speaks of vigour and health even though he was suffering severe gout. Soon after this photograph he returned home to London travelling via Ceylon, the Red Sea, the Suez Canal, Naples and Genoa.

Five years later, in a portrait painted by Herbert Harlakenden Gilchrist by artificial light during the winter of 1901/2, William begins to look like an old man (fig. 34). Gilchrist's parents were Alexander and Anne Gilchrist with

34. Herbert Harlakenden Gilchrist, *William Michael Rossetti*, 1902. Oil on canvas, 125 × 100 cm. Wightwick Manor, National Trust.

whom William had worked on the *Life of Blake* forty years earlier.[52] He is seated in the library of his final home at 3 St Edmund's Terrace, Regent's Park, London. Lucy had chosen it because it was next door but one to her father's house and she had been convinced she would breathe more easily, physically and emotionally, in the clear air of its elevated position. Lucy and Christina had both been dead since 1894. Janey Morris looks out of a picture frame behind the last Rossetti survivor. The shelves are stacked with books, many rare, beautifully bound editions. William stares abstractly out of the picture, his still dark brows contrasting with his white beard. His clothes are as carefully chosen as they were in Australia. He wears his favourite snake-headed tie-pin and his handkerchief is a splash of red. Helen's owl in its 'usual condition of total inoccupation'[53] glowers up at him from its wicker cage. The artist's choice of autumnal tones, natural bark brown and russet, conveys warm admiration for his subject. At seventy-two, William's face seems to bear the weight of years though not everyone thought the artist had quite succeeded. Olive Garnett a young friend of William's children, thought 'Gilchrist's portrait of W.M.R. & the owl's cage promises to be very good, but he has thickened the features & not made the head fine enough'.[54] William and his children liked the picture, although it was not hung when Gilchrist submitted it for the annual Royal Academy exhibition in 1902.[55]

In January 1909, William Rothenstein painted the last major portrait of William Michael at nearly eighty (fig. 35). Rothenstein was about thirty-five when he completed the picture all at one sitting. 'Rothenstein came, & took my portrait – lifesize head in oils. He is a rapid worker, & between 11 & 4, with a full interval for lunch, he had about finished it, tho' I believe he will yet do something additional. It seems to us a fine likeness, with a more energetic expression than other recent versions.'[56] Here a younger man looks at a venerable Victorian. Rothenstein had been introduced to William Rossetti's household by a beautiful young actress, Miss Alice Kingsley, who 'herself might have walked out of a canvas by Rossetti.'

The young artist felt warmly welcome at St Edmund's Terrace and gratefully remembered that 'William Rossetti was the only one of the Pre-Raphaelites who was sympathetic towards the work of the younger writers and painters.' He enjoyed William's wide-ranging conversation and responded to his 'sweet and modest nature'. Rothenstein countered petty criticisms of William, asserting

> he was by no means the 'fool for a brother' that Morris proclaimed him to be; on the contrary, he was an admirable critic of literature and art; he had kept his faith in the power of art bright and clean; and his outlook on life was broad and humane. He didn't like the clatter the younger generation made in the press, and in the social world, so he lived in retirement. But to any who went to see him, he gave himself generously.[57]

Rapport with his sitter and compassion for the ageing process illuminate Rothenstein's portrait. There is pathos in the way the artist depicts the full white beard and walrus moustache compensating for Rossetti's ever lessening hair. In severe profile, the head is thrown into architectural relief against his black overcoat and gloomy background. The veins physically stand out on the domed head. The nose appears to be sculpted out of paint and contrasts with the blue-grey eye, filmy with the faraway look of older eyes. There is a tiny,

35. William Rothenstein, *William Michael Rossetti*, 1909. Oil on canvas, 59.7 × 49.5 cm. Estate of Sir William Rothenstein/National Portrait Gallery, London.

36. Photograph of William Michael Rossetti with Helen and Imogene, *The Graphic*, 15 February 1913.

enlivening flash of red paint beneath the eye. Although the surface paint is very matt, sheen on the head and cheek suggest the authentic qualities of skin – but the neck is muddy, perhaps unfinished by the artist in his haste.

The director of the National Portrait Gallery, H.M. Hake, went to see the picture at 3 St Edmund's Terrace. Although he liked the Rothenstein, he would have preferred to secure the 1853 pencil drawing of William by Dante Gabriel Rossetti, which belonged to Mary Rossetti (see fig. 7). In the event Mary promised to bequeath the drawing to the gallery and Hake and his committee accepted the Rothenstein. On 17 February 1931 Helen Rossetti Angeli thanked the director and trustees for accepting the portrait of her late dear father. 'May I venture to ask you to see that the portrait is placed...in congenial company?'[58] When Rothenstein himself called at the gallery in 1932, he felt dissatisfied with the painting as a work of art. He thought it looked dull and suggested varnishing it. This has not been done to date. Although the portrait spent most of the 1990s on loan to the British Embassy in Rome, it was put into store on its return to London and cannot currently be seen on the walls of the National Portrait Gallery. William is still not in congenial company.

George Porter-Higgins took one of the last known photographs of William, specially commissioned for *The Graphic* on 15 February 1913 (fig. 36). It shows him in his role as grandfather, seated in profile, looking left, with his daughter Helen behind and granddaughter Imogene to the side, both looking out at the viewer. William has opened a portfolio of pictures to show to young Imogene. The group pose is static and solemn but conveys the bonds of family, not only between those in the picture but also those with the unseen dead, suggested by looking into the portfolio. William himself is the lynchpin who connects the next generation with the past, crammed with Rossettis.

Scenes from Family Life

WILLIAM AND HIS MOTHER, FRANCES ROSSETTI

My dearest mother, a pattern to me of everything that is simple, sweet, kind, and noble.
     WMR *Diary* 11 April 1886[1]

That Rossetti family was and is a remarkable one – steeped in finished soil – cultivated, rich in its yield – perhaps a little too refined, too delicate, for the brush, break, of this tumultuous world.
     Walt Whitman, c. 1888[2]

If you were blessed with an unsurpassably good mother, I can with truth say the same of myself.
     WMR to Walt Whitman, 1 January 1885[3]

The Rossetti family is a mythical construction. A gaggle of voices from the past and the present, their own voices as well as later commentators have created a romantic saga comparable only to the Brontë myth. At the heart of the Rossetti family, in the front parlour sat Frances Mary Lavinia Rossetti (fig. 37), née Polidori, who presided over household life 'one and indivisible', where children were treated as adults and father was as playful as one of the children. All four children were united in their opinion of Mamma - she was the source of all affection in the home, a woman of steadfastness and intellect as well as an unpretentious, invincible High Anglican faith. William wrote to her, drew her, tolerated her religion, protected her, considered her, supported her, commemorated her and dedicated books to her.[4]

William Michael Rossetti was born, the third of four gifted children, at 38 Charlotte Street (now Hallam Street), Portland Place, London, on 25 September 1829, 'when matches – first known as lucifers – had not yet been invented'.[5] His elder siblings were Maria Francesca (born 17 February 1827), possibly the most intellectual, who wrote a study of Dante and eventually became an Anglican nun, and Gabriel Charles Dante (born 12 May 1828) the first Englishman since Blake to combine a genius for both poetry and painting. His younger sister, the Poet Laureate England failed to choose when Tennyson died in 1892, was the reclusive Christina Georgina Rossetti (born 5 December 1830), but in childhood 'sprightly and piquant of tongue' and

37. Dante Gabriel Rossetti, *Frances Rossetti*, 1854. Pencil, oval, 152 × 121 mm. Surtees 448. William said his mother had a 'fresh complexion, features more than commonly regular, shapely Madonna-like eyelids, and an air of innate composure.' DGRFLM, I, 1895. Wightwick Manor, National Trust.

William's 'chief chum'. Although their father, Gabriele Rossetti, an Italian political activist and refugee, Dante scholar and writer from Vasto in the Abruzzi, was nominally a Catholic, Frances made sure all four children were christened within her faith of the Church of England – Maria and Gabriel at All Souls, Langham Place; William and Christina at Holy Trinity, Marylebone Road. William's baptism took place on 27 December 1829.[6] He was three months old.

Always worried about money, Frances practised careful economy and strict self-abnegation. 'The most regular and self-postponing of women', she rose regularly at seven, dressed in 'simplicity itself, and out-of-date simplicity to boot', organized (although did not cook herself) breakfast and the main meal, dinner at four in the afternoon. Even a household as modest as the Rossettis', managed to keep at least one servant. The first census of 1841, when William was eleven, showed that Jemima Pocock serviced the family, now living at 50 Charlotte Street.

Frances devoted all her time to her children, educated them, encouraged them and played cards with them – but never for money. As her brother Dr John Polidori had committed suicide in 1821 partly because of gambling debts, there was a family horror of the practice, as well as religious prohibition. But Frances taught her children innocent card games, the Duchess of Rutland's Whim, Beggar my Neighbour and of course Patience. Later they learned whist and Italian *Tre Sette*. The four children associated themselves (with prophetic symbolism) with each of the four card suits. Volatile Dante and Christina claimed glamorous hearts and diamonds, while placid Maria and William were relegated to clubs and spades. Childish amusements were minimal: a rocking horse, a spinning-top, a teetotum, ball and ninepins, games of blindman's buff, puss-in-the-corner and 'animal, vegetable or mineral'.[7] The four children, born within four years, under the aegis of Frances functioned as a self-contained unit whose bonds survived even after the boys went to school. They all contributed to the family magazine *Hodge-Podge or Weekly Efforts* during the summer of 1843, later superseded by the *Illustrated Scrapbook*, which improved with every number, they believed. 'William has written an enormous quantity of *Ulfred the Saxon*', Gabriel told Mamma on 14 August 1843. 'His description of the battle of Hastings and death of Harold is acknowledged by every one to be excellent.'[8]

Although Frances played the piano and sang to the children, it was a home of talk rather than music. William remembered how indulgent she was to them all. His consistent stress on her warm heart was modified by an intimidating impression of high moral rectitude, 'solid qualities of mind, her high and unassuming consistency of character'. He alluded to her natural reticence, a reluctance to put herself forward, concealed behind the façade and 'dignity of self-retirement'. The children all inherited this to varying degrees 'but it has its drawbacks', commented William dryly.[9]

Three-quarters Italian by descent, the Rossetti children were brought up in an unconventional Victorian family. At home they spoke English with Frances and Italian with Gabriele. By day, Gabriele taught Italian at King's College, London. In the evenings he was kind, 'open-hearted, very animated in mind and manner, and on the whole cheerful, in spite of the bitterness of exile and the wrestle with fortune'.[10] Both parents fostered academic and creative activities. The children all drew and painted, read voraciously, wrote poetry from infancy, and at four years old, Gabriel amazed the milkman who 'saw a baby making a picture'.[11] They thrived in their claustrophobic urban home, often filled with visiting Italian intellectuals and dissidents, where there was no separate nursery to be banished to. They had few friends of their own age outside the family, as Frances had no taste for superficial social life. Instead, the children inspired each other in a private world of feverish creativity. Gabriel's later founding role in the Pre-Raphaelite Brotherhood and William's membership was only a logical extension of their childhood Eden of art, poetry and talk.

Born with the century in 1800, Frances was the daughter of Anna Maria Pierce, the English wife of Gaetano Polidori, who came from Bientina near Pisa. Frances's favourite of her three brothers had been tragic Dr John Polidori, who etched a small place in Romantic history when he accompanied Lord Byron to Switzerland as his travelling physician. Dr Polidori wrote *The Vampyre* during the same ghost-story competition that produced Mary Shelley's *Frankenstein*. The children were therefore directly linked to the Romantics, to heightened states of being and intense modes of expression. But of the other Polidori brothers, Philip was 'weak minded and "odd"' and

Henry became an obscure solicitor.[12] Among the four affectionate Polidori sisters, Margaret, Frances and Charlotte ('Substance and Shadow') and the youngest, Eliza, Frances was the cleverest and the only one to marry. She spoke Italian and French and worked as a governess before her marriage. This experience informed the education of her own children, as well as her later attempts to maintain the family finances by running small schools from their home in London, and experimentally in Frome, Somerset.

Duty was the guiding principle of Frances's life and luckily her duty usually corresponded with her affections. She visited her father and his family almost daily in Park Village East, Regent's Park, and with her 'placid, uncraving temperament', and 'great trust in Providence', she worked tirelessly to better and cohere her own small brood.[13]

When Gabriele's health began to deteriorate from 1842 onwards, she stood firm. William confided in his mother that he was expecting promotion and forbade her to think of taking in boarders.[14] By his twenty-fourth birthday in September 1853, the Inland Revenue Board increased his salary to £250.[15] It meant he could repay his mother's lifelong generosity by reuniting the family – divided when Frances and Christina had left London in 1853 to set up school in Frome. William brought the Rossettis back together under a new roof, at 45 Upper Albany Street, on Lady Day, March 1854,[16] just weeks before his father Gabriele died on 26 April 1854.

Frances kept a factual journal of Gabriele's final days, entirely free from sentimentality.[17] Her innate faith sustained her and she bore the loss with unflinching stoicism. Gabriele had practically nothing to leave his wife or anyone, except the copyrights in his esoteric and unsaleable scholarly works on Dante. Her one act of anger in bereavement was to burn the entire stock of his book on Platonic Love, which she thought anti-religious. William considered this the only bigoted gesture she ever made, for 'though religious, she was in no way fanatical'. Her religion was simply an intrinsic, organic component of her everyday life which she sought to instil by 'tender kindness and bright example'. When both her sons rejected confirmation, and teenage William stopped going to church in 1846 or 1847, she maintained an armed truce, preferring 'honest and open disbelief to hypocritical conformity'.[18] Her tolerance was in marked contrast with her anxious, proselytizing daughters who never stopped longing for Gabriel and William to embrace Christianity. When William married without religious ceremony in a register office in 1874, Frances was happy to be a witness.

This 'incomparably kind' Mamma[19] indulged and empathized with each of her children without favouritism. William gravitated towards his mother, in response to his impression, from childhood, that his father centred his hopes on Gabriel. Frances's literary judgment was important to William. Even as a self-conscious young man he showed her his poems, glowing in her response

to his important if tortuous sonnet in 1849 for the front cover of the *Germ*.[20]
And as a man in his fifties, in the excitement of writing his *Democratic Sonnets*,
he delivered a batch to his mother on 17 February 1881.[21] Her literary discrimination was also indicated by Swinburne's respect for her. William
retained an indelible image of his pious mother and the wild poet in disciple-
like pose at Cheyne Walk, 'seated one day in the studio – she in a chair, and
the poet of *Atalanta* close to her feet on a stool'.[22]

Sensible and pragmatic, Frances aspired to intellectual distinction for her
husband and children. 'I always had a passion for intellect', she owned, and she
was rewarded with a glut. But looking back, she wished 'that there were a little less intellect in the family, so as to allow for a little more common sense'.[23]
As the most grown-up and commonsensical member of his family, William
could still be a child to his mother, secure in her concern for his minor health
problems – boils, sore throat, toothache and gout – assuring her (because she
would care) that he took the 'third dose of the green atrocity this morning'.[24]

A bachelor of over thirty, he felt close enough to Frances to take her abroad
twice, on both occasions with Christina, first to Normandy and Paris in 1861,
then in 1865 to northern Italy, Milan, Pavia, Brescia and Verona – the only
time that either mother or daughter ever visited Italy. William involved his
mother in his political allegiances, too, proposing to take her to see the
London arrival of his hero, Garibaldi, at Nine Elms station on 9 April 1864.[25]
Aware that William had been trying to publish his translation of Dante's
Inferno since 1857, Frances made a generous financial offer enabling publication by Macmillan in 1865.[26] William showed his gratitude and honoured
Frances at the opening of his next book *Fine Art, Chiefly Contemporary*:

> In all filial love
> I dedicate
> This little book of criticism
> To my mother,
> Whose dear example ought to have taught me
> The critical virtues of
> Sound judgment, perfect modesty,
> And infallible truth-telling.

The graceful dedication encapsulated Frances's virtues, as William discerned
them, and made public his unchanging love and admiration for her. For her
part, Frances assured William always that she was his 'constantly affectionate
mother'.[27] She treasured his letters, pencilling on one, written in July 1853, in
which he recommended her to read Ruskin's *Stones of Venice*, 'A most dear letter of dear William's. Re-read 1868, 1874, & 1880'.[28]

By one of those few degrees of separation, Frances and her elder daughter
Maria tutored Ford Madox Brown's daughter Lucy between 1855 and 1857. As

Lucy matured from a student into a valued friend, Maria reflected, as she worked a pair of slippers for her, that Lucy was 'one of our very kindest sympathizers, & most effectual helpers in trouble' – referring to Gabriel's breakdown in the summer of 1872.[29] Two years later Lucy married William. The family had therefore known Lucy for years, and after the honeymoon, Frances and Christina (Maria had entered the All Saints Sisterhood in 1873) welcomed her into the Rossetti home, then at 56 Euston Square, Bloomsbury.[30] But William soon ruefully concluded 'that a married couple had better live by themselves than along with other members of the family, however well-disposed'.[31]

The experiment in communal living, certainly less unusual in England in the nineteenth century than it is in the twenty-first, failed to work for a variety of reasons. Christina and Lucy were wary of each other from the start, temperamentally and intellectually incompatible. The unease in the joint household was compounded by the fact that Lucy shared William's unbelief and was quite unsusceptible to Christina's religious arguments. There was nothing for it but to part.[32] Frances and Christina moved to 30 Torrington Square, just around the corner from Endsleigh Gardens. From then on friendly relations were assiduously maintained between the two households. William took care to visit Torrington Square weekly and his regular calls were recorded in Frances's surviving diaries. Lucy also exchanged calls with Frances and Christina, and the rapidly increasing grandchildren underpinned a growing bond of polite but genuine affection. Frances became a thoughtful grandmother and mother-in-law. In her mid-eighties, her account book for 1884 records presents for the children, a scrapbook for Olive, a doll for Mary, but her greatest extravagance was a black cashmere and velvet dress for Lucy.[33]

Having lost her husband and re-established her own identity to some extent in 1854, Frances had to face, twice, the worst losses any mother can envisage, the death of her daughter Maria from cancer in 1876, followed by the decline and death of her brilliant son Gabriel in 1882. At nearly eighty-two years old, partially deaf but retaining all her other faculties, 'enfeebled' but 'not grievously decayed', Frances was with Gabriel when he died in Birchington, attended his funeral, commissioned a stained-glass window in his memory, and was, with William, the joint legatee. Her composure at Gabriel's graveside was exemplary, 'supported by William on one side and Christina on the other – a most pathetic sight. She was calm, extraordinarily calm, but whether from self-command or the passivity of age I do not know – probably from both; but she followed all the proceedings with close interest', as Judge Lushington reported to William Bell Scott.[34]

She who was old had borne most. William later found a little red writing-case that Gabriel had given their mother in 1849. Inside were her poignant lines on a lifetime's losses written in 1876, after the death of Maria. She added the final couplet after Gabriel died in 1882:

No longer I hear the welcome sound
Of Father's foot upon the ground;
No longer see the loving face
Of Mother beam with kindly grace;
No longer hear 'how I rejoice'
At sight of me, from Sister's voice;
No more from Husband loved will be a
'Cara Francesca, moglie mia';
And from dear Daughter sore I miss
'My dearest Dodo', and her kiss:-
I never more shall hear him speak,
The dearly loved who called me 'Tique'.[35]

The sister was Margaret Polidori who died in 1867; Dodo was Maria's pet name for her mother and Tique was Dante Gabriel's contraction of 'the Antique' with which he teased Frances as she grew older.

Four years almost to the day after Gabriel's death, following a fall at home, Frances's energy simply ran out. William had always feared her death. 'There is no calamity in life that I think of with more gloom & terror than the possible loss of my own beloved mother', he had written to Kate Howell, the young wife of entrepreneur Charles Augustus Howell, when her mother died in 1869.[36] Both Christina and William watched Frances draw her last breath. 'My dearest Mother, the pattern to me of everything that is simple, sweet, kind, & noble, died on 8 Ap[ril 1886] at 25 minutes past noon. She had been unconscious for a couple of days or more, & expired in great peace, without any strain or agitation.'[37] For Christina it meant 'the practical close of her own life'. William, with a wife and young family to live for, nevertheless reflected on this monumental change, 'in the death of a mother there is something which, more than aught else, severs one from one's past: it is the breaking of a tie that subsisted in fullest force at the first moment of one's existence, and which has continued in almost or quite the like force ever since. I felt this'.[38]

Six years later as William watched Christina dying of breast cancer through the long autumn of 1894, he kept a record of his last conversations with his sister, however incoherent. 'We talked a little of our mother: and I said that her life might be considered on the whole a happy one, as lives go – much affection bestowed by her, and not a little received. Christina did not reply very definitely, but I inferred that she is less prepared than myself to regard our mother's life as happy.'[39]

One of Frances's and Christina's co-worshippers at Christ Church, Woburn Square, was Maud Newman who never forgot the interdependent relationship of mother and daughter. 'Mrs Rossetti was a particularly pretty and sweet looking old lady…Christina was a truly saintly woman…wrapt and absorbed in devotion, even to ecstasy. One thing only seemed to draw her soul back to this sublunary sphere, and that was her devotion to her mother. If the old lady showed the slightest fatigue, up would spring Christina from her knees and with a tender radiant smile that lit up her countenance, she would draw the mother's arm within her own and lead her gently out of church. If one met them out of doors, the old lady either walking or in a bath chair, they seemed ever engrossed in each other's society and often showed signs of merriment'.[40]

Frances's dominant position in the Rossetti family is mysterious. She may be viewed both as a benevolent and a negative force in all their lives – especially ambivalent in the conspicuous failure of either of her daughters to form enduring relationships outside the family. In fact, William was the only one of her four children to maintain an extended marriage. Photographs and portraits reveal little of Frances's magnetism, but do suggest considerable intelligence kept severely in check. Blind poet Philip Bourke Marston sounded almost the only negative note about Frances. 'William Michael Angelo and Gabriel Rossetti, too, were much attached to her. She never seemed to me a very lovable old lady, but I suppose she was, since she won the hearts of her children.'[41] The conundrum remains that she was far less rigid than either of her daughters. William explained to his young American friend Moncure Conway that 'as for my sisters, they wouldn't go to a theatre to save the British Islands from disappearing off the map: and my mother, though free from such prejudices, never *does* go to any such amusements'.[42]

THE BROMLEYS AND THE BROWNS

Although Lucy was born in Paris on 19 July 1843, in a sense her story began in rural Kent where her parents Ford Madox Brown (Bachelor – Esquire) a youth of nineteen married his cousin Elisabeth Bromley (Spinster – Commoner) aged twenty-two at St John's Church in the parish of Meopham on 3 April 1841.

The death from consumption of Brown's loving, supportive mother, Caroline Madox, early in September 1839, followed swiftly by the death of his elder sister Lyly (Eliza) in June 1840 had been traumatic for the young apprentice artist. Elisabeth Bromley (fig. 38), his Kentish cousin, stayed with the Browns in Antwerp on her way back from finishing school in Germany. To the bereaved boy she embodied mother, sister, sweetheart and wife in one. Painting the portrait of this lovely, accomplished elder cousin and asking her to model for the attendant in his dramatic picture *The Execution of Mary Queen of Scots* had caused 'an ensnaring of hearts' that led to their early marriage. At the ceremony, just thirteen days short of his twentieth birthday, Ford Madox Brown looked so fresh-faced and immature that the vicar enquired 'with some asperity, "Where is the bridegroom?"'[43]

38. Ford Madox Brown, *Elisabeth Brown, née Bromley* (?), 1843. Pencil, annotated later by William Michael Rossetti, ' Seems to be by Brown – From an acc[oun]t. book of his wife ending Nov./43'. Fredeman Family Collection.

The entry in the parish register still exists; the clerk spelled the bride's name 'Elizabeth', she signed herself 'Elisabeth Bromley' and the spelling seemed fluid throughout her short life. When her husband drew the design for her tombstone five brief years later, Brown used the spelling Elisabeth herself seems to have preferred. Entries in Elisabeth's gold-tooled, leather-bound commonplace book reveal a romantic, literary and religious young woman who copied out poetry and wrote her own. In it she recorded the loss of her first child, a boy, 'Born June 29th 1842 died July 4th aged 5 days'.[44]

At the intimate wedding in the ancient, dignified church with its fine nave dating from 1325 and its highly carved seventeenth-century pulpit, the witnesses included Augustus and Helen Bromley, Elisabeth's brother and sister-in-law. Helen was to play a crucial role both in parenting and educating the only surviving child of the union, Lucy Madox Brown, born just a year after the death of Elisabeth's first child.

Brown's mother, Lucy's paternal grandmother, Caroline Madox, came from an 'old Kentish family – among whose ancestors were Crusaders, one of whom, Sir Richard Manning, was knighted by Coeur-de-Lion on the field in Palestine', as the socially striving Lucy herself wrote in 1890.[45] Although her father's early years were spent partly on the continent in Dunkirk, Calais,

39. Ford Madox Brown, *The Bromley Children*, 1843 (?). Oil on canvas, 127 × 101 cm. Christie's Images Ltd.

Bruges, Ghent and Antwerp, Madox Brown retained an affection for his mother's and wife's county of origin, Kent.

This warmth of feeling for family and place is evident in his triple portrait of *The Bromley Children* (fig. 39),[46] probably 1843, showing Augustus and Helen Bromley's three eldest children: Helen junior who died in 1855 aged seventeen, Augustus junior with his hoop and skirts who died in 1845, and baby Louisa (died 1846) one shoe off and one shoe on - exactly as the artist would depict his first grandchild, Lucy's daughter Olivia in 1876 (see fig. 23).

Although Helen, the eldest child, with her hands neatly folded at the apex of the pyramidal design appears wooden and doll-like, her two younger siblings are real children. Augustus turns his head away shyly from the artist while little Louisa twitches her toes and engages playfully with young Uncle Ford. Madox Brown presents the frail children as oddly monumental set against an idealized Kent backdrop on a late summer day. Melliker[47] farmhouse (the children's home) in the idyllic village of Meopham may be indicated at the top left of the picture. An almost surreal, conical featured landscape – possibly

Reculver – appears behind Helen's head, with a surfy sea rolling in on the beach of the Medway estuary just above her shoulders. The trio is framed by overarching branches of trees in full foliage, promising maturity that the children would never fulfil. The census return of 1841, approximately two years before this picture was painted, reveals that Augustus Bromley, the children's father and head of the family was twenty-six and of 'independent means', while his Scottish wife Helen, née Weir, admitted to being nine years older at thirty-five. Their children, who appear in Madox Brown's picture, were three (young Helen), two (young Augustus) and baby Louisa was one month. Augustus and Helen Bromley's last child, Elizabeth Bromley (later Lizzie Cooper) born in 1843 and Lucy's closest friend in childhood and adolescence, does not feature in Brown's picture, which supports the hypothetical date of the triple portrait, just before her birth.

When his young wife, Elisabeth, died on 5 June 1846 in Madox Brown's arms, 'in the post-chaise on the Boulevard des Italiens in Paris, having to the last pointed onwards when words failed', according to Lucy's later restrained but romantic account,[48] the grieving father put his three-year-old daughter into the care of her, now widowed, aunt by marriage, Helen Bromley at Melliker Farm.

The long, low, red-brick building with its tall chimneys still stands today, a generously inviting home, set in green gardens beneath wide, Kentish skies. In Lucy's day, it was a farm of 154 acres. Then as now it is tucked into a safe corner of the comfortable Kent landscape, flanked by barns and outbuildings where a noisy cockerel struts. Its interior is low and beamed, the rooms rambling and informal, ideal for a small motherless girl whose father could only take intermittent breaks from his painting to come down by packet boat from London to see her on special occasions.

However welcome Lucy felt in Aunt Helen's family, she naturally resented not being allowed to live with the father she adored. She told her second daughter years later that after one of Madox Brown's visits to see her in Kent, she stamped on all the flowers in Aunt Helen's garden.[49] She never forgot that early separation from her one surviving parent. The experience underlay her later passion for her own children and for family life, particularly when chronic illness forced another form of separation upon her. Lucy was a spirited child, clearly no angel, as she enjoyed recalling. Once aged about six, she was taken to see Emily Patmore, 'the angel in the house'. 'The angel' greeted her from a top window, which apparently offended the child's dignity. Lucy 'did not like the angel' – or the associated concept of idealised, restricted womanhood – she told a supper party with tart amusement in 1892.[50]

A small watercolour dates probably from Lucy's teenage years.[51] It shows the Kent countryside, probably Melliker Farm, where Lucy spent her childhood

40. Lucy Madox Brown, *Melliker Farm*, undated. Watercolour, 246 × 321 mm. Private collection.

with aunt Helen Bromley and her young family (fig. 40). The old red-brick farmhouse has an unpretentious, welcoming façade and chimneys that indicate cheerful hearthsides within. Although clearly a juvenile piece of work, the picture is ambitiously composed and subtly toned. Ochre and terracotta farm buildings (with suggestions of oast-houses) are counterpointed with a stippled green landscape. Evidently, Lucy saw this place of her motherless, although not un-mothered childhood, as a green Eden.

Helen Bromley wasn't just Lucy's substitute mother; she was her school-teacher as well. Widowed in December 1843, the resourceful Scotswoman had to support her small family by teaching. She rented a large, new house called Milton Lodge at 25 (now 29) Clarence Place, Gravesend, four miles from Melliker Farm, where she established a small preparatory school for young girls and boys. Gravesend was developing as a holidaymaker's and day-tripper's resort in the middle of the century. Visitors came in huge numbers, up to a million a year, to enjoy the amenities of the town and its seaside. Three piers and several bathing stations complete with bathing machines encouraged the new craze for both sexes to take a dip in sea water. The town provided amusements such as theatre-going, shopping and music in its pleasure gardens. It was a diverting journey down the Thames by boat from London until the advent of the railways opened Kent to even more Londoners as the century progressed.

Gravesend is still full of authentic Victorian domestic architecture today. In the middle of the nineteenth century Milton Lodge was newly built and attractively modern, with heavy timbered gables, gothic arched windows and small balconies favoured by contemporary architects. A green-and-white glass lantern on the roof allowed natural light to flood down the stairwell.

The substantial building contained good-sized 'Drawing and Dinner rooms, neat Morning Rooms, Spacious School Rooms, Three principal and Four other Bed Chambers, convenient Kitchen, Scullery, Larder, Two Water Closets, and other Accommodations,' fitted with marble chimney-pieces and a range of cupboards. A pleasing shrubbery within a handsome exterior brick wall and neat iron entrance gates surrounded the house. In 1854 its 'highly respectable tenant' Mrs Helen Bromley paid £70 per annum rent.[52]

There is a surviving 'snapshot' of the residents of the school on the night of 30 March 1851. The census recorded that the head of the household and schoolmistress was Helen Bromley, now admitting to forty-eight years of age. She had been running a school on these premises since at least 1847, and possibly earlier. Her two surviving daughters and 'scholars at home' were listed as Helen, now thirteen and Elizabeth, eight. Her niece Emma Lucy Brown was seven, her birthplace the only exotic one in Milton Lodge's records – 'France British subject'. There were nine boys ranging in age from

41. Aunt Helen Bromley. Cathy Hueffer's photograph album, STH/BH/2/3-6. The Stow Hill Collection, HLRO, and the Hon. Oliver Soskice.

seven to thirteen but only five girls (of whom three were Helen's two daughters and niece Lucy), aged three to thirteen. The unequal ratio of boys to girls may reflect the fact that Victorian parents were more likely to spend money educating their sons rather than their daughters – or could be sheer chance. Presumably the children listed on the census return boarded at Milton Lodge. Two junior teachers, Mercy Salmon and Harriott Robinson both aged twenty-three, assisted Aunt Helen – with two servants, Sarah Shane and Martha Fordham.

It is clear that Aunt Helen's rule was benign both in the schoolroom and in the home. She supplied the mothering which Lucy had lost so abruptly before her third birthday and which she said she mourned for the rest of her life. Aunt Helen could identify with Lucy's bereavement as she had lost both husband and children. Lucy responded to Helen's warm personality and was grateful for the surrogate mothering open-heartedly offered, so that throughout her life she visited Helen in Gravesend (where she continued to run the school until at least 1881)[53] and to be visited by her in London, often for a week at a time,[54] until the old lady's death on 10 June 1886.[55] Years later William called Aunt Helen 'a truly worthy Scotch lady, hearty and amiable' (fig. 41).[56]

Lucy was not included in Madox Brown's new family life in London, although she visited in school holidays, sometimes with her cousin Lizzie Bromley. Later Lucy believed her father kept her away because of her stepmother Emma's increasing alcoholism. She told her daughter Helen that Emma Brown and Lizzie Siddal (who married Gabriel in 1860) were both drunkards, although Lizzie disguised the habit to some extent by taking laudanum. This was their real tragedy, which snobbish Lucy attributed to their lower class origins. But her view was rooted in resentment. Looking back, she felt her early life was overshadowed and spoilt as her father had to keep her out of the house where Emma and Lizzie used to 'carouse'.[57] Even when she left Aunt Helen's school and came up to London in 1856 to continue her education under the tutelage of Maria Rossetti, her father preferred her to board with the Rossettis (at £40 per annum) rather than live at home with the family, first at 1 Grove Villas, Finchley, later at Fortess Terrace, Kentish Town.

It was hard enough in 1850 for seven-year-old Lucy to accept the birth of Cathy, Emma and Madox Brown's first child. Five years later her father broke the news by letter of another usurper to his eldest daughter

> in the shape of a brother for you – he is very little as yet and his complexion is none of the clearest but he will improve in the course of time no doubt, and at any rate his nose is very fine and large for so young a child…I hope to come and see you before long but I cannot name a day at present …[Cathy] sends you her love and kiss and says that she has broken some of her toys – a good many I fear.[58]

42. Ford Madox Brown, *Oliver Madox Brown, Aged Four Months*, 1855. Pencil, 273 × 237 mm. The Attlesey/Shales Collection.

If Cathy broke her dolls on the arrival of Oliver, displaced Lucy may have felt equally murderous, especially as her father gave no definite date to visit. A few weeks later he deferred his visit yet again, assuring her, 'Your mama and little Brother are very well and he is getting quite fat and handsome. He is a regular little pig and only thinks about stuffing himself till he is sick. He is to be called Oliver', and he promised she would at least be present at his christening.[59]

Cathy remembered that with the birth of Oliver she 'was relegated to the background of things'. Her father was delighted to have a son, 'he did not care for girls he always said' (fig. 42). When Lucy finally came to visit, Cathy was 'under the impression she did not know of the existence of myself or my brother till that day'.[60] In spite of, or perhaps because of this sidelining of his daughters, Lucy and Cathy spent their lives trying to please their combative father. He was a constant factor in the element of competition that always subsisted between them.

If Madox Brown often disappointed Lucy during her childhood by not seeing her in person, he wrote warmly affectionate, characteristically unpunctuated letters with a stream of adult news. Early in 1855, Tom Seddon the artist had just returned from Jerusalem, her father told Lucy, 'where he left Mr Hunt who since he left has been to the *Dead Sea* to paint it and on the road was deserted by his Arab conductors and obliged to find his way back alone the youngest Miss Seddon Louisa is still at school in France. Thomas brought me back a very large Arab pipe. I was at the Seddons a few nights ago and Tom dressed himself as a real Arab of the desert and Christina Rossetti as a Sirian [*sic*] girl'.[61]

43. Dante Gabriel Rossetti, *Ford Madox Brown*, 31 January 1867. Pencil, 203 × 162 mm. Inscribed with monogram and 'To E.C.C. Jan 31 1867' (given on the occasion of the marriage of Lucy's cousin Elizabeth Bromley to Samuel Cooper). Surtees 270. Private collection.

A year later, Lucy left school in Gravesend and came up to London. As she grew up, her father came to depend on her competence and intelligence and he and Emma often left the two younger children in her care. 'Tell Cathy and Nol that if they are *good* we will bring them home a present each from Southend and if they are not they will have nothing but whackings instead.'[62]

Madox Brown understood and encouraged an interest in fashion among the female members of his family. Lucy loved shoes and in 1865 he itemized her three pairs of boots (one pair kid), slippers, shoes and tassels.[63] He commissioned Lucy to buy rings for Emma and he cast his artistic eye over 'a very beautifully embroidered dress, black and white on white muslin' that cousin Lizzie Cooper had sent to Lucy. 'Of course it is intended as an imitation of the fashion of last year but by cutting off some of the bottom I think it will make a splendid walking dress', and he enclosed a sketch to explain exactly where the embroidery should be curtailed 'inside the scrolled line'.[64] But he also discussed art with her and sought her advice on English and French poetry he was writing in triolets.[65] Throughout her life, Lucy turned to her father – 'wish I could have your advice' – in illness and in earthquake.[66] She adored him and forgave, if she did not forget, his early absences during her childhood. Cousin Lizzie had no father figure of her own and worshipped Lucy's. When Lizzie married Samuel Cooper, Gabriel's wedding present was a magnificent drawing of Uncle Ford (fig. 43).

Elizabeth (Lizzie) Bromley, Aunt Helen's daughter and Lucy's first cousin and almost exact contemporary, was her closest friend throughout her childhood and adolescence. They grew up together and attended Milton Lodge School together. When Lucy came up from Gravesend to visit her family in

London, Lizzie often came too. Lizzie was light-hearted and fun; she loved Uncle Ford, Emma, and Lucy's half-siblings Cathy and Nolly. Lucy and Lizzie shared secrets, sewed bonnets and frocks and talked about beaux. Lucy was almost as good at making bonnets as she was at watercolours which she presented to Lizzie.

As they both entered their twenties, excitable Lizzie became more and more obsessed with romantic intrigues. She had considerable 'attention', many admirers, and enjoyed the sensation that 'love is not happiness, it is an agony of minds'.[67] She constantly opened her heart to Lucy and expected her more self-contained cousin to reciprocate in a girlish exchange of romantic confidences. But Lucy was cagey.

Then, suddenly, Lizzie met Samuel Cooper, a slightly exotic figure. He was an Anglo-Indian (Eurasian) government official who proposed to Lizzie within a fortnight (figs 44 and 45). She was wild with enchantment and instantly accepted. Lucy told Little Cat (her sister Cathy) that Mr Cooper was

44. Samuel Cooper. Cathy Hueffer's photograph album, STH/BH/2/3-6. The Stow Hill Collection, HLRO, and the Hon. Oliver Soskice.

45. Elizabeth Cooper, née Bromley. Cathy Hueffer's photograph album, STH/BH/2/3-6. The Stow Hill Collection, HLRO, and the Hon. Oliver Soskice.

not very large physically but a great swell. 'We shall wear white ourselves so it will be not great expense but be pretty'. Lizzie's 'trousseau is superb such dresses etc – she got all in 2 days her shoes & gloves are ravishing she says it is the only thing worth being married for'.[68] After the wedding Samuel took Lizzie out to India where she was just as instantly disenchanted. Within weeks, he had become 'detestable' to her. She found the expatriate community small-minded, 'vulgar' and uncongenial. Indian culture was bewildering and threatening and sent her into manic desperation. If she spoke to another man, it set off a scandal. 'All the swells in the place have called upon me, they cannot bear Sam. People with dark blood in them out here are slighted though at home they are tolerated. I consider I have been cruelly deceived and he really is so difficult to understand. He never forgets and brings things up over and over again.'[69]

The climate caused fainting fits two or three times a day and Lizzie never recovered her strength after an early miscarriage. In a series of hectic, densely crosshatched letters on onionskin paper she longed for her mother, Helen Bromley, and to come home. 'I never knew how sincerely I loved you till I left you', she declared to Lucy. 'I am afraid you used to think me very disagreeable, but now I am a regular virago – really!'[70] For her part, Lucy sent her bonnets and frills as well as the *Illustrated London News* and the *Fortnightly Review,* but she had no inclination to follow Lizzie out to India, however much her cousin pressed her.

Eventually, Lizzie did come home, in a flutter about whether to land in England in her 'black silk'. The combination of India and marriage had made her 'so nervous that the least thing makes my heart beat so and I tremble like a leaf'.[71] Vivacious Lizzie was never happy with Samuel Cooper and in 1875, aged thirty-two, she died suddenly 'of apoplexy', shopping in a silk mercer's at St Paul's Churchyard.[72] Only a few weeks after her first confinement, Lucy rushed to be with Lizzie's mother, Helen Bromley. Her presence would be 'the best substitute perhaps for that of her poor daughter', Frances Rossetti wrote sympathetically to Lucy.[73] Although the cousins had been forced apart by geography and different priorities as Lucy took up her career in art, she mourned Lizzie, a symbol of their shared youth spent in the Kent countryside.

Samuel Cooper remarried on 15 September 1881 after another whirlwind courtship and William and Lucy went to the wedding. William thought the bride, Miss Studd, was 'noticeable and rather handsome' with 'strongly marked black eyebrows' and 'a handsome fortune of £1200 a year. They will sail for India shortly.'[74]

46. Cathy Hueffer, née Madox Brown, aged about twenty. Cathy Hueffer's photograph album, STH/BH/2/3-6. The Stow Hill Collection, HLRO, and the Hon. Oliver Soskice

LUCY AND CATHY – HALF-SISTERS

to me even now the memory wrankles [*sic*]
  Catherine Madox Brown Hueffer, *Jottings*, 1922, unpublished MS

Cathy (born 11 November 1850) (fig. 46) was the second daughter of Ford Madox Brown and first child of his wife Emma Hill. She was seven years younger than her stepsister Lucy but exaggerated it to ten in her own mind. Her grandson encouraged her to write her memoirs but she could never quite get down to it, although some unpublished autobiographical jottings recorded a bitter sense of rivalry with Lucy.

In old age, Cathy's resentment was still unabated when she recalled Lucy's snobbery due to her superior education during the late 1850s,

> partly with her aunt Helen Bromley – and later with the Rossetti family – & still later she had many other lessons. She was almost ten years older than myself. We never got on together & only agreed on various points – when we were quarrelling. I remember one quarrel we had was when she abused my mother (to me) & said she did not wonder at my behaviour as I was only a farmer's brat. I retorted there is an old saying Lucy – that 'birds of a feather flock together' meaning that her people had also been farmers. I had my ears boxed for my impertinence & the fray ended. I think I was about 9 or ten at the time. She was a strange mixture with a violent temper and a strong brain which was shown partly by her high forehead & big nose, & I remember she had an odd way – (when talking to anyone who

admired her) of flirting with the ceiling & turning her fine brown eyes up at the corners & smiling at said ceiling…

She was a remarkable woman…She could [not] bear me & when she came to see us sometimes used to push me aside & call me a nasty little brat. She did not approve of my Father having married again: & that only a Farmer's daughter…forgetting that *her* family (my Father's cousins) were also Farmer's children. However that time is long past – but to me even now the memory wrankles.[75]

Cathy's first *Jotting* recalled a frightening encounter in the garden with her father's friend, Dante Gabriel Rossetti. He pulled a funny face at her through a glass door and, terrified, she ran into the back garden where she fell into a bed of nettles. Her tormentor told the two-year-old to rub her inflamed skin with lump sugar but the remedy failed and the nettles stung for hours afterwards. This was not an isolated incident. On 4 December 1854 when 'Kattie' was just four years old, Madox Brown noted Gabriel threatened 'he would put her *in the fire*. Begins to us, on entering, with "That ass of a child" – I stop him with "I've told you before I don't choose you to call my child an ass, it is not gentlemanly to come & abuse persons children to them – If you can't stay here without calling her names you had better go." He did *not go* but was silent for the rest of the eveng.'[76] In complete contrast with the elder Rossetti brother, Cathy always held 'the warmest of affectionate feelings' for William, the younger and gentler brother.

Lucy's resentment of Cathy, the usurper in her father's affections, was compounded when Cathy grew into a distinct beauty and a talented artist. Brown's new wife, Emma, had perfect skin and chestnut hair which she could sit upon. Cathy inherited her mother's bloom but with blue eyes and dazzlingly fair complexion and hair. In 1927 all her obituaries commented on her physical loveliness and natural vivacity. Her daughter Juliet remembered how Cathy could make a room seem pretty as soon as she entered it. Beneath her Victorian traditions was a vivid, impulsive nature, generous and large-hearted, animated by intense likes and dislikes. She could be both very discerning or, alternatively, almost childishly naïve. It was hardly surprising that Lucy, the elder sister, could sometimes find Cathy irritating or that Cathy envied Lucy's superior accomplishments all her life. Effectively, Cathy was debarred from Lucy's academic standards from the age of thirteen when her parents discussed her education. 'Her mother wished Catherine to be brought up conventionally, but her father wanted to make an artist of her. They asked her what she wished and, as drawing was easier to her than ordinary lessons, she asked to be an artist.' [77] So she began her apprenticeship at once, training in her father's studio, like an early Renaissance painter.

As Cathy grew up, her relationship with Lucy matured. Cathy's son, Ford Madox [Ford] Hueffer, believed 'there was of course a long standing feud between my mother and Mrs. W.M.R. [Lucy] (but for God's sake whisper not a word of that to *anyone*)'[78] – an oversimplified analysis. At various times, Lucy and Cathy's relationship was composed of varying measures of rivalry and companionship, both in the studio and at home. They trained together, painted each other, went to parties together, discussed romantic intrigues, were brides-maids together, holidayed together and confided in each other about marriage, pregnancies and children. Sometimes their shared concerns brought them into genuine intimacy, at other times they quarrelled with feral intensity. 'Huffs' and 'scenes' often created unforgivably in front of her children, according to Lucy, were recurring features in their relationship. But when Lucy's baby Michael died and she drew his portrait in death, Cathy made her own companion sketch of Michael, sharing Lucy's unspeakable sorrow. Later that summer of 1883 the sisters holidayed together in Hythe. Cathy drew Lucy's portrait[79] and comforted her when the remaining twin, Mary, was sick in the night. 'Cathy as usual was most kind', knowing Lucy dreaded the convulsions which had pre-saged Michael's death.[80]

As a child of seven, Lucy's daughter Helen stayed with Cathy's family at 90 Brook Green, while Lucy was in San Remo. Helen found Cathy 'one of the most trying and unreasonable women I have ever known – all huffs and excitements and hysteria, fanciful, untruthful and violent', and her husband, Frank, though a man of 'great culture and talent', nevertheless 'very Germanic, unjust and brutal with his sons[81], fanatically devoted to his little daughter[82], and generally detested in his family'.[83] With her intellectual aspi-rations, Lucy admired Frank who had written a book on Wagner, and gener-ally discounted Cathy's confidences about him. Cathy outlived Lucy by over thirty years. When she wrote her autobiographical jottings in old age she was cast back to some of her earliest childhood memories of Lucy and disregarded the many shared, if difficult, years of adulthood.

WILLIAM AND CATHY – IN-LAWS

William had known Cathy since she was born. Her childhood memories of William as a young man in his early twenties were benevolent, the complete reverse of her spooked fear of Dante Gabriel. As a toddler Cathy haunted William to the point of amused exasperation until he had to summon her mother, 'Emma, Emma take this little cuss away, she won't go & I can't get dressed' and the memory was suffused with sunshine for Cathy who remem-bered 'my pretty young mother taking me in her arms down the stairs into the garden, where my father was in his shirt sleeves weeding out candituft [*sic*] .'[84]

From the age of five, her parents took Cathy on theatre visits, which some-times included William. On 19 February 1856 Madox Brown, Emma, William, twelve-year-old Lucy and Cathy sat in the dress circle at the

Princess's Theatre in Oxford Street to see Charles Kean and his wife Ellen Tree play Cardinal Wolsey and Catherine of Aragon in Shakespeare's *Henry VIII*. After the play Cathy informed William, her favourite Rossetti brother, 'who was alluding to the Angels in Henry VIII "that she once saw some real angels up in the sky"'.[85]

Cathy married on 3 September 1872, aged nearly twenty-two, significantly ahead of Lucy who was already twenty-nine. Her husband was Dr Franz Xavier Hüffer (later anglicized to Francis or Frank Hueffer), a musicologist and Wagner specialist from Germany. William wrote Cathy a playful, quasi-romantic letter enclosing an exotic wedding present. 'Will you accept from me the accompanying Indian shawl…for your continuous happiness as bride & wife…May you be as happy, my sweet girl, as your dear father & mother'. He hoped the colours of the shawl would 'match well with your complexion & with gold tint – of which there is a large crop, native to your head'. With male self-consciousness he explained she should 'fold the shawl so that the pattern is all shown on the right side: to you I have no doubt this will present no difficulty, tho to me it wd. be a fit form of discipline preparatory to squaring the circle'.[86] His shawl 'shone among the presents',[87] as Maria reported to Christina, but William himself could not get leave from the office to attend the wedding breakfast for which Lucy had written the invitations.

Both Cathy and William suffered from stressful marriages and supported each other in practical ways at crisis points. When illness forced Lucy to go south in the winters, Cathy or her parents looked after one or more of William and Lucy's small children. Perhaps on one of these visits Cathy painted the watercolour portrait of Lucy's daughter Helen aged about eight, which is recorded in William's 1908 Inventory.[88] Lucy was away in Biarritz during January 1889 when Cathy's husband Frank died suddenly on 19 January, leaving her in 'terrible affliction', as well as acute financial embarrassment.[89] William offered moral as well as realistic support; assured her 'you and yours are hardly a minute in the day out of my thoughts, my dear Cathy',[90] and explored employment opportunities for her two boys. The age of Ford the eldest boy brought back ambivalent memories of William's own truncated youth. He told Cathy that Ford 'ought now to regard his schooling as finished. My schooling closed at the same age, 15, and I at once became one of the scanty bread-winners of my then very impoverished family'.[91] Poor Cathy's eyes 'looked almost extinguished on Sunday…still she bears herself with reason and fortitude' (fig. 47).

William admired the unexpectedly stoical bearing of the three Hueffer children, a Roman virtue of which he had intimate knowledge. 'If the highest ideal of life is to accept everything exactly as it comes, without emotion and without comment,' Cathy's children 'might teach a lesson to all of us'.[92] As Frank's financial affairs unravelled, Cathy's position deteriorated. William contemplated writing to Frank's editor at *The Times*, as well as organizing a

47. Cathy
Hueffer, *Self-
portrait, c.* 1890 or
later. Watercolour,
267 × 229 mm.
Private collection.

memorial concert to raise funds for Cathy. His desire to serve Cathy was 'great, very great' but he acknowledged the prerogative of Madox Brown and the two trustees, and decided to remain quiescent.[93] In summer 1889 Lucy acted as William's secretary, circulating a memorial letter to elicit influential signatures to petition for a Civil List Pension for Cathy.[94] Professor Edward Dowden of Trinity College, Dublin was one of the signatories and suggested other names to approach, but the pension never materialized. Over a decade later Cathy still struggled on an annual income of only £60 and William frequently made loans to her, which she always endeavoured to repay.

When Lucy complained about Cathy's behaviour, William was always prepared to listen - but tried to defuse the Madox Brown dynamite. 'About Cathy, my full belief is that she has some good qualities, and some bad ones: in this she resembles myself certainly, and several other people probably', he commented, and quoted Matthew on forgiveness.[95] Isolated because of ill health in Bournemouth during the spring of 1892, Lucy felt the rebuke. 'It is very kind of you to think of my soul & eternal welfare, I assure you I think of that too…& I assure you I have practised, if not preached, the counsel you quote in the text on forgiveness, I was brought up as a Christian & still honour, I think all, the doctrines of Christ'. Although Lucy at times considered Cathy 'mad if not bad', she told William, 'I was always a friend to her poor mother [Emma Madox Brown had died 11 October 1890] who said so to the last'.[96] Lucy was convinced Cathy had 'insulted' her children, yet again, and that William had shown insufficient sympathy – 'I like a little sympathy'.[97]

Cathy never forgot or underestimated William's affection for her. When he finally had to abandon hope for Lucy's recovery in March 1894, William wrote a bleak postcard to Cathy just before leaving for San Remo. 'Another telegram "much worse" – so Arthur & I must go tomorrow. I have no hope as to result. Goodbye. W.M.R.'[98] As soon as he reached Italy, he wrote immediately to Cathy again, confiding his anguish on onion-skin writing paper that over a century later still feels physically limp with its burden of emotion. 'Lucy is still with us: you may imagine my feelings when at the S. Remo station I learned this from Helen, having travelled all the way from London in the belief that we had lost her.' The immediate crisis had been averted by Dr Ansaldi, so that 'still dear Lucy is here, & goes on from day to day', although William did not alter his view of the final outcome. It was important to him he could tell Cathy that 'Lucy is – & always has been – perfectly clear-minded.'[99]

Around Lucy's death on 12 April 1894, 'in deep dejection',[100] William discontinued his diary for four months and curtailed his usually profuse letter writing. 'The power of expressing myself, save in the baldest terms, seems gone from me for the time', he explained to Cathy.[101] As soon as she heard the inevitable news from Italy, Cathy gathered her thoughts to offer William what little she had that might fulfil his immediate needs and allay his grief. She hesitated to intrude on his sorrow but wanted to give him two suits that had belonged to Madox Brown, her father and Lucy's, as William was the only proper person to wear them. She continued: 'I am selling *everything* in the house except poor Lucy's picture of the "Music Lesson" [*The Duet*, see fig. 80] & her drawing of my brother[102] which she wished back again: my poor little head of Lucy [103] done some years ago & given to Papa on his birthday if you care to have it. (Papa as you may know liked it) Papa's Mother's head & little children's head (My mother's Arthur) for your children…There is also a chalk or pencil head of Lucy[104] when a very young girl if your children would like it as Papa used to say it was very like her'.[105] He replied by return of post, doubting he could ever bring himself to wear Madox Brown's suits but said young 'Arthur *probably* might at some time get them altered, & then wear them.' He was grateful for all Cathy's other offers, although he gently advised her not to give away Madox Brown's portrait head of Emma's baby Arthur (fig. 115), who had died long ago, aged ten months in July 1857. 'You should retain it, the relationship to yourself being so very much closer'.[106]

A year later, close to the first anniversary of Lucy's death, William made sad reciprocation. Deeply absorbed putting the final sentences to his *Memoir* of Gabriel, he remembered to send Cathy a photograph and two books in memory of Christina, a 'shabbyish' copy of *Lorna Doone*, which had been a present from Madox Brown long ago and Gabriel's *Dante and his Circle*. If she would like anything else, he added, 'I could gladly make it yours'.[107]

He continued to keep in touch with Cathy, informed her about the upkeep of Madox Brown's grave (to which he did not expect her to contribute), exchanged lecture and concert tickets with her and took a genuine

48. Photograph of Christina Rossetti in a polka-dot dress. Possibly one of the lost photographs taken by Henrietta Rintoul (see p. 340, n. 19). Fredeman Family Collection.

interest in her children. Cathy sensed concern behind his rectitude – 'you are always just & I think understand my position'.[108] He felt relaxed enough with her to joke about his gout and gout-boots that accompanied him on his voyage to Australia with Helen at the end of 1896. She reminded him how as small girls, Helen and her cousin Juliet used to dig for hours in the back garden to get through the earth to Australia. Now Helen was going in reality.[109]

CHRISTINA AND LUCY – SISTERS-IN-LAW

I do not suppose we are altogether congenial…What a rigmarole, all about my precious self! [110]

Christina Rossetti to Caroline Gemmer[111] about Lucy [2 January 1875]

When Christina (fig. 48) sat down to anatomize the tension between herself and her new sister-in-law, Lucy had been married to William for just nine months. Trying to stress their mutual respect, an undoubted antipathy choked Christina's convoluted sentence structure, or 'rigmarole' as she called it herself. She could not disguise the lack of rapport she felt with Lucy and her letter to Caroline Gemmer, with its copious underlinings and exclamation marks, reads like an outrush of relief (for discussion of the letter, see chapter seven, pp. 230–1). At last she could confide in a friend who would really understand.

Perhaps Christina had habituated herself to an emotional over-reliance on William. He lived at home and was a constant in her life. At a practical level, he supported her financially for at least twenty years, often brokering her arrangements with publishers. Although he did not share her religious outlook, he had a sensibility which accepted and understood her emotional

needs. In a rare moment of frivolity, Christina described to her old friend
Amelia Heimann a party she and William had attended with charades, music,
good food and even dancing. 'Perhaps you know I don't "polk" but that good-
natured William setting at nought fraternal etiquette gave me a turn, and I
enjoyed it much.'[112] William was always sensitive to Christina and felt intuitively that dancing was a release, an innocent stimulant that she rarely allowed
herself. When he danced with Christina at Dr Epps's party in February 1858,
he was still officially engaged to Henrietta Rintoul – although there is no
record that she was present. After his engagement with Henrietta terminated
in 1860, William remained a bachelor for fourteen years, more available than
ever for his siblings' needs.

It had never crossed Christina's mind that Lucy might enter the Rossetti
family on an intimate basis. Before the Rossetti–Brown alliance was
announced in 1873, Christina had been appreciative of Lucy's personality.
When Gabriel suffered a nervous breakdown in June 1872, at the same time
that Christina was seriously ill with Graves's disease, she noted the younger
woman's sensitivity, 'Lucy called this morning full of grief and sympathy'.[113]
And in April 1873, Christina told Gabriel that 'Mrs. Madox Brown and Lucy
called on us before we left London, the latter looking pale but not complain-
ing of illness. What a delightful person she is!'[114] Christina made this observation just before Lucy joined the holiday party to Italy with the Bell Scott
entourage and William Rossetti which was to result in an engagement. This
change in Lucy's status would complicate forever Christina's response to her.

Christina wrote separately to both Lucy and William to congratulate them
in July 1873. During the nine months of the engagement, however, Christina
and Lucy began to grate on one another's nerves. Lucy enjoyed entertaining
her friends, in a way that Christina and William both shrank from. Her un-
Rossettian taste for social life caused immediate difficulties and Christina
offered to move out of 56 Euston Square five months before Lucy was due to
enter it as a bride. Christina apologized to William for her 'ebullition of temper', which years later William could not recall but could 'safely say it was a
trifle'.[115] Christina protested her ill health:

> My sleeping in the library cannot but have made evident to you how
> improper a person I am to occupy any room next a diningroom. My cough
> (which surprised Lucy, as I found afterwards, the other day at dinner), not
> to speak to other far worse matters of noise which with a habitual invalid
> are inevitable, makes it unseemly for me to be continually and unavoidably
> within earshot of Lucy and her guests.

She specifically absolved William: '*You* I do not mention, so completely have
you accommodated yourself to the trying circumstances of my health: but
when a "love paramount" reigns amongst us, even you may find such toleration

an impossibility'. Christina explained she had suffered a serious relapse in her heart condition and was once again under the care of Sir William Jenner for enlargement in the throat. She and Frances, who was 'in grief and anxiety', whose 'tender heart receives all stabs from every side', were ready to move out at once to save further social embarrassment. Indeed Christina could scarcely see 'any way out of the difficulty short of a separation'.[116] Temporarily at least the problem was solved by Christina moving her bedroom out of the library, to share with her mother in the back drawing-room. After William and Lucy's marriage in 1874, Frances and Christina increasingly escaped to the Polidori aunts at 12 Bloomsbury Square until they finally moved to 30 Torrington Square at Michaelmas 1876.

Christina and her mother tactfully stayed away in Eastbourne when William and Lucy returned to London from their Italian honeymoon in mid-May 1874. Christina wrote to her brother 'To think that you two now have one home and one heart – May they be full of peace, love, and happiness', a little rippling subtext suggesting her own doubts on the subject.

One of the most healing factors in the relationship between Lucy and Christina came with the birth of Lucy's children. Although Christina had written verses and stories specifically for children, she believed herself to be un-maternal. But the role of an aunt she could fulfil. In spite of prickly relations with her sister-in-law, Christina was half repelled and half attracted by Lucy's pregnancy in which she took an empathetic interest, expressing keen anticipation at the prospect of owning 'a small nephew or niece!'[117] This proprietorial note was constant in her feelings towards Lucy and William's growing brood. Unlikely at nearly forty-five ever to be a mother, her aunt-hood gave her a valued stake in the next generation, with responsibilities she could grow into, even though she felt consistently 'deficient in the nice motherly ways which win and ought to win a child's heart'.[118]

There was momentary elation in Christina's voice when she reported on Tuesday, 21 September 1875: 'My Dear Gabriel, We have a niece! Born about 8 o'clock (after considerable suffering of poor Lucy) on yesterday evening the 20th. Both mother & child safe, and William our informant this morning'.[119] When William published this letter in *The Family Letters of Christina Rossetti* in 1908 he edited out Christina's parenthetical but distinctly interested remark about Lucy's labour, perhaps for reasons of delicacy, but also because he recalled too painfully how Lucy had 'moaned and cried'.[120] Looking back on family life in general, and on married life with Lucy in particular, he saw a relentless pattern of endless suffering. 'Is there any trial greater or more wearing than that of ever-recurring illnesses and deaths among the persons near and dear to one?' he asked. Although he believed 'that there are some trials still more formidable, as especially those which involve grave self-reproach or public dishonour, merited or unmerited', in his own life he 'found nothing more afflictive than long continued illnesses among close relatives or connexions, followed by death'.[121] Of these, he had extensive experience.

Christina and Frances continued to live with William and Lucy during most of the first year of baby Olive's life but it soon became imperative that they should move to separate accommodation. 'William is cut up, I think, at losing our dearest Mother;' confessed Christina to Gabriel, 'but I am evidently unpleasing to Lucy, and could we exchange personalities, I have no doubt I should then feel with her feelings'.[122] Christina told Lucy that 'a comfortable residence has been fixed upon for our home party in Torrington Sq., No. 30. I hope when two roofs shelter us & when faults which I regret are no longer your daily trial, that we may regain some of that liking which we had as friends & which I should wish to be only the more tender & warm now that we are sisters. Don't, please, despair of my doing better'. Christina berated herself for the breakdown of her precarious friendship with Lucy. In his awkward position as both brother and husband, William did not flinch from publishing this embarrassing letter in 1908 after the sisters-in-law had been dead for a dozen years. 'Christina here takes blame to herself, and imputes none to her correspondent. There might be something to remark about this, but the less said the better', William added, implicitly reapportioning a measure of blame to his dead, combative Lucy.[123]

Although the advent of children was generally restorative to relations between Lucy and Christina, misunderstandings continued to thrive, for instance when a nursemaid reported to Lucy that two-year-old Olive had outstayed her welcome when visiting Torrington Square. Although she did not count on it, Christina hoped that some day her niece would come to love her, and she begged Lucy not to 'check Olive's coming here, or her perfect freedom when she is here…"Kiss and be friends" is a very sound old exhortation: get Olive to be my proxy, and I shall not need to fear the result. Need I?'[124] The pleading question revealed Christina's wariness of Lucy's unpredictability and the emotional distance between them. The unappealing reality had to be faced. As wife and mother Lucy had staked out the upper ground. Even on her own territory of literary production, when *A Pageant and Other Poems* came out in August 1881, Christina craved Lucy's words of approval, '*thin-skinned* I value them'.[125]

Christina continued to be nervous of Lucy's moods. She wrote apprehensively to her sister-in-law just before Christmas 1881. 'My dear Lucy, I dare say you guess what is coming!' Gabriel had suffered a partial paralysis earlier in December, a portent of his final illness, and for his mother and sister the idea of joining William and Lucy's family party on Christmas Day at such a moment of crisis faded 'into extra impossibility'. 'God help us,' Christina prayed, with a deliberate jab at Lucy's humanist position, 'for human help is but a very helpless thing'.[126]

After Gabriel's final ordeal was over, Christina found she could share literary enthusiasms and recommendations with Lucy. 'You were talking about books the other day, – have you read Wilkie Collins's *Moonstone*? It was the last I read to poor dear Gabriel, and it interested us.'[127] Both Christina and Lucy found it easier to offer each other compassion and understanding in writing rather than in person. 'My dear Lucy,' wrote Christina in 1882, 'We cannot hear from William of your Father's being ill, without my writing to express my Mother's and my own affectionate sympathy.'[128]

At this moment Christina's sympathies were particularly acute as she was engaged in reading and sorting all correspondence from her dear, dead brother. Lucy's daughterly concern for a parent was an emotional area Christina could fully understand. She also shared Lucy's passion for educating the children and praised Lucy for her high academic standards. Lucy had played the piano from childhood. By her early twenties, her repertoire included difficult pieces by Beethoven, Clementi, Handel, Haydn, Meyerbeer, Mozart and Weber.[129] On their marriage in 1874, William bought her a Broadwood piano for £80, which took him three years to pay off in instalments. But Aunt Cathy was more naturally musical and encouraged Olive to sing. Christina was conscious this was a talent she had never possessed. If Mamma ever 'hears Olive warble forth a sweet soprano melody, it may do something towards supplying the defects of her own unmusical daughters. So Cathy cultivates graces while you train intellects among your young people: a capital exchange', Christina commented benignly on 22 August 1883.[130]

But two days later Christina's mood of self-denigration and self-abasement resurfaced. She apologized to Lucy for her temper, although even she felt she had come a long way since her youth, 'Ask William, who knew me in my early stormy days: he could a tale unfold.' However, apart from some early childhood fractiousness, William recalled 'she had really never been ill-tempered or exasperating with me, that I can remember, and I had no "tale to unfold"'. Christina continued to prostrate herself before Lucy, 'indeed I am sorry to recollect how much you yourself have undergone from my irritability, and how much there is for you to bury in kind oblivion. I fear you may detect me in many an inconsistency, yet I assure you that in theory you do not deem consistency more essential than do I.'[131]

It is difficult to assess whether Lucy ever made any similar apologies to Christina, as Christina was in the habit of destroying nearly all incoming correspondence. They both exerted a strenuous effort to remain on good letter-writing terms, at least. When Lucy was away in Ventnor during the winter of 1886, trying to avoid another critical attack of bronchial pneumonia, Christina responded expansively to Lucy's 'last delightful letter' with literary news and considerable female flattery. She trusted Lucy would rejoice William's heart by flourishing in the warmer atmosphere of the Isle of Wight and would come 'into fuller bloom before his eyes'. She tried to coax Lucy into loving her, hoping that Katharine Tynan, the attractive young Irish poet, had told William what she had told Christina – that she preferred Gabriel's portrait of Lucy (fig. 22) to that of Lizzie Siddal. 'I wonder whether you will think this worth telling you! (I should appreciate it, were it I.)'[132]

Christina conveyed her love more naturally from a distance, commiserated over the children's illnesses, and relished the idea of bucket and spading close to the seashore. 'To this day I think I could plod indefinitely along shingle with my eyes pretty well glued to the ground.'[133] She rejoiced that Lucy was not suffering the severe London winter of 1886 and consequent rioting in the capital,

> but, however one may deplore lawlessness, it is heart-sickening to think of the terrible want of work and want of all things at our very doors, - we so comfortable. Emigration is the only adequate remedy which presents itself to my imagination: and that, of course, may leave the mother country to die of inanition a stage further on: yet no one can call upon people to starve to-day lest England should prove powerless to hold her own tomorrow. You see, my politics are not very intricate.

Christina and Lucy could debate subjects such as politics, books and art with relative safety. The territory only became combustible when they moved to religion and personal behaviour. Christina concluded by reminding Lucy that tomorrow would have been Maria's birthday, 'my irreplaceable sister and friend', a role she implied Lucy could never fulfil.[134]

When Frances Rossetti suffered a fall in her bedroom which heralded her final illness in 1886, Lucy was quick to send sympathy to Christina, which elicited an open and honest reply. 'Love responds to love...weakness at 85, – you can well imagine what are my fears and my feelings. And indeed I am not venturing to fix my wishes on either result: I see my dearest Mother suffer much, though very patiently; I could not wish her to suffer on indefinitely for my own selfish sake. God's will be done'.[135] The children sent little tokens to try and anchor their grandmother in this world. Ten-year-old Olive sent a play she had written about Theseus. With Lucy distressingly weak and absent from London in the health resort of Ventnor for the first five months of 1886, Cathy was attentive to Christina and Frances. Christina continued to keep Lucy informed of the long, slow dying which eventually took place on 8 April 1886. William noted that 'as Dante Gabriel had died on 9 April, 1882, the interval between the two deaths was exactly four years'.[136] For Christina it was a cosmic change, as she told Lucy:

> It has become a different world since last I wrote to you. Yet I rejoice that it is I who am left in the grief of this separation, and not my dearest Mother.

Please thank your dear children one by one for each instance of their love towards either of us. And my thanks and love to yourself, dear Lucy. Grateful thanks too for the pretty wreaths you and they sent...I am glad Cathy and Mr Hueffer were with us in church and at the grave.[137]

Was Christina aware of the double pang her last remark might cause? Lucy was gratified that part of her own family represented her at the matriarch's funeral but she could not fail to be aware that, yet again, her own frail health excluded her from significant family events.

In her grief, Christina valued the sisterliness that even a Lucy had to offer. 'I am glad to believe that a letter of mine crossed your sisterly one, for this is the last moment at which I could wish to loosen the ties which remain to me. Love and thanks to you, my dear Sister, for all you have felt and expressed for us'. Consciously or unconsciously, Christina had elevated Lucy to fill partially the gap left by Maria. Now she wanted to show Lucy she would cement emotional goodwill with financial intent.

Did William tell you of a conversation we had? – when I said that I hoped finally to leave at least as much as £2000 to him. I have long felt in his debt for all those years when his munificent affection provided me with a most ungrudged home, and he and we all think that, if we loosely compute this debt as for 20 years at £100 a year, I shall pay back the *money* in full; the *love* can only be repaid in kind...Now I particularly want you to know all this, because, if I were so unhappy as to lose my dear William, I should (so far as I foresee at present) feel that his claim lapses in full to yourself or to the children. Please be sure of this...[138]

That summer of 1886, Christina took her niece Olive away to Brighton and chose to see some of Lucy's better qualities in the 'very nice child, docile and independent, which is a very fine combination...In face I think her a good deal like Lucy. She is full of intelligence'. But Christina could not resist a small negative thrust. 'I cannot give any adequate reason for the doubt, yet I feel in doubt whether she has not some tendency towards a jealous disposition'.[139] Christina had been the youngest of four children in her family, inevitably the spoiled darling and, by her own admission, given to temper tantrums. She had no knowledge of the suppressed jealousy which an eldest child like Olive might feel with the birth of every subsequent sibling, or the false maturity a child in that position so often assumes.

Geographical distance between Lucy and Christina always smoothed relations between them. In winter 1887 Lucy exchanged Ventnor for San Remo and enjoyed making graceful gestures in Christina's direction. She sent and encouraged the children to send letters, cards, flowers and plants, a little heath 'for thought' which looked 'charming planted' and promised to flourish even in the bleak London winter. Office duties kept William in London over

Christmas 1886 but he looked forward to joining Lucy in January.[140] Christina told Lucy, 'A great slice of my heart travels about with him now, he being the only one of his own standing left to me'.[141]

Did Lucy find Christina's love for William natural and sisterly or did she consider it another symptom of Christina's threatening over-dependence? Christina tactfully declined William's offer to travel with him to San Remo and found herself dispatched by the doctors to Torquay, telling William tortuously, 'I am glad you have more happy and endeared ties than I have, – I am glad, as so it is: otherwise I should be afraid of wishing it for you any more than for myself, and for myself I do not wish it'.[142] From Torquay Christina sent her love and snowdrops out to San Remo, responding again to affectionate kindness from Lucy.

The snowdrops reminded Christina of Lucy's 'never-to-be-forgotten drawing' of infant Michael in death four winters before. Because of their unbelief, Lucy and William baptized none of their children, an omission which distressed Christina. As baby Michael's life had ebbed away on 24 January 1883, she begged William to allow her to baptize him with her own hand. After consultation with Lucy, tolerance of Christina's position prevailed. Dr William Gill who was present in the Rossettis' large double drawing-room at 5 Endsleigh Gardens, remembered observing Christina in a retired corner 'with the little corpse across her knees and a vessel of water by her side, engaged in the most profoundly devotional manner in baptizing the little dead boy'.[143] Privately satisfied, she committed Michael into her God's keeping.

She prayed again for William's family during the San Remo earthquake in February 1887 and exchanged concerned and loving letters with Lucy. So confident did Christina feel of their delicate new rapport, that she returned to that subject dear to her but anathema to Lucy – baptizing the children. She agreed the Rossetti children were 'happy' children in an ordinary mundane sense, 'But I cannot pointedly use that word *happy* without meaning something beyond the present life. And baptism (where attainable) is the sole door I know of whereby entrance is promised into the happiness which eye has not seen nor ear heard neither hath heart of man conceived...please do not take offence at what I say'. In her great cause, Christina was prepared to risk being an interfering sister-in-law. 'I constantly pray for you and William and my dear nephew and nieces'. She offered her own humility to appease Lucy. 'Yet I feel and acknowledge that every one of you is setting or has set me an example'.[144]

When it came to suffering ill health, Christina was a specialist and quick to offer sympathy. 'My dear Lucy, I am shocked and pained to know what you are suffering. For though I never myself endured a carbuncle I have seen my dearest Mother more than once ill with one, and so I know the keen pain and exhaustion which ensue. Dear Sister, I would help and ease you if I could', she commiserated in June 1888 when Lucy was in Worthing.[145] Christina's recipe for a mustard footbath survives, carefully written out, perhaps to ease one of Lucy's frequent 'colds'.[146]

In spite of the mustard baths, in winter 1888 when Lucy was compelled to move to the French Pyrenees, Christina distributed her letters equally between William and Lucy, careful not to 'forfeit by neglect the continuance of [Lucy's] "esteemed favours"'. She continued to flatter Lucy's educational ambitions. 'Although I had heard two or three times of Olive's play, never till this morning did I understand that it was written in French! Still more impressive is the German journal!! My love to my polyglot niece and the juniors. I hope the four will not leave Italian out of their "curriculum"'.[147]

Christina was determined to build sound relationships with all her nieces and nephew and wrote separately to Olive, Arthur, Helen and Mary, reminding them of a game their 'sober old aunt' had once invented, remembering birthdays, discussing books, plays and cats. Arthur had a special aptitude for languages and, as Christina had a soft spot for her only nephew, she taught him Italian by a correspondence course of her own devising. She sent him word puzzles and stamps for his collection when his interest in her stringent course lapsed.

Ill health both bound and separated the sisters-in-law. Christina's condition meant that she put on weight while Lucy gradually wasted to wraith-like proportions. Christina hoped Lucy might 'hit the happy mean between her actual girth and *mine!!!* But I recommend her to stay as she is, rather than the full alternative.'[148] She shared therapies, cures and quackeries with Lucy. In autumn 1889 Christina sent Lucy a printed leaflet recommending cork slabs in the bedroom 'as a remedy against bronchial or pneumonial troubles; and Christina gave her some of those slabs. My wife used them for many months together, with apparent benefit', reported William.[149]

During the summer of 1890, while Lucy was quarantined with Arthur and Mary who had measles, Christina took the other two children for walks in Highgate Woods. Lucy commented that 'Christina's kindness has gone for not a little'[150] and she gave her sister-in-law her biography of Mary Shelley just published, inscribing it – 'To my dear sister Christina with Lucy Rossetti's love'.[151] She asked William to 'give my best love & thanks to Christina for all her kindness & care & trouble', adding a convoluted insight into her thinly masked feelings about her sister-in-law: 'but I feel you are so near & dear to her that what I feel is in this case almost superfluous, I am not sure that this expresses what I mean'.[152]

When Lucy began to spit blood alarmingly in the spring of 1893 so that 'each day seemed likely to be her last', Christina shared William's anxiety 'for our dear Lucy' and hoped that some early warming sunshine would temper the chill April winds 'allowing flowers in general, and especially our own

Flower de Luce, to drizzarsi in sullo stelo' (to straighten on the stem). In the circumstances Christina, well aware of her austere effect, was even more reluctant than usual to call unexpectedly on Lucy, 'as I am such an exceptional phenomenon'. She bleakly asked William instead to convey her love and let her know 'if ever it would give [Lucy] the slightest pleasure to see me.'[153]

As the year progressed, it became obvious that Lucy could never survive another English winter. William made plans for her to travel to Italy again but he worried about money. His bank account had reached its lowest ebb, less than £76, when Christina relieved William by generously giving Lucy £100 'on the ground that our mother had wished to leave a like sum to Lucy, but had not found it manageable. This of course is true, in its direct sense: not less true is it that Christina has acted from spontaneous impulse of good-feeling', recorded William.[154] Then just before Lucy made the 'anxious and painful' step of leaving England for what her sister-in-law guessed would be the last time, Christina took the risk of arriving unannounced. 'You know I called and saw Lucy last week?' she asked William, 'I did not like her to leave England without my at least trying to see her once more, and when I got to your house she consented to admit me. As to looks she quite surpassed my expectation, but I know that looks are not always to be depended upon.'[155]

After Lucy's departure on 3 October 1893, Christina, like William, feared the sheer 'incalculability' of the shock of Ford Madox Brown's almost immediate death (on 6 October) on his frail daughter, so far from home. 'I hope she is at Pallanza ere this, and so may have caught the alarm from your letters before the final blow falls on her.'[156] On the day of Madox Brown's funeral, Christina thought constantly of Lucy, remembering 'her great affection for her Father'.[157]

By Christmas, news of Lucy from Pallanza, on Lake Maggiore, was increasingly discouraging, although she managed to dispatch a box of flowers to Christina. Treading ancient tinders again, Christina told William she had written Lucy 'a sisterly letter, not I hope one in any way to try her'.[158] Although by now Christina's cancer was advancing, she made what William considered a totally inappropriate – but generous – offer to go out to Pallanza herself. 'Is it imaginable that my going over could be of any use or help or comfort?' she asked William. If her doctor agreed, she would set off in the New Year, accompanied by a nurse. 'Of course I would not be an expense to my family, and perhaps the girls might find some sort of support in the presence of one who might be their grandmother'.[159] The tentative wording of Christina's offer reflected the long years of difficulty in all her dealings with Lucy. Of course the offer would be declined, especially as Lucy was in the final stages of disintegration, but it was genuinely made.

Christina made one further, practical gesture to the dying Lucy. On 26 March 1894 she offered another £100 to send William Gill, Lucy's own London doctor, out to Italy. No more could be done or said, although

Christina continued to send anxious loving thoughts to Lucy in Italy. By then Lucy was 'far past any hope of recovery or improvement: she continued alive and suffering up to 12 April. It was a kind thought of Christina to commission our family-doctor, Mr Gill, to go over to San Remo, if wanted by the patient. But there was truly nothing to be done, beyond what a young Italian physician, Dr Ansaldi, supplied by his daily and judicious attendance.'[160] Christina's relationship with Lucy was finally dispatched. In the short remaining months of her own life, her need for 'my most dear brother' William whom she had once said 'I love better than any man in the world'[161] would be uncomplicated by Lucy. 'Be sure my heart is with you in your grief, desolation, and general harass and anxiety. Every word of your letter is full of interest to me: I am glad that poor Lucy's last day was of diminished rather than of increased suffering'.[162] It had always been an uneasy triangle.

WILLIAM MICHAEL AND DANTE GABRIEL ROSSETTI – BROTHERS

Few brothers were more constantly together, or shared one another's feelings and thoughts more intimately, in childhood, boyhood, and well on into mature manhood, than Dante Gabriel and myself.

    WMR in the preface to the *Complete Works of Dante Gabriel Rossetti*, 1911, xx

Your love, dear William, is not less returned by me than it is sweet to me, and that is saying all.

    Gabriel on William's forty-third birthday, 25 September 1872[163]

With the founding of the Pre-Raphaelite Brotherhood in the autumn of 1848, both William and Gabriel acquired five new 'brothers', but none ever replaced the other as 'first brother' in their mutual affections. Only sixteen months separated Gabriel (born 12 May 1828) and William (born 25

49. Photograph of Dante Gabriel Rossetti and William Michael Rossetti arm in arm, 1853. Fredeman Family Collection.

September 1829) but Gabriel's unalterable seniority was a shaping factor in William's temperament and self-esteem. Gabriel and William grew up in an empathetic, creative union more often associated with twins (fig. 49). But the almost uncanny twin-like sympathy between them was based on complementary rather than similar personalities.

The peculiar dynamic between William and Gabriel was established early. Headstrong, imperious and self-willed, Gabriel was the dominant 'leopard-cub' while more equable William was his subordinate, peaceful kid to 'lie down with'.[164] As junior brother and the 'calm' to his 'storm', William followed where Gabriel led, read 'the same authors, coloured prints in the same book, collected woodcuts for the same scrapbook'.[165] From infancy onwards, they were 'the very best of friends', inter-dependent and self-involved.[166] Their favourite books were simply inscribed 'Rossetti' because they unquestioningly belonged to both, and 'the initials of either [brother] would have been out of order'.[167] Until Gabriel left school, they were rarely apart, but 'rose, talked, walked, studied, ate, amused ourselves, and slumbered, together'.[168]

Neither William nor Gabriel relished schooldays. Both attended first the Reverend Mr Paul's day school in Foley Street, Portland Place in 1837, before proceeding to King's College School. Gabriel left to become a painter in 1841 although William continued his education until February 1845. As a member of King's College teaching staff, Gabriele Rossetti was entitled to free tuition for his eldest son, which was transferred to William when Gabriel left school. William had been moderately studious until the moment Gabriel left, when he instantly became 'audaciously lazy'.[169] Released from the tedium of school, Gabriel was 'free to choose his own intellectual pabulum', and William simply decided he would do the same, drifting far away from the school curriculum.[170] His real world of mental thought lay outside the schoolroom, with Gabriel.

Although Gabriele and Frances Rossetti showed no overt favouritism between their children, William nevertheless sensed his father's 'predilection for Gabriel', and his mother's for himself. These parent–child demarcations deeply marked William's character. Gabriel, the eldest son, named after his father Gabriele, unconsciously modelled himself on his excitable and exotic father. William, by contrast, absorbed the feminine ideals, if not the religion, of his ministering, stoical mother. Like her, he learned to suppress hostility, writing to his father at the early age of seven, 'As to *anger* I certainly think that it is one of the worst of passions. Think how many have been killed when others have been *angry* with them.'[171] In spite of repressing aggressive feelings, William remained in tune with his emotional life, although he learned to disguise it for outsiders. The adult relationship between the brothers was founded therefore on the paradigm of their parents' marriage. William repeated the dynamics he saw enacted every day between his parents. As

Frances had been handmaiden to her husband's intellect and temperament, William became the foil and facilitator to Gabriel's genius.

Genius and its demands shaped William's life and the development of his character. He could not 'remember any date at which it was not understood in the family that "Gabriel meant to be a painter."'[172] Accordingly, William aged fifteen, was harnessed to paid employment without demur. 'It was a hard necessity, and was felt as such', William told his sister-in-law, Cathy Hueffer, over forty years later.[173] 'Genius, like every other possibility for man', Holman Hunt observed shrewdly, 'claims cultivation, and this cultivation W.M. Rossetti forewent by consideration of circumstances that his brother might have the better opportunity'.[174] A different brother might have been jealous, but William never exhibited any outward resentment towards Gabriel, or his parents, for categorizing him in this secondary rank. From childhood he had been subtly undermined and told he was uncreative. 'His [Gabriel's] mind was inventive, mine un-inventive.'[175] He absorbed the family myth about his inferiority. It is impressive that in spite of this early typecasting in a supporting role, William went on to make a major career in nineteenth-century art criticism and literature, unrelated to his livelihood at the Board of Inland Revenue which supported many Rossettis over fifty years.

As a ten-year-old, William began to write a chivalric romance, inspired by Gabriel. Gabriel supplied the first incentive although he did not influence what William wrote. 'This was characteristic', explained William, 'of our relations throughout our joint lives.' William believed he owed the impetus for his subsequent literary career to Gabriel. 'If it had not been for him, I might perhaps never have attempted anything in the way of literature, art-criticism, and the like'. But once motivated by Gabriel, William 'relied entirely on my own resources, not consulting him at all as to how I should fashion the work, or what code of opinions I should adopt.'[176] In his autobiography, William pointed out that his career in art criticism had led to a separation from Gabriel, not a symbiosis. Many people supposed that he was the 'mere mouthpiece of [Gabriel's] suggestions', particularly during the years that Gabriel was a Pre-Raphaelite painter and William a Pre-Raphaelite critic. 'But I did not criticize in a certain tone at his dictation, or to subserve his opinions, but because I myself entertained the views which I expressed.'[177]

If William was prepared to act as Gabriel's editor, proof-reader, Italian linguistic adviser, moneylender, protector, supporter, mediator, confidant, memorializer and general gofer throughout a lifetime, these functions were all willingly espoused out of William's absolute belief in his brother's artistic and poetic genius. This faith was built on William's huge capacity for hero-worship. His heroes were drawn from literature – Dante, Blake, Shelley, Whitman – or from contemporary politics – Garibaldi, Mazzini, Lincoln – but his brother Gabriel was his first, nearest, and greatest hero. Hero-worship was the outlet for William's natural and inculcated diffidence, indeed it was a logical outcome of his own lack of self-belief. He accessed his heroes' glamour and independence of thought by writing about their achievements and establishing their reputation with the public. Later, William showed particular gifts for recognizing neglected or unknown talents and nurturing them – Walt Whitman, James Thomson, Francis Adams, Katharine Tynan – because he knew from first-hand experience, however resiliently he controlled and sublimated it, what it felt like to be marginalized.

William's relationship with Gabriel was constant, although it did not run on an even continuum. Shared interests in literature and the arts always cemented it. In autumn 1848, it was Gabriel's initiative and force of will that established William, although not an artist, as one of the seven founding members of the Pre-Raphaelite Brotherhood. Although he spent his days as a government clerk, in the evenings William was translated into Gabriel's world. Predictably, the P.R.B. probably meant more to him than it did to the other 'brothers'. He basked in the 'heart-relished luxury' of their meetings, their authentic undergraduate discussions on art and literature (although none of the group were university men), moonlit strolls by the Thames and joint 'studies, aspirations, efforts, and actual doings'.

Encouraged by Gabriel, William wrote a long poem, first called *An Exchange of News*, then *A Plain Story* and finally *Mrs Holmes Grey*, strictly adhering to the Pre-Raphaelite code of realism.[178] Gabriel who was with Holman Hunt in Paris – 'the females, the whores, the bitches – my God!!' - responded enthusiastically and in detail. 'The arrival of your poem yesterday was about the best thing that has happened'. He summed up each verse paragraph, excellent, admirable, first-rate, capital, remarkably fine, not quite so good, exceedingly powerful:

> Your Inquest is, on the whole I think, a very clever and finished piece of writing – wonderfully well-managed in parts and possessing some strong points of character. The woman's letter is exceedingly truthful and fine. The rest of the poem is very first-rate indeed – some passages really stunning…I think your poem is very remarkable, and altogether certainly the best thing you have done. It is a painful story, told without compromise…Perhaps it is more like Crabbe than any other poet I know of .[179]

In several pages of close practical criticism, Gabriel paid great respect to William's essay in poetry. But he also teased his younger brother for slipping into 'Malvolio's vein', when he used pretentious language in one of his reviews in the *Critic*.[180] By writing poetry and articles, acting as the P.R.B.'s secretary, editing their private journal as well as their magazine, the *Germ*, William's links with Gabriel, his personal hero, expanded and consolidated. Gabriel specifically reassured William that he had every right to edit the *Germ* as 'we have excluded from the title the words "Conducted by artists." You are thus on exactly the same footing as all other contributors'.[181]

The P.R.B. was an extension of their boyhood. They still shared literary and artistic enthusiasms for a list of immortal heroes ranging from Homer to Robert Browning, and from 'that real stunner' Leonardo to Raphael.[182] They also shared new friendships. 'Being of a very retired and self-poised character', William felt he might not have made these friendships on his own initiative. 'It was almost invariably through Gabriel that I got to know people, to like them, and sometimes to love them'. Gabriel transported William from the bureaucracies of government office where he found no 'genuine comradeship of mind' to the exciting liberation of a place among artists.[183] In his turn, William was useful and highly efficient. He was well read, well informed and an asset to the Brotherhood. Some of his most enduring friendships with the Pre-Raphaelite Brothers, such as William Holman Hunt and Frederic George Stephens, were deeper and more lasting than Gabriel's. William's day job may have lacked glamour but his Italianate good looks and undoubted personal presence kept him in demand as a model for Pre-Raphaelite pictures. Between 1849 and 1850 he sat twice to Holman Hunt, for *Rienzi Swearing Revenge for his Brother's Death* and *A Converted British Family Sheltering a Christian Missionary from Persecution from the Druids*, for the figure of the angel in Gabriel's *Ecce Ancilla Domini!*, and for the head of Lorenzo in John Everett Millais's *Lorenzo and Isabella*. Without Gabriel's fraternal love for William, he would never have made those early contacts that shaped his life in the art world. As his contribution, William publicized Pre-Raphaelite artists and their radical new principles in popular articles he wrote for the *Spectator* and the *Critic*. Between the brothers in their early twenties, Gabriel the commanding new artist and William his promoter and supporter, relations continued to be interactive.

Early in the 1850s, two significant new factors entered fraternal relations. Money and women. 'Tin is no more',[184] became Gabriel's habitual refrain as he repeatedly besieged William: 'Please don't forget – but I know you won't – about that tin – as soon and as much as you can manage like a brick. I have an awful lot of claimants.'[185] 'I am really ashamed to plague you but could you lend me £10 for a fortnight…£5 would be better than none – or anything indeed – but if you could lend me 10 it would be the greatest service now that I am so engrossed with my picture and so wanting to get it finished.'[186] Frances Horner, daughter of William Graham, Gabriel's patron from Glasgow, remembered tales of William's legendary forbearance. She recollected that Madox Brown 'said one day: Gabriel, you really ought to pay William; it isn't the thing, my dear fellow, to be so much in his debt.' And Gabriel said, 'Pay my brother William? Good God, Brown, you must be mad.'[187]

The 1850s was also the decade of women. William courted Henrietta Rintoul and Gabriel fell in love, then out of love with the attenuated Lizzie

Siddal before he finally married her in 1860. Gabriel pursued golden Annie Miller, the girl Holman Hunt put into *The Awakening Conscience* and planned to marry. In August 1856, Fanny Cornforth (born Sarah Cox in January 1835, from Steyning in Sussex)[188] entered Gabriel's life and some of his most suggestive and sensuous pictures – *Found*, *The Blue Bower*, *Bocca Baciata*, *Fazio's Mistress* and *Lady Lilith*.

In 1857, Gabriel's life was further complicated. He was in Oxford, painting the Oxford Union murals – the charismatic focus of a second circle of younger Pre-Raphaelite artists including Edward Burne-Jones, Arthur Hughes and William Morris. A new raven-haired stunner, Jane Burden, the daughter of a groom, bewitched him. In retrospect, he should have taken his chance with Janey then but he was tied by the guilty old connection to sickly, languid Lizzie. By 26 April 1859 it was too late – when Jane made an upwardly mobile marriage to William Morris. A year later, after a decade long relationship, Gabriel finally married Lizzie.

Thus in the 1850s there were, at least, four major women in Gabriel's life. All would model for him. All came from working- or lower-middle-class backgrounds, propelled by their contrasting types of beauty into a bohemian world of artistic aspiration and self-improvement. Lizzie, the most intellectually ambitious, learned to paint and write poetry under Gabriel's passionate tutelage. William admired her abilities in both fields and found a graceful purity 'stamped upon everything she did'.[189] Ruskin agreed, and settled £150 per annum on her. Holman Hunt wanted to transform Annie Miller – an Eliza Doolittle figure – by education, and then marry her, but Gabriel's attentions caused an acrimonious rift between the two artists and ruined Annie's chances with either. Janey was the most successful in a worldly sense, outlived them all, managed to keep her husband in a social arrangement, and inspired her lover to create some of his most iconic images, even though his compulsive love for her was one of the component factors that precipitated his nervous breakdown of 1872. Fanny was the only one who gave Gabriel sustained happiness and uncomplicated sexual fulfilment. During his dramatic illnesses in the 1870s, it was her financial security he wanted to safeguard. She never bothered to disguise her Sussex vowels, her lower-class origins or her blatant sexuality. The Rossetti women had to be protected from too much knowledge of her central presence in Gabriel's life. Consequently, she was not mentioned in Gabriel's will, and William barred her from the funeral.

William was worldly and privately non-judgemental about Gabriel's women. The one about whom he was publicly most obfuscatory was Janey Morris, concealing the exact date when the relationship began, partly because it was adulterous, and partly because she was still alive when he published his brother's biography in 1895. That December he sent Janey a copy inscribed with his 'sincere regard',[190] for once her influence could have no more potency after Gabriel's death in 1882, she and William continued to maintain a social relationship. (Janey's daughter, May Morris, sent William a telegram when her mother died suddenly, years later, on 26 January 1914.)[191] William was susceptible to feminine allure and women found him attractive throughout his life. Visually alert, and like Gabriel whom Mrs Gaskell called 'not mad as a March hare, but hair-mad', William responded to the physicality of his brother's women. During the same period he was in love with Henrietta Rintoul who also had abundant ringlets of hair. Lucy, whom he eventually married, arranged her auburn hair in complicated coils. Descriptions in William's later biography of Gabriel and his own autobiography linger over massive wreaths of gorgeously rippled hair, either with a 'deep-sunken glow' like Janey's or coppery golden like Lizzie's.

He showed genuine admiration for and delicate understanding of Lizzie's quality of mind and the interiority that fuelled it. 'All her talk…was like the speech of a person who wanted to turn off the conversation…she seemed to say – "My mind and my feelings are my own, and no outsider is expected to pry into them"'.[192] William fully accepted Lizzie's premarital relationship with Gabriel. Their closeted interdependence between 1850 and 1854, *tête à tête* in his studio at 14 Chatham Place, Blackfriars, supplanted the boyish comradeship of the P.R.B. as a priority in Gabriel's mind. In William's view, the Lizzie–Gabriel *entente* hastened the breakup of the Brotherhood.[193] Her long-anticipated marriage to Gabriel was delayed, as Gabriel admitted 'almost beyond possibility',[194] and only took place when Lizzie, 'ready to die daily and more than once a day',[195] was wrecked by illness and opium addiction. Later observers have found it hard to credit William's opinion that the premarital relationship was not a sexual one, although he admitted 'it may have gone beyond the conventional fence-line'.[196]

After ten years of vacillation, even William was surprised when the couple suddenly decided to marry in Hastings. Gabriel agonized over Lizzie's ragged and dramatic ill health. 'My dear William,' he wrote, 'Many sincere thanks for your brotherly letter. I assure you I never felt more in need of such affection as yours has always been, than I do now.' William was the 'one person' in whom he could confide, 'as I could not bear doing it to any other than you'.[197] 'She is a beautiful creature, with fine powers and sweet character,' William told Bell Scott on 14 May 1860, adding hopefully, 'if only her health should become firmer after marriage, I think it will be a happy match'.[198] On 23 May 1860, the marriage Lizzie had longed for to ratify her insecure position in Gabriel's life and affections finally took place, but only doomed the affair. Less than two years later on 11 February 1862, Lizzie's addictive and addicted personality was extinguished, when perhaps due to post-natal depression following the birth of a stillborn child, she took an overdose of laudanum. She had written elegiacally, prophetically:

> Oh never weep for love that's dead,
>   Since love is seldom true[199]

and Georgie Burne-Jones recalled an indelible 'impression that never wore away, of romance and tragedy' between Lizzie and her husband.[200]

Fanny was a total contrast to Lizzie and was established in Gabriel's life both before and during his marriage to Lizzie. Shortly after Lizzie's death, Fanny was reinstated as Gabriel's live-in mistress. William accepted her and was easy with her. Gabriel was occasionally absent from his new home, Tudor House, 16 Cheyne Walk, the 'strange, quaint, grand old place with an immense garden, magnificent panelled staircases and rooms – a palace'.[201] During the mid-1860s William contributed to the rent and stayed the night on a regular Monday, Wednesday, Friday basis. Sometimes he spent evenings alone with Fanny trying to summon spirits, absorbed in their joint passion for séances.[202] William signed himself 'affectionately yours' to Fanny and sent her thoughtful little presents such as two Chinese flowerpots he bought for £1 4s 0d in Great Russell Street,[203] and a blank book for newspaper cuttings that she wanted.[204]

The 1860s were fruitful years for Gabriel as an artist. His income far exceeded William's – but so did his expenditure and his debts. In 1865 Gabriel made about £2,050, though a little less in 1866. In 1867 his income was about £3,000,[205] the same year that William was promoted to the post of Committee Clerk at the Board of Inland Revenue on a scale of £575–£650, a fraction of Gabriel's incomings. Gabriel continued to borrow freely from William but repaid some of that generosity when William was robbed on holiday in Venice in 1868. Gabriel continually expected clerical and scholarly assistance from his younger brother. 'Can you help me at all, do you think, in collating my *Vita Nuova* with the original, and amending inaccuracies…It ought to be done immediately', he demanded in January 1861.[206] In 1867 William made a lengthy catalogue of all the books in Gabriel's collection.[207]

They continued to share enthusiasms but now they were for visits to Cremorne Gardens,[208] blue china, Chinese artefacts and exotic beasts. In 1867 Gabriel kept a series of calamitous animals in the garden at Cheyne Walk. William noted their fates with interest: Jessie, a barn owl whose head was bitten off by a raven, two grass-green parakeets starved to death, a green Jersey lizard killed by a servant, a dormouse with a hole in its throat, a dog split up its back by a deerhound, a shrivelled tortoise, a cardinal grosbeak and a salamander which met sudden deaths, a rabbit eaten all but his tail, and a pigeon devoured by a hedgehog.[209]

William was not just banker, zoo attendant, copy editor and personal assistant; he also tried to act as his brother's mediator. After a beneficial relationship with Ruskin, Gabriel fell out with the influential critic. Over dinner with the Ruskins on 4 December 1866, William heard that Ruskin wanted to renew the friendship. He recommended Ruskin should call on Gabriel but tactfully refrain from 'overhauling his work too brusquely'.[210] Ruskin acted on his advice the very next day but although the meeting was cordial enough, and Ruskin warmly praised Gabriel's picture of 'Beatrice in a death-trance', the breach was never healed. Six months later, Gabriel mischievously reported to William that Ruskin had published a letter in which he claimed William had derived all his knowledge on art from the older critic, and had no rights to express any opinion on matters of public interest. William noted the criticism in his diary but made no comment.[211]

William's daily diary was a long-standing friend to him over more than half a century. In it he recorded not only his day-to-day doings, details of his literary work, family news but also close accounts of what pictures and poetic projects Gabriel was currently engaged in. But in moments of intense emotional crisis William usually abandoned his diary, sometimes for months, occasionally for years at a time. One of the most painful events that bound him to his brother was Gabriel's nervous breakdown and suicide attempt in June 1872. 'This diary-work is becoming too painful now if important matters are to be recorded, and too futile and irritating if the unimportant are made to take their place. I shall therefore drop it', which he did until November when Gabriel had made an unexpected recovery, resumed work and was living at Kelmscott with Janey Morris.[212]

During the summer of 1872, when Gabriel was *in extremis*, William's friends realized how close he came to following his brother into despair, but not into delusion. Gabriel's breakdown was compounded by many factors, but they all involved feelings of guilt: Lizzie's death, the exhumation of her body to recover the poems he had impulsively buried with her, his obsession with Janey Morris, the successful publication in 1870 of *Poems* inspired by dead or illicit loves, and Robert Buchanan's subsequent attack on that volume, which he had dreaded for months.[213]

Gabriel did not involve William in recovering his poems from the tomb but he did ask him to help transcribe their rotting pages. 'I do not know if you would have time or inclination to assist in so unpleasant a job. If so, you could do some of the more difficult parts while I did others.' As a rather backhanded sop he added 'You know I always meant to dedicate the book to you', which he would do, 'failing only one possibility [presumably Janey] which I suppose must be considered out of the question'. [214] William offered him absolution for the act of desecration. 'Under the pressure of a great sorrow, you performed an act of self-sacrifice: it did you honour…You have not retracted the self-sacrifice…but you now think – and I quite agree with you – that there is no reason why the self-sacrifice should have no term.'[215] When Buchanan's long-awaited attack on Gabriel's *Poems* came in an article called 'The Fleshly School of Poetry' in the *Contemporary Review* in October 1871, it was partly in settlement of old scores with William, who had reviewed Buchanan's own poetry disparagingly and aggravated the insult by calling him 'so poor and pretentious a poetaster' on the opening page of *Swinburne's Poems and Ballads: A Criticism* (1866). When Buchanan expanded his article and published it in pamphlet form in May 1872, it was the trigger which sent Gabriel, a raging insomniac already addicted to a pernicious regime of chloral and whiskey, into persecution mania, conspiracy theory, hallucinations and derangement.

Looking back on the summer of 1872, William remembered the day the crisis broke, 2 June 1872, which he spent entirely with his brother, as 'one of the most miserable days of my life, not to speak of his'.[216] In Bell Scott's contemporary opinion, William's own state symbiotically began to mirror his brother's. William was desperately fearful of the effect of Gabriel's illness on his elderly mother and sisters (particularly as Christina was suffering from Graves's disease at the time) and equally anxious to fend off Gabriel's creditors during the unquantifiable period that his brother might be unable to work. In his *Autobiographical Notes* (1892) Bell Scott claimed that in 1872 William had been 'so prostrated by anxiety, loving Gabriel much and fearing him not a little' that Ford Madox Brown had to share the business side of Gabriel's affairs.[217] William countered briskly over thirty years later: 'I was not prostrated, though I assuredly was afflicted, and, had I not been so, the more shame to me'.[218] Although both William and Gabriel had been close friends of Bell Scott, William believed that for unexplained reasons, Scott's purpose was to blacken Gabriel's reputation – 'under cover of writing his own Autobiography'.[219]

When Bell Scott went to dinner at the Rossettis' a year after Gabriel's recovery, on the night before Maria left home to join an Anglican Sisterhood, they all discussed William, before he arrived.

> They both, but especially Christina, confided to me how very much alarmed they had been for William ever since Gabriel's illness, and that they were truly glad of the Lucy advent,[220] as they wd. of anything else that might break the spell that seemed to hold him. For weeks they said he never uttered a word to any of them, and now he talked 'when Lucy is here'…Lucy duly turned up Billy accompanying, and we were all very cordial, although William is manifestly just the same morose brother they described him, and also not very hospitable, leaving his guests to amuse themselves.[221]

Undoubtedly, William's overpowering sense of responsibility for Gabriel, which went through several acute phases, notably in 1872, 1877, 1879 and 1882, profoundly affected his sensitive personality and pitched him into varying degrees of social withdrawal. At the time of the 1872 breakdown and in its aftermath, Bell Scott noted that everyone around Gabriel had become his 'absolute slave'.[222] While Gabriel was out of London, mostly in Scotland with a rota of carers during the summer of 1872, William was constantly sent on missions to Cheyne Walk to collect books, green drawing paper, round brown chalks, handkerchiefs, thick trousers and waistcoats. He had to see to all Gabriel's business and domestic concerns, liaise with a succession of doctors, minders and friends, authorise treatments and placate Fanny. He was asked, peremptorily, to copy manuscripts, send money and deal with insurance pay-ments. Later, he was even expected to find saveloys to send down to Kelmscott where Gabriel, in recovery, had arrived by the autumn. And through all these tasks and preoccupations, he continued to attend daily at Somerset House. As he recovered, Gabriel became aware how much William had suffered in his heightened exchange of sympathy. 'Indeed', he proffered thoughtfully, 'perhaps your suffering may have been more acute than my own dull nerveless state during the past months'.[223] This letter continues 'Your love, dear William, is not less returned by me than it is sweet to me, and that is saying all.' He began to see the strain showing in William's face. 'By the bye, when I saw you, I thought you showed fearful signs of fagging and overwork, as well you might', yet he carried on setting William endless tasks.[224]

But from 1873 onwards, William's relationship with Lucy marked a new phase in the relationship with his dominant brother. In October 1874, Gabriel complained, 'I never see you now'.[225] Henceforward, William would have a regular proof-reader – Lucy – to help him with his own literary works, instead of always acting in that capacity to Gabriel. A mundane enough occupation, it was emblematic of a distinct shift in relations. From now on he would be a planet himself, instead of always a lesser moon.

However, the emotional interdependence between the two brothers was never severed, just subtly altered. When Gabriel plunged into further chloral-ized declines, William was still unfailingly loyal, visiting him regularly every Monday evening. On 26 January 1880 William read Gabriel the first part of his lecture on 'Wives of the Poets'. The following Monday, he read him the second instalment and Gabriel responded with three 'Songs of the Beryl Spirits'. They talked about the old days on William's visit on 1 March 1880. There had been a time when Marie Spartali, the Greek beauty whom Madox Brown had hopelessly loved, would have accepted Gabriel. Apparently, Marie's father would have equally welcomed an offer from William.[226] But now he could share Gabriel's intensity with Lucy who accompanied William about once a month. She admired Gabriel immensely and enjoyed discussing art and poetry with him. But Gabriel never wanted to see William and Lucy's children. Perhaps they recalled too painfully the stillborn child he and Lizzie had lost in 1861 and the fact that his lifestyle now made it unlikely he would ever become a father.

William felt no resentment about Gabriel ignoring his children. He accepted it as part of the eccentric licence he had been taught since boyhood to accord to genius. Instead he was charmed when in February 1881 Gabriel asked to see Lucy (who was away in Brighton) and 'in course of talk said that you & I [William and Lucy] are exactly suited to each other. To this I assented except on the score of my over-age – wh. however he wouldn't admit'.[227] The brothers discussed painters and poets, heroes and stunners, Shakespeare, Blake, Shelley and Michelangelo in a continuum of debate that had persisted since their joint childhood.

William monitored Gabriel's state of mind – 'better', 'very melancholy' or 'more depressed' – with every visit. Gabriel continued to be susceptible to notions of personal persecution. When *Patience* opened in April 1881, he saw references to himself in the 'fleshly poet' Bunthorne. On 2 July 1881, William 'went with Mathilde Bl[ind] to see the comic opera of Patience (Gilbert & Sullivan) in ridicule of sham-aesthetics: very amusing....I don't see that any individual is pointedly aimed at'.[228] Bunthorne was a conflation of all the major figures associated with aestheticism, including Ruskin and Whistler but he became most popularly associated with Oscar Wilde. Depression had sunk not only Gabriel's *joie de vivre* but his old sense of humour.

Towards the end of 1881, Gabriel told William he was very ill. William kept his regular Monday evening appointment on 7 November when Gabriel vomited and drank champagne. He had been used to turning night into day, never retiring until 5 a.m. Now he went to bed early at 9 p.m., had a nurse in attendance and was 'much dejected and unstrung' in William's foreboding opinion. He increased his evening visits to twice a week. On the same date that he made his usual brotherly visit, 14 November, William applied for promotion to the Secretaryship at the office, his logical career goal. His concerns about Gabriel were deepening. Then on 17 November he recorded tersely: 'My candidature for the Secretaryship has failed – [Charles] Forsey appointed. Pazienza.' It was the Italian exhortation he had heard at home throughout his childhood, which had governed his strictly controlled temperament thereafter, or especially his relationship with his dynamic elder brother.

The medical crisis came in mid-December 1881. A 'paralytic numbness' seized Gabriel in his left side, arm and leg, and he had to be carried to bed. Doctors and friends debated Gabriel's whiskey and chloral addiction and Dr Marshall proposed injecting morphia near the wrist as a substitute. Dr Maudsley was called in, chloral discontinued and spirits reduced to a wineglass a day. Gabriel's sleep was punctuated by opium-dreams and weird hallucinations, 'seeing writings & printed sheets where none existed' and replying to questions that had never been asked. Maudsley diagnosed that these were due to withdrawal from chloral rather than to effects of the morphia, but William was unconvinced.[229] On 20 December Gabriel did not recognize his friend Frederic Shields (ironically also a chloral addict) when he visited, but babbled a mixture of French, English and Italian. William called the next day to hear improved reports from Theodore Watts-Dunton and Dr Maudsley but decided not to risk being unrecognized himself.

In the New Year 1882, Gabriel rallied a little, although his left hand was comparatively useless and his spirits low. William briefly took heart when he found Gabriel painting a small replica of his *Proserpine*. But the artist oscillated between fretful and listless. On William's suggestion, it was decided to move him from old dismal associations in Chelsea to the new marine health-resort of Birchington-on-Sea near Margate in Kent. Here John Seddon offered Gabriel free use of Westcliff Bungalow within sight of the sea. Installed with a relay of paid companions, concerned friends, medical advisers and a nurse, Gabriel began to read and write again but was beset with his old furies and feared his sight was failing. In March, old Frances Rossetti and Christina arrived to augment his care. Theodore Watts-Dunton called on William at Somerset House with the latest perturbing reports.

On 1 April 1882 William arrived in Birchington for the weekend and found Gabriel 'in a very prostrate condition physically, barely capable of tottering a few steps, half blind, & suffering a good deal of pain'. On Sunday, Dr Harris, a local Birchington doctor, examined Gabriel and gave William the prognosis he dreaded – that Gabriel's brain was likely to be permanently affected by his long-term chloral abuse. William was cast into gloom but returned to London that evening to seek Dr Marshall's advice and perhaps Sir Andrew Clarke's. At the end of the week, on Good Friday, 7 April, William went back to Birchington. The doctor told him Gabriel's disease was uraemia, a form of kidney disease. About 5 p.m. on 9 April, Easter Day, William helped Mrs Abrey the nurse 'to put on his loins a large linseed-and-mustard poultice, and his drawers were put on at the same time – both processes much against his will, as he disliked and dreaded the heat in bed'. Both William and nurse 'reasoned with and coaxed him on the subject'. After supper at 7 p.m. William dozed briefly on the drawing-room sofa until Shields ran in for him at 9.20 p.m. Just before that, while Frances was rubbing her son's back, Gabriel 'fell back, threw his arms out, screamed out loud two or three times close together' in a convulsive fit that distorted his face, and immediately collapsed. Frederic Shields flew round for Dr Harris who pronounced 'he still lived – then said he was dead'. At his bedside, William recorded, were 'my mother, Christina, Watts, Shields, Caine, Dr Harris of Birchington, & myself'. It was 9.31 p.m. Within three minutes Lucy appeared, having travelled all day from her father's in Manchester.[230] 'Lucy's arrival at the very moment almost', William told Madox Brown, 'was an unspeakable comfort to me, & so continues'.[231]

50. Frederic Shields, *Dante Gabriel Rossetti in Death*, 10 April 1882. Pencil on cream paper, 305 × 256 mm. Private collection.

The following day William asked Gabriel's devoted friend, Frederic Shields, to make a drawing of him. Being 'the most high-strung and susceptible of men' this was 'a truly self-sacrificing act of Shields'. The artist inscribed the drawing 'in anguish of heart'. William kept the drawing (fig. 50). [232]

After three weeks leave, William returned to the office. Three months later he began writing his diary again.

3

The Victorian

Day – the office

As William spent such a substantial proportion of his life between the ages of fifteen and sixty-five, working full-time at the Board of Inland Revenue – probably in excess of 50 per cent of his waking hours – it is surprising that his autobiography devotes just two out of its thirty-three chapters to his career in public service. He felt he had been overworked, especially in the second half of his career, and undoubtedly he spent many hours each week at the office. He worked officially 10 a.m. to 4 p.m. (but often stayed until 5 or 6 p.m.) five days a week, plus a half-day every Saturday. Yet in spite of spending over a half a century with a succession of colleagues, in retrospect he considered he had made no intimate friends through his work.[1] His true friends came from his other worlds of art and literature. However, the Board had then, and retains to the present day, a reputation as a billet for intellectuals, experts and eccentrics who are able to pursue lives outside Board hours, without comment or raised eyebrows. The apparent brevity of his working day (by modern standards), generous holidays rising to six weeks a year, and the fact that William could receive callers on art or scholarly business, and even do literary work and private letter writing at the office, were positive aids to balancing a double life.

On the recommendation of a family friend, Sir Isaac Lyon Goldsmid, William began employment as a clerk in the Excise Office in offices[2] north-east of the Royal Exchange at Old Broad Street, on 6 February 1845. He would have preferred to train as a doctor but the Rossetti finances were in decline with the ill health and near-blindness of Gabriele, the head of the family. The first son Gabriel with his genius was not expected to work. Maria (regularly) and Christina and their mother (intermittently) earned money from teaching. At fifteen and a half, William became the main breadwinner of the family without complaint or resentment. His official title was 'Extra clerk' or 'Officiator', his starting salary £80 per annum. There was no qualifying examination, although in his *Autobiography*, Trollope reported taking the entry exams for the Post Office as early as 1834. He exploited their terrors and absurdities in his novel *The Three Clerks* (1858) and William was equally

51. Dante Gabriel Rossetti, Study for *Found*, taken from William Michael Rossetti, 1851. Pencil, 273 × 191 mm. Surtees 64L, pl. 76. Gabriel made this drawing from William during his junior days as an Excise Office clerk. Private collection.

opposed to the entry-by-exam system which was not introduced for Excise Office applicants until 1848.

William took an oath affirming he was 'well affected to the present Government' and began work filling up forms before progressing to letter writing and the custody of official documents. Two years later in 1847 his position was ratified when he was promoted to a permanent clerkship, or 'put on the establishment' (fig. 51).

He worked in a branch of the Secretary's Office called the English Correspondent's Office, whose main business was to liaise with members of the Excise Service and traders in England (there were equivalent Irish and Scottish Correspondent's Offices). In 1848 the English Correspondent's Office was abolished and William was promoted to the main Secretary's Office. On 10 April all the Excise Office clerks were sworn in as special constables ahead of the Chartist demonstration. In spite of his oath of government loyalty, William's reforming principles made him a natural Chartist sympathizer, so he was considerably relieved when, in the event, his services were not required.

In 1849 the Revenue administration was streamlined. The Board of Stamps and Taxes amalgamated with the Board of Excise to form the new Board of Inland Revenue, with responsibility for land and assessed taxes, stamps, property tax and the Post Office. The newly formed Board gradually moved into offices in Somerset House between the Strand and the Thames. By November 1852[3] William found himself back on the site of his lazy schooldays where he had attended King's College School for nearly eight years between 1837 and 1845.

A new wing to house what Trollope called this 'nest of public offices' was erected, an early example of purpose-built office space. A Renaissance palace dating from the 1550s and designed for Lord Protector Somerset originally stood on this site. In spite of several architectural reincarnations over the centuries, Somerset House, one of London's most elegant government buildings, faced in classically beautiful Portland stone, preserved its palatial character with spectacular views across the river and the heart of London. During most of his career, William worked in his own room behind a wooden door, one of many opening off a maze of generous, high-arched corridors. Fine circular staircases in Somerset House led the eye upwards to glass lanterns that let light flood down. In October 1867 he was promoted to Committee Clerk on a salary scale of £575–£650.

The boardroom where William attended meetings was large and well proportioned. The Victorian board table at which he sat still remains, although superseded now by a modern version. The nineteenth-century table was not rectangular but consisted of two hexagons linked by a bridge where the Chairman of the Board sat at the centre.

In 1869, William was promoted to Assistant Secretary in the Excise Section at an annual salary of £800[4], which rose to £900 ten years later.[5] In this post, either daily or every other day, he attended meetings of the Board, headed by the Chairman – in 1869 Sir William Stephenson.

On a typical working day, 21 September 1874, William's numerous official visitors, as he told Lucy, included

> 1, a Mr. Penny, brother of a discharged officer of Excise…2, an old gentleman 'from the North' who wanted to see [Adam]Young [the Secretary] – a private acquaintance. 3, the afflicted Mrs Brett, of whom we have so often spoken…4, two of our own officials, who want to get a Civil Service pension for the widow of a late colleague in the Solicitor's office – a most meritorious man indeed, & I gladly signed the application drawn up. 5, a suspended Excise officer in London, lately fined for an act of intemperance…6, the wife & daughter of another Excise officer who had also been fined along with the preceding. This lady came prepared with a photograph of her son, & of an American her son-in-law, wanting particularly to deprecate the removal of her husband from London – wh. however I think can't well be avoided, even if no worse befall him. The old lady was a little incoherent in her pleadings; &, tho' I really felt for her distress, I cd. not help saying that I did not exactly see why, because she had a son-in-law in America, her husband shd. be retained in a post in London.[6]

It is clear William dealt with a whole gamut of harassed petitioners with good-humour, impartiality and decisiveness (fig. 52).

William explained the function of an Assistant Secretary in the Civil Service, which was (and is today) far more prestigious than its job title would suggest.

52. William Michael Rossetti. Cathy Hueffer's photograph album, STH/BH/2/3-6. The Stow Hill Collection, HLRO, and the Hon. Oliver Soskice.

> In the Inland Revenue an assistant secretary is not a person who assists the secretary, but one who performs work similar to that of the secretary, although it is (in theory, and to some extent in practice) of a rather less important kind. This work consists essentially in reading and considering a number of letters addressed to the office on a variety of subjects; making orders upon some of them; presenting others to a commissioner or to the Board, to obtain signatures to orders, or to have the orders made; revising the drafts of the letters written to carry out all those orders; and signing the letters themselves. There is plenty to do; and it could only be done by a person who understands the law and practice of the department.

By the time William retired in 1894, the ten-man structure of the Board was made up of the Chairman (who invariably received a knighthood or higher honour), a Deputy Chairman, two Commissioners, two Secretaries (to whom William directly reported) and four Assistant Secretaries (two for Excise, two for Stamps and Taxes). Although he saw business conducted fairly and promptly, William ultimately took the view that administration by Boards was a mistake, restricting the scope for individuals to take responsibility. 'Numerous matters, but only those of minor moment, were definitely settled by myself', he commented with a note of regret.[7]

He reported to a number of Excise Secretaries during his half-century with the Board, Freeling, Keogh, Dobson, Corbett, Young and Forsey, but his personal favourite was Sir Robert Micks who retired just before William in 1893. 'He was highly considerate towards myself, and courteous to all; a man of strict honour' whose intelligence William valued.[8] Micks was particularly sensitive in allowing William extended compassionate leave, on occasions when he needed to visit his sick wife abroad.

It was originally part of William's private career plan to achieve the Secretaryship which would have meant a substantial rise of approximately one third in his annual salary. However, throughout his years at the Board, he was able to significantly supplement the official salary with income from his literary work. His position at the Board as Assistant Secretary should not be underestimated. The Board itself recognized William's extracurricular expertise by assigning him to a special role he was uniquely qualified to fulfil, valuing art collections for the purposes of death duties. In 1891 he reassessed the Wallace Collection and earned the Revenue £7,000.[9] He enjoyed this work in its wide variety for sixteen years from 1888 to 1904, ten years after official retirement; it provided him with satisfaction and travel all over the country until he was seventy-five.[10]

In 1897 he took on the additional role of assessing works of art for tax exemption under the new Tory Act of 1896 whereby art or objects deemed to be of 'national, scientific or historic interest' would be tax exempt, a measure ostensibly to prevent art of national importance in private hands from being sold to foreign buyers, but really to relieve British art owners from the burden of crippling taxation. William reported on hundreds of private art collections for the Board. His democratic-socialist principles combined with his immense knowledge of art made him the perfect man for the job and the Revenue could be confident that works of art under his scrutiny would be shrewdly and fairly assessed.

It was particularly appropriate that his career should culminate in a position so compatible with William's lifelong interests. Earlier he had toyed with the idea of applying for administrative posts in the British Museum or the National Gallery. He confided in Lucy and his diary on 1 January 1878:

> I of course shd. in essentials prefer the post of Sec. to Nat. Gall. to that of Asst. Sec. or even Sec., to the In. Rev., & my advancement to the post of Sec. here is, to say the least, not a certainty: so, if the money aspect of the N.G. post compares favourably, or not quite unfavourably, with that of my present berth, I wd. be quite inclined to take the risks of transferring myself, at the age of 48, from an office wherein I have been ensconced ever since the age of 15.

He concluded accurately: 'I don't much expect the N.G. project will come to anything, because (1) I suspect the emoluments are not up to the mark, & (2) the appointment wd. probably be conferred on some better-qualified or more influential candidate'. The incident reveals just how trapped he was for fifty years in a profession he never chose.

Evening – the séance

He sees angels: they cannot be described
   William's Séance Diary, 25 November 1865

What seemed genuine was unimportant, and what was tolerably important was ascertained or might be surmised to be not genuine.
   William's Séance Diary, June 1866

Between November 1865 and August 1868 William attended over twenty séance sessions and kept a Séance Diary in which he recorded and attempted to make sense of what he saw and heard. By his mid-thirties, William had been close to deathbed scenes, his father's in 1854, and Gabriel's wife, Lizzie Siddal's, more recently in 1862. Séance mania and the discussion of apparently paranormal experience was at its height during the mid-nineteenth century – and even a cause of dissension in the legendary marriage of Elizabeth and Robert Browning. Elizabeth was a passionate believer in psychic phenomena and Robert a complete sceptic.

First invited to a séance by Captain Ruxton (his co-organiser of the British Art exhibition that toured America in 1857–8, see pp. 131–5), William went to séances in the spirit of research. As an agnostic who continually asked himself questions about religion, it was an awkward but intriguing subject for him. Believers secure in their faith tended to reject spiritualist paraphernalia such as turning tables, ouija boards, automatic writing, ghosts, guardian angels and migrating souls. Unbelievers found faith of any persuasion difficult to accept either intellectually or emotionally.

William and Ruxton carefully concealed their identities when, on Saturday, 11 November 1865, they visited Mrs Marshall, a professional medium and former washerwoman. She tried to persuade William she had conjured the spirit of John Cross, an artist friend of Thomas Woolner. Although the Marshalls 'asked no fishing questions whatever, nor did I detect either in any deception', their boisterous behaviour made William dubious.[11]

The next day, Sunday, 12 November, William, Gabriel and Fanny Cornforth convened an intimate, private session without a professional medium. Gabriel tried to summon the spirit of Lizzie, his dead wife, but the séance degenerated into a muddle and nothing happened. On Friday, 17 November, William joined William and Letitia Bell Scott, Holman Hunt, his sister Emily Hunt and Mrs Woolner, nearly all 'more or less decided disbelievers' for an uproarious session of 'laughing and nonsense' when the 'whole affair was treated lightly' especially when the table gyrated across the floor.[12]

William returned to Mrs Marshall's for a professional session with William Bell Scott on Saturday, 25 November. Seven other men they had never seen before participated, 'some at any rate obvious believers'. Bell Scott who had dismissed spiritualist evidence until now was 'staggered...hugely' by the uncanny correctness of answers supposed to emanate from the spirit of

53. Photograph of William Michael Rossetti and William Bell Scott (wearing wig), 1858. Photograph by W. & D. Downey, Newcastle-upon-Tyne. Fredeman Family Collection.

Spencer Boyd,[13] who had died suddenly on 1 February 1865 at Scott's home.

'Uncle John' next entered the session, apparently Dr John Polidori, William's maternal uncle. With his Byronic connections, Polidori had always been a source of Romantic speculation to William. He now cross-questioned the spirit. 'Will you tell me truly how you died? Yes. How? Killed. Who killed you? I.' William believed Polidori had committed suicide in 1821 and was not afraid to say so in his expurgated edition of *The Diary of Dr John William Polidori*. (Aunt Charlotte Polidori, Dr John Polidori's sister, had physically removed incriminating passages from the diary, much to William's regret.)[14]

Bell Scott crawled under the table to look for the source of knocks vibrating through its surface. 'Whilst he was thus looking, and the people obtaining messages through the table, came this message "Mind your wig." They all laughed, not seeing any applicability in the message: Scott alone guessed it might be meant for him', William confirmed, knowing his friend wore a wig (fig. 53).

William now partially revised his opinion of Mrs Marshall. In spite of her vulgar bearing, she saw visions in the streets and ghosts 'like the shadows of living people, only white'. During this session she became very excited, talked volubly and fixed William with a mesmeric stare. He 'took it cool, and the fit soon passed'.[15]

But the fit had not passed for William. After leaving Mrs Marshall's that Saturday he went on to a smaller séance where contact was made with Frank Oliphant, a glass painter Bell Scott had known. 'He sees angels: they cannot be described', William reported. Then came a closer, more poignant contact – Lizzie Siddal. The spirit spelled out that she 'had during her life a liking for me; considers that I acted as an affectionate brother to Gabriel. Saw Gabriel and me at breakfast this morning at Chelsea (correct); but could not say who else were present (my mother and Christina)'.[16]

William was becoming addicted. On the evening of Monday, 27 November after work he joined Gabriel, Fanny and Charles Augustus Howell (Gabriel's agent) in the studio at 16 Cheyne Walk. This time William tried (in Italian) to contact his father Gabriele. But the messenger from the spirit world was elusive and insolent. 'Are you a bad spirit?' asked William. 'Yes. Have you been telling us a pack of lies? Yes. Are you what is termed a devil? No. Are all devils the souls of men? No reply'.[17]

Early in 1866, Lizzie reappeared at a séance which included, among others, William, Alfred Lyster (William's friend and colleague from the office), his wife and Louisa Parke whom Mrs Lyster had adopted. Louisa was an intelligent woman, a lifelong friend and correspondent of Christina Rossetti. She and William once went to the theatre together with Lizzie and Gabriel. Lizzie's spirit volunteered, 'Gabriel loves somebody here very much: will you go and tell him love Lou. I could not at first conceive what Lou could be, and went on trying in vain to get a completion of the word; at last I guessed it must be the beginning of "Louisa" (Parke): the awkwardness of the situation inclined me to evade the finish of the word: yet I still made an effort or two to get the finish, but failed'.[18] Although Gabriel had made a head and shoulders portrait of Louisa around 1855[19] there was no record of any intimacy between artist and sitter.

Lizzie Siddal rematerialized on Sunday, 25 February 1866 at an impromptu séance at 16 Cheyne Walk while Gabriel was working on his old design of Hamlet and Ophelia – for which Lizzie had modelled. William and Fanny sat at a small japanned table that almost at once moved in response to their questions. When Lizzie's spirit seemed to be present, Gabriel took William's place and asked the question tormenting him ever since his wife's laudanum overdose four years before. 'Are you now happy? Yes. Happier than when you began communications of this sort? Yes.' Gabriel wanted to know whether Lizzie had any knowledge of his current work. 'Did you like the picture I sent off the other day [this was *The Beloved*]? Yes'.[20] Gabriel tested the spirit briefly before going back to his design. Like Hamlet, he seemed to accept that this was 'an honest ghost'.

William, however, continued to probe. 'Did you consider that picture which Gabriel sent away the other day one of his very best? Yes. Do you know to whom it has gone? Yes. Give initial of surname. R [correct for Rae].[21] Have you seen Rae in this house? Yes. Has he dark hair? Yes. Tall? No. Have you seen his wife? Yes. Is she good-looking? Yes. [all correct which Fanny indicated her not being aware]. Do you know in what room of Rae's house that picture is now placed? Yes. Dining-room? No. Drawingroom? Yes…Were you present when Rae received *The Beloved*? Yes. Did he express a high opinion of it? Yes'.

William deepened his examination, enquiring whether spirits communicate only with living people with whom they are in sympathy. Yes, came the answer. 'Can you give me any idea of the process by which you pass from one place to another? No. Is it in any way like a human being doing the like thing? Yes.'[22] William's relentless catechism seemed to tire the spirit whose answers became erratic and eventually faded away.

The next interaction William recorded with Lizzie Siddal came on Saturday, 12 May 1866. This time the group consisted of the two Rossetti brothers and the Howells. 'We all pledged ourselves to abstain from any tricks'. In the suggestive flickering of the firelight, the delicate, ornamental table soon began to tilt distinctly. Once or twice

> at request, the table moved very steadily & decisively towards one of the sitters. When motion in the table became evident, Gabriel asked Is there any spirit present? Yes (the ordinary 3 tilts). Will you spell out your name? Yes. Spell it – Christian? Name? Eli…Now surname? Ros. Here G stopped, & I said Give the last letter of the surname? I. (This G. & I understood to be Elizabeth Rossetti). G. Will you give a message? Yes. Give it? Love *yor*? Liz. (This word *Liz* had not been at all anticipated by me, nor, as he said, by G: When *Li* came, we both were rather expecting *Life*?)[23]

Perhaps the message of absolution emanated from Gabriel's subconscious or from the unspoken comfort William longed to offer his brother about Lizzie. Or was it was spontaneous fraternal collusion? There were no messages at all for the Howells.

Later that year, in October 1866, William and Bell Scott attended a daylight session with Mrs Marshall, the professional medium. Bell Scott wanted to contact Pauline, Lady Trevelyan who had died five months before and William would try to communicate with the spirit of Pre-Raphaelite artist Walter Deverell who had died young in 1854. Nothing persuasive happened until Bell Scott's artist friend, Frank Oliphant, claimed to be 'not dead' but present in the room.

William asked Oliphant's spirit some of the eternal questions that exercised him.

> Are you happy? Yes. Do you see God? No. Do you see Christ? Yes. Is he like a man? Yes. Is he the same as God? Two taps in reply, meaning "not exactly". Is there such a being as God? Yes. Is he a being separate from the material universe? No. Is the whole material universe, including the intellect of it, the same as God? Yes. In other words what is called pantheism is the true theology? Yes. Is my intellect a part of the whole which constitutes God? Yes.

These answers corroborated William's agnostic position and his lifelong rejection of conventional religion. But William conscientiously recorded one further answer, which contradicted what had gone before. 'Is Christ God? Yes'.

After Oliphant's spirit had dematerialized and a few less convincing spirits had come and gone, William's guardian angel professed to be present. Angels of any kind had no place in William's cosmic view. Nevertheless, he asked a series of questions, prosaic and profound. 'Have you wings? No. Are you like a man? No…Is there such a place as hell? No. I mean a place where people are roasted & so on? No. Is there any place of punishment for souls? Yes. Do any souls remain there eternally? No…Is there any devil? No. No such being as is ordinarily understood by the name Satan? No.'

Throughout their association with the Marshalls, William and Bell Scott believed they had successfully concealed their identities and their connections. Although the sessions had been 'somewhat unsatisfactory', they concluded it could not 'be denied that some of the messages were curiously right'.[24] William continued to participate in ad hoc séances during autumn 1866, once alone with Fanny Cornforth,[25] once by candlelight with Mrs Anne Gilchrist 'a total disbeliever in all spiritualist manifestations' when there were no mani-festations,[26] and again with the Lyster family when Lizzie Siddal resurfaced.

The next day Saturday, 15 December 1866, William and Gabriel went round in the winter twilight to Madox Brown's house at 37 Fitzroy Square. Lamps were turned low as they took their places round the heavy table. Present but not always participating at the same time were Brown and Emma, Lucy, Cathy, eleven-year-old Oliver (Nolly) Brown, and Lucy's aunt, Helen Bromley, who had no belief in spiritualism. Cathy suspected Nolly of playing schoolboy tricks and Lucy told William much later that Nolly had eventually confessed to making the table move.[27]

After this William's appetite for supernatural phenomena declined, and it was over sixteen months before he recorded the next session on 1 April 1868, a supper-séance in the presence of the well-known professional mediums, Mr and Mrs Guppy and Mrs Faucett, This time every ray of light was excluded and the group included Janey Morris, Gabriel, Mr and Mrs Tebbs, Bell Scott, Fanny Seddon (sister of Mrs Tebbs and of the painter Thomas Seddon) and William. The solid, polygonal table made no movements. Any 'verbal' com-munication came through tapping sounds beneath it.

At first nothing happened. There was much talking and hilarity. After quar-ter of an hour some of the group, including Janey Morris, said they were con-scious of a rush of cold air over their hands. William felt nothing and when he touched the back of Janey's hand 'it was ordinarily warm'. Tebbs asked a spirit to bring flowers to the table. Fanny Seddon asked for roses but Mrs Guppy objected that roses were not in season. But flowers materialized. 'Mrs Morris named cowslips: she got polyanthus'. William asked for primroses and got a geranium thrown into his hands followed by two primroses that landed on his knees. 'Gabriel asked for hyacinth, & got it, a good-sized sprig. Violets and daffodils were also asked for & were among the flowers found when the light came.' The flowers were fresh, mostly single sprigs 'as if pulled off one by one: the whole together made a smallish bundle for the hand, such as I suppose as would sell for 1d or 2d in the street. The room contained no flowers at all, so far as any one knew'.

The next phenomenon was a brilliant light like a star or a diamond, which Mrs Faucett and Mrs Guppy both professed to see. 'Mrs Morris said that one of these lights was perfectly visible to her', although to no one else. After supper the group became more riotous and 'a sudden shower of eau-de-cologne struck us', followed by a further shower of plain water although there had been no liquid in the room as far as anyone could tell.

Although William could not detect the Guppys or Mrs Faucett in any trickery, he reflected that a competent conjurer could have easily produced both flowers and showers. The problem remained that Janey who was certainly no spiritualist impostor had professed to seeing an unnatural light. William later discussed with Howell, Faulkner and Holman Hunt various physical explanations for Janey's vision. Hunt's suggestion seemed particularly feasible, that the light might have been 'a mere optical spectrum; such as one sees in the light after keeping one's eyes shut hard, or in the dark after some lapse of time'. William discovered that Mrs Faucett had publicly exhibited her magnetic powers – indeed as a child she had been known as the 'Living Magnet'.[28]

Nearly the same group reconvened for another supper-séance with the Guppys on Friday, 24 April 1868. Mrs Faucett and Bell Scott were absent. New participants were Alaric Watts and Lucy Madox Brown who sat next to William. Gabriel and Janey sat side by side. Flowers (mainly jonquils) and showers rained down. Lucy whispered to William that she could not keep her hand still, and touching it, he found that it moved about, apparently involuntarily, over the surface of the table. Guppy suggested Lucy might prove to be a writing or drawing medium but when a pencil was put in her hand she produced nothing.

Next, raps came 'purporting to be from Thomas Seddon', the artist. As it was his sister Mrs Tebbs's birthday she asked the spirit, 'Will you give me a message? Yes. Give it. – Dear Sister, God bless you now & evermore. Can you give us a drawing? No. Why not? My drawing power has left me. Gabriel here asked; When I die, will my drawing power leave me? No... Mrs Tebbs resumed questioning: Do you still take an interest in Gabriel Rossetti's work as a painter? Yes. In Fanny's efforts as a painter? Yes. Do you approve of her continuing to exert herself to do her best in that way? Yes'. The responses of the revenant, or the will of the assembled group, which contained at least three artistic women, Lucy Madox Brown, Janey Morris and Fanny Seddon, endorsed the rights of creative women. Several people felt currents of cold air although William 'felt nothing'. Then suddenly 'several heavy volumes of books were bundled on to the table – Froissart, Weldon's Register'. William immediately suspected trickery. Most of the session had been unconvincing, the Rossetti brothers later agreed.[29]

William recorded his last séance in his special diary on Friday, 14 August 1868. The craze had lasted just under three years. Very late that night between midnight and 2 a.m. at Gabriel's studio, William, Treffry Dunn (Gabriel's studio assistant) and Fanny Cornforth gathered on a whim round a solid table in 'quasi-darkness'. Gabriel joined the group as soon as rapping was heard under the table. Inevitably, perhaps, it was Lizzie's spirit that invaded Gabriel's mind with recurrent, torturing themes. 'Are you my wife? Yes – Are you now happy? Yes – Happier than on earth? Yes – If I were now to join you, should I be happy? Yes – Should I see you at once? No – Quite soon? No. Tilt the table to the person you like best: it came to G[abriel]. Do you now like F[anny]? Yes – But some while ago you used not to like her? No – Did you pull her hair on a particular occasion?' (William had witnessed it) 'Yes – Will you pull her hair now? Yes.' But nothing transpired.

Gabriel asked Lizzie's spirit if it knew his father 'in the world of Spirits? Yes.' He asked her to bring his father to the table. After a short delay, he was thought to be present although, unusually, he 'spoke' in English rather than Italian. William asked the former Dante scholar, 'Do you see Dante in your present condition? Yes – Were your Dantesque theories correct? Yes – is Dante then really an atheist? Yes – Is Atheism true? Yes – Then there is no God? No – is there such a being as Christ? Yes – In other words, Christ is not God? Yes (i.e. he is not). Do you know where Christina is? Yes – Is it the South of England? Yes (Wrong: she is at Leeds.)' His answers faded out until 'the manifestations came to a standstill'.[30]

William's Séance Diary came to a standstill, too, with this final entry. In the old spirit of Pre-Raphaelite realism he had aimed to record objectively everything he observed. He had worried about logical plausibility and physical explanations for psychic phenomena. He had suspected trickery but he was open to experience. He had treated levitating tables without levity and listened to 'messages' from the long and newly dead. When his daughters tried ouija boards at the beginning of the twentieth century, he could not resist joining in. 'Gabriel professed to communicate with me, & to be happy', William noted. He put some questions to test the genuineness of the spirit 'but nothing satisfactory came of them. As of old, I remain unable to account for what happens'.[31]

4

Pre-Raphaelite

SKETCH-BOOK

William's acumen as an art critic, art historian and connoisseur was founded on his own early attempts at drawing. From a young age he was told, and he accepted, that his particular aptitudes were literary and critical, but nevertheless he drew from time to time, as did his sister Christina. His childhood delight in the natural world is apparent in two surviving coloured drawings, *Moth* and *Viola* (see p. ii), the latter dated January 1841, when he was eleven.

Paints and colours were an essential part of Rossettian childhood. William remembered how their usefulness could be enlarged from the merely artistic to conceal a poor boy's social embarrassment:

> I was invited, perhaps in the autumn of 1844, to pass a day at the house of my school friend, Edward Nussey, in Cleveland Row, close to St James's Palace; his family were very well off – I dare say opulent. I had only one blue cloth jacket possible to put on for such an occasion. The elbows of it were whitened by wear; so I took some of the Prussian-blue water-colour paint which I was wont to use in colouring woodcuts, and daubed upon those elbows, in the hope – mainly a vain one – of making them less unpresentably white.[1]

At fifteen, William left childhood behind for ever when he took up what he thought was temporary employment at the Excise Office. Long days of unremitting routine meant little time for creative work of any sort. No art work dating from the next four years survives. However, as soon as the Pre-Raphaelite Brotherhood came into existence in autumn 1848, William attended life classes at a Bond Street studio and drew other artistic exercises, designs, copies and portraits. In his role as keeper of the *P.R.B. Journal*, William noted not only what his 'Brothers' had painted, but also what they intended to paint. John Everett Millais's mind was fecund with ideas:

> Millais said that he had thoughts of painting a hedge (as a subject) to the closest point of imitation, with a bird's nest, – a thing which has never been attempted. Another subject he has in his eye is a river-sparrow's nest, built,

as he says they are, between three reeds; the bird he describes as with its head always on one side, 'a body like a ball, and thin legs like needles'. He intends soon to set about his subject from Patmore, Sir Hubert, and Mabel, 'as she issues from the trees'.[2]

On 24 May 1849 William took practical artistic advice from the sculptor, Thomas Woolner who 'has recommended me to follow out one of the designs I had begun, and laid aside, for "Maud's madness". This I shall probably do, tho' the idea of painting two children is very frightening.'[3] On Sunday 'Gabriel and I were engaged, the greater part of the day, on our respective Designs.'[4] The following week William arranged a first sitting for Miss Saunders, a new model. Late on Tuesday, 29 May, William and Holman Hunt, and probably Gabriel, 'talked and did portraits'.[5] The next day he complained about a middle-aged, overweight model at the life class – William preferred to copy drapery, folds of material rather than folds of flesh. On 30 June 1849 he wrote to Frederic George Stephens, booking in both the Rossetti brothers 'for perspective purposes' on Friday week.[6] During mid-August William and Gabriel drew fairly regularly from life models at a different drawing school run by James Leigh in Newman Street while Holman Hunt was working on a picture of a mother and children coming over a hill 'on which he has painted various buttercups and dandelion puffs. He has painted up the sky, put a plume onto the casque of one of the troopers.'[7] *Rienzi Vowing to Obtain Justice for the Death of his Young Brother* became the first picture publicly exhibited with the opaque but thrilling initials 'P.R.B.' It was a time of concerted creativity among the Pre-Raphaelite brothers.

Undoubtedly the most conspicuous aspect of William's art output is the dozen or so pencil portraits of friends and members of his family. They bear witness to his genuine response to individual characters as well as to technical expertise. In her book *Pre-Raphaelite Portraits*, Andrea Rose reproduced what may be the first and only self-portrait by William (fig. 54).[8]

It is a disarming piece of work, showing William two days after his seventeenth birthday. An unstructured, wide-lapelled jacket, casually unbuttoned over waistcoat and high-collared shirt, sporting an artist's droopy bow-tie, all indicate an attention to sartorial detail which lasted a lifetime. William's sophisticated pencil work and cross-hatching plays up contrasts between light and dark, effectively suggesting shadows and the solidity of a three-dimensional figure in its space. The study also hints at private awareness of his divided self, exploring inner conflict in a young man who appears both dreamy and assured, an office clerk who is also a bohemian.

In the same year, 1846, Gabriel drew a very similar portrait of William, and it may even record the same occasion (see fig. 5).[9] The striking similarities between the two pencil portraits have caused some confusion. In *Ford Madox Brown and the Pre-Raphaelite Circle* (1991), Newman and Watkinson credit

54. William Michael Rossetti, *Self-portrait*, 27 September 1846. Pencil. Private collection.

William's self-portrait as a portrait by his brother[10] and say it is in the National Portrait Gallery, which does indeed hold the very similar sketch by Gabriel. However, Andrea Rose confirms that the different drawing she saw in a private collection is an authentic self-portrait by William.

In the late 1840s and early 1850s, Gabriel and William's widening circle of friends, first in the Cyclographic sketching club – a precursor of the Pre-Raphaelite Brotherhood itself – and from 1848 in the Pre-Raphaelite Brotherhood, were all enthusiastically making their own and each other's likenesses.

The finest of William's portrait heads is a speaking likeness of the young Millais, in profile looking left, showing off to full advantage his sculpted, high cheek-bones and Roman nose (fig. 55). The young man's complexion is delicately expressed in subtle, cross-hatched shading which contrasts with the rampant curls of his bohemian coiffeur. The eye beneath its feathery eyebrow is the observant eye of an artist. William has captured something of this young man's double appeal, a male 'stunner', his face almost feminine but not effeminate, with a romantic beauty that only youth can impart. 'His face came nearer to the type which we term angelic than perhaps any other male visage that I have seen', thought William.[11] Millais was not quite twenty-four, William a few months his junior, when he described the marvellous boy. Apart from the face,

55. William
Michael Rossetti,
Millais, 12 April
1853. Inscribed
'To Thomas
Woolner' signed
in monogram
and dated. Pencil,
270 × 190 mm.
Mrs N. Murray-
Smith, Australia.

the rest of the portrait is loosely sketched; large expanses of white merely indicate Millais's high winged collar and the lapels of his fashionable jacket. William inscribed the portrait, 'To Thomas Woolner', added his own initials 'WMR' entwined in a careful monogram, and the date '12 April, 1853'.

This was 'the day fixed for the grand meeting of Woolner's friends, when each is to make a drawing to be sent to him in Australia', as Gabriel wrote to Emma Brown. The hour appointed for the drawing party was midday exactly. The brothers were due to breakfast at Millais's at eight and then 'go somewhere into the country for the sketching' before rounding off the day with an evening of conviviality.[12] Gabriel's portrait sketch of William, now in the National Portrait Gallery, was drawn on the same occasion (see fig. 7). Gabriel told Bell Scott that William had sketched 'the whole lot of us in his own striking style',[13] commenting accurately when he sent the results of the sketching party out to Woolner, that 'some of William's sketches are very rich', although only the ones of Millais (above) and Holman Hunt (below) have been traced. Gabriel was also full of wonder at Hunt's sketches, made with Swiss chalks, so much softer and more beautiful in colour than Creta Levis, he thought.[14]

56. William Michael Rossetti, *Holman Hunt*, 12 April 1853 (?). Pencil, 270 × 190 mm (on verso of fig. 55). Mrs N. Murray-Smith, Australia.

In the light of Gabriel's comment about Hunt, there is an added bonus behind William's portrait of Millais. The verso reveals a less beautiful but highly characterful likeness of Hunt, also sketched by William (fig. 56). The youthful Hunt has a rugged, earnest expression, perplexed frown-marks, retroussé nose, and profuse side-whiskers. The sketch is not as finished as William's picture of Millais but nevertheless is drawn with swift, vigorous authenticity. Next to his likeness of Hunt, William playfully experimented to achieve an elegant monogram and inscribed the best of these overleaf, beneath his portrait of Millais.

Only two days before drawing Millais on 12 April 1853, William struggled to capture Christina's likeness, as he ruefully reported to his dearest Mamma, recently arrived in Frome, Somerset in order to set up school with her youngest daughter. 'I have just been attempting two successive portraits of Christina to send you: but they came out such shameful Guys that they found their legitimate home in the fire instead.' William continued self-deprecatingly: 'Will you tell her that I have not forgotten her so utterly as my portraits, had she seen them, might have led her to suppose'.[15] Christina was a far more complex, 'interior' personality to render in pencil than the gorgeous, dandified Millais. His physical appeal was apparent, hers much more subtle, elusive and metaphysical. A few weeks later William made a further attempt to capture Christina's likeness. This time, recognizing his near-success, he did not cast his efforts with disgust into the grate but preserved the portrait (see fig. 60).[16]

William was visiting his mother and sister in Frome when he portrayed Christina on 22 June 1853. Released from office routine and buoyant from the clear success of his recent Millais portrait, he drew with new freedom and confidence. For once he had time, as well as enthusiasm, as on that same, long, summer's day he produced one of the most uncompromising, analytical portraits of Frances Rossetti that survives (fig. 57).[17]

Frances has a massive face, a suggestion of a jowl, large, regular features, inexpressive eyes, a smooth high brow, and heavy, dark, corkscrew ringlets beneath her frilled cap. She is neither masculine nor feminine but dominant

57. William
Michael Rossetti,
Frances Rossetti, 22
June 1853. Pencil,
353 × 255 mm,
signed with initials
and dated '22 June
1853 – WMR'
lower right and
'Head of my
Mother' on verso.
Private collection.

and eternal. A fine-toothed bone comb secures a ringlet that dared to stray. William's feeling for his mother was unfailingly affectionate and all four siblings adored her. Yet William may have subconsciously referred to an unknown side of Mrs Rossetti in his stern visual account.

William had a fair enough opinion of his portrait sketches to frame four of them together.[18] One profile head of his father Gabriele in a peaked cap (fig. 58) and another (second portrait) of young Millais (fig. 59) are flanked left and right by two tender images of William's sister Christina (figs 60, 61). *Gabriele Rossetti*, dated 1852 when his father was nearly seventy, is almost a caricature.

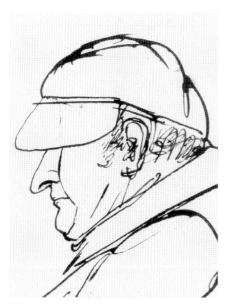

58. William Michael Rossetti, *Gabriele Rossetti*, 1852. Pen and ink, 70 × 89 mm. Private collection.

59. William Michael Rossetti, *The Young Millais*, c. 1849. Pen and ink on buff paper, 89 × 127 mm. Private collection.

60. William Michael Rossetti, *Christina Rossetti*, 22 June 1853. Pencil, 121 × 171 mm. Private collection.

61. William Michael Rossetti, *Christina Rossetti*, c. 1855. Pencil, 121 × 171 mm. Private collection.

By totally concealing the eyes and drawing swiftly, perhaps in a moment when Gabriele was unaware, William has caught the sense of isolation of the nearly blind. The economy of line in the simple head of Millais placed next to Gabriele's makes a poignant contrast with the withdrawn old man. Millais seems to face the future head on. In a few vigorous strokes William suggests the unruly curls that, at just twenty, accentuated Millais's extreme youth.

The stars in this quadruple frame are the two pencil portraits of Christina, also in her twenties. On the outside left, initialled 'W.R.' and dated '22nd June 1853', is a head-and-shoulders profile, showing Christina with downcast eyes beneath elegant brows, strongly sculpted nose, lips and chin (fig. 60). Her smooth centrally parted hair, is caught up in a knot at the nape and a long, artful lock sweeps down below her unseen ear to loop up at the back. William has conveyed a sense both of the outer and inner Christina, the delicate calm of her outer appearance set against the tension of interior, mental capacity behind her wide brow. The portrait acknowledges Christina's reserve, restraint, and unknowability.

On the right hand side of the frame is another pencil drawing of Christina, striking because of its utter simplicity of line, showing her face only in downcast left profile (fig. 61). In no more than ten separate curving lines, William has expressed mood and character. Everything is pared down here but the force of personality is apparent in the jut of the jaw, the up-tilt of the nose, the down sweep of the lashes. Christina is caught in a moment of reverie, inwardly musing, forever remote. William monogrammed this drawing and dated it 'c.1855'. The four highly contrasted studies exhibit William's capabilities in character drawing, his deft assurance, as well as his wide raft of sympathies for differing personalities.

William drew friends such as James Hannay[19] but more often his fellow-brothers in the P.R.B.: Gabriel[20], Holman Hunt and Thomas Woolner,[21] and an almost breathing likeness of Frederic George Stephens (fig. 62). William was not the only one of the Pre-Raphaelites to admire Stephens's debonair good looks. 'Millais is painting him for Ferdinand listening to Ariel',[22] William told Frances Rossetti in September 1849,[23] and Madox Brown chose his head for *Christ Washing Peter's Feet* two years later. Although he exhibited two portraits at the Royal Academy during the early 1850s, Stephens soon gave up any notions of being a professional artist, preferring to develop his literary career.

However, Stephens was the honorary secretary and William one of the co-founding committee members of the Hogarth Club, a late sprig of the by-then defunct Pre-Raphaelite Brotherhood. Inspired by Madox Brown's initiative, between 1858 and 1861 the club aimed to provide an alternative salon to the Royal Academy, with exhibition facilities and a congenial social milieu for artists, their patrons and friends. Its short-lived fortunes, noted William later, were anything but brilliant.

62. William Michael Rossetti, *Frederic George Stephens*, undated. Pencil, 175 × 120 mm. Reproduced with kind permission of Roger W. Peattie.

Stephens became the established art critic on the *Athenaeum* for over forty years from 1861 to 1901. William's instantaneous sketch captures Stephens at a moment of youth. It was a lifelong friendship between the two art critics. William 'was from the first fond of Stephens' and recorded that this 'kindliest and most persistent of friends' had always been as fond of him.[24]

William drew some small, undated, female pencil heads labelled in his hand, '*Mrs O.*' and '*R.O.*' These are probably Mrs Eliza Orme (elder sister of the original 'Angel in the House', Emily Augusta Patmore, née Andrews*)* and her daughter Emily Rosaline Orme (figs 63, 64), and therefore the sister-in-law and niece respectively of poet Coventry Patmore. Patmore had warned

63 and 64. William Michael Rossetti, *Mrs O[rme]* (far left), and *Emily Rosaline Orme* (left), both undated. Pencil, each 120 × 100 mm. Private collection.

Thomas Woolner about Eliza Orme[25] whom he considered his pushy, manipulative sister-in-law, but William always found her warm and seductive, 'of rich physique, with luminous dark eyes'. Eliza had married distiller Charles Orme when she was only sixteen but when William first met her she was an 'older woman' over thirty. She had refined tastes and cultivated a salon of artists and writers. She sang beautifully and played the piano with an erotic charge, 'there never was such playing as hers – so delusive, so persuasive, so altogether dramatic', recalled her granddaughter, Flora Masson. 'She was a wonderful hostess – really interested in hearing about other people's joys and sorrows…It was a family habit, on summer evenings, to walk in the garden in groups of twos and threes, up and down the lawn, and round and round the gravel paths under the pear trees. William Michael Rossetti has described the scene:

> "All calm, the dusk condenses round;
>   The lawn is changing green to grey,
> Our voices take a softer sound,
>   Light words are hushed we had to say,
> And graver eyes peruse the ground."[26]

Thirteen years younger, William fell under Eliza's spell. Walking together in her magical garden at Avenue Road, Regent's Park, William felt awkwardly shy but was not entirely afraid to voice his own opinions. Once the beguiling Eliza teased William for being 'sarcastic'.[27] She flirted with him and boosted his ego. They discussed Blake and he responded to her voluptuous blend of intellectual sympathy and physical attraction, reflected not only in his anecdote about their skirmish in the garden but also in the slightly overblown image he drew of her.

Forty years later he noted her death on 28 April 1892, and told his wife Lucy, 'I must have first known Mrs Orme, I think, in 1850, or even 1849; and for some 5 or 6 years ensuing no one did more than she to make me feel at my ease and give me some self-confidence on my entrance into life'.[28] By the mid-1850s, after he became engaged to Henrietta Rintoul, his intimacy with the Ormes subsided but he always remembered Eliza Orme as one of his 'earliest and most indulgent friends'.[29]

William also made several attempts to capture the fresher charms of Miss 'R.O.', which bear a striking resemblance to a drawing of a young woman reproduced in *The Rossetti Cabinet*.[30] William identifies her on the verso of Gabriel's pen and ink drawing (c.1852–4) as Coventry Patmore's niece, 'Miss Orme by Gabriel', presumably Emily *Rosaline* Orme, Eliza's eldest daughter. W.E. Fredeman showed that the last four letters of 'E*mily*' are visible beneath Gabriel's drawing. William found Miss Orme almost as 'pretty and engaging' as her mother, as he divulged just after her marriage in 1853 to David Masson, the scholar and biographer of Milton.[31]

65. William Michael Rossetti, *Maria Rossetti, c.* 1869. Pencil, 122 × 115 mm. Troxell Collection of Rossetti Manuscripts, Department of Rare Books and Special Collections, Princeton University Library.

William's small clutch of surviving portraits – about a dozen – all exhibit his genuine human compassion, his sense for beauty even in plainness, his clear-sighted lack of sentimentality. A rough sketch of his eldest sister Maria is truthful and touching.

He drew Maria in profile looking left and downward, a strong, reflective face (fig. 65). Her dark Italian hair is severely drawn back, setting off a carved simplicity of line from brow to chin. Her heavily accented eyebrow highlights a fine eye. Maria was considered the most intellectual of the Rossetti siblings and William conveys a thoughtful gravitas. Around her neck a beaded rosary indicates both inward and outward piety. Her gaze is not on this world, but a world beyond, or a world within. In this undated drawing Maria is neither young nor old but simply ageless[32]. William drew this portrait on the back of one of Christina's manuscripts and later identified it, 'This must be mine – meant apparently for Maria – very bad W M R'.[33] But it is not very bad; it is far more perceptive than any of the unflattering photographs of Maria.

William's humanitarian generosity is not the only feature apparent in his collection of portraits. The other marked trait is his sense of humour, his eye for the absurd, the eccentric detail that tells you more about a character than whole pages of description: the froth of curls on Millais's head, the upturned nose and expanded chest of Holman Hunt, the cap crammed down over the failing eyes of his scholar father, Gabriele, the little comb denoting a small female vanity in his mother's hair, a floppy artist's bow telling of aesthetic longings in the dreams of the Excise Office boy.

William wasn't just interested in the human world; he had world enough within him for an unsentimental response to the animal. Throughout his life his greatest love among domestic animals was reserved for cats, but if William drew any cats, none of them appear to have survived. William Bell Scott had a dog called Olaf, a legendary canine with a Jekyll and Hyde personality. In

66. William Michael Rossetti, *A Caricature of Olaf*, 1859. Pencil on cream paper, 115 × 185 mm. Private collection.

67. William Michael Rossetti, *Alligator*, August 1859. Pencil on blue paper. Private collection.

1859 William made a bristling and lifelike *Caricature of Olaf* (fig. 66) whose shiny wet nose, beady eye and flapping ears balanced by an over-arching tail, indicate he is ready for anything. Bell Scott loved the dog and loved his friend William enough to paste this drawing into his personal album.

Olaf was still in rude good health nine years after William's caricature and Bell Scott was forever making excuses about his behaviour. 'Olaf made the most tremendous row' when Gabriel came to visit, 'and as he was standing by my studio's fire he trod on the beast's tail and Olaf seized him by the foot and fairly bit through his boot. By and bye my friends will keep out of my way on account of this dreadful dog, who is after all harmless as a lamb except when trodden on'.[34]

In his version of the story, Gabriel embroidered on the demonic character of Olaf who

> first greeted me with a selection from some opera of his own, probably 'Scotus le Diable' – and when, after an hour or so, he had subsided and appeared at rest, he suddenly sprang up from the hearth and produced an indented pattern in the style of Morris and Co. round the toe of my boot – the different ornaments composing it being varied in the fanciful style of that firm so as to avoid monotony...I directed W. B.'s attention to this instance of Olaf's adding decorative art to his musical studies; and the remark I received in reply (uttered with slow complacency) was 'Ah! then he has some teeth yet, you see!' I may mention in conclusion that I am *not* lamed for life, and that is all I can say.[35]

William's *Olaf* lies at rest, meditating his next opportunity to pounce.

Three other animal drawings by William survive. Two pencil sketches on a single sheet of blue paper were probably made during one of his many visits to the Zoological Gardens in Regent's Park. On the recto, dated 'Aug 59', is a supine alligator with a wide toothy smile, glittering eye and strong scaly limbs

68. William Michael Rossetti, *Blackbacked Jackal*, undated, possibly August 1859. Pencil on blue paper. Private collection.

(fig. 67). William was fascinated by amphibians. At the Jardin Zoologique in Brussels, he unashamedly prodded with his umbrella a six-foot long American alligator. The reptile naturally responded, 'opened his pale pink mouth wide and gave vent to a double outbreathing, approaching a snort or hiss'.[36] On the verso of *Alligator* is another predator, a blackbacked jackal with pointed, whiskery snout and a deceptively indolent eye (fig. 68).

Like *Olaf*, these appear to have been observed from life, with the added dimension of anthropomorphic caricature.[37] William was not only mesmerized by fierce beasts. He always had an eye for the small and disregarded. 'Picked up a mole in coming along the only one I ever saw walking about above ground: he was going along at a good trundling pace'.[38] He was a man who used to notice such things. Another piece of miniature animal observation shows a densely furry wombat (fig. 69).

She sits in a patch of feathery grass and may depict the wombat that arrived at Gabriel's back garden menagerie at 16 Cheyne Walk in 1869. 'The wombat, whom I saw yesterday, is the greatest lark you can imagine: possibly the best of wombats I have seen', enthused William to his brother. 'She (for I believe it is a she) is but little past babyhood, and of a less wiry surface than the adult wombat: very familiar, following one's footsteps about the room, and trotting after one if one quickens pace – and fond of nestling up into any hollow of arms or legs, and nibbling one's trousers.'[39] William always loved wombats and when he visited Australia in 1897 he had to be dissuaded from bringing one home.

69. William Michael Rossetti, *Wombat*, undated. Pen, ink and pencil, 41 × 55 mm. Private collection.

William's animal drawings are evidence of his connoisseurship of the natural as well as the artistic world. He and Christina regularly visited the Zoological Gardens in Regent's Park and William habitually sought out zoos when travelling abroad. He was interested in every animal from beetles to elephants. At Marseilles he was, as ever, irresistibly drawn to the Jardin Zoologique where he had an adventure with 'a very grand elephant, who made an unprovoked assault upon me'. William tempted him with a lump of bread but stood too close to the bars of his enclosure. 'He thrust his trunk into my face; wound it round my neck, knocking my hat off; and I scarcely know why he didn't strangle me outright while he was about it' but noted without rancour that the beast 'afterwards accepted my bread without further demonstrations'. He handled a docile young hyena 'doux comme un chien' and discussed zoo policy with a female keeper who explained to his bemusement that London had a wider variety of animals on account of 'England's being so much nearer to Africa!'[40]

But William's delight in nature was not solely for the exotic. He always had an eye for the unassuming animal or mineral. His pen and ink study of a *Shell* (fig. 70), executed with aesthetic precision, is a characteristically Victorian exercise which Ruskin at the Working Men's College might have set him during one of the practical drawing classes William attended after office hours. The graceful curves and whorls on what is probably a giant tun shell, are intimately described, its hard, exterior carapace texturally contrasted with its dark, inner cavern. Ruskin was an inspiring teacher who published *The Elements of Drawing* in 1857, followed by *The Elements of Perspective* two years later. He taught the working men who were his students to look long and carefully at objects they were drawing, to notice things in depth rather than cast a cursory glance. William's mineral study *A Piece of Coal*, in pen and ink, dated April 1860 would have tested even the most inspired natural observer. A

70. William Michael Rossetti, *Shell*. Pen and ink on grey paper, 76 × 105 mm. Private collection.

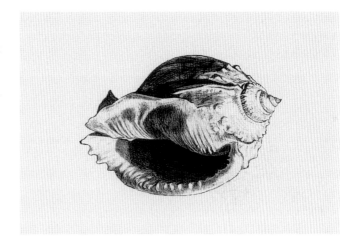

71. William Michael Rossetti, *The Young Mother*, c. 1857. Pen and ink, 178 × 133 mm, signed with initials WMR. Private collection.

piece of carbon, aeons old, an organic curiosity, it appealed to his taste for the unnoticed and disregarded.

Much more ambitious was his highly effective copy in pen and ink of Millais's etching *The Young Mother* published in 1857 (fig. 71).[41] This was one of only thirteen plates Millais etched in his career, in spite of being one of the most sought-after and productive of all the illustrators of the 1860s, creating designs for over 270 illustrations between 1854 and 1869.

William's copy is extremely faithful to Millais's model.[42] It shows a contemporary mother and child, probably in a Scottish Highland setting. The monumental figure of a young mother with her braided head curves around the child whose hand she is kissing. The curve is repeated in the baby's head and arm. The central image of immovable maternity set in an elemental land/sea-scape succeeds both emotionally and technically. Behind mother and child, a vast space is sporadically filled with hills, coast, boats and children playing. Although the original conception was of course Millais's, it is interesting that William chose this subject to copy, many years before experiencing parenthood himself.

Two more seascapes or landscapes by William, like *The Young Mother*, may be exercises or copies from another artist, both drawn with significant technical accomplishment. *On Yarmouth Beach, Norfolk* (fig. 72), in charcoal and chalk on sepia paper, shows a bare, empty stretch of coast dominated by a clutch of lobster pots, intricate cages that mean death for some creatures but a living for others.

72. William
Michael Rossetti,
*On Yarmouth
Beach, Norfolk,*
undated. Charcoal
and chalk on buff
paper, 255 × 353
mm. Private
collection.

Highly textured and complex, every individual strand of each lobster pot is intimately described and contrasted with the central, tactile wooden plank that diagonally bisects the whole *nature morte.* Sand and rope, water and sky, light and shadow, even unregarded small pebbles are given solidity in space and time. The unassumingness of the subject matter makes an observer look afresh at seashore objects that denote not just a livelihood but also a way of life.

In the same medium is bleak *Colnbrook Dale* (fig. 73). Another huge diagonal cuts across this picture. A collection of driftwood signifies that human activity once took place here. Grandeur and decay lie displayed across the blank sand dunes. The only life is in the contrasting, diagonal line of birds, wheeling on the wind, a metaphor for human existence, like *Ozymandias* by William's favourite poet, Shelley.

73. William
Michael Rossetti,
Colnbrook Dale,
undated. Charcoal
and chalk on buff
paper. Private
collection.

Both these elemental landscapes are titled and signed in red crayon, 'Rossetti W' or 'W Rossetti'. Neither of these is William's hand, but instead in the characteristic style of his sister Christina. It was natural for brother and sister to authenticate and label each other's work from time to time and Christina here confirms and records that the two landscapes are indeed William's work. It has been suggested that the drawings are 'too good' to be by William, that they may be by John Sell Cotman (a member of the Norwich School of Painting) who had been William's drawing master at King's College School, or that they are, at least, 'Cotmanesque'. An interesting connection with the Norfolk landscape was the tall figure of a young widower, Joseph Crome whom William met in his early days at the Excise Office. Joseph was the son of 'Old Crome', a well-known painter of the Norfolk coastline whose work can be seen at Norwich Castle Museum.[43] William may have been influenced by atmospheric paintings of East Anglia by Joseph's father when he visited the area with his office colleague and drew his own pictures.

William's drawings are far more numerous and more varied than Pre-Raphaelite commentators have cared to discover or admit. They are significant because they show that the connoisseur reviewer was, in his early days at least, also a practising artist. By undertaking a range of drawings that gave him insight into the technical and emotional challenges of creative art, as well as developing his expertise as a connoisseur, William intuitively fulfilled the qualifications Hogarth thought essential for successful art criticism. Moreover, all his artworks showed his devotion to the fundamental creed of Pre-Raphaelitism – to confront the natural world 'with earnest scrutiny of visible facts, and an earnest endeavour to present them veraciously and exactly'.[44] Artistic practice as well as his crucial position within the Pre-Raphaelite Brotherhood made William a critic with a difference and not merely a pontificating theorist, throughout his career as a commentator on modern art.

Art Critic

Extracts from a two-page document in William's hand reveal his most dearly held views on the function of an art critic.

> The moment I see a picture I receive a first impression from it, wh. is very generally the abiding impression: I know in an instant whether it is to my judgment good, bad, or indifferent – &, if good, whether it is good in a great way or in a small one.
>
> Lay great stress upon your first impressions, & don't readily fritter them away.
>
> Form a sincere opinion whether you like a picture or not…in total disregard of the question whether other people share it or the contrary.

> Be prepared to admit the merit of any & every sort of painting, provided only it is a good thing *from its own point of view.* The severity of David or Ingres, & the latest experiment in Impressionism, can equally meet this condition.[45]

The advice is undated (except for its reference to Impressionism, the word to denote the French art movement first used in English in 1881)[46] and it reads as if offered to a younger critic just starting a career in art journalism. William's instructions are practical, fearless and entirely free from jargon or theory. This is how I do it, he says. First impressions are often best impressions, but you must support these with first-hand technical observations about colour, tone, texture, drawing and composition. Beyond the purely technical, dare to voice an opinion about qualities such as invention, intellect, beauty and expression in a picture. Have the courage to express your own individual opinion without bowing to fad or trend. Above all, acknowledge the achievements of past masters and be open to the shock of the new. This is no starchy scholar speaking. This is the authentic, autobiographical voice of William Rossetti, liberal pragmatist, autodidact, professional reviewer, critic, connoisseur, man of letters, popularizer, interpreter and demystifier of contemporary art to an avid audience of Victorian gallery-goers.

It was the *Germ* that launched his career as a critic. Through Major Calder Campbell who had written a sonnet for the *Germ*, William met the barrister, later judge, and newspaper editor, Edward William Cox. Cox had enjoyed the *Germ* and said so, twice, in a weekly he edited called the *Critic*. He entertained William and offered him the unpaid job of reviewing exhibitions for his paper. As William had haunted art galleries throughout his adolescence, this was an exciting offer, especially as Cox allowed him total freedom to express his views on art and develop his own individual voice. Even though he only wrote for the *Critic* from February to November 1850, it was a launch that led directly to more art reviewing in the periodical press, at a more visible level, for the influential *Spectator*.

In October 1850, Smith & Elder's publisher's reader, William Smith Williams – most famous for discovering *Jane Eyre* – was on the point of resigning as the *Spectator*'s art-critic because of a libel case pending against the journal. With his usual generosity in forwarding young people's careers, Ford Madox Brown proposed Rossetti as Smith Williams's successor. William wrote a sample piece for R.S. Rintoul, founder-editor of the *Spectator*, about the choice of Sir Charles Eastlake as incoming president of the Royal Academy. Rintoul was impressed and appointed William the next art critic of the *Spectator*. The salary was substantial, £50[47] per year, almost half William's annual salary at the Inland Revenue, approximately £110 in 1850. It wasn't just about money, although it made William 'almost…a capitalist' among the rest of his Pre-Raphaelite Brothers. Only Millais made more than £160 per year and 'most of the others, much less or hardly anything'.[48] At just twenty-one, William was not only a promising young clerk at the Inland Revenue but, with an energy and versatility reminiscent of the double life of Anthony Trollope, was also establishing a second career as a critic.

In the press William promoted the work and ideas of the radical young Pre-Raphaelite artists, mainly William Holman Hunt, John Everett Millais and Dante Gabriel Rossetti. In addition, he wrote discerningly about the movement's less mainstream associates, such as Arthur Hughes and John Brett.

For more than a quarter of a century, from his appointment to the *Spectator* in 1850 until 1878, he produced nearly 400 art 'critiques' for English and American periodicals.[49] From his earliest beginnings he was a thoughtful and honest reviewer, studying works of art and poetry long and intently, always making notes as he read or on gallery visits. William's rapt attention to detail was paralleled by the way Pre-Raphaelite artists looked at the natural world 'stamen by stamen'.[50] This approach, based on close observation of pictures and first-hand examination of texts, gave him confidence in his own taste and opinions even as a very young man. He won and deserved the admiration of contemporaries such as Thomas Woolner, George du Maurier, John Ruskin and John Brett. One of his Pre-Raphaelite 'Brothers' Thomas Woolner praised his unpretentious tone when he commented shrewdly to poet William Allingham on 8 November 1850: 'I am glad to hear from W. Rossetti that you liked his review on your poems; he bids fair to be one of our best in the review line – he takes more pains to discover the author's intention and less to display his own learning than most journalists'.[51]

William's critical impersonality was not, however, bland. He wrote with attitude, but not with cruel destructiveness. All reviewers bring personal history, if not prejudice, to their targets and although William consistently aimed at 'unbiassed opinion',[52] he confessed to some only human 'smoothing down of edges' when evaluating works by friends and 'a little tartness' when reviewing those outside his charmed circle.[53] George du Maurier warmly commended Rossetti's successful impartiality as well as his insight as a critic: 'You mention William Rossetti's critique in *Fraser* of this month. Have you read it? I think he's the *only* critic who's not a hack and whose opinion[s] are genuine & felt – and strange to say he appears to me to have wonderfully little party feeling considering his bringing up & associations. His article on Millais' Moonlight is enough to stamp him as a genuine critic to my mind.'[54]

As an old man, Rossetti felt he should apologize, and did, for any unwitting partisanship he might have shown in his youth. He maintained that although inevitably filtered through personal perception, his appreciations of works of art and literature had always aimed at the 'strict truth. If all my old critiques were to be reprinted…I do not believe that I should in a single instance be compelled to confess to myself, "There I said what I knew to be neither true nor fair; a bad personal motive was at the bottom of it."[55]

As a critic he was full of opinion but never arrogant. He believed the critic fulfilled an honourable but humble function which could never displace the artist or author. The critic was not God, nor should he pretend to be. When John Ruskin recommended him to American William Stillman, he said that Rossetti possessed a 'peculiar power of arriving at *just* critical opinions; and I hardly know anyone else who I could – in his default – recommend to you…I do not say this lightly for I see that the spirit in which you conduct your journal is indeed very different from that with which such periodicals are usually managed – and I look for very great good from your influence over your countrymen'.[56]

Practising artists trusted Rossetti's critical acumen. John Brett wrote to his sister Rosa about the reception of his picture *The Hedger*, that 'W. Rossetti thinks satisfactorily of it and he is the best judge I know after JR [John Ruskin]'.[57] At its height, his career in criticism was ratified when, after the success of his pamphlet *A Criticism* in 1866, in defence of Swinburne's *Poems and Ballads*, Macmillan approached him for a collected edition of his best reviews. Although Macmillan had wholly disagreed with William's attack on the prudish mid-Victorian press, which had crucified Swinburne, the publisher was quick to sense commercial opportunity in the stir it had caused. 'Macmillan wants my Selections to form a volume only about as big as Arnold's Essays in Criticism.'[58] Bound to Arnold's model, William had to make a succinct selection confining himself to his essays on art, which appeared as *Fine Art, Chiefly Contemporary* in 1867.

> *One must embrace art, indeed, as a beautiful body; but a body actuated by a soul*
> WMR, *Fine Art, Chiefly Contemporary*, x, 1867

The collection put together by William encapsulates his best, most characteristic, topical art journalism between 1850 and 1866, ranging from Ancient Egyptian art with its 'changeless mystery of calm'[59] to the cutting edge pictures of Whistler. The two epigraphs he chose were signposts to critical principles upheld throughout his career. He explained, quoting Petrarch,[60] that he was offering his own individual artistic judgement, not a view on art that other people must follow slavishly. Or as Blake put it, in William's second epigraph, 'Always be ready to speak your mind, and a base man will avoid you'.

William chose articles that had all appeared previously in journals, weeklies and magazines such as the *Spectator, Fraser's Magazine, Edinburgh Weekly Review, Saturday Review, London Review, Pall Mall Gazette, Reader, Weldon's Register, Liverpool Post* or in specialist art publications like the *Fine Arts Quarterly Review*. In these reviews he responded to key exhibitions of the day: the Royal

Academy exhibitions that marked each London summer season; Crystal Palace displays; international exhibitions in Paris and London in 1855 and 1862; exhibitions by individual artists and illustrators, including Ford Madox Brown, George Cruikshank and John Leech. He reviewed a book on Turner and another art criticism collection, by Francis Turner Palgrave, parallel to his own. He also reprinted his seminal article *Præraphaelitism*, which had first appeared in the *Spectator* in 1851, and included radical discussions of unfashionable 'British Sculpture, its Condition and Prospects' (1861) and esoteric 'Japanese Woodcuts' (1863).

William declared his manifesto as an art critic in a frank and personal preface. He freely admitted that his opinions on art had developed and changed over the sixteen years he had been in the field. He intended that *Fine Art, Chiefly Contemporary* should show his thoughts on art developing and changing over the years. To stand still would have meant stagnation, and he explained how his priorities in looking at a picture had shifted from subject matter to style. His taste for 'directly decorative art' had grown with maturity as he developed an eye for the innovatory aesthetics of Whistlerian art that was to lead to the new *cri de coeur*, 'art for art's sake',[61] among artists and *cognoscenti*.

Absolute fairness in criticism was his ideal, so while he included copious notices of works by Madox Brown, Millais, Holman Hunt, Leighton, Frith and Whistler, he specifically excluded discussion of his brother's pictures, partly because they were not seen in public exhibitions, although he maintained that Gabriel had been the 'brains' behind the Pre-Raphaelite movement, 'its intellectual impulse and originating *vis*'.[62]

One logical outcome of William's ideal of honest impartiality in criticism was his open dislike of the Victorian convention of unsigned, or anonymous reviews. His opinion won praise from Henry James who described William in 1868, jointly with F.T. Palgrave and P.G. Hamerton, as one of 'the three principal art-critics now writing in England – the only three, we believe, who from time to time lay aside the anonymous, and republish their contributions to the newspapers'.[63] Critics should have '*le courage de leurs opinions*', William believed, and the reading public had a right to know where those opinions came from. 'When one is vaccinated, one likes to have a reasonable assurance that the virus came out of a cow, not possibly out of a dog in a mangy or hydrophobic condition', William concluded in a bizarre image.

So personal was William's art-critical credo that he noticeably used the first person singular throughout his preface, whereas in the collected articles that form the body of the book he retained the conventional authority (or timidity) of the royal 'we'. His tone similarly hovered between the forthright and the diffident, clearly apparent in the contrasting words he attached to himself. On the one hand, his role and his voice were 'subordinate', 'non-artistic', 'weak', 'tentative' and 'humblest'. But on the other side of the scale, his opinions marked by 'genuineness', 'exactness' and 'authority', were 'sensible' and 'entirely my own'. In a characteristic negative circumlocution, fusing modesty with self-belief, he claimed his articles were 'not quite unworthy of being rescued from oblivion'.[64]

Reissuing his reviews of Royal Academy summer shows of 1861–4 allowed William scope to expound his views on contemporary art – always his area of special interest and, therefore, one half of his title. Using the Royal Academy shows as a springboard, he produced essays on the current state of British art and how it should develop. William's aesthetic position by the late 1860s prioritized style above subject matter, particularly in the field of visual art, although style was not his chief criterion in assessing literature. He attributed advances in style by modern British artists to 'the stern and true discipline of Præraphaelitism', believing that 'if you have good style, you have simply and entirely good art'. A picture's content was secondary to its 'style' because 'good style will make a good picture out of the most ignoble subject'.[65] However, he advocated that modern artists should choose modern subjects, either drawn from life as they saw it, or from history as they interpreted it, because 'life still is life all the world over, and all the centuries through'.[66] The artist's range of possible subject is 'as endless as the range of life and of society' and the artist's job was to give his subjects 'real palpitating life', not historic pomposity or laboured didacticism.

As usual, William stressed the importance of trusting first impressions when looking at any work of art, allowing the critic or spectator to see at first glance, 'by a sort of instinct', based on sympathy and experience whether the work is 'on the whole A SUCCESS' or merely 'an affair of shreds and patches'. However, any general opinion should be supported by remarks on imagination, conception, style, expression, beauty, composition, design, draughtsmanship, chiaroscuro, texture, colour and execution.[67]

William always makes valuable and illuminating generalizations but is often most perceptive and idiosyncratic when he discusses individual works of art. As he said of Ford Madox Brown, 'strong men have strong idiosyncrasies.'[68] His strengths lay in his visual memory, the result of looking long and deep at pictures, such as Millais's *The Woodman's Daughter* (1851), set 'deep in summer' when 'the air throbs with penetrative light and warmth'.[69] The best pictures inspired him to empathetic interpretation. He sighed with *Mariana in the Moated Grange* (Millais, 1851) where 'throughout the long day's watching, the moist leaves have drifted in, and lie unheeded on her table; a mouse, fearless of disturbance, has come out from "behind the mouldering wainscot"; and sunset lights up in the casement the emblem of the broken lily'. Mariana's bed 'waits to receive her but not to comfort her, after one more day gone in the heartsick vain longing'.[70]

William compared his two Pre-Raphaelite 'Brothers', Hunt and Millais, acutely tracing Hunt's reflective art to its origins in thought and intellectual effort, while the more naturally creative Millais worked out of flair and intuition. When Millais moved away from pictures that 'told a story', towards suggestive, mood subjects such as *Autumn Leaves* (1856), William immediately hailed his innovatory achievement. He continually praised Millais 'the unapproachable' for 'power, brilliancy, suavity, ease and "go"' but was not afraid to take him to task for increasing carelessness that came with success, 'look at the mere smear of formless umber which stands for the boy's hand' in *A Dream of the Past, Sir Isumbras at the Ford* (1857). As the years went on, William lamented that Millais produced too many glib commercial canvases, 'knocking off picture after picture of little girls and boys'.[71]

In Holman Hunt's more literal art, William noticed, with a corresponding literality of his own, the odd jarring detail. Appreciating Hunt's *Claudio and Isabella* (1853), William observed with bathos that in spite of its subtlety of thought and expression, its moral dignity and complexity, Claudio's hair looked like a wig. Totally unattuned to Hunt's religious fervour and generally opposed to overt symbolism, he nevertheless loved the exactitude of Hunt's rendering of the details that composed the English countryside in *The Hireling Shepherd* (1852), 'from the marsh-mallows, elecampane-plant, and thickly-tangled grass of the foreground, to the August corn-field and pollard-willows, and above all the elms and bean-stacks of the distance'.[72] When *Our English Coasts* by Hunt was shown in 1853, William hailed it not only as 'the most triumphant vindication yet seen of the Præraphaelite principle' but as 'a new experience in art'. The small sheep-picture 'barren of a single human figure, and confining itself to strictly ovine expression, contains as deep a human interest as any in the gallery' and was distinguished in William's opinion by its 'absolute truth, and beauty'.[73]

Turning from perfection on a small scale to overweening ambition on the grand scale, William always had misgivings about the sleek artificiality of Frederic Leighton. His *Cimabue's Madonna carried through Florence* (1855), certainly had 'largeness, but not greatness; style, but not intensity; design rather than thought', quiet put-downs expressed in deadly antitheses.[74] William would never concede that Frith's immensely popular crowd scenes such as *Ramsgate Sands* (1854), *Derby Day* (1858), or *The Railway Station* (1862), were more than 'sparkling, airy, well put together…full of spirit, facility, ingenuity, and lifelikeness'. He felt that nothing in these broad canvases of Victorian social life went 'deeper than the surface' although they had value, he felt, as time capsules, snapshots of actual life in the 1850s.[75]

When it came to the more challenging, genuinely new art of Whistler, William had no hesitation in acclaiming his 'pictorial genius'. Describing the river scenes with their 'fogs, beauties, and oddities' that were the American's specialities, he painted his own word-picture of the river shown in Whistler's *Etchings* (1863), the Thames that he saw daily from his vantage point at the office at Somerset House. 'Broad sheen of full-tided river-surface; ridged tide-marks creeping up the beach; ripples gleaming and dancing to the eye near at hand, or lending an ambiguous comminution to the more distant space of water; clouds blowing over an uncertain sky, or dispersed by gleams of sunshine'. The familiar scene shown in *Wapping* with 'the whitish Thames flecked with barge, boat, and steamer, under a sky of indistinct blue' had never before been 'so triumphantly well painted. Everything is literal, matter-of-fact – crowded, dispersed, casual.'[76]

True as ever to his Pre-Raphaelite aesthetic, William's terms of praise derive from realism. William's choice of vocabulary in *Fine Art, Chiefly Contemporary* is simultaneously direct and quirky, sometimes concrete and expressive, at others more ungainly and coagulated. He can be plain-spoken and call a picture 'its author's masterpiece'[77] or 'frankly a blunder, and there an end'.[78] Or he can be circuitous, over-dependent on 'perhaps', 'seems' and 'maybe', calling Millais's *Ferdinand Lured by Ariel* (1850), 'a work which *might* be said to *hint* of new opportunities to art' [my italics].[79] He never made any claims as a prose stylist but his endeavour to do the impossible, to capture art in words, is always genuinely communicative.

Criticism could be compared with the emerging new art of photography, William thought – but not only because of photography's capacity for realism. Instead, both were interpretative arts which, at their best, could 'well-nigh re-create a subject; place it in novel, unanticipable lights; aggrandize the fine, suppress or ignore the petty; and transfigure both the subject-matter, and the reproducing process itself, into something almost higher than we knew them to be.'[80] This is the aim and function of both photography and criticism. (Perhaps this is why William allowed himself to be photographed by the grandiose and stagey photographer, Julia Margaret Cameron, see fig. 14) 'The golden age', William conjectured mischievously, 'might include the silence of critics; but that is the golden age, and this is the iron one'.[81] By selecting from his hundreds of disparate art reviews in the periodical press to produce a single representative volume, William ensured that readers would hear his critical voice, which, if neither golden nor iron, was unmistakably authentic.

Fine Art, Chiefly Contemporary was hailed in the press. 'Mr Rossetti is a real representative of modern criticism', possessing an 'extraordinary delicacy of discrimination, and an equal facility of summing up his judgment in a word that speaks entire paragraphs. We know of no other critic with his power of artistic definition.'[82]

In spring 1868 the publisher John Camden Hotten, encouraged by the initial press reception of selected *Poems by Walt Whitman* (1868), invited William, the volume's editor, now thirty-eight, together with Swinburne, seven years junior, to produce jointly some *Notes* to accompany the forthcoming Royal Academy exhibition. 'I should like to issue such a critical pamphlet each year – after the manner of Mr Ruskin in time gone by', Hotten wrote flatteringly to William.[83] The co-authors conferred over the next few days and agreed William should cover the whole exhibition while Swinburne would append a free-ranging essay of his own choice – rather 'a dislocated scheme' in William's view. It became even more haphazard when Swinburne had a dramatic accident on the night of 28 April. Carrying an unlit lamp, he crashed into a mirror in the dark, fell over, shattered the lamp and cut open his head, right knee and left foot, losing a great deal of blood and unable to mobilize help until morning. 'I do hope it won't cut me off from my chance of being your coadjutor', he moaned, lame in both legs, but making the most of the story. His bloodstained room, he regaled William, 'looked as if M. de Sade had had a few friends to a small and select supper party'.[84]

In the event, it was far more constructive for the public to take William's *Notes* with them as they toured the exhibition rather than Swinburne's more hectic literary companionship and distinctly more purple prose. William wrote the longer first half of the pamphlet (which sold at one shilling) and Swinburne the shorter second half in which he focused mainly on the great artists, such as Whistler and Dante Gabriel Rossetti, conspicuous by their absence from the Royal Academy exhibition, and indulged in grand generalities about art, beauty, pain, pleasure and horror.

With his characteristic 'liberty of selection and candour of statement', William's vade-mecum put an arm round the shoulder of the ordinary visitor, imparting practical advice and confidence about looking at pictures.[85] These really were 'notes', sometimes not even complete sentences, giving the reader an authentic sense of strolling round the gallery. William recorded his detailed reactions to seventy-seven works of art on show, mostly paintings, but also highlighting drawings and sculpture. In addition, he named eighty-six more creditable works that he didn't have scope to discuss within a short pamphlet.

William pronounced 'no little dissatisfaction' with the 'rather cheap outcome' of the 100th Royal Academy exhibition in 1868 and complained about the 'ever-recurrent hanging controversy'.[86] Sometimes he damned individual works with the deadliest of faint praise, as here, politely concluding his remarks about a picture based on *Othello, The Life's Story*, which 'cannot, I think, be counted among Mr Cope's successes'.[87] Mr Ward's 'overblown style', which had 'about as much retirement and repose as a peony the hour before it falls to pieces', roused him to a poetic image that momentarily masked rebuke.[88] He cheekily sighed: if only Mr O'Neil could 'get somebody else's colour to exude through his brush, with texture and surface to correspond!' in *Before Waterloo*.[89] Maclise's *The Sleep of Duncan* conveyed an 'impression of unreality huddled and oppressed with decorative exuberances'[90] and he was even more disappointed by that artist's *Madeline after Prayer*, which simply lacked the poetry of Keats's original conception. There was no 'real luminosity in the moonlight which Keats has made so resplendent' and even the needlepoint Maclise put in Madeline's embroidery frame was tasteless and of 'horrible pattern'.[91]

Although he called himself 'a non-practical critic',[92] William repeatedly made practical suggestions about how pictures might be improved. He was particularly observant about telling details in a picture, such as Houghton's *H. Bassett, Esq., in his Laboratory* with its 'scientific plethora' and vivid sense of a room shut away from the world. A pipe-smoker himself, William noticed the scientist was smoking a pipe 'to indicate some enforced pause in his work while an experiment is maturing'.[93]

Whenever he could praise artists, he did so, both his friends and those unknown to him, great contemporary names like Watts, Landseer and Leighton, as well as striving amateurs. He declared Millais to be 'in pure, unforced, untrammelled possession of his mastery' in the portrait of his three daughters, *Sisters*.[94] Arthur Hughes's *Sigh no more, Ladies, Sigh no more* as always was 'full of refined sentiment' with a 'genuine but real poetry' that was quite different from most of the other offerings on show.[95] William could throw off graceful remarks – looking at the face of G. Richmond's *Mrs Brereton* was 'like making Mrs Brereton's acquaintance – or like wishing to make it.'[96] He could combine grace with perception as when discussing the portrait bust of Carlyle's magnificent head by Woolner, 'who searches under the surface of his sitter's face, and records on its surface what he has found beneath'.[97] He could enthuse when he saw pictures such as Albert Moore's *Azaleas*, 'for a sense of beauty in disposition of form, and double-distilled refinement in colour, this work may allow a wide margin to any competitors in the gallery, and still be the winner.' It was an innovative decorative picture that also provoked intellectual debate about 'the innermost artistic problem of how to reconcile realization with abstraction'.[98]

William was prepared to challenge major reputations and to tussle with himself to describe exactly what made him uneasy about too facile an acceptance of smooth professionalism like Leighton's. While acknowledging that *Ariadne Abandoned by Theseus* was the 'loftiest work' Leighton had produced, William sensitively identified 'a certain hiatus between his perception of the poetic in art, and his power of expressing it' which led to a strained artificiality in the picture that was 'glaringly and even irksomely apparent'. Yet he commended the mood of yearning calm Leighton had created, 'profound as the blue sea violet-tinted in its distant intensity' which inspired treatment at length, culminating in a moody quotation from William's favourite poet, Shelley's *Stanzas Written in Dejection, near Naples*.[99]

William's *Notes on the Royal Academy Exhibition 1868* are forthright and opinionated, always honest, rarely unkind and often vivid and thought provoking. Walking round the show with him is an enlivening and immediate experience and gallery-goers of the day agreed. Meeting his author in the street at the end of July, Hotten told him he was pleased the pamphlet had sold about 1,500 copies, although William recorded his private disappointment in his diary that night.[100]

IMPRESARIO

Moving in an international arena as commentator and analyst of contemporary art gave William a sense of personal status. It added another dimension to his working life, taking him far beyond the confines of his office in the Inland Revenue at Somerset House. His annual foreign holidays always had an underlying purpose, to build up his knowledge of European art and to widen the scope of his artistic sympathies. His openness to developments in international art helped him to feel active and purposeful in his own sphere, rather than overpowered by the contiguous dynamic talents both within the Rossetti family and in his wider circle of Pre-Raphaelite friends.

As art critic and connoisseur, William Rossetti's part in the construction of popular aesthetic taste was a direct outcome of his cosmopolitanism. His place in the contemporary British art world was pivotal, as an original Pre-Raphaelite 'Brother' and keeper of the *P.R.B. Journal*. A prolific journalist, he acted as a cultural conduit, interpreting British art to a global audience and bringing foreign art, especially Oriental and French, to the attention of art lovers at home, aiming always to democratize and demystify the discussion of art. William contributed to trans-Atlantic dialogue, writing 'Art News from London' for Stillman's New York *Crayon*, 1855–6, beginning a lifelong relationship with America which occupied a symbolic, emotional locus in William's socio-political landscape.

On significant occasions throughout his life, William took practical action within the art world, demonstrating that the function of the critic was neither passive nor parasitic. A connoisseur with a cosmopolitan perspective, he was easily persuaded to turn entrepreneur to promote an exhibition of modern British art across the Atlantic and to act as its secretary. In 1856 Captain Augustus Ruxton, an ex-army officer, proposed the idea to William who was ideally placed to negotiate both with British artists and with receptive Americans. William knew all the in-crowd among young British artists. Coincidentally, Ernest Gambart the leading London picture dealer was considering a similar exhibition and, following uneasy negotiations, the two forces combined, Gambart supplying most of the watercolours and Rossetti procuring the oil paintings. 'The American Exhibition of British Art, which opened in the autumn of 1857, proved by no means a success', William later admitted:

> except indeed that the artists in New York, and in their degree the art-lovers and public there as well, showed a great amount of goodwill, and

made a reasonably fair show of paying visitors. The like was the case at Philadelphia, Boston, and Washington, to which cities the Ruxton section of the works travelled afterwards. Several sales were effected, including Leighton's *Romeo and Juliet* (the scene where Juliet is supposed to be dead) and a smaller duplicate of Holman Hunt's *Light of the World*; Longfellow purchased another painting. In other respects most things went wrong.[101]

It had been a thankless, and at times an acrimonious, task for William who felt Gambart, determined to compete instead of co-operating, had constantly undermined him. 'I am told on every side, you represent only a *very small body of men* & have no support of the academical body & the generality of artists', sneered Gambart in August 1857 just before the exhibition was due to open in New York.[102] Market forces as well as petty annoyances dogged the whole undertaking. As ill luck would have it, the paintings arrived in New York 'just in the thick of one of the most calamitous money-crashes' of the nineteenth century. Captain Ruxton and Gambart's agent constantly disagreed and the American public 'had very few dollars to spend, and not much heart for thronging to places of amusement'. At twenty-eight, William was amazed and amused by American prudery, which consigned a nude *Venus* by Leighton firmly to the back of a closet, 'huddled out of sight by request, lest the modesty of New Yorkers should be alarmed'.

Problems were compounded when

a sudden and violent storm of rain damaged several of the water-colours, including a work by Madox Brown. Besides, the British artists had not after all come forward with adequate zeal. It was the year of the great Art-treasures Exhibition in Manchester, and several men had really nothing to contribute; there was no important oil-picture by Turner, no Millais, no Dante Rossetti — and the American devotees of Ruskin, and sympathizers with Præraphaelitism, had been specially looking out for all these. Ruxton was a loser by his spirited speculation — Gambart, I dare say, not a gainer.[103]

But William's account was overly downbeat and pessimistic. The exhibition in America was a landmark — because of the Pre-Raphaelite pictures that he managed to assemble.

It was a moment of cross-cultural fertilization. It brought mid-century British art with its startling new focus and techniques, to American critics, artists and gallery-goers. More particularly, it put the tenets of Pre-Raphaelitism into the American public arena. And it was Pre-Raphaelitism itself which caused most heated debate in the American press. When the exhibition first opened at the National Academy of Design in New York on 20 October 1857, with a huge number of over 350 art works, the *New York Times* complained that 'the paintings are disposed after a strange, incoherent fashion, which dazzles the eyes as you enter and leaves the brain bewildered when you

go out....Pre-Raphaelite intensities killing "naturalistic" composure, and fla-
grant oils literally burning the life out of quiet aquarelles'.[104] W.J. Stillman
criticized William's principles of selection feeling that

> the Pre-Raphaelite pictures have saved the Exhibition so far as oil pictures
> are concerned, but even they should have been culled more carefully. You
> should have thought that the eccentricities of the school were new to us,
> and left out such things as Hughes's *Fair Rosamund* and *April Love*...with
> Miss Siddal's *Clerk Saunders*...all of which may have their value to the ini-
> tiated, but to us generally are childish and trifling. Then you have too much
> neglected landscape, which to us is far more interesting than your history
> painting.[105]

William's comments on some of the artists and their works exhibited in New
York survive as a holograph manuscript, divided into two parts for oil paintings and watercolours.[106] Although attributed to Dante Gabriel, the manuscript is undoubtedly in the handwriting and characteristic vocabulary of
William Michael. The notes show he admired a number of the British artists
shown in the American exhibition but others decidedly underwhelmed him,
implying that he was prepared for a mixed reception in America. He commented that Mrs Bodichon (Barbara Leigh Smith) 'well known as a woman
who writes and exerts herself for public objects in England – and I fancy,
known to many persons in America' was an amateur of great power. He had
already written in the *Crayon* that she was 'full of Pre-Raphaelitism, that is to
say full of character and naturalism in the detail, as well as the multiplicity of
it.'[107] He pointed out that Ruskin admired Miss Siddal's power 'greatly, thinking her (I believe) possessed of more natural genius for art than any other
woman'. On the other hand, he admitted that Cattermole's contribution to
the exhibition was 'rather a slight specimen', and although Corbould was an
'extremely popular painter: clever, dexterous', William judged him 'flashy' and
lacking in genuine emotion. Ford Madox Brown, Holman Hunt, William
Henry Hunt, Arthur Hughes, Frederic Leighton, John Ruskin, William Bell
Scott and William Lindsay Windus were some of the other significant
exhibitors whose work he admired.

The exhibition, now reduced to 232 items, moved to Philadelphia in the
New Year, and ran from 3 February to 20 March 1858. The Philadelphia press
entered the fray, some, like the *Pennsylvania Inquirer*, exclaiming about the 'surpassing excellence' of many of the canvases that 'excited surprise as well as
intense admiration'.[108] Other commentators blamed Ruskin for championing
the Pre-Raphaelites whom they found medieval, barbaric, and, moreover,
'Catholic'.[109] Nearly on the New York scale, with 321 items, the show moved
on to Boston from 5 April to 19 June 1858. Again, although Pre-Raphaelite
paintings were in the minority, they continued to excite the most contentious

comments. Some elements in the Boston press appeared to feel personally affronted by Pre-Raphaelite naturalism.

Curiously, the show's mildest or most incandescent artists aroused the most dissension. Tender works by Arthur Hughes were variously described as childish, fearsome, or an abortion. His *Ophelia* might have been 'a powerful representation of a maniac, but not of *our* Ophelia', but the same journal, the *Crayon*, in spite of editorial misgivings, eventually fell under the spell of his *April Love*, admitting 'the more we look upon it, the more we become absorbed in its simple embodiment of deep, pure intense feeling'.[110]

Pre-Raphaelite pictures spoke to ordinary people, as Ruxton told William after listening to his workmen hanging Hunt's *Light of the World*: 'Never mind the gas, the picture will light us up'. Ruxton was moved by his picture-hangers' immediate response, 'they look, and they look, and they look, and they say something that the author of the picture would be pleased to hear. *The Sailor Boy*, *Try and Remember*, *King Lear* – above all, *The Light of the World*, *Innocence*, *April Love*, are immensely popular among my hangers'.[111] Press response to *The Light of the World* diverged wildly. The *New York Times* admitted the painting's 'true power'[112] but the *Christian Register* shuddered at its 'strange, spiritless, galvanic life'.[113]

America longed for the apparent simplicities of landscape. When the British artists fulfilled this longing for a kind of innocence, they won lyrical approval from the *Atlantic Monthly* which described the Pre-Raphaelites' view of Nature 'as full of beautiful facts, and like children amid the flowers, they gather their hands full...crowd at their laps and bosoms, and even drop some already picked, to make room for others which beckon from their stems – insatiable with beauty'.[114] But other critics were irritated by the extremism of Pre-Raphaelite practice which they saw as a near-orgasmic concentration on details of 'all the weeds, dandelions, bits of straw, old glass, fence-rails, and pokers that can be found in Great Britain'.[115] Major Pre-Raphaelite landscape artists including Madox Brown, John W. Inchbold and John Brett were shown, as well as a single picture by Ruskin himself, *Study of a Block of Gneiss*, which excited particular mirth at the expense of the ladies who enthused about it. 'Oh! look what Ruskin has done!' they cried, to the ridicule of the *Philadelphia Sunday Dispatch*. 'We have seen gneiss, but never such a piece as this of Ruskin's; it looks like an unfortunate elephant's back that has been subject to the whip, full of niches elaborately worked out...It is really incorrigible - nay, contemptible'.[116]

In *Some Reminiscences* William remembered, perhaps incorrectly, that the exhibition also visited Washington. Washington had been included on the original schedule but no records survive confirming this venue.[117] But William did remember correctly that among the several sales made in spite of the American stock market crash, the first picture sold was *The Reeks*, showing Ireland's wildest mountainscape, the MacGillycuddy Reeks in Killarney, by Miss Fanny Steers. William's exhibition memorandum records that she was 'one of the very best, I think, of the water-colour landscapists. Always paints small & finished (sunsets particularly beautiful) and gets unfairly treated & overlooked. Thackeray bought one of her pictures last year or the year before.' It was characteristic of William to champion an artist or a cause he felt had been neglected or vilified. Fanny Steers' American buyer was another literary man, Henry Wadsworth Longfellow, who paid £20.

The American exhibition had brought British art in all its multifarious variety to the Americans. It had caused hilarity and admiration, praise and scorn almost equally. Above all, it had incited debate and given an international dimension to Pre-Raphaelitism which was pronounced by the *Atlantic Monthly* to have taken 'its position in the world as the beginning of a new Art – new in motive, new in methods, and new in the forms it puts on.'[118] Pre-Raphaelitism was on the global art map.

EXPERT WITNESS

William's second public intervention in the art world twenty years later was in court. He was called as the opening expert witness for the plaintiff, James McNeill Whistler in the notorious libel case he brought against the defendant, John Ruskin. But for William the keynote of the whole affair was embarrassment.

Since the early days of the Pre-Raphaelite Brotherhood when Ruskin had famously championed the iconoclastic new movement, William had revered the older man as a great critic. He was personally indebted to Ruskin for giving him a start in international art journalism. He and Ruskin had enjoyed an open, if not an intimate relationship. Since early Cheyne Walk days in 1862, both Rossetti brothers had enjoyed a quite different friendship, full of *joie de vivre*, with the boisterous and provocative young artist Whistler. He had a 'natural gift for epigram and repartee' all delivered with a 'spontaneous impromptu air'.[119] His art was a challenge to middlebrow gallery visitors who cheered great crammed pictures like Frith's *Derby Day* or *The Railway Station* that reflected society's own face. Whistler challenged spectators to look in a totally new way at colour compositions which could not be read as pictorial versions of narratives, or illustrations of morality, but were most expressively paralleled in suggestive, musical titles he chose, such as *nocturnes, harmonies* or *arrangements*.

As a commentator on modern art, William was instantly sympathetic to Whistler's intentions. Indeed one of his practical policies in criticizing art was to judge a work by how far it fulfilled its artist's intentions, rather than by evaluating a picture or a sculpture against either its contemporaries, or the conventions and masterpieces of the past. Other critics condemned Whistler for being 'loose and sketchy' but in William's view the artist's 'rapid style' with 'its perfect understanding and keeping according to its own standard', achieved incomparably 'more than minor men could do with tenfold effort'.[120] This aesthetic principle of judging a picture by the artist's intentions, or 'own standard', gave William the freedom to recognize new genius when it appeared, so he was quick to salute Whistler's avant-garde art, warmly reviewing his pictures almost annually from 1862 to 1878. The 'shore-life, river-life, boat-life, barge-life' with their 'old wharves, jetties, piers, rigging, bow-windows' and 'hard-fisted, square-shouldered, solid and stolid-faced men' reeking of tar and tobacco, so evocatively captured in Whistler's *Etchings* (1863), had not been bettered since Rembrandt, thought William, and he said so.[121]

Superlative comparisons like these made William an obvious choice for Whistler's solicitor, James Anderson Rose, to choose to testify on the artist's behalf in November 1878. Whistler had always been hot-headed and contentious. In 1867 the Burlington Fine Arts Club had expelled him by 19 votes to 8 for throwing his fellow club member and brother-in-law, Seymour Haden, through a window in Paris. William had instantly resigned from the club in protest, followed a few days later by his brother Gabriel. Whistler was certainly not innocent in the matter but the club, said William, 'had no claim to interfere in an affair wh[ich] had not occurred in the Club premises, nor even in the United Kingdom'.[122]

So when Ruskin launched his swingeing attack on *Nocturne in Black and Gold: The Falling Rocket*, after seeing it at the Grosvenor Gallery in 1877, Whistler predictably became litigious. 'I have seen, and heard, much of Cockney impudence before now, but never expected to hear a coxcomb ask two hundred guineas[123] for flinging a pot of paint in the public's face', Ruskin wrote in *Fors Clavigera* in July 1877.[124] Whistler responded by suing Ruskin for libel, claiming huge damages of £1,000 plus his costs for bringing the case.

In early March 1878 William noted in his diary, to his 'great regret' that Ruskin was dangerously ill, 'I fear he is dying'. He had not talked to Ruskin at any length since dining at his house in 1866.[125] By the end of the month he heard that Ruskin's disease was 'softening of the brain' and recovery seemed hopeless.[126] In April the seriousness of the diagnosis was mitigated to 'brain-fever' but although Ruskin gradually rallied, he was not well enough to appear in person at the November trial. When William was finally subpoenaed to appear on Monday, 25 November 1878 at the London law courts, Queen's Bench Division, then in a building beside Westminster Hall, he confided his 'vexed' and divided loyalties to his diary. He had begged Anderson Rose 'to let me off if he can, but don't at all suppose this can be managed'. Long before Ruskin's condemnation of Whistler, William had published 'a high estimate' of one of the pictures Ruskin attacked. But he would feel deeply awkward to aid 'personally in bringing Ruskin in for damages'.[127] The weekend following the trial he wrote regretfully to Ruskin, explaining he had testified against him only under compulsion.[128]

The frequently monosyllabic and guarded evidence William gave to the court is a snapshot of his discomfiture. Under barbed cross-examination from Ruskin's counsel, Sir John Holker, the Attorney-General, William's unease and desire to say as little as possible is transparent:

> HOLKER: What is the peculiar beauty of the *Nocturne in Black and Gold*, the representation of the fireworks at Cremorne? It seems very dark. Is it a gem? (*Laughter*)
> ROSSETTI: No, I would not call the painting a gem.
> HOLKER: Is it an exquisite painting?
> ROSSETTI: No.
> HOLKER: Is it very beautiful?
> ROSSETTI: No.
> HOLKER: Is it eccentric?
> ROSSETTI: It is unlike the work of most other painters.
> HOLKER: Is it a work of art?
> ROSSETTI: Yes, in my opinion it is.

William was careful to avoid repeating Holker's word 'eccentric' which had louche, pejorative implications. He preferred to explain an avant-garde picture by its 'peculiarity', focusing on its individuality, its right to be judged according to its own, new criteria. Sir John Holker continued:

> HOLKER: Why is the *Nocturne in Black and Gold* a work of art?
> ROSSETTI: Because it represents what was intended. It is a picture painted with a considerable sense of the general effect of such a scene and finished with considerable artistic skill.
> HOLKER: Has there been much labor bestowed upon the painting?
> ROSSETTI: No, but I don't think it is at all necessary for a painting to show labor and finish….I could not form an opinion with the light and short-sightedness.

Holker tried to persuade William to assess the picture's commercial value. William squirmed. Critics did not price works of art, he demurred. He was pressed. He appealed to the judge, Sir John Huddleston, who supported the defendant's counsel. Holker pursued his advantage:

> HOLKER: Is two hundred guineas a stiffish price for a picture like this?
> ROSSETTI: I would rather not express an opinion as to the value of the picture, but if I am pressed I should say two hundred guineas is the full value of it − (*Laughter*) − not a 'stiffish price.'
> HOLKER: Do you think it is worth that money?
> ROSSETTI: Yes.

HOLKER: And would you give that for it?

ROSSETTI: I am too poor a man to give two hundred guineas for any picture.[129]

The outcome of the case was stalemate. Whistler carried the day but the court awarded derisory damages of one farthing.[130] Whistler's solicitor was delighted that William had remained authoritative as well as wary under cross-examination. But in his desire to be absolutely even-handed to both Whistler and Ruskin, William's evidence sounded cagily dry. However, as there was just cause on each side, he struggled to betray neither. Ruskin as a critic had a right to say what he believed about pictures and indeed William had relished his 'audacity of phrase' when the attack was launched.[131] Whistler as a practitioner could explore suggestive techniques and new realms in his art. He might benefit as well as suffer commercially from the comments of critics. Although William had consistently praised Whistler for his remarkable gifts, he had more recently sounded a warning note, 'a little less of personal whim, and more willingness to take the world on the same terms on which other people take it, would by this time be of advantage to him as to most of us'.[132]

By the time William wrote this in the *Academy*, his nearly decade-long association with the intellectual journal (1869–78) as its chief art critic was almost over. To William's displeasure, the editor Charles Appleton determined to replace him with the younger critic J. W. Comyns Carr. Apart from the personal humiliation, being bundled out 'neck and crop' as he confided in his diary,[133] William stood to lose an income from the *Academy* of about £100 a year, an extremely useful supplement to his salary at the Inland Revenue for a married man with two children.

Losing his billet at the *Academy* affected his 'self-opinion', but it opened a new opportunity to enhance his reputation as a literary critic – with the *Athenaeum*. The editor Norman MacColl took William on with alacrity, on the recommendation of Theodore Watts-Dunton. His association with the journal, after an initial mishap involving a libel case against the *Athenaeum*, became a long and fruitful one, giving him a platform to become one of the most influential contemporary literary critics, on a whole range of classic and contemporary authors and especially on his best loved poets Dante and Shelley.[134]

In spite of Whistler's 'volcanic temperament', William and Lucy always remained on 'the easiest and pleasantest terms' with the fiery artist. They attended his maverick Sunday morning breakfasts and Whistler came to Lucy's evenings 'at home'. Although William modified his enthusiasm for Whistler's art, he continued to hail its originality.

In September 1895 William's prominence as an international authority on art was ratified when he was invited to head the jury at the first Venice Biennale, a responsibility that pleased him deeply in the phenomenally hot Venetian autumn, although he modestly explained the committee appointed him because of 'my age rather than my deserts'. The organiser of the Biennale was a Venetian, Professor Fradeletto, with whom William remained friendly for years. His fellow jurymen were 'all critics of high distinction', Italy's Adolfo Venturi, France's Robert de la Sizeranne, Germany's Richard Muther and Professor Lange from Copenhagen.[135] Not only did William present a special prize of £16[136] out of his own purse to a promising young Italian artist V.A. Cargorel, but he was specially gratified that the committee voted an international prize to Whistler for his *Little White Girl* which had been 'an object of [William's] admiration from a much earlier date'.[137]

CONNOISSEUR

Collecting is often a critical element in connoisseurship and William enjoyed collecting in an eclectic fashion. It was an enthusiasm rather than a mania. He collected fine art, Pre-Raphaelite and Rossettian art, blue china, papers, documents, letters, press cuttings, articles, antiquarian books, curios and curiosities. He kept diaries, compiled anthologies of poetry as well as scrapbooks called *Miscellanies* and wrote biography and autobiography, all strategies for preserving or shaping the past.

In pursuit of his collecting craze, he loved visiting Oriental boutiques in Paris and London, making modest purchases of 'Japanese crape-pictures' that took him on magic carpets far away from mundane reality and office routine.[138] Still a bachelor, with no thoughts of marriage in spring 1873, he indulged in a pair of 'Japanese swords with some capital metalwork, £1.10'. Well aware of the spiritual as well as aesthetic qualities that Japanese samurai ascribed to these unique weapons, he considered 'the swords a very good bargain, & don't remember having ever seen a true *pair* for sale before. They must be fifty to eighty years old at least, I should fancy'.[139] In a linked retail indulgence a few days later, he couldn't resist 'eleven Japanese & Chinese books (£1.10) at Wilson's'.[140] Perhaps £1 10s, or thirty shillings, was his mental cut-off point when making escapist purchases.

An essential factor in collecting is list making, classifying and cataloguing. William often made lists of art works in his house, letters received, books owned, pictures for sale, finances and expenses when travelling. He became, in 1905, the bibliographer and ultimate list maker of his brother's works. At some deep level, perhaps, he shared Queen Victoria's feeling, identified by Lytton Strachey, that in meticulous list making 'the transitoriness of this world had been arrested'.

Collecting and cataloguing provided William with tactics for exerting control over the huge mass of papers and objects that he accumulated over a lifetime. He was not an aggressive collector of things; it was almost as if the things collected him and were an intrinsic part of the autobiographical record of his life. Faced by the chaos of moving house in 1890 from Endsleigh Gardens, where he calculated he had lived for over a third of his life, to a much smaller home at St Edmund's Terrace, his thirteen-year-old son Arthur observed censoriously, 'I should think it extremely probable that a large proportion of my father's books will be lost, or at least seriously damaged.' 'Don't say that, Arthur', Lucy instantly retorted, 'if anything happened to your father's books and pictures I should certainly die.'[141]

After the deaths of Gabriel in 1882 and Christina in 1894, William was obliged to draw up lists for exhibition, sales or probate, which he did with precision, as if these were the last services he could offer the dead. Each item, art work or book was conscientiously listed, its value noted without sentimentality.

On 6 December 1908 William drew up an inventory of all the works of art framed or otherwise displayed at his final home, 3 St Edmund's Terrace. It runs to almost thirty closely handwritten pages, detailing 497 framed items alone, the subject matter, medium and brief description of each one noted with its estimated market value, in a hand still flowing and confident, the information from memory still invaluable.[142] This task undertaken at the age of nearly eighty was clearly in anticipation of his own death. But every collector or connoisseur hopes to achieve much more than just an inventory, a disparate hoard of rare books, art works or *objets d'art*. Instead, the collector seeks a unifying sense of the necessary and inevitable relationships within the collection. When Henry James invented Adela Gereth, a hardnosed general who had bagged 'The Spoils of Poynton', he gave her the creativity collectors aspire to, a flair for arrangement, a true genius. She could make things compose – a gift 'that will never be in an inventory!...a kind of fourth dimension. It's a presence, a perfume, a touch. It's a soul, a story, a life'.[143]

As a young man Richard Curle, the writer, bibliophile and Conrad specialist, visited William at home in St Edmund's Terrace.

> Everything in it was old and beautiful. There were pictures by his brother, Dante Gabriel Rossetti – especially a lovely portrait of their sister, Christina Rossetti – and pictures by his father-in-law, Ford Madox Brown; also blue and white china, Japanese prints, mellow furniture, including the sofa on which Shelley, in Italy, slept the night before he was drowned, rows of ancient books; and everything seemed somehow to have been part of the house for generations and to have cast a spell of peace and finality upon the rooms.

Transported at a step into a past world, Richard Curle found the secret, cohering factor in all these collections was William himself, 'this tranquil old man, with the grave, kindly eyes, who was the magician'.[144] In old age William had become the Prospero figure which he had modelled for Lucy more than four decades previously (see fig. 87). Although the collections at 3 St Edmund's Terrace can never be re-created (the house was bombed during the Second World War), William's 1908 inventory is a potent reminder of the wealth and individuality of his personal collection. In its own way it is a testament to a soul, a story and a life.

William's 1908 inventory is also evidence of a catholicity of taste throughout a lifetime. One of his most appealing characteristics was his apprehension of genius in art wherever it might be found. With his cross-cultural heredity, and his lifelong enthusiasm for foreign travel, he was more open to influences from abroad than many Victorians of his generation. In this personal inventory, Japanese or Chinese artists accounted for nearly a quarter of all items. He and Gabriel began collecting Japanese art and artefacts as early as 1863, although William had begun to be aware of them almost a decade previously when he had reviewed for the *Spectator* the earliest exhibition in England of Japanese decorative arts, held at the Old Society of Painters in Watercolours in 1854. William was enchanted by the innovative mannerism of 'Japanesque' and predicted that among enthusiasts it would become 'a rage to be the possessor of something or other from Japan.'[145] He would be in the vanguard of that rage, scouring specialist oriental shops such as Madame Dessoye's in the rue de Rivoli in Paris and Farmer & Rogers in Regent Street, London where the foreman, Arthur Lasenby Liberty, later founded his own world-famous, design-driven, aesthetic emporium on the opposite side of the street. When William visited Liberty's in 1877 he was gratified when the proprietor hailed him as 'the first pioneer of Japanese art in London' although he modestly demurred that this was not strictly accurate.[146]

At the 1862 International Exhibition in London, when a Japanese diplomatic party graced the capital for the first time since 1613, William was able to see a more extensive selection of lacquerware, ceramics, textiles, carvings, enamels, cloisonné, prints and books than had been shown in 1854. In commenting on the exhibition, William challenged the distinctions between decorative and fine arts:

> The painting of a picture, the carving of a statue, the design of a building, the setting of a jewel, are all exemplifications of the faculty of fine art...the extreme division and subdivision of art in the present day is one of the most baneful features of it – one of those which most cramp the artist...There ought to be much less of this distinction, and a much freer field for the artist to work in.

After collapsing conventional demarcations between fine and applied arts, he dared to declare almost artistic heresy: 'about the very best fine art practised at the present day in any corner of the globe is the decorative art of the Japanese'.[147]

William reviewed a book of Japanese woodcuts by Hokusai in the *Reader* in 1863, probably the first public notice of Japanese art in England. Whistler had introduced Gabriel to 'Japonnerie', a mania that had filtered through from Impressionists such as Manet and Tissot in Paris. Both Rossetti brothers were 'astonished and delighted with Japanese designs; their enormous energy, their instinct for whatever savours of life and movement, their exquisite superiority to symmetry in decorative form, their magic of touch and impeccability of execution'. When Gabriel began collecting triple-colour printed designs and woodcut books, for every one print or book that his brother bought, William purchased half a dozen more (figs 74, 75).

> A continuous band of the colour prints, lightly framed, was hung around my dining-room after I had removed to Endsleigh Gardens. They made a gorgeous decoration, which was highly commended by Dante Gabriel, Trelawny, and some others. They were not much to the taste of Madox Brown, nor yet of my wife; so, when we removed in 1890 to St Edmund's Terrace, Regent's Park, they were not replaced in any living-room, but they make a brilliant, and to unaccustomed eyes a rather startling, show in the entrance-passage.[148]

William's inventory includes works by Baruko, Bukuro, Hokusai, Hiroshige, Ikka, Shansho, Sugaku and Utamaro, landscapes of a floating world, rivers, lakes and mountains, scenes of geishas, actors, grotesques, hermits, fireworks, warriors and dragons.

As Lucy didn't share his passion for oriental art, William was gratified when his children adopted his taste for art from the land of the Mikado. The most artistic, Helen, crammed her bedroom walls with Hiroshige landscapes. William allowed himself unusual flights of rhetorical questions to convey his enthusiasm:

> Was there ever, in real insight and superlative strength, the grace that comes of strength, a better landscape painter than Hiroshige? Yes, there was Turner. Who else? Or was there a more stupendous master of whatever he set his hand to than Hokusai? or one who understood a tiger – the essence of a tiger, not to insist upon his skeletal scaffolding and his "anatomy fig-ure" – better than Ganko? or an inventor of bird and flower groups, a seer of the life of flower and bird, equal to Kitao Shigemasa or Sugaku? How pale and petty, how anaemic and indecisive, do most European things appear beside such mighty handiwork! [149]

William collated not only 'mighty handiwork' but also the flotsam and jetsam of a life spent in art and literature. In his later years he physically assembled dozens of curious *Miscellanies*. He pulled together scores of press reviews and articles with little regard for common themes or chronology and simply bound them up into volumes, cutting and pasting with a vengeance. Whole

74. *Geishas Picnicking*, mid-nineteenth century. Japanese coloured woodcut, 254 × 356 mm, from William Michael Rossetti's collection. Private collection.

75. Kuniyoshi, *Fisherman*, mid-nineteenth century. Japanese coloured woodcut, 356 × 254 mm, from William Michael Rossetti's collection. Private collection.

shelf loads of these compilations survive in the University of Minnesota Library, Minneapolis. Another aspect of his passion for archiving, preserving and collecting, it was also an activity to defy the passing of time. Yoking them by violence together in bound volumes, he felt he was giving permanence to these miscellaneous, ephemeral articles.

In his declining years William continued to write, to record, to collect and to help other collectors. His prime motive at this stage was to memorialize those inspired individuals whose times he had lived through, whose lives he had commemorated. He assembled and annotated several volumes of Pre-Raphaelite memorabilia, *Ruskin: Rossetti: Pre-Raphaelitism* (1899), *Prœraphaelite Diaries and Letters* (1900) and *Rossetti Papers 1862–1870* (1903). He produced these authentic compilations, instead of original work of his own, because, he explained, still subscribing to the propaganda absorbed since childhood, 'I have not an originating mind'.[150] But his conscientious labours proved invaluable first-hand resources for generations of art and literary historians. Collecting and memorializing satisfied deep creative needs in William. When the ache of old age became unbearably numbing, William the collector could fly into the past as well as project his taste into the future. In Susan Sontag's *The Volcano Lover*, her Cavaliere, the great collector Sir William Hamilton, delivers his manifesto: 'while there are more exalted destinies, I maintain that to discover what is beautiful and share that with others is also a worthy employment for a life'.[151] William the elderly collector and inventory maker confronted the brevity of life and prepared for death (the ultimate Collector) by keeping busy, charting his collections, labelling his furniture with notes of provenance and making lists that attested to a lifetime of connoisseurship.

5

Artist

Lucy's exposure to art began as a baby when she first modelled for her father. She grew up constantly aware of the impedimenta that cluttered his studio. Sometimes she modelled for him for so long that she fell asleep. But there is no record that she was specially gifted as a child in drawing or painting. Her education at Helen Bromley's school in Gravesend tended to be academic rather than creative and this intellectual streak, inculcated in a family that prized cleverness even in babies, became a major component of Lucy's adult approach to art. William identified this as her 'elevated tone of thought, loyal to the high things in life and in art and literature'[1] and even William Money Hardinge, Lucy's great admirer and confidant towards the end of her life, felt exhausted by the sheer amount of thought that informed each of her canvases.[2]

Although Lucy frequently acted in an administrative capacity in her father's studio, little evidence remains to indicate artistic inclinations as a teenager. However, a record of a crayon life drawing by Lucy, *Nude Female* dated 1860, appears in the probate inventory of William and Lucy's final home together, 3 St Edmund's Terrace, Regent's Park, drawn up soon after William's death in February 1919.[3] Opportunities to draw from life were rare for women artists at this time. Lucy had access to life models only because she was able to work in her father's studio. But this single inventory entry suggests she was studying drawing years earlier than has hitherto been thought. In the first half of the 1860s, because of her quick brain and application, Lucy was mainly employed as amanuensis to her father rather than as a hands-on studio assistant. When Lucy's half-nephew, Ford Madox Hueffer,[4] eventually wrote Madox Brown's biography – originally begun by Lucy herself during her final, tragic illness in 1893 – he noted that his grandfather's art generated an enormous amount of paperwork. 'This correspondence alone was a weighty matter, spread over five years. I have in my possession upwards of two hundred lawyers' letters, and a very large number of copies of answers on the subject.[5] They must have cost a considerable amount of thought and an almost equal amount of manual labour, although in many cases Madox Brown's daughter Lucy acted as his amanuensis'.[6]

In December 1865 the Madox Browns moved from Kentish Town to a larger, more fashionable address at 37 Fitzroy Square which 'became distinguished as a centre for men of letters and from the world of art'.[7] Lucy attended a constant round of sparkling evening parties, recorded in the letters and diaries of William Bell Scott, George Price Boyce, William Allingham and William Michael Rossetti. On 21 August 1867 she and Cathy were bridesmaids at St Matthew's Church, Brixton for the wedding of the Portuguese entrepreneur Charles Augustus Howell to his cousin, Frances Catherine Howell, always known as Kitty. The couple invited William – aged thirty-seven – to be best man but he declined, advising Kitty to find someone 'less middle-aged & less glum'.[8] Lucy and Cathy gave an aesthetic blue and white teapot as their wedding present.[9] Maria and Christina Rossetti chose an ivory card case, William a small Japanese cabinet but Gabriel's present outdid them all, 'a Persian dinner service green and white with a *dragonous* pattern', as Christina reported to her friend Amelia Heimann.[10] The Morrises, Burne-Joneses, Madox Browns and Rossettis all gathered for the splendid occasion. But it was an agonizing day for the twenty-four-year-old bridesmaid Lucy, 'suffering greatly from neuralgia, a recent accident with a leach, [e]tc – & at times barely able to stand or sit it out: her teeth have got distressingly black – so much so,' William Rossetti observed in his diary, 'that I almost suppose it must be due to some remedy she is taking.'[11] The 'remedy' that caused the staining was either iron tonic that Victorians took in vast quantities for every complaint, or mercury-based and probably more dangerous than the original infection.

Like her father, Lucy relished social life. On 15 October 1867, a rainy day, William Allingham called in at convivial Fitzroy Square where he found upstairs, 'Madox Brown, Mrs B., Lucy, in a green dress, Katty, [Cathy] young half-sister with fair hair; Marshall, Dunn. Piano, Grog.'[12] After watching the races, on Derby Day 1868, Allingham sat in his informal velveteen jacket at a full dress dinner party between Lucy Madox Brown and Miss Faulkner – ten ladies present – 'Banquet, – "Earthly Paradise", I suggest, & Ned writes this atop of the menu. A storm of talking'.[13]

Until the late 1860s when she was in her mid-twenties, Lucy's art education had been peculiar or almost non-existent, according to contemporary commentator and art historian Ellen Clayton. 'With the exception of drawing for two or three months, at the age of eight or nine', Clayton claimed Lucy showed no inclination for art.[14] But one or two interesting juvenile drawings, including a watercolour probably showing Melliker Farm (see fig. 40), appeared in a Christie's sale in 2000,[15] the *Nude Female* life study of 1860 was thought accomplished enough not to be discarded, and a study of a dog, monogrammed and dated 13 May 1867, still remains in the hands of descendants. So evidence suggests that Lucy dabbled in art but did not make sustained efforts during her early years. Clayton implied that Lucy was biding her time and that 'a special kind of mental development' was subconsciously preparing her for a late entry into art.

It was one day early in 1868 that Lucy apparently stepped in to complete an unfinished (and unidentified) picture by Albert Goodwin (fig. 76), Madox

76. Albert Goodwin. Cathy Hueffer's photograph album, STH/BH/2/3-6. The Stow Hill Collection, HLRO, and the Hon. Oliver Soskice.

Brown's regular studio assistant. Her younger half-siblings Cathy and Oliver were already training with great promise in their father's studio. Until this defining moment Lucy may have felt that art was their territory and, by default, hers was academia. But her unexpected and obvious proficiency alerted her father to the fact that his eldest child also possessed talent. His approval gave her a new confirming sense of herself. She began to believe she too could make a professional career in art, as the younger Madox Browns intended. So Lucy, aged twenty-four, joined art classes in her father's studio with Cathy and Oliver, and students Theresa Thorneycroft and Nellie Epps (who later married Edmund Gosse). They were all precociously talented. At seventeen Cathy had already been training for four years

> like one of the early Florentines. At eight every morning she was in her father's studio preparing his painting things for him. After that she would draw whatever he placed before her, sometimes plaster casts, sometimes his own head. If he did not approve what she had drawn, he would scratch a line right through it and make her begin again and again until she had got it right. The aim was to draw exactly what she saw. Thus she was disciplined. 'Drawing,' she said, 'can be taught, but colour comes naturally to an artist.' There was no theory about the mixing of colours, no rule as to how they should be put on…In the studio from early morning she painted until midday. After lunch they would rest for half an hour and then work again

until 4.30, the tea-hour. Then, whether she liked it or not, she went for a walk with her mother. At 5.30 they would return and help Madox Brown to receive his friends; and at 6.30 the first bell would go and they would dress for dinner, at which William Rossetti, Swinburne, Edmund Gosse, and P.P. Marshall would often be present, Dante Gabriel Rossetti coming in afterwards, when they would all return to the studio for the evening.

This extract from one of Cathy's obituaries in 1927 vividly evokes the routine of student days under Madox Brown's tutelage.[16]

The studio atmosphere was competitive, absorbing and highly charged, particularly when Marie Spartali joined the group. Daughter of Michael Spartali, a wealthy Greek shipping magnate, the classically beautiful young artist unconsciously inspired *Love's Problem* in the heart of her teacher, Lucy's father, a married man old enough to be Marie's father:

> Pale rose of purity that feeds love's fire
> With tantalizing lips that none may kiss. [17]

A series of Petrarchan sonnets, the form so often used for unrequited love, survives in a battered exercise book, bearing witness to Madox Brown's painful and impossible love. Oxymoronic titles express agonies of inner conflict, *Cruelly Kind*, *Absent Presence*, *Amor Incendiaris*, *Mute Worship*, *Change in Constancy*, *Angela Damnifera* and *Pleading Contraries*. Others frankly address *Hopeless Love*, *Late Love*, and *Voiceless Love*. Marie's speaking eyes are a recurring image. Several poems look for hidden meanings in paintings she undertook for her art master but there is no indication that she returned his love, simply that her generous heart understood his pain. Madox Brown felt trapped in his teacher's role:

> As I with quivering lip the mentor played,
> With moistened eyes – unteaching as I taught! [18]

He was also trapped in his marriage to his second wife, the voluptuous but problematical Emma Hill. They had been united since 1849 when she was in her mid-teens. Together they had brought up their children, faced financial worries, the death of a baby son, Arthur, in 1857, and Emma's increasing alcohol addiction. He felt so confused and guilty about her that on 7 December 1869 he addressed a sonnet to Emma, 'Sweet love of twenty years, still young and fair/Impassioned mistress, friend and wife in one,' trying to convince himself that Emma 'still shall be my heart's best care.'[19]

A few weeks later, at midnight on 16 January 1870, Gabriel came round to tell Madox Brown his 'unwooed love would wed another man', William Stillman, an American widower whom Marie eventually married in 1871. Gabriel stayed while Madox Brown sobbed on his shoulders till dawn brought confirmation of the news from Marie's own lips. Madox Brown remembered:

77 and 78. Marie Spartali Stillman (left) and William Stillman (right). Cathy Hueffer's photograph album, STH/BH/2/3-6. The Stow Hill Collection, HLRO, and the Hon. Oliver Soskice.

> Never did the rainbow's span
> Show lovelier nor could wrecked men scan
> More hopelessly the undrinkable salt sea! [20]

However, as Marie's parents initially opposed her marriage to the 'brilliant and erratic' American, whose first wife had committed suicide, Madox Brown recovered his equilibrium in time to host the wedding breakfast at his home in Fitzroy Square (figs 77, 78).[21]

In spite of these deeply awkward emotions which permeated the studio atmosphere, Lucy and Marie maintained an intimate friendship. Marie gave Lucy one of her earliest paintings, *Shanklin Chine* (1867),[22] and the Spartalis often invited Lucy to stay with them in Clapham, and in their country home on the Isle of Wight, decorated in the most exquisite aesthetic taste. Visitors during the 1870s admired their Walter Crane wallpapers, marble mantelpieces, Minton tiles and black and gold Japanese furniture in the bedrooms.[23] After their marriages, Marie and Lucy continued to meet to discuss art and children, and corresponded for many years. Marie's future stepdaughter Lisa (from Stillman's first marriage), an 'all but blood true daughter',[24] and a promising artist of only eight years old, who later portrayed Lucy's eldest daughter as a child (see fig. 112), was sometimes included in Madox Brown's art lessons. Lisa Stillman remembered thrilling days when she painted her first portraits and had her first encouragement. She wrote later to Lucy's daughter and Madox Brown's granddaughter, Helen Rossetti Angeli:

> There was a sense of peace & kindness under his roof, of earnest work & freedom of spirit. His great protective fatherly presence gave a sense of safety from the fears of childhood partly because he gave children a feeling of equality. With him and with Rossetti I never realized I was a child & never felt that my work or opinions were negligible. I never feared a snub. Madox Brown was to every young & growing being the ideal father & protector.[25]

Lucy too blossomed under Madox Brown's art training which inculcated his early Pre-Raphaelite ideals of realism and strict truth to nature, disdaining the later slide into decorative aestheticism. Lucy's first picture for exhibition, a watercolour called *Painting*, was shown at the Dudley Gallery in 1869, the year when all three junior Madox Browns made their first public appearances. Its apparently ambiguous title referred directly to its composite subject of a picture within a picture. A young woman artist at an easel (modelled by Cathy) was shown painting a picture of an old woman holding some faggots, 'a very remarkable first work in point of quiet efficiency of tone and general keeping: all seemed right in intention as if by a kind of instinct', thought William Rossetti, years before he had any romantic attachment to the artist.[26] Ellen Clayton noted how warmly received this first picture was, how 'remarkable for its harmonious, quiet unity and solidity of tone. All the critics warmly commended this essay…The usually stern critic of the *Athenaeum*' also praised it, albeit from the sexist perspective of the day: 'It is seldom that so deeply toned and soberly coloured a picture comes from the hands of a lady; rarely have we seen an example of such high technical merit from those of a tyro.'[27] Lucy's special taste for ambitious composition and intense depth of colour were already apparent, principles learnt in her father's studio but reimagined through her own unique perspective.

However, *Painting*'s small success failed to relieve Madox Brown's financial worries or his sense of persecution. 'I have not for years known anything like it – not apparently the faintest chance of effecting a sale on any hand or obtaining a commission', he wrote to Frederic Shields on 9 February 1869. 'Nothing seems ever now to approach the house except Christmas bills, which come tumbling in with a will…They have skied poor Nolly's *Jason* most infamously – put it, in fact, entirely out of sight; otherwise there was a good chance of its having sold. Cathy's pretty head is likewise in the dark. Lucy's, however, is well hung and spoken of, only the papers seem more or less in a combination to run even it down'.[28] A few months later Madox Brown was able to relax briefly and report to Shields that Lucy, Cathy, and Nolly 'selling four pictures for small sums have helped to keep things square'.[29]

Art critics today, particularly male commentators, tend to trivialize the achievement of the Madox Brown sisters, implying they had no ideas of their own. 'It isn't that the work of the sisters Lucy and Catherine Madox Brown isn't technically accomplished, but that they imitate the work of their father so closely that one can often name the specific work of art by Ford Madox Brown that inspired each picture', complained a reviewer of the Pre-Raphaelite Women Artists exhibition in 1997–8.[30] In 1895 an article on Lucy in the *Magazine of Art* pointed out the peculiar way Madox Brown's work 'impels to imitation…you cannot see much of it without becoming attempered…and she had seen it always'.[31] This observer believed Lucy's work was far more vital whenever she resisted the osmotic influence of her father or of Dante Gabriel Rossetti and painted out of her own innate and unerring dramatic sense. But copying has traditionally been an essential exercise in any student's art training and one of Lucy's surviving art works bears witness to this aspect of her tuition. Byronic subjects were the talk of the studio during 1869–70 when Madox Brown and his son Nolly were collaborating with editor William Rossetti to illustrate Byron for *Moxon's Popular Poets* series. Lucy sketched *The Two Foscari*, after Ford Madox Brown's much larger watercolour, *Jacopo Foscari in Prison*, 1870.[32]

The subject was familiar to Madox Brown and Lucy from Lord Byron's tragedy *The Two Foscari*, 1821, and Verdi's opera *I Due Foscari*, 1844 (fig. 79). Inspired by a love story set in a Venetian dungeon, it shows Jacopo Foscari taking his final farewell of his wife and Venice before going into banishment. Madox Brown's watercolour technique of applying opaque layers of pigment to achieve a depth of colour more usually associated with oil painting was one of the lessons he taught Lucy. It was a Pre-Raphaelite characteristic to make oils shimmer with the delicacy of watercolours and vice versa, to give watercolours the intensity of oils. Comparing Lucy's faithful, small copy with Madox Brown's finished picture, it is obvious Lucy learnt to paint in her father's style. It is less well known that in the studio she and her sister often worked up and completed Madox Brown's pictures. 'How is the painting getting on?' Madox Brown asked Lucy. 'I am finishing the Cordelia you painted in', he wrote when she was staying with the Spartalis in the 1860s.[33] The picture was probably *Cordelia's Portion* (1866), developed from drawings he had made in Paris in 1844 when Lucy was an infant.

At twenty-six Lucy was still unmarried. Her thoughts and the subject matter of her pictures often focused on love. Though documentary evidence from Lucy's girlhood is tantalizingly sparse, it is reasonable to speculate that these years contained friendships, flirtations and skirmishes. If Lucy had any affairs of the heart in the years before her marriage, the letters and diaries, which might have supplied evidence, have simply vanished or been self-censored. However, some fragments of youthful verse remain in Lucy's hand, either reflecting an early heartbreak or simply experiments in writing poetry. At times her pencil script becomes very faint, almost physically suggesting romantic disappointment:

79. Lucy Madox Brown, *The Two Foscari*, c. 1870. Watercolour and coloured chalk, 210 × 130 mm. Fredeman Family Collection.

> He gave me love and joy for one short hour
> To make all joy and love henceforth lose power...
> I blame thee not...If my heart break
> O love forever lost – I blame thee not...
> How shall we meet my love?
> > After long years.

Lucy invokes an image of herself as a solitary, elemental figure on the seashore, a favourite Victorian motif:

> Oh Love the sea the self-same time did play
> Last year, when thou, who now art far away
> Wert here, on this same spot where now must I
> In loneliness pass on to live or die.

The language and imagery is conventional; nevertheless, the heartache is keen:

> O thou! if thou hast doubted love
> Think of the pains that have been borne
> And by it hearts that have been torn.[34]

It is not surprising, then, that one of Lucy's earliest and most accomplished pictures examined the theme of love.[35] *The Duet* (fig. 80) makes playful reference to Orsino's contemplation in *Twelfth Night* whether 'music be the food

80. Lucy Madox Brown, *The Duet*, 1870. Watercolour on paper, 571 × 425 mm, signed with monogram and dated 'LMB – 70' lower left. Exhibited Royal Academy 1870. Private collection.

of love'. Two lovers, both in nostalgic eighteenth-century dress, play the game of love across a pianoforte. By setting the tryst so obviously in a bygone age, the artist employs an instantly 'readable' Victorian form of visual shorthand. The two young lovers are not facing the complications of modern love. Their love is set back in time, in a supposedly simpler age, a lost golden age of innocence and harmonious values. The lovers are both particular and universal. They transcend time and make music together. Singing a duet, they find romantic unity; in duality, wholeness.

Seated at a pianoforte the young woman's eyes gaze up towards her musical partner. Her long brown hair, caught at the nape, flows down her back. To complement her warm colouring, her suitor wears a blond wig tied in a black velvet bow. The girl's head glows against the gleaming halo provided by a chinoiserie screen decorated with birds, sculptural twigs and oriental script. A wall-hanging on the right shows blue mountain peaks, towers, foliage, woodland with knights on horseback and a huntsman blowing a horn. It could be the interior of the Madox Brown home at 37 Fitzroy Square. The young pianist's faintly striped dress picks up the amber of the screen and hanging, then deepens to cerise. Her underskirt in softly textured black lends voluptuousness to the whole costume. Soft muslin is tucked into the bosom and the dress has an airy train.

Inlaid on the side of the pianoforte is a plaque that underscores the picture's musical theme. It shows Orpheus charming the animals with his lyre. The pianist's eyes are not on the music, they are only for her lover as he bends across the pianoforte, elegant and youthful in his buff jacket, cuffs double buttoned and a froth of lace at wrist and neck.

It is a picture of wooing, a courtship full of tenderness. The lovers are on the brink, forever silent but about to break into a love song or romantic ballad. It is a study of anticipation. The girl is just about to touch the keys, the exact position of her little finger showing the artist herself was an able pianist. The young man studies his sheets of music like a love letter. It is the moment before declaration, the moment of eternal silence in the dialogue of lovers. The artist explores the conundrum of evoking strains of music in silent paint, and solves it by choosing the sprung moment of expectation before the love duet begins. Technically accomplished, *The Duet*'s sensitive brushwork and palette of subtle amber, rose madder and sage green prompted Gabriel to tell Madox Brown, 'Lucy has painted a really perfect picture.'[36]

The Duet was the only one of Lucy's pictures exhibited at the Royal Academy, in 1870, when it was sold to F.W. Craven of Manchester for fifty guineas, although he later rejected it. Subsequently it went to Liverpool, priced at sixty guineas, and was shown again in 1877 in London at the Dudley Gallery, housed in the Egyptian Hall on Piccadilly which had become the primary showcase for the secondary wave of Pre-Raphaelites and early Aesthetic Movement artists.

81. Lucy Madox
Brown, *Après le
Bal*, 1870.
Watercolour.
Exhibited Dudley
Gallery 1870.
Private collection.

In 1870, the same year as *The Duet*, Lucy exhibited another watercolour, *Après le Bal* (fig. 81), at the Dudley Gallery. Contemporary reviews of the picture mixed praise with criticism. The *Art-Journal* called it 'a work of something better than promise, and yet far from completeness. Great is the sense and harmony of colour; yet the tone is dreary, the forms are ill-defined, and the execution muddled. But these faults, which in another work were fatal, are more than counterbalanced by merits'.[37]

Après le Bal examines contemporary social pressures on young women. Lucy depicts a private feminine moment when one young woman comforts another after the public competitiveness of dancing and matchmaking. Both composition and colours relate to *The Duet*. But the duality in this picture alludes to sisterliness and only indirectly to invisible lovers. The older girl on the right leans forward extending a consoling hand to the younger girl slumped in a chair. The hair colouring of the two girls, one corn yellow, the other auburn brown, may imply that Lucy was thinking of her own relationship with her younger sister Cathy who had coils of fair hair. Cathy certainly modelled for this picture, as did Marie Spartali and Miss Nesbitt. The 'Lucy sister' on the right, whose elegant turn of the head suggests the beautiful Marie Spartali, wears a dress whose colours, although in reversed proportions, link back to the girl in *The Duet*. A soft, unstructured, medievalized black gown, set off by a long floating evening scarf of coral *devoré*, connects her physically to the 'Cathy sister', with her harvest hair, gold chains over her bosom, the flower she holds and flame-coloured chair where she sinks. Her romantic full white dress is secured with a narrow dark girdle at the waist and she trails a mantilla of black lace across the train of her skirt, which leads the eye back across the picture to the comforting sister.

Again the background is crammed with importance, a cropped window on the extreme left and a large picture centre right behind a partly drawn curtain. Two china vessels on the window-sill, one a fashionably aesthetic Chinese dragon vase, entice the viewer through the window to an idealized townscape with water running through it – Bruges perhaps, or Amsterdam or Venice. On the extreme right is a china cabinet stacked with the blue-and-white china the Pre-Raphaelites loved to collect and, to its left, a classical bust on a plinth. The classical motif is picked up in the fillet that binds the 'Lucy' sister's hair, a piece of kingfisher feather jewellery from China, an echoing bracelet on her arm, and the almost Greek simplicity of her draped gown. An exotic oriental carpet in the foreground reiterates the warm colours in the rest of the picture.

This is a report back from that feminine world the artist inhabited. It tells a deeper truth than the superficial impression of the Madox Brown girls' effortless superiority left in Laura Hain Friswell's account.[38] Laura described the sisters' external brilliance and charisma. Lucy's report is from their inner lives, expressed through outer symbolic signs.

Death or parting is always implicit in love and Lucy was not unusual in being interested in the agony of loss – indeed she was no stranger to it. She had lost her mother, her baby half-brother Arthur and her elder cousin Helen who had died of consumption at sixteen. This delicate cousin had taken a particular delight in Lucy's insouciance even before she joined the Bromley family at Melliker Farm in 1846, aged three, 'Mamma tells me that Lucy runs on the parade and shakes hands with all the gentlemen. I am quite shocked at her'.[39]

When Lucy's knowledge of death and romance combined, she became lyrical. The subject she chose was archetypal, *Romeo and Juliet in the Tomb* (fig. 82).[40] It is true that her father had worked on his *Romeo and Juliet* (fig. 83), first a watercolour study and later an oil painting between 1868 and July 1870 but

82. Lucy Madox Brown, *Romeo and Juliet in the Tomb*, 1870. Watercolour on panel, 610 × 815 mm. Signed with monogram and dated 'LMB-70'. Exhibited Dudley Gallery 1871. Wightwick Manor, National Trust.

83. Ford Madox Brown, *Romeo and Juliet*, 1870. Oil on canvas, 135.5 × 93.98 cm. Delaware Art Museum, Samuel and Mary R. Bancroft Memorial, 1935.

he had chosen a completely different scene, the moment after consummation of the secret marriage. Lucy undoubtedly admired her father's version and quoted unrestrained praise for it from French critics in her 1890 *Magazine of Art* review of her father's career. 'It is the loftiest and most admirable interpretation of Shakespeare ever conceived by artist, poet, painter, or sculptor'.[41] He chose the second balcony scene from Act 3, Scene 5 when Romeo must leave before the 'envious streaks' of sunrise betray him. Madox Brown had warned his purchaser that he 'must expect a scene of passion' as his Juliet is in a post-coital trance of abandonment while Romeo, a figure of vital masculinity is caught between the tension of staying and going. His head is buried in Juliet's neck, absorbing her body scent whereas his left leg and arm are already over the edge of the balcony and away. Both figures are active and upright in complete contrast with the supine composition of Lucy's picture.

Lucy chose instead the tense moment when Romeo, defying the banishment order imposed on him, has returned to Verona. In the gloaming vault of the Capulets, Romeo mistakes Juliet's pallor for death itself. He does not know that, counselled by Friar Laurence, she has merely swallowed a sleeping draught that mimics death, in order to escape the horrors of an arranged marriage to Count Paris. Juliet lies bisecting the picture, a figure of delicate transparency in wedding dress and veil, apparently in her last sleep. Her beauty lights Romeo's appalled face as he leans over her. 'It is a moment of absolute stillness, preluding fierce action – one of those moments in which, the mind being at a standstill, the senses take note of infinitely small things, the flowers on the bier, or the whisper of the bat's leathern wings'.[42] In his left hand Romeo grips the phial of poison symbolically poised over Juliet's heart. Juliet will wake to find her lover dead beside her and she too will commit suicide. Swords lie ready on the floor beneath her bier, in poignant contrast with the Pre-Raphaelite detail of flowers and birds scattered in the foreground. The picture is built on such contrasts: life and death, sleep and waking, active and passive, standing and proneness, agony in the tomb and dispassionate light from the outside world. In the top right-hand corner, above the steps leading out of the charnel-house, is another of Lucy's pictures within a picture, opening here on the steeples and rooftops of an imagined Verona under an angry streaked sky, half obliterated by a bleak winter tree. Nature, suggests the artist, is impervious to human agony; the seasons will simply go onwards the same in their relentless cycle. Love and loss will flare and fade and endlessly repeat.

Lucy's finest picture was exhibited at the Dudley Gallery (no. 336) in 1871 the same year Whistler showed his *Harmony in Blue-Green – Moonlight* (no. 265).[43] *Romeo and Juliet* was praised by French art critic Ernest Chesneau, who told her father he admired it 'more than any thing else I have sent him' and visitors from New York declared it '*quite a revelation to them*'.[44] Years later when

84. Lucy Madox Brown, study for *Romeo and Juliet*, undated, probably 1870–1. Black chalk on grey paper, 280 × 336 mm. Private collection.

Lucy was in Avignon en route to the Italian Riviera, the picture was admired at a party in London and Marie Corelli 'improvised a pianoforte toccata upon the theme of it.'[45]

The Christie's sale in November 2000 included some drawings by Lucy. All the items which surfaced either amplified Lucy's *oeuvre* or brought her life into sharper focus. Three drawings gave insight into her working methods and underlined her technical accomplishment. A few smaller sketches shone a new light on undocumented areas of her personal story.

Most striking was Lucy's strong and confident study in charcoal on Ingres paper for *Romeo and Juliet* (fig. 84), concentrating on the faces of the two lovers, idealized and real at the same time, clearly drawn in a moment when Lucy managed to get Cathy and Oliver to pose for her. Their youthfulness is almost tangible, Romeo's even more affecting because the real boy Oliver died before his nineteenth birthday. The phial of poison in Romeo's hand is far more prominent than in Lucy's finished watercolour. In her drawing, she makes it the dramatic focal point of the picture, literally poised between the bodies of the lovers, the physical agent of their final destruction, symbolizing the wider forces of a poisonous society. Swift and assured, the drawing reveals Lucy as an instinctive romantic, unerringly drawn to literature's archetypal romance. Her lovers are equally realized as prototypes of tragic lovers and as individuals. The scraps of poetry that survive in Lucy's handwriting remind us she understood love and its losses, through both lived and imaginative experience.

The Christie's sale also included a large rectangular study of a powerful male nude, drawn in black chalk, inspired by one of Lucy's many visits to the

85. Lucy Madox Brown, *The Dancing Faun*, signed in monogram and dated 2/12/[18]69. Black chalk on grey-green paper, 585 × 333 mm. Private collection.

antique galleries at the British Museum. 'I am off to the British Museum',[46] explained Madox Brown to Frederic Shields in April 1869, showing how seriously he took his duties as art teacher, 'to see after Lucy, Cathy and Nolly who go there twice as much now to draw'.[47] Ellen Clayton explained that Lucy 'drew from the antique and from life under the guidance of her father. For the antique studies, Mr Brown engaged the rooms of the Branch Government School of Art in Bolsover Street, Portland Road, for the three mornings in the week when the ordinary pupils were not in attendance.'[48] Drawing from copies of ancient classical statuary was central to Madox Brown's training of his students. When Lucy and William married in 1874, Marie Spartali Stillman sent several plaster casts as wedding presents, all copies from antique art works: *The Boxer, Jason* and *Venus of Milos*.[49]

Lucy's fine drawing, *Dancing Faun* (fig. 85), the faun also known as 'Faun with clappers', is a copy of a statue from classical antiquity in the *tribuna* at the Uffizi in Florence.[50] A superb bronze cast by Soldani was kept in the gardens at Blenheim Palace in the nineteenth century but it is more likely that Lucy made her drawing from one of many contemporary engravings or from a plaster cast, either at her father's studio, or at Bolsover Street, or at Brucciani's gallery of classical casts in Covent Garden, where art students and amateurs were admitted free of charge. The *Dancing Faun* was illustrated in Brucciani's 1914 catalogue, no. 2580.

Lucy's observation of the male body is accurate, vigorous and appreciative. Although drawn from a classical model, its candid sexuality raises the question whether, in the privacy of Madox Brown's studio, Lucy and her fellow students had opportunities to draw the male as well as the female nude. The *Dancing Faun* has an immediacy that may not come merely from observing sculpture. Educated artistically in the free-thinking, free-talking atmosphere of her father's studio, Lucy saw no need for fig leaves actual or metaphorical. She was noted as 'a woman of very liberal opinions, and not frightened at anything that might be said within the bounds of reason'.[51] Her faun is ecstatically absorbed in music and dance, muscles tensile in hands, torso and thigh.

The Greeks associated the faun with Bacchus and the Romans identified him as Pan. A mischievous, even devilish, mythological figure with horns in his hair and Puck-like, pointed faun ears, he is perhaps forever enticing some nymph to join the dance. 'He is not supernatural, but just on the verge of nature, and yet within it', reminiscent of Nathaniel Hawthorne's *Marble Faun* (1859/60) who had 'nothing to do with time' but had 'a look of eternal youth in his face'. A faun 'had no conscience, no remorse, no burden on the heart, no troublesome recollections of any sort; no dark future either'. It is likely that Lucy read Hawthorne's novel after it was published to great acclaim in England as *Transformation* in 1859. Hawthorne lived in Liverpool from 1853 to 1860, serving as the American consul between 1853 and 1857, and attended the important Art Treasures exhibition in Manchester in 1857.

After Hawthorne's death, the Madox Browns 'had an ailing daughter' – probably the consumptive Una Hawthorne – 'fastened' on them 'for awhile in some family crisis of hers' which rather reduced working hours in the studio towards the end of summer 1871.[52] *The Marble Faun* (referring to a different but associated classical faun by Praxiteles) figured in the Madox Brown literary as well as sculptural landscape. However, the beautiful young Italian, Donatello, in Hawthorne's novel bore such a striking resemblance to Praxitiles' *Faun*, that when he took a whirl round the sculpture gallery in the Capitol at Rome, his seemed like 'the very step of the Dancing Faun'. Like Kenyon, the sculptor in Hawthorne's novel, Lucy found qualities in her faun that were touching and impressive. 'In some long-past age, he must really have existed. Nature needed, and still needs, this beautiful creature; standing betwixt man and animal, sympathizing with each, comprehending the speech of either race, and interpreting the whole existence of one to the other'.[53] Lucy distilled similar feelings into her powerful drawing of the *Dancing Faun*, and was satisfied enough with it to add her monogram, 'LMB', and the date '2/12/69'.

The third important drawing in the Christie's sale was a large charcoal study for *The Tempest* (fig. 86), Lucy's first finished oil painting. As in the *Romeo and*

86. Lucy Madox Brown, study for *Ferdinand and Miranda Playing Chess*, undated, probably 1870–1. Black chalk on grey paper, 591 × 482 mm. Private collection.

Juliet sketch, the artist focuses only on the two central figures, and particularly on the faces of Miranda and Ferdinand for whom the models were again Cathy and Oliver (who painted *Prospero and the Infant Miranda* in a different scene from *The Tempest* also in 1871[54]). Miranda is active and dominant, the total reverse of the comatose figure of Juliet. Glimpsed through the cave's mouth is the stern of the expensive ship that has brought a lover from the outside world to Miranda's magical island. The chess table, which is a major symbolic feature of the finished painting, is merely sketched in here, showing only a single chess piece. It is a striking preliminary study and shows again the appeal for Lucy in the games people play and the interaction between lovers.

Lucy used the study as the basis for her next major painting to explore the theme of love. Like *Romeo and Juliet* it is drawn from Shakespeare and has Italian connections. A scene from Shakespeare's most experimental play, *The Tempest* (1611), inspired *Ferdinand and Miranda Playing Chess* (fig. 87).[55] Once Duke of Milan, Prospero was deposed by his brother Antonio and ship-wrecked with his baby daughter Miranda onto a miraculous island, inhabited only by spirits. Miranda has grown to innocent womanhood, knowing no other human being except her father.

87. Lucy Madox Brown, *Ferdinand and Miranda Playing Chess*, 1871. Oil on canvas,
68.6 × 61 cm. Signed in monogram and dated lower left, 'LMB –71'. Exhibited
Dudley Gallery 1872. Private collection.

On the far right of Lucy's composition, Prospero indicates to incredulous
King Alonso the scene in his cave where their two children are playing chess,
Ferdinand dreamily entranced by imperious Miranda. The circular chess table
carved from a tree-trunk repeats the circularity of the cave's exit to the outside world beyond. The game of chess is charged and symbolic. Miranda (playing white) is winning, leaning over the board to take Ferdinand's coral red
Knight. Lucy chose coral for Ferdinand, to echo Ariel's song:

> Full fathom five thy father lies;
> > Of his bones are coral made;
> Those are pearls that were his eye.[56]

Chess mimics the language and imagery of courtly love itself. The lady has already taken several of her opponent's coral pieces, which lie piled on the books at her feet. Ferdinand clasps one of Miranda's white ivory pieces, suggesting the exchange of hearts between the two lovers. The game of chess is the game of love itself:

> MIRANDA: Sweet Lord, you play me false.
> FERDINAND: No, my dearest love,
> > I would not for the world.[57]

Miranda accuses Ferdinand of cheating, which he denies in cosmic terms. But is he telling the truth or lying? The ambiguity of the dialogue reveals the seeds of a genuine tussle between the sexes, a real relationship between lovers rather than just a saccharine island idyll. Lucy's picture explores Shakespeare's implication about the future battle between the sexes in her symbolic treatment of the battle of the chess pieces.

King Alonso fears this glimpse of the son he believes drowned may be merely a 'vision of the island.' But Prospero restores father to son and, at the same time, introduces his innocent daughter to her first rapturous view of humanity:

> MIRANDA: O, Wonder!
> > How many goodly creatures are there here!
> > How beauteous mankind is! O brave new world
> > That has such people in't![58]

This blend of wonder and reality ranges from the expressions on the lovers' faces to the artist's closely observed details of flowers, fruits, chess pieces, green lizards and lapis-blue parrot. Miranda's basket in the extreme right foreground holds a collection of 'Shakespearean' fruit, hips, haws and medlars. A symbolic passion-flower in bloom is pinned back at the top left of the cave's entrance. A salamander, also an emblem of passion, scuttles down the right-hand side of the picture. Russet in the passion-flowers is repeated in touches on the parrot's beak and tail, the chess pieces, and the ribs of the ship framed through the cave's entrance. Red is picked up in Ferdinand's doublet and hose. His stockinged feet suggest humility before his beloved but the golden chain and elegant pearls at his cuffs signify his undeniable royalty. His dark curls are counterpointed with her auburn tresses, enhanced by a loose, corn-yellow, Pre-Raphaelite robe, striped with pale sea-green. Her sleeves and bosom are bound with iridescent sea-pearls and on her wrist is an amber coloured bracelet. The artist implies that Miranda's nobility is innate and needs no outward marks of crowns or chains.

A diaphanous, flower-sprinkled curtain across the mouth of the cave is drawn back to reveal the lovers – exactly as it would have been on the Shakespearean stage. Lucy has inserted her trademark 'picture within a picture', echoing Shakespeare's device of a play within a play (*Hamlet*) or a masque within a play (*The Tempest*). A circular watery image shows the rosy-fingered dawn (of a new world) emerging over distant white cliffs, while a green surf laps the ship and breaks on the beach.

Members of Lucy's family modelled for this ambitious composition, providing a double interest for the viewer today.[59] This is undoubtedly one of the richest and most allusive of Lucy's surviving pictures. Its literary subject matter ensures that it is a picture to be 'read' as well as enjoyed for its exquisite visual impact. It was Lucy's first oil painting for public exhibition and it hangs today in its original frame, exactly as it did when first shown at the avant-garde Dudley Gallery, London, in 1872, priced at £105.[60]

For her next picture Lucy chose a more obscure literary text but an equally romantic theme. She was just completing it when William Rossetti called round at the Madox Browns on Sunday, 31 December 1871. 'Very good indeed,' he recorded in his diary and 'greatly more satisfactory than I had (from what Gabriel had told me) expected to find it.'[61] The subject of *The Fair Geraldine* or *The Magic Mirror* (fig. 88), a richly detailed watercolour, is drawn from Thomas Nashe's *The Unfortunate Traveller* (1594).[62]

When the poet and early sonneteer, the Earl of Surrey, fell in love with stately Geraldine, he declared: 'her high exalted sunbeams have set the Phoenix nest of my breast on fire, and I myself have brought Arabian spiceries of sweet passions and praises to furnish out the funeral flame of my folly'. However, he was committed to travel abroad, to Italy, for which he asked Fair Geraldine's permission. 'She very discreetly answered me that if my love were so hot as I had often avouched, I did very well to apply the plaster of absence unto it, for absence, as they say, causeth forgetfulness.' While abroad, the Earl of Surrey met Cornelius Agrippa, a famous scholar and the 'greatest conjuror in Christendom'. Surrey's servant persuaded him to test Geraldine's fidelity by asking the magician to show him 'the lively image of Geraldine, his love, in the glass, and what at that instant she did and with whom she was talking'. Has she forgotten the anguish of her poetic lover? 'He showed her us without any more ado, sick weeping on her bed, and resolved all into devout religion for the absence of her lord.' Geraldine had been faithful to her one true love and the magic mirror reflected a tearful image of legendary female loyalty.

In Lucy's picture, Cornelius Agrippa (modelled by William Stillman, husband of Marie Spartali) draws aside a curtain from a huge circular mirror. But Lucy has transformed the story and the image in the mirror. Geraldine is still

88. Lucy Madox Brown, *The Fair Geraldine* or *The Magic Mirror; Cornelius Agrippa showing the Fair Geraldine in a Magic Mirror to the Earl of Surrey*, completed 1871, exhibited Dudley Gallery 1872. Watercolour on paper, 736 × 635 mm. Private collection.

faithful but she is no longer lachrymose on her bed. Instead she is discovered in nature, seated in a garden of courtly love, reading by a lake. The book in her hands, absorbing her totally, is appropriately *The Songs and Sonnets of the Earl of Surrey.*

When William Rossetti first saw the picture he was taken aback by the startling vision of Geraldine dominating the whole composition and her poet-lover, kneeling in spellbound adoration of his constant mistress. Love may be changeable, suggested by the chameleon running down the top right-hand side of the canvas, life itself transmutable by death, indicated by a turning globe, a skull and a 'Vanitas' book, but fair Geraldine has remained true to the Earl of Surrey. Human love, suggests the artist, is perfectible, even in the face of adversity and separation. Accordingly, Lucy's palette is warm and life enhancing. An oriental, man-made, mulberry patterned carpet in the foreground complements the greenery-yallery of Geraldine's natural garden of love. The viewer is led ever upwards in a series of subtle reds from a small flight of steps to the magician's claret robe, via Surrey's slashed russet costume to the copper pot of flames and curling smoke that frames the vision of Geraldine. Lucy has provided not just one but two pictures within a picture. The magic mirror is the central focus but at the top-left corner a Tudor lattice window opens onto the rooftops of an elaborately timbered town, perhaps Wittenberg or the court of the Emperor Charles V, both staging posts in the Earl of Surrey's travels.

A year later Lucy chose as her subject a macabre and dramatic moment from English history (fig. 89). On the reverse of the oil painting, a descriptive label reads 'Margaret Roper by night stealthily removes the head of her father Sir Thomas More from London Bridge AD 1534 – painted by Mrs Rossetti, 37 Fitzroy Square W. Oil price 250£.' This was the picture's price when exhibited in Manchester in 1875, having been previously shown in Liverpool in 1873. In 1875 it went to the Dudley Gallery at the reduced but still substantial price of 128 guineas.

Morbid historical subjects appealed to Lucy. On her honeymoon in April 1874, although suffering one of her perennial chills and general malaise, she particularly admired another decapitated subject, *Judith Beheading Holofernes* (1869) in the Musée des Beaux Arts at Marseilles. The artist was Frenchman Henri Regnault, romantically killed in the Franco-Prussian war at only twenty-eight, who had specialized in oriental themes which combined terror with high emotion, in rich, glamorous colours. 'Haine au gris, c'est là mon cri de guerre', he told Mallarmé.[63] Spectators fainted when his towering picture *Exécution sans jugement sous les rois maures de Granade* was first exhibited in Paris in 1866. Gabriel believed that had he lived Regnault could have been France's greatest painter since Géricault, although he found the 'repeated tendency to head-chopping' in his principal works extremely strange.[64] Another

89. Lucy Madox Brown, *Margaret Roper Rescuing the Head of her Father, Sir Thomas More from London Bridge*, 1873. Oil on canvas, 63 × 49 cm, signed in monogram and dated lower left 'LMB – 73'. Exhibited Liverpool 1873, at the Dudley Gallery and at Manchester 1875. Private collection.

French artist, Pierre Puvis de Chavannes, also captivated by the theme of head-chopping, painted several versions of *The Beheading of Saint John the Baptist* during the years *c.*1865–70, contemporary with Regnault's *Judith*.

Lucy's gruesome subject allowed her to focus on issues of moral rectitude and the theme of mutual father/daughter love, which passionately interested her. She was attracted to the figure of Margaret Roper, an iconic heroine and famously educated woman, so she located Margaret Roper as the central figure in a drama both personal and political.

Balancing precariously in a small rowing boat on the swirling Thames, deep in the shadow cast by London Bridge, Margaret is receiving the head of her father lowered to her in a basket from the pike where it was displayed after execution. Henry VIII's Lord Chancellor More had wrestled with his conscience and found himself unable to support Henry's divorce from Catherine of Aragon or his Act of Supremacy, repudiating Papal rule from Rome. For this, Sir Thomas More paid the ultimate price. Margaret had always been his most brilliant, most studious and favourite daughter. Her husband, and More's son-in-law, William Roper, immortalized in literature Margaret's last moments with her father – a scene that had been painted in 1863 by William Frederick Yeames:

> Desirous to see her father, whom she thought she should never see in this world after, and also to have his final blessing, [she] gave attendance about the Tower wharf, where she knew he would pass by, before he could enter into the Tower…As soon as she saw him, after his blessing on her knees reverently received, she hasting towards him, and without consideration or care of herself, pressing in among the middest of the throng and company of the guard that with halberds and bills went round about him, hastily ran to him, and there openly, in the sight of all, embraced him, took him about the neck and kissed him. Who, well liking her most natural and dear daughterly affection towards him, gave her his fatherly blessing and many godly words of comfort besides. From whom after she was departed, she not satisfied with the former sight of him, and like one that had forgotten herself, being all ravished with the entire love of her dear father, having respect neither to herself nor to the press of the people and multitude that were there about him, suddenly turned back again, ran to him as before, took him about the neck, and divers times together most lovingly kissed him, and at last, with a full heavy heart, was fain to depart from him.[65]

Biblical echoes in Roper's language emphasize the almost Christ-like dimensions of More's figure swept along by the throng as he is led to certain sacrifice. Lucy's choice of the rescue of More's severed head depicts a different stage of the drama from Yeames's earlier picture. Her treatment of the head recalls Roper's implicit analogy and traditional, pictorial views of

Christ on the cross, but in Lucy's picture the Virgin Mary's saintly mother-hood is replaced with saintly daughterhood.

When I first saw the picture, the custodian had arranged for a lineal descendant of Sir Thomas More to show it to me. It was an uncanny link, not with Lucy, but much further back into the historical past that inspired her picture. Margaret Roper died about nine years after More's execution and her father's head was buried with her in the More family grave. Margaret nurtured and cherished her father to the end and beyond. Lucy identified with this relationship. She saw her father as a major artist crucified by criticism and cruel lack of recognition. In her own mind, she was his champion, as Margaret had been More's rescuer.

Lucy's figure of Margaret Roper expresses daring combined with tenderness. Margaret is the proactive protagonist in her own story; kneeling in a religious pose, her loving arms reach upwards to receive the head from its grisly cradle. She is wearing a dark, fur-edged, Pre-Raphaelite hooded robe, sleeves puffed at the shoulder, fitting tightly down to the wrists. A flash of red braid enlivens her costume, symbolizing the blood that has been shed. The drama and danger of her mission is underlined by the straining figure of the Tudor boatman, perhaps Margaret's husband William Roper, struggling to steady his oar, cropped off at the left-hand edge of the picture, brilliantly suggesting in the moonlight the motion of his fragile craft and the threat of discovery in mid-rescue. Lucy's daring use of cropping or cut-offs heightens the sense of instantaneity.

Blank slabs of impersonal brickwork facing London Bridge emphasize Fate's indifference to More's end and Margaret's predicament, but this is offset by the Christian symbolism of a three-spired church at the extreme right of the picture, and a jet cross and rosary centre-foreground in the bottom of the boat. Sir Thomas More died for his religion and his religion did not forget him. The Roman Catholic Church beatified him in 1886, thirteen years after Lucy painted this picture.

Lucy's treatment of history is original and provocative. Shifting Sir Thomas More from the centre of his own story to a bit player, she directs the spotlight instead onto Margaret, a secondary actor in the drama. Writer and feminist Mathilde Blind may have modelled for the figure of Margaret Roper. Certainly, Margaret's Pre-Raphaelite robe is similar to the dress Mathilde chose to wear when Lucy painted her portrait (see fig. 90), but the bright gold halo of Margaret's hair suggests Cathy Madox Brown as the model. Lucy's treatment of her subject is unflinching as the head swings down to Margaret's waiting arms, the dark scene lit only by expectation of dawn in the night sky and livid flashes of moonlight on the faces of the living and the dead. The artist was particularly interested in chiaroscuro and her light effects are always subtle and dramatic. In this picture Lucy addressed life and death, belief and

90. Lucy Madox Brown, *Mathilde Blind*, 1872. Black, red and white chalks on grey paper, 770 × 550 mm, signed in monogram and dated 'LMB – 72'. By kind permission of the Principal and Fellows of Newnham College, Cambridge.

unbelief, mortality and immortality within an elemental setting of unearthly light and swirling waters. It is not a comfortable picture. It was not intended to be. But it is dramatic and unforgettable.

In addition to such complex and ambitious compositions, Lucy produced a number of single-figure portraits.[66] Her striking portrait of Mathilde Blind (fig. 90) shows one strong creative woman seen through the eyes of another. Although born in Germany, Mathilde Blind (1841–96), poet, biographer, translator, editor and feminist, came to England with her stepfather Karl Blind where both became close friends of the Madox Browns. In April 1883, Lucy and Cathy felt that Mathilde had become too close a friend to their father and usurped their role as daughters, let alone Emma's role as wife. Bitter rows ensued. Madox Brown was deeply distressed, his daughters patched up relations with Mathilde for his sake, but in the last years of her life when both Mathilde and Lucy were sick women, unforgiving Lucy refused to see her old friend. But even William entertained suspicions that Madox Brown might have secretly married Mathilde, who had been in her youth a person 'of extreme beauty and fire'.[67] Ford Madox [Ford] Hueffer told William in 1905 that his grandfather had wanted to marry Mathilde after Emma's death in 1890. He consulted Cathy 'with a view to preserving harmony in the family'. (Lucy was not mentioned in Ford's account, but by then she had been dead for over a decade.) Apparently Cathy waived her objections and the marriage would have taken place if Madox Brown had been in better health.[68]

However, at the time of the portrait sittings, artist and subject, who were almost exact contemporaries, were at least intellectually compatible. Lucy's study shows a freethinking woman of the mind, presented with the tools of her profession. A mane of wavy, dark hair frames Mathilde's 'fine, animated, speaking countenance'.[69] Her eyes are fixed on a faraway object beyond the right outside edge of the picture. Instead of conventional Victorian dress, she wears an aesthetic robe in sage green, trimmed at its deep neckline and cuffs with grey fur. A vivid orange wrap is arranged with artful carelessness around her shoulders. In her capable hands are pen and paper from which she has raised her gaze, apparently lost in thought. The poet fills the canvas, a commanding, monumental figure, although she was in fact petite. Lucy has used the soft versatility of pastel chalks to create a picture composed of textures that contrast provocatively with one another – fur and hair, textiles and skin.

In 1867 Mathilde published her first volume of *Poems* under the pseudonym Claude Lake. She was committed to the emancipation of women and in particular to their education. She wrote biographies of George Eliot (1883) and Madame Roland (1886) – and gave an inscribed copy of the latter[70] to Lucy – in the same Eminent Women Writers series edited by John Ingram, for which Lucy wrote *Mrs Shelley* (1890). Mathilde met the young artist Marie Bashkirtseff in Nice where both had gone to seek relief from consumption. Mathilde's 1890 English translation of Marie's dazzling *Journal* has still not been superseded. Women's right to a better education was a concern Mathilde shared with Lucy, who was grateful for the superior education her father had managed to provide for her, first at Helen Bromley's school, then privately in the Rossetti household, and finally, artistic training in his own studio.

Lucy grew up proficient in languages, music and art, avid for academic discipline. It is fascinating to speculate what Lucy and Mathilde talked about during sittings for this portrait – intellectual pursuits or family gossip or both. Mathilde's face has a nakedness about it, but Lucy herself, a modern 'girl of the period', was not averse to some touches of strategic make-up, as William Bell Scott noted disapprovingly at a party: 'all the ladies at least Mrs B and Lucy – quite fluffy in the faces with white powder, I can't think Brown ought to let them.'[71] Seeing the portrait in 1906 after the deaths of both artist and sitter, William considered it a 'correct likeness' but only valued it at

91. Lucy Madox Brown, *Maria Rossetti as an Anglican Nun, c.* 1873/4. Pencil. Published in Georgina Battiscombe's *Christina Rossetti*, 1981. Private collection.

'£22–£25', as 'heads done in tinted chalks do not, as such, command very high prices'.[72]

Lucy drew her old tutor Maria Rossetti in about 1873–4 (fig. 91). Large, free pencil strokes depict an enveloping wimple beneath which Maria's broad, Italianate features are strongly delineated. In spite of her own lack of conventional religious belief, Lucy sympathetically conveys Maria's commitment to her faith and to the life she has chosen. Maria already guessed she had cancer and Gabriel worried about the Spartan regime in the convent that, all too soon, might make her 'noviciate for another world', as he shuddered to William.[73] She had entered the All Saints Sisterhood when Lucy began the portrait. Details of her habit would change when she exchanged the robes of a novice for those of a nun. Maria provided Lucy's 'artistic eye' with a punctilious list of what should and should not be included. Apart from a white hood, cap-strings, collar, and black rope girdle knotted at the side, Maria wrote very affectionately to her old pupil, now her sister-in-law, explaining there should be 'no cross on the breast, but a large black one at the end of the girdle, too low I believe to come into your drawing at all.'[74]

Much later, in 1887, Lucy painted a watercolour portrait of Signorina Carsini who, William recorded, 'gave Italian lessons to our children at San Remo'.[75] Lucy's *Portrait of a Parisian Landlady* was seen in the north of England during the 1960s by the artist L. S. Lowry, together with Mrs Phyllis Marshall of the Stone Gallery, now in Burford. Mrs Marshall told me that she and L. S. Lowry 'agreed that it was an excellent work'.[76]

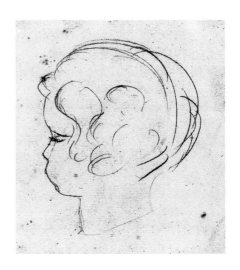

92. Lucy Madox Brown, *Head of a Child*, undated. Pencil, 105 × 98 mm. Private collection.

Lucy also produced portraits of at least two of her children. In February 1879 she was working on a portrait of Olivia in coloured chalks and a year later she worked up an oil portrait of her eldest daughter, then aged three and a half.[77] Her father wrote to her from Manchester, their symbiotic relationship deepened by mutual discussion of work, 'I hope you are getting on in some wise with your picture, I almost want you here as you want me'.[78] When Michael Rossetti, Lucy's youngest child and Mary's twin, died on 24 January 1883, Lucy tried to calm herself by working on a crayon-tinted picture of the eighteen-months-old baby who probably suffered tubercular meningitis. She made in death what Christina called 'one never-to-be-forgotten drawing',[79] a *Posthumous Portrait of Michael Rossetti, his Pillows Strewn with Snowdrops*,[80] as he had bloomed as briefly as the winter flower. A tiny pencil drawing by Lucy of a child's head about the same age as Michael came to light at the Christie's sale (fig. 92). Its swift simple lines captured the essence of babyhood.

After the death of Michael in 1883, Lucy often externalized her grief and lamented to William that she was a 'failure'. He tried to empathize with her feelings of inadequacy and to encourage her to paint again. 'I feel very much for you, dear Lu, in the dejection wh. comes over you now & again at the thought that you had it in you to do something conspicuous in art, & that time & tide are drifting the chance away. But it is still in your power, if you like, to resume some amount of art-work & do good things', he wrote.[81] Increasingly, though, her subjects were drawn from the domestic arena.

Cathy's daughter Juliet stayed for a while with her Rossetti cousins at the end of the 1880s when she vividly remembered Aunt Lucy's educational methods. Juliet also remembered the boy who may have been the model for *André* (fig. 93), a sulky 'anarchist page-boy...the son of my aunt's French cook. He had red hair and a cross, spotty face...he never seemed to do much work.

93. Lucy Madox Brown, *Portrait of André, c.* 1889. Chalks on coloured paper, 560 × 458 mm. Private collection.

He disliked work because it tired him so.' Like all children in the Rossetti household, André held Marxist political views. The difference was that he was 'a uniformed slave of the capitalist system' and hated wearing a coat 'with a long row of degrading buttons up the front as a token of servitude.' Lucy's *André* certainly seems to be wearing some sort of uniform, with a row of buttons up to his chin, a handkerchief in his top pocket, and braid round the sleeves of his jacket. His expression is passive rather than revolutionary but maybe he is biding his time.

Juliet reports that he called himself 'a son of France' and chillingly warned her and the Rossetti children

> that in France they had once got up a revolution and chopped the heads off all the tyrants. Tyrants' heads rolled off into the basket underneath the guillotine as quickly as peas out of the shucks into the basin when his mother shelled them. One day, he said, the same thing would happen here, and then '*our*' turn would come, and he and his mother and their kind would triumph...we used to sit round him on the floor, and hug our knees and listen. We felt ashamed and apologetic, and it was very difficult to think

of anything to say to comfort him. Of course, it wasn't our fault, and we longed for the revolution. It was in our programme. Once my aunt [Lucy] came in and found him lying on the sofa, and she grabbed him by the ear and led him straight out of the room, right to the top of the kitchen stairs. She said she only kept him for his mother's sake. We all got up from the floor and stood close together. I shall never forget how angry we were, and how terrible our faces looked when she was doing it. It seemed to come just as a proof of what he was always saying: how unjust the world was, and how the tyrants always got the best of it.[82]

If Lucy's relationship with young André was as tempestuous as Juliet remembers, it is surprising that she chose him as a subject for a portrait at all. Perhaps the portrait was a peace offering between them, Lucy's democratic validation of André's identity, which nevertheless captured all that locked-in resentment of a servant for a 'tyrant'. André stares fixedly ahead, his hands loosely clasped in his lap, a study in muted brown and cream against a deeper yellow background and green curtain folds. His mouth is set as if he has refused to speak to the artist.

Lucy's artistic taste more usually tended to the literary and historic rather than to the domestic. In 1875 she triumphantly bought 'cheap' from a shop in Cleveland Street, very near her home, a sixteenth-century Venetian painting *A Legend of St John*, an epic scene which she attributed to Veronese although William thought it might be a Tintoretto.[83] After marriage, her own artistic subjects mostly contracted to studies of her children or landscapes drawn on seaside family holidays. These were the years in the mid-1870s when Lucy had an account at the leading suppliers of artists' materials, Roberson's of Covent Garden – where Gabriel had bought his colours since 1850. Several landscapes by Lucy were recorded in William's 1908 inventory: *Trees* (1868–70, unlocated); *Lynmouth* (1872, unlocated), watercolour landscape, exhibited at the Dudley Gallery; *Charmouth, Dorset* (see fig. 96), a watercolour painted in 1878 and sent to a provincial gallery in March 1879, together with *Broadstairs*, probably begun in April 1876, dated '79',[84] (fig. 94); and three Biarritz sketches (1889), watercolour sketches of sea and sky (unlocated)[85].

Her father considered *Lynmouth*, which Lucy painted during a Madox Brown summer holiday in 1871, a 'fine' landscape and planned to price it at 12 or 15 guineas.[86] Lucy exhibited *Lynmouth* at the Dudley Gallery in 1872, at the same time as *Ferdinand and Miranda Playing Chess* and *The Fair Geraldine,* or *The Magic Mirror*. She was able to perceive the dramatic potential in landscape, as well as in literature and history. *Lynmouth* showed 'the houses of the rock-environed Devonshire village, and the brawling Lynn running close below and between'.[87] Years later in 1888 when writing her biography of Mary Shelley, Lucy remembered 'that terrestrial paradise in North Devon, Lynmouth.' She conflated Shelleyan myth with her own nostalgia. 'This

94. Lucy Madox Brown, *Broadstairs*, signed in monogram, lower left and dated [18]79. Watercolour, 305 × 457 mm. Private collection.

lovely place, with its beautiful and romantic surroundings loved and exquisitely described by more than one poet, cannot fail to be dear to those who know it with and through them. Here, in a garden in front of their rose and myrtle covered cottage, within near sound of the rushing Lynn, would Shelley stand on a mound and let off his fire-balloons in the cool evening air'.[88]

William went ahead to Charmouth to find suitable lodgings for Lucy, Olive and Arthur for their summer holidays of 1878. He described the picturesque outlook from his breakfast table for his 'Dearest Love' on 5 July, and enclosed a sketch too (fig. 95).[89]

Lucy's intense watercolour (fig. 96)[90] retains and amplifies strong compositional features suggested by William's swift sketch. She and the children stayed on until late August in Charmouth, painting and fossil hunting on the beach after high tides when the sea was calm following a storm. William in

95. William Michael Rossetti, *Charmouth*, in a letter from William to Lucy, 5 July 1878, 8.30 a.m. Pencil, 113 × 179 mm. University of British Columbia Library, Rare Books and Special Collections, Angeli-Dennis Collection 7-8.

96. Lucy Madox
Brown,
Charmouth,
1878/9.
Watercolour.
Signed with
monogram and
dated 'LMR 79',
lower right.
Private collection.

particular loved searching for ammonites but professional duties meant he
had to return earlier than the rest of the family to his office at Somerset
House.

Lucy continued to draw landscapes even as her physical strength declined.
On her first therapeutic visit to San Remo during the winter of 1886/7 with
her two eldest children Olive and Arthur, Lucy still had energy and inclination
to work at her art. But she felt isolated from the professional art world and
feared her father would find her efforts pitiful. 'I send a roll containing 3
sketches', she wrote home to William, 'one sunset for Maizy [Mary] – a head of
Signorina [Carsini, the children's Italian tutor][91] for you & the other view from
window to be sent on to Nelly [Helen] – I am afraid Papa will think them very
bad but they will give some idea to the babes'.[92] The two youngest children,
Helen (Nelly/Coodle) just seven and Mary (Maizy) aged five, were being cared
for in England respectively by Emma and Madox Brown, and Cathy and Frank
Hueffer. Lucy's consumptive illness increasingly split up the family.

Further items of Lucy's *oeuvre* remain undiscovered or ambiguous.
William's 1908 inventory recorded a chalk *Female Life Study c.* 1876, now
untraced, [93] and in his diary for Friday, 12 April 1878, he noted, 'L. has
resumed of late her picture of Clarissa Harlowe: is also drawing from the
model at her father's, and speculates on the ambitious work she had long
thought of – Venus staying the hand of Aeneas, about to slay Helen.' None of
these pictures has surfaced, but William's record suggests that four years into
marriage and after the birth of her first two children, Lucy still proposed
working on major projects drawn from literature and mythical history, such as
Richardson's great, complex heroine Clarissa and Virgil's epic treatment of
interaction between gods and mortals. The diurnal round had failed to crush
Lucy's ambition.

Other pictures have been attributed to Lucy. An undated watercolour *A Girl at a Lacquer Cabinet* is mentioned as a footnote in William Money Hardinge's eulogistic article after her death,[94] and may or may not be the same as *Mary Anne and Chinese Cabinet*, a large gilt-framed but undated watercolour that appears on Helen Rossetti Angeli's single-page handwritten inventory of 1948.[95]

Another conundrum is *The Fugitive*, reproduced in *Women and Art* (1978) by Elsa Honig Fine who attributes the picture to Lucy (fig. 97).[96] *The Fugitive* is unlocated but Elsa Honig Fine was able to reproduce it from a photograph. Responding to my enquiry, she wrote: 'On the back of the photo is written Mrs. W.M. Rossetti "The Fugitive" 22 ½ × 16" Collier Sale, Christie 11. 2. 21. I don't know who wrote it or where I got the photograph from. The signature is FR.'[97] Christie's records of the Thomas Collier Sale confirm that *The Fugitive*, a picture on panel, attributed to Mrs W.M. Rossetti, was sold by A.L. Nicholson for eighteen guineas to 'Gamanalza', or a similar name, difficult to decipher accurately.

The black and white reproduction in Elsa Honig Fine's book shows a scene dramatic enough for Lucy. A young barefoot girl is sheltering against the trunk of a mighty tree, her long, loose hair dishevelled, an apron reaching midway down her calf-length dress. She also wears two individual conical breastplates so that her costume is a curious blend of the domestic and the military. Is she aware of the Lear-like figure spying on her from behind the tree? The two figures are caught in a mysterious relationship and the unidentified situation is pregnant with menace. Tempting though it might be to

97. *The Fugitive*, attribution uncertain, undated, signed in monogram, lower left, FR (?). Panel, 57.2 × 40.6 cm. Unlocated.

accept Christie's 1921 attribution to Lucy, it seems unlikely to be right. As far as can be made out from the small reproduction, the painting style seems quite different from Lucy's – and the initialled signature 'FR', totally different from the way Lucy signed or monogrammed her pictures, usually but not invariably, 'LMB + date.' Rossetti descendants are unable to recall any picture of Lucy's that corresponds to *The Fugitive*. One explanation might be that the picture once belonged to 'Mrs. W.M. Rossetti' and in 1921 Christie's staff may have mistaken a note of provenance for one of attribution.

When the young artist William Rothenstein dined with William Rossetti a few days after painting his portrait in January 1909 he was beguiled by the art from a past era all over the house at 3 St Edmund's Terrace. But the pictures that he praised most wholeheartedly and emphatically were Lucy's.[98] Almost a century later the town where she died, San Remo, gave Lucy rebirth when it welcomed her back as a key artist in their Millennium Exhibition during April and May 2000.

6

Man of Letters

A pioneer in critical judgment
    Helen Rossetti Angeli, letter to H.M. Hake, director of the National Portrait
    Gallery, 20 December 1930[1]

I myself should always have liked to be a literary personage, doing literary work of my own the best I could: my position did not allow of this, and what I had to be was a Government-clerk giving his spare hours to newspaper-critiques etc.
    William Michael Rossetti to Elsie Hueffer (Mrs Ford Madox Hueffer),
    1904[2]

When Helen Rossetti Angeli offered Rothenstein's portrait of William Michael Rossetti to the National Portrait Gallery in 1930 she described it as 'a powerful and vivid piece of work' (see fig. 35). She wanted her father represented in the gallery where other Rossettis were already included, 'on his own merits, for his own distinction...as a critic and a man of letters. It is perhaps, at the present moment, not as widely recognized as it should be, that he was in a sense a pioneer in critical judgment – one of the first, if not the first, to recognize and affirm without hesitation the genius of Shelley, Blake, Whitman and other immortals – let alone what he did for his own family.'[3]

In old age, William underestimated the effect of his output, his 'great literary influence and eloquent pen' – in the words of the young Oscar Wilde.[4] In fact, the sheer variety, scope, industry and energy of William Rossetti's literary career was overwhelming. Looking at random at the first half of 1886 when he was fifty-six years old, working full-time for the Inland Revenue, apprehensive about Lucy's incipient tuberculosis, children's chickenpox, his own increasing deafness and the decline and death of his mother, his diary reveals a huge range of literary commitments. In these months, January to July 1886, he contributed to Arthur Mackmurdo's Century Guild *Hobby Horse,* the *Athenaeum* and the *Pall Mall Gazette* on subjects ranging from Ford Madox Brown's art, Dante's *Paradiso,* the truth about Shakespeare, a new biography of Longfellow, Mathilde Blind's poetry, an obituary of his mother and proportional representation in Ireland. He researched entries for Encyclopaedia Britannica on Titian, Solario and Shelley. He prepared a *Collected Edition* of Gabriel's poetry with a biographical preface, wrote a preface to the *Letters of Anne Gilchrist,* attended to reissues of his 1868 selection of Whitman and his

98. William Michael Rossetti, photographed by Richard Randall, Broadstairs. Cathy Hueffer's photograph album, STH/BH/2/3-6. The Stow Hill Collection, HLRO, and the Hon. Oliver Soskice.

1870/8 *Memoir of Shelley*, chaired the Shelley Society, wrote a lecture on *Prometheus Unbound*, wound up the Whitman subscription fund, conferred with Furnivall about publishing *Cor Cordium* – his own compilation of Shelley's autobiographical documents – and finally accepted a commission to write a biography of Keats. Such a catalogue of activity completely belies his modest assertion on 5 July 1886 that 'My habit is to put off the evil day of added work of whatever kind' (fig. 98).[5]

William's most important literary works were those acts of scholarship and remembrance he undertook to establish not only the whole Rossetti family myth but also much of Pre-Raphaelite history. He outlived all the Rossettis to conserve their fame in his editions, biographies and memoirs and in published collections of their personal papers and letters. In so doing, he became literary executor not only to the Rossetti family but also to the Pre-Raphaelite Brotherhood. Scholars of the movement today are indebted to his pioneering work.

As one of the seven original members of the Brotherhood, founded in autumn 1848, he reported on it from a unique standpoint. Reproduced in Holman Hunt's autobiography in 1905,[6] a swift sketch takes us in to an early P.R.B. meeting where an Italian coffee pot simmers invitingly on the range and all the excitement of shared passions for art and literature, the stimulus of youthful talk and debate are instantly captured (fig. 99). On the left, Millais reads aloud to Gabriel, propped against the back of his armchair in poetic pose. Woolner is pointing to Collinson's sketchpad. On the right of the picture,

William, in an elegant, long-limbed pose mirrors his brother's attitude as he leans over Collinson's shoulders to comment on the invisible drawing.

Nearly half a century later, it was William who explained the fundamental aims of the new, secret Pre-Raphaelite society: '1, To have genuine ideas to express; 2, to study Nature attentively, so as to know how to express them; 3, to sympathize with what is direct and serious and heartfelt in previous art…and 4, and most indispensable of all, to produce thoroughly good pictures and statues.'[7] Presenting modern issues through the palimpsest of medieval art gave Pre-Raphaelitism its shock and excitement. In style and technique the 'Brothers' looked to early Italian masters (literally pre-Raphael) but their themes and subject matter – fallen women, prostitution, illegitimacy, suicide and adultery – all challenged social taboos. In effect, they made the medieval modern. They were realists. Through their peculiarity they also made English art universal or at least international. 'Consider for a moment', wrote Ford Madox Ford, the novelist who saw himself as the 'last of the pre-Raffaelites [*sic*]', to his fifteen-year-old daughter in 1935, 'the pre-Raffaelites are the only English artists who cut any ice at all outside England. They are admired in these other countries for a certain dogged sincerity – and they are not more admired than they are because they were muddle-headed beings born into a very bad period'.[8]

As secretary to the Pre-Raphaelite Brotherhood and its 'catalytic agent',[9] it was William's special function to keep a diary of their informal meetings and day-to-day doings in the *P.R.B Journal*. In a slightly bizarre reflection of his minute-keeping duties at the Inland Revenue, he kept an invaluable record of Pre-Raphaelite activities between 1849 and 1853. The document was subsequently stripped of up to a third of its material by unknown hands, probably Gabriel's. But William's *Journal*, in the restored version published by William E. Fredeman in 1975, gives us the only first-hand insight, apart from surviving letters, into the early days of this radical new art movement. At their most vivacious, perhaps when William took annual leave from the day-job, his *Journal* entries are concise, informative and amusing:

99. Arthur Hughes's copy of Holman Hunt's sketch, *The Pre-Raphaelite Meeting 1848*. L to r, DGR, Millais, Woolner, Collinson, Stephens and WMR. From Holman Hunt's *Pre-Raphaelitism*, 1905.

Tuesday 29th May 1849: I went in the morning to the Society of British Artists, calling in the way, with Gabriel, on Hunt, who was out; – he having proposed to take a night walk. Scarcely anything good at the Gallery…Between 10 and 11 Hunt called, when we finally resolved to postpone our walk. Talked and did portraits. We have received a letter from Millais, who says that there's a most splendid critique of his and Hunt's work in the *Builder.*

Wednesday 30th May 1849: …On going to the Class in the afternoon, I was told that, on her unrobing [the Model's], she was unanimously requested not to give herself so much trouble; and we have determined, as the preferable alternative, to draw her dressed almost entirely. She is very fat and at least 45.[10]

William himself was a far more graceful (and clothed) model – he was often asked to pose in the evening and at weekends for the full-time artists in the group.[11]

William's minutes record the birth of the *Germ*, the experimental literary arts magazine produced by the Pre-Raphaelites, offering the public a stimulating mix of poems, short stories, illustrations and reviews. It survived for just four issues in 1850 under William's managing-editorship. It is now a coveted collector's item. Contributors included Ford Madox Brown, Dante Gabriel Rossetti, Christina Rossetti, Coventry Patmore, William Bell Scott, Thomas Woolner, Frederic George Stephens, Walter Deverell and John Lucas Tupper. William wrote a sonnet for the *Germ*'s cover, so tortuous that William Bell Scott complained 'it would almost need a Browning Society's united intellects' to unravel its meaning'.[12] But Arthur Hughes found it inspiring.[13]

In this studiedly avant-garde arts magazine William, aged only twenty, printed some of his own poems but more importantly the first of his perceptive reviews of contemporary poetry, thus launching his career as a literary critic. As with modern art, his instincts never failed to direct him to the best of the new in contemporary literature. He was one of the most enthusiastic reviewers of Arthur Hugh Clough's brilliantly witty extended poem, *The Bothie of Toper-na-fuosich*[14] (later re-titled by the poet *The Bothie of Tober-na-Vuolich*, because some critics, not William, had complained the original title meant 'the bearded well' – Gaelic slang for the female genitalia).[15]

William welcomed the poem's fresh treatment of sexuality and feminism, as well as the sheer novelty of Clough's risk-taking text 'that unites the most enduring forms of nature, and the most unsophisticated conditions of life and character, with the technicalities of speech, of manners, and of persons of an Oxford reading party in the long vacation.'[16] His fast developing democratic ideals were matched in the romance and the message of Clough's poem – that true love may be found in humble places. Like Clough's clever young hero Philip Hewson, 'the Chartist, the poet, the eloquent speaker', in 1848 William was a Chartist sympathizer. Philip was as bored with Victorian middle-class courting rituals as the daring Pre-Raphaelite Brothers. Like so many of them, Philip found love and inspiration not in 'your Lady Augustas and Floras' but in working-class women, such as Elspie in Clough's poem, discovered in her earthy toil:

> Bending with three-pronged fork in a garden uprooting potatoes.
> Was it the air? Who can say? or herself, or the charm of the labour?
> But a new thing was in me; and longing delicious possessed me,
> Longing to take her and lift her, and put her away from her slaving.
> Was it embracing or aiding was most in my mind? Hard question!
> But a new thing was in me...[17]

In admiration for what he acutely identified as Clough's 'peculiar modern-ness'[18] William quoted page-long extracts from *The Bothie*. Clough asked Professor Heimann who had given him a copy of the *Germ* to convey his appreciation, 'I do not know who has honoured my almost forgotten Pastoral with so kind a criticism as I find in its pages', he wrote on 24 January 1850, 'but I must beg my thanks to the writer.'[19]

In the *Germ*'s second issue, William reviewed Mathew Arnold's collection *The Strayed Reveller; and other Poems*.[20] The youthfulness in William responded to and admired the maturity in Arnold, the constant evidence of a 'well-poised and serious mind', which the new critic again exemplified with generous quotation from the text. In the fourth and final issue of the *Germ*, William discussed Robert Browning's poetry in general and *Christmas Eve and Easter Day* in particular, which allowed him to air his theories about a critic's duties, 'to state facts, and to suggest considerations; not to lay down dogmas.' The critic has a right to speak with his own authority. 'He condemns, or gives praise; and his judgment, though merely individual and subject to revision, is judgment.'

William also theorized about poetic style, which in his opinion could never be an absolute, static value but depended on three variables, 'firstly, national; next, chronological; and lastly, individual.' His penetrating discussion of poetics built up to a powerful defence against those Browning detractors who accused him of ruining 'fine thoughts by a vicious, extravagant, and involved style'. On the contrary, William found Browning's works 'replete with mental and speculative subtlety, with vivid and most diversified conception of character, with dramatic incident and feeling; with that intimate knowledge of outward nature which makes every sentence of description a living truth; replete with a most human tenderness and pathos.' Nearly always faithful to the opinions of his youth, he continued to admire Browning's music and metre that were never merely lyrical but 'expressional & emphasising' and often 'absolutely transcendent'.[21]

In 1850 he had nothing but contempt for those carpers who moaned they couldn't read *Sordello*. Why did people think they should be able to understand

Browning at a mere first reading, 'to know Browning's stops, and to pluck out the heart of his mystery?' The young critic was implacable. 'Read Sordello again', he thundered.[22] In August 1850 the *Guardian* commented that some of the best pieces in the, by then defunct, *Germ* were 'by two brothers named Rossetti'.[23]

BEATS EVERYTHING BUT BALZAC

The critic turned practitioner in 1849 when William wrote a long poem *Mrs Holmes Grey*, a unique and daring creative experiment, which aimed to fulfil in poetry the principles the Pre-Raphaelites applied to their works of art. The essential Pre-Raphaelite credo was to see the world with rigorous naturalism, following Wordsworth and Coleridge's manifesto in their 1798 preface to the *Lyrical Ballads* fifty years earlier. William specifically aimed to exclude any elaborate, conscious poetic tropes from his language, 'which professed to be speech uttered in ordinary real life'.[24] *Mrs Holmes Grey* retold an actual crime of passion which William had read about in the press. The sensational story centred on the 'death of a lady, a surgeon's wife, who had died suddenly in the house of another medical man for whom she had conceived a vehement and unreciprocated passion.'[25] William cast the lurid material in the form of discussion and newspaper reports of the coroner's inquest. Even though his medium was blank verse, he tried to convey the tone and language of authentic journalistic reportage:

> *Coroner's Inquest – A Distressing Case.*
> An inquest was held yesterday, before
> The County Coroner, into the cause
> Of the decease of Mrs. Mary Grey,
> A married lady. Public interest
> Was widely excited.
>
> When the Jury came
> From viewing the corpse, in which are seen remains
> Of no small beauty, witnesses were called…
>
> Witness: 'She would clasp
> Her arms around me in speaking tenderly,
> And kiss me. She has often kissed my hands.
> Not beyond that.'
>
> The Juror: 'And did you
> Respond – ' The Coroner: 'The witness should,
> I think, be pressed no further. He has given
> His painful evidence most creditably.'[26]

It was an ambitious attempt to write a genuinely Pre-Raphaelite poem and both Gabriel and Swinburne praised the stark result that culminated in a final night scene 'Equal, unknown, and desolate of stars.' As editor of the *Germ*, William felt he could not print his own creative work. The poem remained unpublished until it appeared nineteen years later in February 1868 in a monthly magazine, the *Broadway Annual*.[27] Swinburne reread William's experimental poem 'with renewed admiration and quite intense interest' on New Year's Day 1868.[28] A month later, he was still enthralled by William's daring project to transfer criminal court proceedings into poetry. 'I *can't* get that blessed poem of yours out of my head. It's all very well, but you beginning in that way ought to have knocked us all out of sight....Do write something more in my line and I'll be the first to admit your superiority. I'm not writing "chaff" – but I have today re-read your poem – and I *can't* hold my tongue, or my fingers. That idea of yours in "Mrs Holmes Grey" beats everything but Balzac. I can't tell you how its choice impresses and excites me.'[29] It seems extraordinary that Swinburne genuinely admired William's stark, unadorned poem. It couldn't have been more different from his own alliterative, assonant, lulling lyricism.

Swinburne, an unlikely but enduring friend for nearly fifty years, dedicated his *William Blake: A Critical Essay* to William, to mark their fervour for another shared enthusiasm – the then unfashionable, visionary poet-painter. 'I can but bring you brass for the gold you send me', wrote Swinburne with 'affectionate admiration', and 'grateful remembrance, which needs no public expression'.[30]

William and Gabriel helped Anne Gilchrist edit her husband's *Life of William Blake* in 1863, for which William supplied the *Annotated Lists of Blake's Paintings and Drawings*. Later, William significantly supplemented Gilchrist's *Life* when he edited *Blake*, with a *Memoir*, for the Aldine Poets' series in 1874. Such wide-ranging literary work firmly established him as a creator and arbiter of cultural taste, often voicing dissenting views from the literary establishment during the central years of the Victorian age. Insightful on both art and literature, he was at the centre of the moral and cultural debate about what and whom art was for. His aesthetic agenda was based on foundations of quiet but unshakeable democratic ideals, endeavouring to move art beyond the orbit of the *cognoscenti*, to demystify and interpret it for ordinary people. It was the same programme as Matthew Arnold's, who wrote in *Culture and Anarchy*: 'The great men of culture...have laboured to divest knowledge of all that was harsh, uncouth, difficult, abstract, professional, exclusive; to humanise it, to make it efficient outside the clique of the cultivated and learned...'[31] Rooted in William's cosmopolitan upbringing, a European dimension underpinned his literary objectives which developed an international perspective as his progressive politics and advanced aesthetic tastes crystallized.

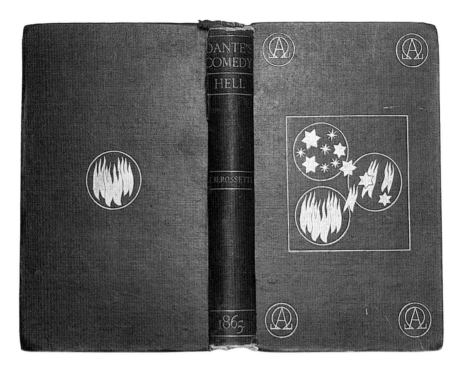

100. Bookbinding by Dante Gabriel Rossetti for William Michael Rossetti's translation of *The Comedy of Dante Allighieri* [sic]. *Part 1 – The Hell*, 1865. Black cloth, 178 × 117 mm. Private collection.

WILLIAM'S 'HELL', 1865

Dante was an elemental figure in William's personal literary landscape. As children, the Rossetti siblings absorbed Dantean culture almost by osmosis – both from their father, Gabriele and from their maternal grandfather, Gaetano Polidori. Christina said that the young Rossettis' Italian roots made the *Divine Comedy* an intrinsic part of their birthright. William recalled that 'Dante Alighieri was a sort of banshee in the Charlotte Street houses; his shriek audible even to familiarity', long before any of them could fully understand his poetry.[32] As an adult, William freely ranked Dante with the greatest. 'I think the height and depth of poetic totality in Dante, power and performance, do entirely outweigh the like in Milton. In fact I think the *only* poetic figure in modern Europe that equals Dante – and he no doubt exceeds him in the general compendium of endowments – is Shakespeare'.[33] In 1861 William translated the prose arguments of Gabriel's version of Dante's *Vita Nuova* and published his own blank verse translation of Dante's *Inferno*, as *The Hell* in 1865.

William's translation is a seductively tactile volume to handle, compact in format, bound in black cloth, now faded to deep sepia (fig. 100). It was the only one of William's books to have a cover design by Gabriel who completed it just weeks before publication at the end of February 1865.

The decorative, wordless front cover is strikingly geometric, blocked in gold on black, emblematic of the flames of hell intermittently bisecting the inferno's perpetual darkness. Within a simple square gold outline in the centre of the front cover are three equally simple gold circles, representing the tripartite structure of Dante's *Divine Comedy* – Hell, Purgatory and Paradise, underlining the Trinity of Christian belief, and echoing the *terza rima*, a three-lined rhyming stanza which Dante invented especially for his epic work. The lowest circle on the left (*sinistra*) contains three tridents of pronged flames, emblems of Hell. Another smaller three-headed flame links this circle upwards to the next circle, Purgatory, containing both flames and aspiring stars. A single star leads the eye upwards and onwards to the highest point of the design, a third circle beatifically sprinkled with stars representing Paradise, the apex of Dante's poetic and theological design. Outside this perfect square containing the three circles, on the outer edges of the front cover are four further smaller circles, each encircling an entwined Alpha and Omega, the beginning and the end of all things, as if bounding the medieval cosmos known to Dante. Thus seven circles emblazon the front cover, seven being the mystical, perfect number.

On the spine these few words appear in elegant, simple capitals:

DANTE'S COMEDY

HELL

W.M. ROSSETTI

1865

The back cover is entirely plain except for a single circle at the centre, Hell's sphere repeated from the front cover to indicate Dante's *Inferno* within the covers, here in William's translation.

Alexander Macmillan had rejected William's translation in 1857 but was prepared to publish in 1865 when William's mother, Frances Rossetti, generously put up funds of £50,[34] partly in appreciation for William's long-term financial support for the family, partly because the Dante project was close to her heart and recalled her husband Gabriele's lifelong devotion to arcane interpretations of the great poet.

In the weeks after publication, William distributed copies of *Hell* among friends and family. At least two survive that are personally inscribed, one to his sister 'Maria Francesca Rossetti with her Brother's love' and one to 'John Ruskin from his affectionate fellow student of Dante W.M.R'.[35] Ruskin sent Rossetti 'a thousand thanks', for the 'very nice' book, tactfully referring to its physical appeal, without embarking on a detailed response to the translation within its hyper-aesthetic covers.[36]

There are hundreds of both Victorian and modern translations of Dante's *Comedy* and it is intriguing to compare a representative modern translation with William Rossetti's. Mark Musa's version of *The Inferno* was first published in 1971, just over a century after William's. The Royal Academy chose extracts from Musa's translation to accompany an exhibition, Botticelli's Dante (2001), because of its direct appeal to modern English-speaking readers.

In their introductions, both Rossetti and Musa refer to Dante's letter to Can Grande della Scala, the ruler of Verona, in which the poet explains that 'a comedy is that which speaks in lowly style, and, beginning harshly, ends prosperously.'[37] Musa quotes the letter at greater length, although both translators keep its implications in mind, together with those conflated from Dante's *Convivio*. 'For the clarity of what will be said, it is to be understood that this work [the *Comedy*] is not simple, but rather it is polysemous, that is, endowed with many meanings. For the first meaning is that which one derives from the letter, another is that which one derives from things signified by the letter. The first is called "literal" and the second "allegorical" or "mystical".'[38] Musa continues, 'The literal level of a work must always be exposed first…you must prepare the wood before you build the table'.[39] If the poet's first intention is to enrapture the reader at a basic level of meaning, then any translator ignores this advice at his peril. Musa reminds himself 'that it is the literal sense of the great poem that contains all its other possible meanings'.[40]

Rossetti's similar manifesto as translator is stated in his opening words: 'The aim of this translation of Dante may be summed up in one word – Literality'.[41] So plain does this plain (Anglo-Italian) speaker intend to be that he prefers the English word *Hell* to Dante's Italian *Inferno*. 'Strict faithfulness, constantly amounting to literality' remained Rossetti's constant watchword to later Dante translators. He praised Dr Edwards's version at the end of the century for its highly literal 'efficient and effective' merits, reminiscent of his own aims as a translator in 1865.[42] But the literalness so prized by Rossetti brought him adverse criticism on the resulting oddness of his translation from the reviewer in the *Athenaeum*.[43] Rossetti was the first to acknowledge that his style was marred by awkwardness; he knew 'singularity, or even oddity of phrase is one of my chief shortcomings'.[44]

Rossetti's apparently simplistic approach can be compared positively with the literalness advocated by a great twentieth-century translator Vladimir Nabokov, who asked, when he published his version of *Eugene Onegin*, 'Can Pushkin's poem, or any other poem with a definite rhyme scheme, be really translated?' Only a literal approach, 'rendering, as closely as the associative and syntactical capacities of another language allow, the exact contextual meaning of the original' can result in 'true translation', Nabokov believed.[45]

Here are the two translations compared at two points in Dante's poem:

Dante's *Inferno* translated by Mark Musa [46]
Canto I: opening lines

> Midway along the journey of our life
>> I woke to find myself in a dark wood,
>> for I had wandered off from the straight path.
>
> How hard it is to tell what it was like,
>> this wood of wilderness, savage and stubborn
>> (the thought of it brings back all my old fears),
>
> a bitter place! Death could scarce be bitterer.
>> but if I would show the good that came of it
>> I must talk about things other than the good.

Dante's *Hell* translated by W.M.Rossetti [47]
Canto I: opening lines

> In midway of the journey of our life,
> I found myself within a darkling wood,
> Because the rightful pathway had been lost.
> And ah! How hard a thing it is to say
> What this wood was, savage, and rough, and strong,
> That in the thinking it reneweth fear.
> But, of the good to treat which there I found,
> I'll tell the other things I saw in it.

Neither Musa nor Rossetti use Dante's original *terza rima*. Instead both choose unrhymed blank verse, although Musa echoes Dante's three-lined stanzas by setting out his translation in three-lined verse paragraphs whereas Rossetti divides his into verse paragraphs of varying lengths. Musa observes that Dante's style is sometimes purely prosaic and therefore his translation 'should be simple where Dante's is'. The modern translator explains his aims in restrained vocabulary. 'I have set as my goal simplicity and quiet, even, sober flow – except when I feel the moment has come to let myself go, to pull out the stops…I have consistently tried to find a style that does not call attention to itself'. [48]

It might almost be Rossetti speaking over a century earlier, not only of his aims and intentions as a translator, but also of himself, 'I have aimed at unconditional literality in phraseology, and at line-for-line rendering…I have kept to the metre, which is the same as in blank verse, but not to the rhyme…To follow Dante sentence for sentence, line for line, word for word – neither more nor less – has been my strenuous endeavour…My aim was not originality, but truth'. [49]

For Musa and Nabokov, the most effective verse translations must be unrhymed, a decision with which Rossetti entirely agrees. However, Musa believes the translator may sin against the simplicity of Dante's diction in other ways, by using inappropriate flowery language or allowing deliberate archaisms. Although Rossetti's portfolio of vocabulary throughout his *Hell* is admirably direct, plain and workmanlike, he nevertheless adopts archaisms consistently, notably using the King James Bible endings for verbs such as 'reneweth' instead of the current 'renews' (line 6 above). However, Musa himself is not entirely guilt-free. 'Death could scarce be bitterer' (line 7 above) he offers, harking back to earlier poetic usage when today 'scarcely' would be the natural form of the word. 'I found myself within a darkling wood' (line 2 above) translates Rossetti. Unlike Musa's monosyllabic 'dark', Rossetti's 'darkling' is an evocative Victorian usage recalling Keats, 'Darkling I listen; and, for many a time/I have been half in love with Easeful Death',[50] and prefiguring Arnold's pessimistic vision of the 'darkling plain' in *Dover Beach*.[51] Rossetti's rendering of Dante's 'darkling wood' is one of his most allusive poetic effects.

Translation, like biography, is an interpretative art; it is essentially of its own time and echoes contemporary linguistic taste and idiomatic style. Biography reinterprets the works and lives of the past for people of today and is equally ephemeral. Like translation, biography may need to be rewritten for each new generation. Rossetti's honest, well-intentioned translation was for his time and place. It is unfair to expect it to sound colloquial to our ears.

Compare Rossetti with Musa here:

Rossetti's version:
From *Canto V:* closing lines, p. 37 (Dante's response to the story of Paolo and Francesca)

> Meantime as the one soul was saying this,
> The other wept so that, for pitying,
> I failed at heart, as though I should have died;
> And down I fell as a dead body falls.

Musa's version:
From *Canto V:* closing lines, p. 113 (Dante's response to the story of Paolo and Francesca)

> And all the while
> the one of the two spirits spoke these words,
> the other wept, in such a way that pity
> blurred my senses; I swooned as though to die,
> and fell to Hell's floor as a body, dead, falls.

In this instance, Rossetti's almost entirely monosyllabic rendering is very successful, more compact and direct than Musa's. 'Swooned' is an archaism and 'blurred my senses' less heart stopping than 'I failed at heart' with its suggestion of heart failure. Nevertheless, Rossetti was perfectly conscious of the inadequacy of his final line and added an apology. 'The original line, "*E caddi* come corpo morto cade," is noted for representing the fall by its sound, – a beauty which has vanished, or nearly so, in the translation'.[52] In his efforts to let Dante speak plainly, to transfer strict Pre-Raphaelite principles to translation, Rossetti knew he sometimes lost touch with the poetry.

In 1866 Charles Eliot Norton's *North American Review* carried an article on current Dante translations which recognized the limitations of Rossetti's exercise in the genre but praised him for having 'preserved the substance, and in good measure the spirit, of his original'. But it identified the flaws, 'a certain tendency toward the use of expressions more quaint than exact...and a certain want of rhythmic grace and harmony in the structure of the verse.'[53] Rossetti for his part found it an 'excellent article' and accepted both its praise and its blame.

In a note to his translation, Rossetti pointed to the symmetry of Dante's poetic construction, in which all three sections, Hell, Purgatory and Paradise, culminated in an image of human aspiration, looking towards the stars. And, just as the poet imposed his stellar pattern, so a biographer may sometimes discern life-patterns or 'thematic designs', such as Nabokov uncovered in his autobiography *Speak, Memory*.[54] Rossetti's translation of *Hell* had been written in the context of his doomed relationship and ultimately broken engagement to Henrietta Rintoul. Once out in the public arena, and dedicated out of a last loyalty to her, he was liberated. A few weeks after publication, on 12 April 1865, Gabriel gave a party at 16 Cheyne Walk, an evening when the 'wide river was lit up...by a full moon'. Georgie Burne-Jones remembered the conviviality of the occasion and listed all the guests, William Michael Rossetti, William Bell Scott, Swinburne, William and Janey Morris, the Munros, Mr and Mrs Arthur Hughes, Alphonse Legros with his pale, handsome English wife. The Madox Browns, including the half-sisters Lucy and Cathy, created hilarity by arriving two-and-a-half hours late 'smiling and unruffled' – they had been trying to save the cab fare. Georgie recalled that there had been 'nothing further from expectation at the moment than a marriage that took place nine years later between the elder of these and William Rossetti.'[55] Publishing his *Inferno* gave William a sense of resolution. At last he could put Hell and Henrietta firmly behind him.

SWINBURNE'S 'POEMS AND BALLADS. A CRITICISM'

Finally putting an end to his unfulfilling relationship with Henrietta Rintoul, William knew that 'the passionate and the sensuous' were needs he could not ignore. He believed these were also the 'two ultimate and indestructible elements of poetry'.[56] It was a direct allusion to Milton's definition of poetry in *Of Education*, as 'simple, sensuous and passionate'. In August 1866 Moxon published Swinburne's fourth volume of poetry, *Poems and Ballads*, but swiftly had to withdraw it in the face of critical uproar at its sensuality, atheism and blasphemies. It was a perfect cause for William and although the *North American Review* turned down his article in praise of Swinburne, it was quickly scooped up by John Camden Hotten, who had cannily reissued Swinburne's volume. Hotten published William's defence, *Swinburne's Poems and Ballads. A Criticism* on 3 November 1866 in a slim cloth-bound edition priced at 3s 6d.

In his opening sentence William lit a fatal fuse. In cavalier journalese he joked that in the cultural climate of the day, 'even so poor and pretentious a poetaster as a Robert Buchanan stirs storms in teapots'. Buchanan could not shrug off the Rossetti jibe. It festered and partially motivated his eventual destructive attack on Gabriel's *Poems* (1870) for the very sensuality that Swinburne so dangerously exhibited.

William's essay hailing Swinburne as a 'new great poet' was powerful precisely because it was a critical vindication and not just a paean of praise. He explained that Swinburne had challenged critics to be horrified but his *Atalanta in Calydon* in 1865 was the best poem since *Prometheus Unbound*, a modern poetic achievement comparable with but probably superior to *In Memoriam*. In 1866 *Poems and Ballads* was a 'scorching and explosive production' in which William identified the four main currents in Swinburne's poetry that had offended critics, the passionately sensuous, the classical Greek subject matter, the religiously 'mutinous' and the 'assimilative' (presumably derivative) literary forms.[57] William defended Swinburne's right to present the lesbian loves of Sappho, 'aberrations of passion which were vital enough to some of the great of old'.[58] The poet was a pagan 'in intellectual sympathy', and his literary liberty to hold and express speculative opinions, including atheism, must be defended.[59] The 'indecencies' that most enraged Swinburne critics, 'of positive grossness or foulness of expression' or even of 'light-hearted, jocular, jovial libertinism' were simply non-existent.[60]

Like William's romantic idol Shelley, Swinburne 'had a fatal facility…for saying the most alarming things on the unsafest subjects'.[61] William conceded that Swinburne was drawn towards subjects of 'moral repulsiveness' but this was offset by his 'deep and eager sense of beauty', his 'subtilizing' eloquence, 'carved' diction and intuitive melodic faculty.[62] His limitations meant he could be at times overlong, over alliterative, and obscure but at his best William judged him 'dazzling' and 'sublime' with 'an impulse, a majesty, a spontaneity' superior to the common run of poets.[63] William's essay was both a lively, persuasive defence and a provocative attack on mid-Victorian prudery. Such causes triggered his best writing and his most independent criticism.

101. Photograph of Walt Whitman sent by the poet to William Michael Rossetti in 1869. Private collection.

WILLIAM AND WHITMAN

William's lack of sexual embarrassment coupled with his literary taste for the innovative meant he was one of the first critics in Britain to recognize the 'entire originality' of American poet Walt Whitman (fig. 101).[64]

William admired Whitman from the moment Bell Scott gave him the American poet's *Leaves of Grass* for Christmas 1855. Thomas Dixon, the cork-cutter of Sunderland to whom Ruskin wrote his *Letters to a Working Man*, had previously alerted Bell Scott to its publication. William told Dixon later that although he loved Browning so much 'both as a writer and personally', he believed 'Whitman to be, all things considered, the *greatest* poet now writing in the English language', one of the noblest men and greatest intellects in the world, whose 'fame, wide and vast is certain and inevitable.'[65]

George Henry Lewes (Mr George Eliot) discerningly noticed the American publication of *Leaves of Grass* in 1855 in the *Leader*, a weekly review he edited. But the first major public reception in Britain of Whitman's 'positive and entire originality' came from William in an article he contributed to a short-lived, liberal, Catholic weekly, the *Chronicle*, on 6 July 1867. Since Whitman was derided and ignored in his home country – except notably by Ralph Waldo Emerson – William seized the opportunity to hon-our the poet abroad. He unerringly analysed how Whitman had remade modern poetry, comparing him to the greatest literary innovators, Homer and Shakespeare.

Whitman had dispensed with rhyme but invented his own 'rolling, rhap-sodic, metrical, or semi-metrical prose-verse', galvanizing an 'electric shock…running from writer to reader.' Whitman uncompromisingly took the universality of his individual soul – 'that wondrous thing, a single, separate person' – as his subject. William instantly recognized that 'the flame from which it catches fire' was Americanism, inventing new spheres of poetic opportunity, an achievement both 'intensely modern and intensely American'. His democratic politics and his poetry appealed to William. As a Unionist and inclusivist, Whitman had nursed soldiers from both sides during the American Civil War. He continually trumpeted 'the full coequality of the sexes.' Minor blemishes such as his allusions to 'gross things and in gross words' could be contained and forgiven. William called him 'Walt' and passionately declared his new genius. Unlike his youthful literary criticism for the *Germ* in 1850, which had depended on the use of overlong quotations, William's mature voice was a blast of opinion incorporating hardly any quotation. It was as if by chemistry Whitman's theme – 'I celebrate myself, and sing myself' – had been transmitted to William.[66]

Less than a month later, on 10 August 1867, William's article was reprinted in the *New York Citizen*. It had 'a certain *retentissement*'[67] in America and the British voice gave Whitman credibility in his own country. In London, publisher John Camden Hotten read William's rave review in the *Chronicle* and promptly commissioned him to edit a selection of Whitman's poetry.

William set to work at once, cutting up and pasting from his own copy of Whitman to produce an anthology the publisher and the public would accept. In deference to 'a nervous age', he told Swinburne he 'thought it absolutely necessary (*mânes de l'auteur de Justine, ne m'en voulez pas*) [spirits of the author of *Justine* (Marquis de Sade) do not be angry with me] to exclude everything decidedly offensive', preferring to omit a poem altogether rather than to wield 'the literary gelding knife' and cut indecent expressions or lines within a single poem.[68] His author's proof copy of the book still survives with his introduction handwritten on paper exactly the same size as the eventual published book, and his meticulous proof corrections showing exact knowledge of printers' marks.[69]

William used his *Chronicle* article as the basis for his preface to the book, extending and personalizing it to great effect, heightening if possible his earlier fervent tone. So confident was William that he used his own voice, in all its first person singularity to applaud and rejoice in Whitman, whose 'self-assertion is boundless', '*the* poet of the epoch', 'the poet of democracy' whose 'iconoclastic boldness' and 'Titanic power' exploded the canon of subjects available for poetry. It is easier to forgive one of William's oddest editorial decisions – to supply titles of his own to poems untitled by Whitman – when he asks himself and the reader some fundamental questions: 'Is he powerful? Is he American? Is he new? Is he rousing? Does he feel and make me feel?'[70]

In spite of its omissions, William's edition of *Poems by Walt Whitman* (1868) gave Whitman his first British readership. The editor of the *Evening Sun*, Charles Kent, hailed publication with 'the most affectionate & overflowing tribute to Whitman's great gifts' that William had ever seen in print.[71] The book also enraptured Anne Gilchrist[72] who became one of Whitman's most ardent British fans and even proposed to him. After Madox Brown gave her William's edition in June 1869 she could 'read no other book; it holds me entirely spell-bound, and I go through it again and again with deepening delight and wonder'. William responded elatedly: 'That glorious man Whitman will one day be known as one of the greatest sons of Earth, a few steps below Shakespeare on the throne of immortality'[73] and encouraged Mrs Gilchrist to publish her ecstatic views on Whitman, which she eventually did in an American journal, the *Radical*.

When the Rossetti *Whitman* first appeared, the poet considered it 'a beautiful volume' and always thought of William as one of his first friends in England, 'one of the staunchest – right along: has never qualified his allegiance.'[74] He had further reason to be grateful when, after writing to President Cleveland of the United States to no avail on Whitman's behalf on 13 June 1885,[75] William masterminded a subscription fund for the elderly, disabled poet now living in near penury after a stroke. Many figures from British arts and letters subscribed, including William and Lucy, Robert Louis Stevenson, Henry James, Professor Dowden and the tragic young novelist Amy Levy who was William's neighbour in Endsleigh Gardens. The sum collected was equivalent to about £10,000 today.

In retrospect, of course, Whitman would have preferred a virgin selection of his poems with no editorial cuts or additions. But on 16 November 1867 Whitman had sent William a message in a letter to Moncure Conway, authorizing him to make such alterations that William might 'consider needful for decency'.[76] Horace Traubel asked Whitman in 1888 if he had been satisfied with William's selection. 'On the whole – yes. Yet any volume of extracts must misrepresent the Leaves – any volume – the best. The whole theory of the book is against gems, abstracts, extracts: the book needs each of its parts to keep its perfect unity…Take it to pieces – even with a gentle hand – and it is no longer the same product.'[77]

William maintained his admiration of Whitman's work. E. Moxon, Son & Co. commissioned William to edit a range of authors for his 'Popular Poets' series and asked him to produce a selection from Longfellow but not Whitman. In the biographical introduction to his Moxon *Longfellow* in 1870, William trumped the publisher with his final sentence. 'The real American poet is a man enormously greater than Longfellow or any other of his poetic compatriots – Walt Whitman.'[78] Two years later he dedicated his anthology, *American Poems*, to Whitman and represented him with thirty-two poems, by far the greatest space accorded to any contributor.

Discussing Whitman with Swinburne's guardian angel, Theodore Watts-Dunton, Watts predicted that William's excessive admiration for Whitman would 'in 20 years hence destroy [his] reputation as a critic'.[79] Watts was no literary forecaster. ('Whose Who and What's Dunton?' sniggered Whistler.[80]) More than any other literary intervention, it was William's prophetic recognition of

Whitman's genius within the context of largely hostile contemporary opinion that ensured his reputation for risk-taking and discerning criticism.

WILLIAM AND SHELLEY

decidedly the greatest figure and phenomenon in English poetry since Milton

not a vague dreamer, but a strenuous leader of modern thought
        William Rossetti on Shelley [81]

Perhaps William's greatest poetic hero was another radical libertarian, the restless visionary Percy Bysshe Shelley, whose dangerous reputation he promoted unflaggingly. He edited *Shelley with a Memoir*, in two volumes in 1870, and revised it in three volumes in 1878 in response to harsh criticism of his too invasive editorial practices. Between 1878 and 1895 he wrote about sixty articles for the *Athenaeum*, mainly on Shelley or on Italian literature. He lectured on Shelley and was a chairman of the Shelley Society from 1886 until its dissolution in 1895. Although he wrote a *Life of Keats* in 1887 for the 'Great Writers' series, he frankly preferred the more overtly political Shelley. One of his most cherished projects was an autobiography that Shelley never wrote, compiled from extracts of the poet's letters and works. Called *Cor Cordium*, it came from William's own heart of hearts but remains in manuscript form and was never published.

William first read Shelley 'with rapture' in boyhood in about 1844. On a rereading in 1860 he found the poet 'more admirable than ever'. When he was preparing his first Shelley edition in 1869, he discussed the poet avidly with George Eliot, another autodidact and Shelley admirer. He noticed that 'in animated intellectual talk' her face became 'incomparably superior to what it was at other times'.[82] Shelley cemented many of William's most meaningful later friendships with Dr Garnett, Professor Dowden, Mathilde Blind, and above all with the maverick old adventurer, Edward John Trelawny, who had known Shelley in Italy during the crucial last months of his life and had exploited the memory ever since. William observed, 'there seems to be in Shelley, more than in other poets, something which binds his sympathizers closely together.'[83]

Why did William in middle and later life love and revere Shelley the wild child so unrestrainedly? On the face of it, there would seem to be vast temperamental chasms between them. William relished connections and a sense of a cultural continuum as well as paradoxes, and he found the Shelley/Rossetti links and paradoxes particularly piquant. The Pre-Raphaelites, like their Romantic forbears and their Bloomsbury descendants, were essentially unclubbable, and yet all three 'groups' achieved cult status in public perception. Shelley was an aristocrat who thought like a radical; William was a sober civil servant who thought like an anarchist. Of all the Romantic poets, Shelley was by far the most political. His relevance was still fresh, as William pointed out. Only as recently as 1867, the Tories had found it in their interests to pass the Second Reform Act, almost the same scheme of political enfranchisement which Shelley, poet, dreamer, atheist and democrat, had envisaged in his *Proposal for Putting Reform to the Vote* in 1817. Out of all the Pre-Raphaelite Brothers, William was by far the most revolutionary, sharing ideals of political freedom and near atheism with his idol. 'Shelley had as good a right to form and expound his opinions on theology as the Archbishop of Canterbury had to his,' William pointed out crisply in his third version of Shelley's life, the *Memoir* (1886).[84] He described his own position as closer to a fatalistic agnosticism, epitomized by the motto he saw daily over Covent Garden Market, '*che sarà sarà*'.[85] Like Shelley, William 'had no belief whatever in a *personal* God'.[86]

Shelley believed poetry should have meaning and moral content, the opposite of Aestheticism's creed by the 1890s of 'art for art's sake', first exemplified by Swinburne. Mirroring his own ideals and delighting his sensitive poetic ear, William exalted Shelley's work both for its radical content and its poetic inventiveness, especially in his masterpiece, *Prometheus Unbound*. As a prose writer himself, William appreciated the brilliance of Shelley's prose, particularly *The Defence of Poetry*. William the critic extolled Shelley the creative artist.

Shelley was an advocate of sexual freedom who behaved like an innocent. Outwardly appearing to subscribe to Victorian respectability, William was inwardly a free spirit, extremely susceptible to female sexuality. Both men were involved with clever, complicated, intellectual women. In writing Shelley's life, William believed that sexual irregularities could not be glossed over. Urged to dig the dirt by Swinburne, he assured him his full intention was 'to state plainly everything I can find: he who comes to me for biographic reticence is (as old Shelley said about *Epipsychidion*) like a man going to a gin-shop for a leg of mutton.'[87] So William spoke plainly about Shelley's doctrine of free love and the shocking suicide of his first wife Harriet. However, although protesting he positively liked Harriet, characterizing her as 'amiable, good, accommodating, affectionate', he damned her in a single word, 'commonplace'. It was indisputable in William's view – 'the fact is a fact' – that she lived with other men, successively, after Shelley left her for Mary Godwin, but what was a noble principle of free love in his hero was tawdry in the abandoned wife. In spite of believing in equality between the sexes, William failed to see the discrepancy in his treatment of Harriet and Shelley, probably because Harriet was unredeemed by genius.

William thought what he called the 'sympathetic bond' between author and subject essential to biography. He decried, in Milan Kundera's description, the tendency for biography to become 'criminography', and determined not to present Shelley as an Arnoldian 'ineffectual angel'.[88] On the other hand, accuracy, not prurience, was his principle. 'Painful' aspects of Shelley's life had to be addressed; William found 'no adequate ground for biographic reticence in the case of so important a man as Shelley'.[89] So in order to retain biographical freedom, William kept his distance from the poet's son and his wife, Sir Percy and Lady Shelley. He did not want to allow himself to be controlled by the family by agreeing to write the authorized *Life*. This was his biographer's manifesto: 'If I care myself to read anything at all about a man, I like to know what he really was, and, when I become the informant, I like my reader to do the same. An important personage does not in the long-run suffer by our understanding what were his faults, blemishes, or weaknesses; he thus becomes more human to us, and therefore more endeared. A photograph with the wrinkles burnished out is always a bad photograph.'[90] William was a Pre-Raphaelite biographer. Realism was always his intention.

William's biographic independence and his preference for short biographies prefigured Lytton Strachey (although Strachey rejected any notion of a 'sympathetic bond'). Although he claimed biography as 'the most delicate and humane of all the branches of the art of writing', Strachey thought it was not part of the biographer's brief 'to be complimentary: it is his business…to lay bare the facts of some cases…dispassionately, impartially, and without ulterior intentions.' With his Romantic credentials, William also anticipated the late twentieth-century romantic biographer Richard Holmes who literally 'foot-steps' his long dead subjects. William made a special journey to Viareggio to absorb the scene where Shelley's body was cremated on the beach, interviewing eyewitnesses who provided a pulsing link with his hero. 'I have stood on the very spot,' against the noble Apennines, by a pellucid sea, under an Italian summer sky. 'I spoke to an old Italian, who had himself in boyhood witnessed the memorable event, and recollected how strange it had been considered.' William quoted his other key witness: '"The heat from the sun and fire", says Trelawny, "was so intense that the atmosphere was tremulous and wavy." '[91] In his eloquent *Memoir* of Shelley, William combined genuine re-imagining of the life with coherent sifting and ordering of the then known biographical facts, including critical evaluation of the works to produce an excellent short introduction. His purpose to establish Shelley in the canon of poetic greatness was essentially fulfilled.

Trelawny, 'the hero of a hundred exploits', gave William access to Shelleyan myth and manuscripts. Fuelled by Shelley-mania, their friendship lasted from 1869 until Trelawny's death in 1881. Trelawny sent William on an 'Aspern Papers' mission to Florence on 14 and 15 June 1873 (when he was wooing Lucy) to interview Claire Clairmont, once Byron's mistress and possibly Shelley's, as she retained some of the poets' letters and papers. The Shelley connection was a romantic factor in William and Lucy's Italian courtship. The old buccaneer also fed William's passion to collect, by giving him a macabre relic, a fragment of Shelley's charred skull that he had snatched from the funeral pyre. William took it round to a party at Madox Brown's on 29 February 1872 and was intrigued at the differing reactions aroused. Many,

102. Photograph of Helen Rossetti [Angeli] seated on the Shelley sofa in the library at 3 St Edmund's Terrace, *c.* 1900. Reproduced as the frontispiece to volume II of *Some Reminiscences* by William Michael Rossetti, 1906. Private collection.

including the Madox Browns, William Bell Scott, Philip Bourke Marston and Mathilde Blind were reverentially moved whereas Swinburne 'paid next to no attention' and Gabriel passed it off as a joke. William treasured two hairs supposed to have come from Shelley's head. He also lost them. Trelawny made him one further gift, an elegant beech or walnut-wood sofa that Shelley had bought in Pisa in 1821, on which he was said to have slept the last night of his life (fig. 102). It became one of the biographer's most valued possessions. It 'faces me as I write these words', he noted, providing an uncanny tangible link from Shelley himself forward to William's readers.

To reciprocate, in 1875, William helped Trelawny prepare for the press an extended version of his colourfully reconstructed *Recollections of the Last Days of Shelley and Byron* first published in 1856. After Trelawny's death, Charles Lamb, a solicitor from Brighton, unexpectedly gave William two drawings by Shelley to add to his collection of Shelleyana.[92]

'This Shelley job has delighted me immensely. I have always adored Shelley, & to have my full swing with him (both poems & life) as has now fallen to my lot, is a satisfaction such as chances to few men', rejoiced William.[93] It was ironic that William's editorial work on Shelley, which brought him such intense pleasure, should have proved so contentious to both contemporary and later scholars. Once he had signed the contract with J. Bertrand Payne, 'a large sleek man' of the publishing firm E. Moxon, Son & Co., who had noticed his contributions to debate on editing Shelley in *Notes and Queries*, William 'set to work with the utmost zest – scrutinizing the text, reading-up the biographical materials, jotting down and collating the details in them, compiling my notes to the poems, writing the memoir, and subsequently revising the proofs'. The enormous project took up every moment outside (and sometimes within) his working hours at the Revenue, from mid-1868 until the end of 1869, but William knew he would have been his own tormentor had he 'stinted or slurred work in any particular'.[94] He tried to convey the nature and intensity of his huge task. 'I am satisfied that a person who has not gone through some similar experience has no conception of the amount of trouble and painstaking involved in close editorial work of this nature.'

In retrospect he shuddered at the minutiae of persuading the printer to indent Shelley's poetic lines, in accordance with their rhyme and metre. Editing the unstable texts of Shelley's poetry is still debated. Shelley texts are endlessly difficult to determine. Some were privately or posthumously published, printed abroad, uncorrected by the poet in his lifetime or even appeared in pirated editions. William's proactive editorship was bound to be controversial. But he was convinced he was right to correct 'absolute blunders' as long as he clearly stated where 'conjectural emendations' were his own. But he added, deleted or altered words, 'corrected' rhyme, metre and grammar and generally transgressed against emerging principles of good editorial practice. An unusual alliance of Swinburne and the other Shelley expert Buxton Forman (whom Swinburne fixed as 'Fuxton Borman') derided William for his pervasive emendations. On the other hand, Gabriel and William Bell Scott wished William had made even more textual revisions.

William himself was ready to accept criticism up to a point, so he made some alterations in subsequent re-printings although he never succeeded in producing an acceptable edition. Wounded by criticism of his beloved project he felt privately vindicated when, after making a detailed study of *Prometheus Unbound* in 1902, C.D. Locock found some of William's 'conjectural emendations to be correct' when correlated with Shelley's manuscripts in the Bodleian Library.[95] When his extensively annotated three proof volumes were offered for sale in 1922,[96] London bookseller John Jeffery described them as a testimony to 'the greatest expression of genuine hero-worship in the whole history of literature'.[97] But his editorial practices had incited outrage and denigration from scholars. Nor did he retrieve his editorial reputation when the Clarendon Press published his edition of Shelley's *Adonais* in 1891.

A further irony about William's love affair with Shelley was that it brought him the chairmanship of the Shelley Society from 1886 to 1895 – ironic to have untamed Shelley memorialized within the constraints of an academic society, and incongruous that William, who was more likely to resign from a club than to join one, should have agreed. But promoting Shelley was, in another irony, an almost priest-like task.

The idea came from Frederick James Furnivall, tireless scholar, a 'tough customer' according to William, and a prodigious former of societies. Since 1864 he had set up a series of learned societies to promote Early English texts, Chaucer, ballads, Shakespeare, Wyclif and Browning. At about 1.30 p.m. on Sunday, 6 December 1885 'on the hill between Hendon and Hampstead' he was inspired by Henry Sweet to found his last, the Shelley Society.[98] At its height there were about four hundred members, including Mathilde Blind, Bertram Dobell, Dr Furnivall, Harry Buxton Forman and the young George

Bernard Shaw, who each paid a stiff annual subscription of one guinea. This financed a programme of lectures, ambitious performances such as *The Cenci* (banned by the Lord Chamberlain) and *Hellas*, Shelleyan concerts, facsimile editions of Shelley's works and reprints of early criticism. In the end, debts mounted up alarmingly (much to Lucy's disapproval) until William reckoned he had paid over £120[99] out of his own pocket by the time the society's affairs were finally wound up in November 1902.

The society had three secretaries, of whom the last was the notorious Thomas J. Wise, collector and forger, who faked and sold transcripts of Shelley correspondence he had disarmingly purloined from William, charging up costs through the Shelley Society's accounts. During the years when Lucy's health and brittle personality were at their most demanding, William found absorption, as well as added aggravation, in the affairs of the society, conscientiously arranging speakers and delivering his own lectures. Some people though, who attended early meetings in April 1886, like the blind poet Philip Bourke Marston, found it a great bore.

> On Tuesday we all went to the Shelley Society and heard Buxton Forman expound *Queen Mab*, and tell us how it was written, and that kind of thing. I do think these societies are such nonsense. As for paying a guinea to belong to one, No thank you. By-the-bye Buxton Forman cannot speak at all, and that made it difficult for one to keep one's eyes open…Then, a man called Bernard Shaw, who frankly declared himself at the start an atheist and a socialist, a man who I know slightly and much hate, an Irishman who speaks with a strong accent, arose in his glory and said that he regarded *Queen Mab* as a much greater work than the *Cenci*. I wanted to get up and murder him…Then, Aveling addressed us, and we were all very glad when it was over.'[100]

Dr Edward Aveling planned to give a lecture to the society on 'Shelley and Socialism' (the Society's subtext), co-written with his lover Eleanor Marx. They had been openly living together since July 1884. His application to join the Shelley Society caused a furore. The committee members wanted to exclude him on grounds of immorality, 'an inquisitional act', thought William, who failed to see that a literary society had 'anything to do with the sexual morals' of aspiring members.[101] It was 'absolutely monstrous and ludicrous'[102] for a society devoted to Shelley of all people to reject Aveling 'who may be a bad lot'[103] on the grounds that he was not formally married to the so-called Mrs Aveling. William had no personal knowledge of Aveling but in protest resigned from the society from 10 February to 10 April 1887 until Aveling's application was accepted. When the Avelings finally presented their lecture on 14 December 1887, William appropriately chaired the meeting. The Aveling affair exemplified both his lack of prudery and his adherence to principles.

His connection with Aveling underlined his innocence, as well as his political and moral independence. William tried to enlist George Bernard Shaw
and other members of the Shelley Society to sign a petition to the Governor
of Illinois to spare the lives of seven anarchists accused of a bombing incident
in Chicago in 1887. In the end only William signed and Aveling, who undertook to dispatch a second petition, never did so.[104]

William promoted Shelley studies by lecturing to the society on Harriet
Shelley; the Shelleys near Geneva; Shelley and Leopardi; *Prometheus Unbound*;
and on 'Shelley and the element of water'. Since 1875 he had lectured on
Shelley to keen audiences all over the country – the most avid listeners were
in Scotland, he noted. Always respecting his audience, he prepared carefully
and enjoyed lecturing. Identifying all the watery references in Shelley was an
original thematic approach but William bombarded the society with such
extensive strings of extracts relating to saltwater/freshwater/ships/
boats/drowning and shipwreck that by the 103rd quotation he was forced to
inwardly admit 'people didn't care for this.'[105]

In fact, this sort of careful, analytical, cumulative work, although hardly
suitable for the lecture-hall, gave William satisfaction and even a sense of security. His daughter Helen called it his 'queer taste for methodical routine
work', which she felt she had inherited, announcing she would have been
happy to spend her life in a library cataloguing books.[106]

WILLIAM AND SCHOLARSHIP

William was a natural and self-taught scholar. He never had the benefit of
higher education but he relished academic research for its own sake. On the
invitation of Dr Furnivall in 1866 he annotated *The Stacyons of Rome*, a
descriptive list of relics to be found in Roman churches, compiled with the
aid of a book by Girolamo Francino, dated 1600, which belonged to his
mother, and produced *Italian Courtesy-Books* in 1869. Both of these were published by the Early English Text Society, founded in 1864, the first of Dr.
Furnivall's 'family' of great Victorian literary societies.

Another academic endeavour was to compare Chaucer's *Troylus and
Cryseyde* line by line with the source of Chaucer's poem Boccaccio's *Filostrato*,
issued in two parts in 1873 and 1883 by Furnivall's Chaucer Society. (The
society advertised Part One for 1875 but William delivered the manuscript
two years early.) He discovered that less than a third of Chaucer's lines were
'traceable to his Italian prototype'.[107] At the invitation of the Philological
Society, William became one of the earliest contributors of quotations used to
define words in the *Oxford English Dictionary*. He estimated that he had read
over a hundred books for this task alone, 'some of them big affairs, such as all
the dramas of [Philip] Massinger'.[108]

By 1882 his reputation for scholarship brought him an invitation to examine Italian at the Taylor Institution in Oxford. He returned to Oxford on 24 November 1891 to give the Taylorian Lecture – on Leopardi, 'the most important and consummate poet of Italy' – in a distinguished lecture series that included speakers Stéphane Mallarmé on 'La Musique et les Lettres', Walter Pater on Prosper Mérimée and W.P. Ker on Boccaccio.[109]

This invitation came in March 1891 from Dr Edward Moore of the Dante Society, who invited William to lecture to Oxonians on any subject from Italian literature. At first, although feeling 'hardly competent for such a task', he thought he would choose Dante's Beatrice, but soon changed to Leopardi whose work was little known in England. Research at home and in the Reading Room at the British Museum occupied him until mid-July when he began writing the lecture, worried that his mass of material would overspill the allotted hour. He decided to organize his talk under three headings, dealing with Leopardi's life, character and literary work. Academic audiences today might find William's approach over-biographical, but he felt it necessary to supply such information, partly because Leopardi was relatively unknown in England at the time, partly in order to link the life psychologically to Leopardi's philosophy of pessimism, and partly because of his own fascination with life stories.

Forty years earlier in an anonymous, erudite and largely sympathetic article for the *Quarterly Review*, it was no surprise that Gladstone (later the great Liberal Prime Minister) had been ultimately unable to endorse the absolute pessimism of Leopardi's tragic poetry.[110] Unconstrained by the dictates of conventional religion, William was able to assess the full extent of Leopardi's poetic achievement. Where Gladstone found Leopardi's poetry too negative to be true art, William traced the psychological origins of that negativity to the poet's chronic invalidism, and a resulting intellectual view of human life partially consistent with his own. Living daily with Lucy's life of illness, William understood the effect of the body's unremitting debility on Leopardi. 'We read his personal sorrows into his abstract cogitations', William explained, but he believed Leopardi would have arrived at the same mental position even without his physical handicaps. Happiness for any human being was merely a delusion, the only consolation in Leopardi's scheme of the universe was death, his continual theme 'inscrutable and unappealable Fate, Nature hostile and Man the shadow of a shade'. William could not subscribe to this depth of gloom, but sharing Leopardi's anti-Christian position and total disbelief in an afterlife freed him to respond to the 'firm and thrilling grasp' of his lyric poetry. Like Whitman, Leopardi struck William as 'one of the most personal of poets; all that he says comes out of himself'.[111] Working on Leopardi, William soon realized there was a compelling comparison to be made with his other great hero, Shelley.

Even before delivering his lecture at Oxford on 24 November 1891, William was planning a further talk analysing the similarities and differences between these two English and Italian poets who had been almost exact contemporaries but had never known each other. Like his earlier essay, this too was built on a tripartite structure. William explicitly compared Shelley and Leopardi under three clear headings, their lives, poetry, and respective theories of semi-optimism and pessimism. In the most engaging section of his talk he contrasted and analysed specific pairs of poems, Shelley's *The Triumph of Life* with Leopardi's *Appressamento alla Morte* (Nearing Death), Shelley's *Mont Blanc* with Leopardi's *Ginestra* (Broom-plant). William described Shelley as a 'Perfectibilist' and 'Necessitarian' with a passion for reforming the world. By contrast, Leopardi's absolute and unqualified pessimism gave him no passion for reforming the world. Leopardi saw humanity as 'constantly weak and mostly bad', whereas Shelley felt 'deep sympathy' and 'earnest active benevolence' towards mankind. Marked contrasts and uncanny points of contact between the two poets made a strong lecture and William delivered it twice, on 10 February and 17 March 1892, first to the Shelley Society and then for an audience of about eighty at Hampden House in London's Somers Town, an institution he compared with Toynbee Hall in the East End.

POPULAR POETS

Although ambivalent about the value of publishing poetic 'selections', William's belief in democratic principles of 'literature for everyone' was the underlying rationale for the twenty-one selections he edited in Edward Moxon's series of *Popular Poets*, most of them between 1870 and 1873. The list included major English poets Milton and Pope but was weighted towards the Romantics, Wordsworth, Coleridge, Byron, Shelley, Keats, the contemporary James Thomson, Felicia Hemans, and Americans Longfellow, Lowell and Whittier. William also compiled two anthologies for the series, *Humorous Poems* and *American Poems*. As objects, these editions offended his innate, aesthetic good taste but they were affordable, pocketable and user-friendly.

Five years later, consciously echoing Dr Johnson, William collected his own introductions to the Moxon *Popular Poets* series in *Lives of Some Famous Poets* (1878). In order to provide a guided tour through English literature for the general reader, he added seven extra essays on writers not issued in the Moxon series, Chaucer, Spenser, Shakespeare, Butler, Dryden, Gray and Goldsmith. Gabriel praised William's collection of short *Lives*,[112] which reversed the Victorian tendency towards comprehensive, heavyweight biographies, anticipating instead the radical, selective approach of Lytton Strachey in the early twentieth century. William's volume was successful, 'sold somewhat briskly'[113] and went into a second edition in 1884. Christina was not surprised at the continued demand for it. 'Do you remember how *our* Maria was impressed by the impartiality of your *Lives* of the Poets? Now I am so too, as well as by the admirable lucidity of your style. The facts would be interesting under any treatment, but you help instead of hindering readers.'[114] With similar readability but even greater concision, he contributed over fifty short, critical biographies of artists – mostly Italian – from Canaletto to Tintoretto to *Encyclopaedia Britannica*'s ninth edition between 1876 and 1888. Years later William revised these entries for the eleventh edition of 1905, in collaboration with his half-nephew, Ford Madox [Ford] Hueffer, as a tactful way of helping the young writer financially.

Playing Horatio

On the celebrated Rossetti family, William was his own and the public's best informant. But for years he held back, conscious of what the public would say about the partiality of a brother as biographer, hoping that Theodore Watts-Dunton would fulfil his promise to write the life of Dante Gabriel Rossetti. When this pledge was still unredeemed over a dozen years after Gabriel's death, William took up the task himself, finding absorption in the aftermath of Lucy's and then Christina's deaths, diffident at first but gradually fulfilled. Unconcerned with displaying his own ego, he saw his function not merely as 'keeper of the flame' of the Pre-Raphaelite Brotherhood and Rossetti family history but also as its interpreter and transmitter to posterity. Sharing unbelief in a personal afterlife with Madox Brown and Lucy, literary work gave him solace and purpose.

With his appetite for collecting and archiving documents, publishing editions of letters and poetry, memorializing and writing biographies, he was the most effective public relations officer the P.R.B. never appointed. In carrying out such tasks, this conscientious and honourable man aroused bitter controversy and personal opprobrium in his own day that has persisted into modern times. Some critics thought they detected motives that were self-serving and self-seeking. Edmund Gosse was still grumbling about 'publications, revelations, sales of objects [that] followed in a terrible succession', a few days before his own death in 1928, long after William's.[115]

Following the deaths of Gabriel (1882) and Christina (1894), William collated and published successive editions of his siblings' major works. 'Tell William', Madox Brown wrote to Lucy, 'I found I had not read his notice of his brother in the new edition [of 1886]. Tho' so very short, it is very new and instructive and like all he writes most readable.'[116] William edited Gabriel's collected works in 1886, 1891, 1904 and 1911, produced his own account of *Dante Gabriel Rossetti as Designer and Writer* in 1889 and a major biographical work *Dante Gabriel Rossetti: His Family Letters with a Memoir* in two volumes in 1895.

Although he claimed to dislike biographies that deliberately debunked their subjects, he published an unflattering biography of Keats in 1887. He was the only nineteenth-century commentator to point out that Keats's social origins were 'undistinguished'.[117] Other biographers who tried to elevate Keats did so in 'concession to that deadly spirit of flunkeyism in the British people'. But he explained to Madox Brown, 'I have tried to express a reasonably *balanced* opinion…keeping my eyes open to faults and weaknesses. As to his character I do certainly believe that what I have done comes nearer to being a serious *étude* than is to be found in other books on the subject.'[118] However, Oscar Wilde berated him for 'separating the man from the artist. The facts of Keats's life are interesting only when they are shown in their relation to his creative activity.' With hindsight, it is ironic how deeply Wilde detested the 'keyhole and the backstairs' tactics of modern biographers. He complained that Rossetti's detailed account of Keats's life 'spares us nothing', dwells on sexual misadventures, dissipation and 'hysterical and morbid ravings of the dying man.'[119] Today very similar attacks are made on biographers - those 'wretched flesh-eating bacteria' in Germaine Greer's punishing phrase. Wilde, it seemed, found Rossetti outrageously intrusive as a biographer. In comic reversal, modern commentators have been infuriated by William's discretion in relation to the Rossettis.

In the preface to his *Memoir* of Gabriel, William asserted his moral rights to reticence in a statement that most biographers and autobiographers today would find alien. 'I have told what I choose to tell,' he said, but added tantalizingly, 'it does not follow that I know nothing beyond that which I write. In some cases I do know a good deal more; but to cast a slur here or violate a confidence there would make me contemptible to myself.'[120] Rossetti clearly felt there was a qualitative difference between his biographer's duty to Keats, a man who died in 1821 almost beyond living memory, and his fraternal duty to his brother who had not died until 1882, leaving so many of the key players still alive in 1895.

In his *Memoir* of Gabriel, William rejected Wilde's strictures about detaching the life of an artist from a discussion of his works. Initially he had held back, as he felt he would be accused of the partiality of a brother, but ultimately he turned what he feared might be disadvantage into a special strength. Imbued with natural authenticity, William's account knits autobiography with biography to achieve unique texture. When Gabriel wailed tragically or indulgently, 'What I *ought* to do is what I *can't* do', he implicitly underlined how William's life, the converse of his own, was perennially constrained by moral imperatives. As biographer, William presents facts that only he could know, marshalling illustrative anecdotes, quotations, letters and reviews. He uses extended quotations from Holman Hunt and Frederic George Stephens to describe Gabriel's physical presence and to give the biography a three-dimensional objectivity. Short chapters lead the reader swiftly through childhood and family, school and friendships, reading and art training, student life and the founding of the P.R.B., Lizzie Siddal, Ruskin, Morris,

Burne-Jones, Swinburne, models, art, money, séances, wombats, Cheyne Walk days, Janey Morris, 'the sunshine of his circle', exhumation, *Poems*, the disastrous *Fleshly School* attack – to the emotional heart of the book, Gabriel's breakdown, suicide attempt, long slide into chloral addiction, depression and death. William included, discussed and disputed countless 'mis-statement and over-statement[s]' made by William Bell Scott in his *Autobiographical Notes* published posthumously in 1892.

The biographical task for William was deeply complex. Aware of the inevitable subjectivity of his opinion of Gabriel, he juxtaposed his hind-sighted narrative with his diary extracts written in the heat of events, and called in evidence from other key eyewitnesses. He assembled testimony from Frances and Christina Rossetti, John Ruskin, Frederic George Stephens, Holman Hunt, William Bell Scott, Frederic Shields, Dr Hake, Hall Caine, Dr Maudsley, Harry Quilter and Frederic Leighton. The technique multiplied the angles from which Gabriel could be viewed and had an almost cinematic effect.

William justly estimated his brother's vital contribution to nineteenth-century British art, inspired by 'the pure loveliness and self-withdrawn suavity' of Lizzie Siddal and Janey Morris's 'face of arcane and inexhaustible meaning'.[121] He agreed with Gabriel's own opinion that his finer achievement was in poetry rather than in painting, an assessment that probably would be reversed today. For William, Gabriel was a tragic and divided Hamlet figure who had 'that within which passeth show', a man 'of astonishing genius, ardent initiative, vigorous and fascinating personality, abundant loveableness, many defects, and in late years overclouded temperament and bedimmed outlook on the world, whom it was once my privilege to call brother.'[122] Although Gabriel could be 'imperative, dominant, self-sustained, and stiff-necked',[123] William affirmed if 'his work was great; the man was greater.'[124] His personal tragedy was that though Gabriel's work was done 'it did not prove to be its own exceeding great reward'. If Gabriel was Hamlet, then William was his devoted Horatio, left alone in this harsh world after the deaths of brother, mother, sister, wife, to tell his story, 'a faithful biographer' who had 'no wish to thrust [him]self constantly forward.'[125] In writing the life stories of both Gabriel and Christina, William had no hidden agenda to aggrandize his own function. His mission was simply to ensure the lasting reputation of siblings he considered geniuses.

Although he felt himself a brother 'of very minor pretensions',[126] William judged his *Family Letters with a Memoir* of Gabriel 'certainly the most considerable performance of my lifetime'.[127] As for Oscar Wilde who read the two volumes in Reading prison in April 1897, he slated Gabriel's *Letters* printed in William's second volume as 'dreadful. Obviously forgeries by his brother.' But from his cell of bitter humiliation, he judged Robert Louis Stevenson's evocative *Vailima Letters* 'most disappointing also.'[128]

William's volumes of the *Family Letters* of both Gabriel in 1895 and Christina in 1908 showed his editorial skills at their best. The letters were catalogued, dated and accompanied by his own contextual and biographical notes, which often provided more fascinating data than the letters themselves. If he cut lines within letters, he scrupulously indicated omissions. As acts of scholarship, retrieval and reanimation, these editions could not have been produced by anyone else at the time and have formed the basis of biographical research for over a century.

For his sister Christina, William edited *New Poems* (1896) and wrote a perceptive life for the *Poetical Works of Christina Rossetti with a Memoir* (1904). Blame for this collected edition, 'cramped and crowded, poorly printed, meanly published, two columns to a small page', pursued him into the twentieth century.[129] But for William, a complete edition of Christina's poetry could never be assembled. He had been at work on it since 1898, aware that 'after my death there wd. not remain any one very well qualified to undertake anything of the kind'.[130] His editorial practices were over-invasive by modern standards, but he was motivated by impossible constraints of protective brotherly love. In his short memoir of Christina, he strenuously aimed at objectivity and conveyed an authentic impression of her personality without the anodyne sentimentality of Mackenzie Bell's biography.

As an act of loyalty to his long-dead father, he translated Gabriele Rossetti's *Versified Autobiography* into English blank verse in 1901. He explained to his publisher, Mr Metcalfe of Sands, that although his father was mainly known in England as the parent of Gabriel and Christina, in Italy there was 'very considerable interest in *himself* as a poet, patriot, and Dante scholar'.[131] With William's extensive explanatory notes, Gabriele's *Autobiography* is still an invaluable source of information about the Rossetti family in Italy. In all these works William tried to observe an almost impossible double loyalty – both to his famous family and its right to privacy, and to the public's right to know. William believed absolutely in both these principles and tried to resolve the inevitable conflict between them with firmness and tact. Cynics attacked him for the duplicity they perceived in observing such double standards and ignored the tension of the tightrope he was teetering on. Where he had shown an excess of conscience, they accused him of the sin of commercialism.

AUTOBIOGRAPHY

In his autobiography, *Some Reminiscences* (1906), William looked back over his own life from his unique perspective on Pre-Raphaelite history. Reading William's autobiographical documents today, his tone of genuine feeling and candour is unmistakable even though he rejects the wilder temptations of more colourful autobiographers. Like all autobiographers he has his own agenda and his own case to present but he is not a devious manipulator of evidence. Instead he provides a rich eyewitness testimony of appealing and varied texture, a collage in words, blending memoirs, biography, autobiography, poetry, reviews, letters, anecdotes, opinion and detailed art criticism. His instinctive, prophetic sense for modern historical practice is evident in his conscientious quotation from contemporary supporting material. In urbane tones he unpicks fabrications and arbitrates on opposing views.

He tactfully countered Holman Hunt's misconception about the true origins of the P.R.B., advanced in *Pre-Raphaelitism and the Pre-Raphaelite Brotherhood*, his autobiographical manifesto published the previous year, 1905. Hunt had claimed that in 1848 he and Millais were the co-founders of the P.R.B. William had always stressed the tripartite balance. 'Some writers have said that Rossetti was the originator of Pre-Raphaelitism. This ignores the just claims of Hunt and Millais, which I regard as co-equal with his.'[132]

Unusually for an autobiographer, William confessed to a 'decidedly bad' memory, especially for conversations over fifty years old, which he categorically refused to reinvent, the total reverse of Holman Hunt who did choose to reconstruct long-forgotten conversations. William's primary motives were to memorialize the dead, explain them to the living and to bear witness to the extraordinary art and personalities he had known, but not to claim the final word either on the Rossettis or the Pre-Raphaelites. These are only 'some' *Reminiscences*, his version from his standpoint in time. 'If you want more,' William tells us tartly, 'be pleased to consult some other informant.'[133] With its modest disclaimer, *Some Reminiscences* obviously appealed to Joseph Conrad as a title for autobiography. Possibly by subconscious connection through his friend Ford Madox [Ford] Hueffer, William's 'half-nephew', Conrad initially called his slim recollections *Some Reminiscences* too, when they first appeared in the *English Review* (1908–9), before eventually settling on the more definitive *A Personal Record* for book publication in 1912.[134]

William's autobiography of 1906 disclosed a pivotal literary figure of the late nineteenth century – not only by association with great artists such as Madox Brown, Hunt and Rossetti. During his long career he had created for himself a major reputation as literary critic and historian.

Some Reminiscences had been written, in part, as a response to Holman Hunt's of 1905, in order to readjust some of his old friend's claims and assumptions. Historical sparring did not undermine their long friendship. Hunt was Rossetti's 'oldest surviving friend, and of late years again a very warm one. His work was done, and well done, and death must have been a relief to him from blindness,' thought William. On Monday, 12 September 1910 William was observed at the burial of Holman Hunt's ashes in St Paul's Cathedral (following cremation at Golders Green).[135] John A. Hipkins (1851–1933), a deaf artist who specialized in caricatures, caught the pride and gallantry of William's old age in a few swift economical lines (fig. 103).

William Rossett.
AT Holman Hunt's Funeral
St Paul's.

Sep 1910

at St Paul's Cathedral at the Funeral of W.H.H

103. John A. Hipkins, *William Michael Rossetti at Holman Hunt's Funeral*, 12 September 1910. Pencil, 105 × 80 mm. The National Library of Scotland, Edinburgh.

Edith Hipkins considered a typical caricature by her brother was 'curiously exact in supplying touches seldom revealed in the posed photograph. It is also unique for certain mannerisms with hands and feet, as individual to the owner as his head.'[136] At Hunt's funeral, William gazes dismayed into the future. His head is exaggeratedly ovoid; a darkly etched eye speaks of emotion repressed. His hands are concealed within a voluminous cape. The artist sees an old man disempowered, planted on absurd, perfunctory feet stiff with gout.

Hunt's widow, Edith, asked William to be one of the eight pallbearers at St Paul's. Others included Forbes Robertson the actor; Sir Charles Holroyd, director of the National Gallery; Professor Israel Gollancz of King's College, London, a founder of the British Academy, and Solomon J. Solomon the painter. William was particularly pleased to see his old friend the artist Arthur Hughes, looking older but 'still well and upright'. Agnostic William neverthe-less found the ceremony full of 'dignity and impressiveness' as he took a long 'last look at the casket, within the crypt enclosure, containing the ashes of my old friend'.[137] William went home from St Paul's to perform his last service for Hunt, characteristically assuaging grief by writing a memoir for the *Contemporary Review*.

7

Marriage

FITZROVIA TO SAN REMO, 31 MARCH 1874 – 12 APRIL 1894

Dearest Sweet – keep for yourself the great mass of my love, inter-changed as I know it is for all the warmth and profusion of yours.
   William to Lucy, 18 September 1874[1]

I think I love you more every day if it is possible.
   Lucy to William, 19 September 1876[2]

A great multitude of people have believed, and will continue to believe, that their life consists of a balance between unhappiness and happiness. Some will go so far as to say that the happiness visibly predominates.
   From William Rossetti's Lecture on Leopardi, 24 November, 1891[3]

Married life cannot be exactly happy when one of the spouses is perpetually and grievously ill. Affectionate and tender it may be, but not happy; indeed the very affection bars the possibility of happiness.
   From William Rossetti's biography of Dante Gabriel Rossetti, 1895[4]

How much of William's later feelings about Lucy and his marriage could he have foreseen on their wedding day, Tuesday, 31 March 1874? Looking back twenty years later after Lucy's death, on 12 April 1894, how much former happiness could he recall? Is previous happiness eroded or falsified by the fact that eventually it ended unhappily? There was realism on both sides on that day in 1874. Both bride and groom were mature adults – Lucy was thirty, William forty-four. It wasn't just a marriage between individuals; it was an alliance of two major Pre-Raphaelite families, the Madox Browns and the Rossettis.

   William had been engaged before, almost two decades previously, to Henrietta Rintoul. From October 1850, William, the rising young art critic of the *Spectator*, had been a frequent visitor to its editor, R.S. Rintoul, his wife and daughter Henrietta in their rooms above the office in the Strand, where he said he always felt at home and was 'treated with most abundant kindness.'[5]

   It has been suggested that during the later 1850s William may have modelled, or have been one of several models, for a beautiful drawing by Dante Gabriel Rossetti, now called, *Dante in Meditation Holding a Pomegranate* (fig. 104) (perhaps a study for or after the watercolour *Giotto Painting the Portrait of Dante,* 1852).[6] The head is exquisitely graceful and finished[7] in comparison

104. Dante
Gabriel Rossetti,
*Dante in
Meditation Holding
a Pomegranate*,
probably later
1850s . Pen, black
ink and graphite,
229 × 200 mm.
Yale Center for
British Art, Paul
Mellon Fund.

with the rest of the study, which is sketched in more loosely. If William did model for this figure of Dante, perhaps this is how Henrietta saw William, glamorous, poetic and Italianate in the heydays of their courtship.

Henrietta was a bluestocking, intellectual and high-minded. She and William were mutually attracted and shared passionate literary conversations. William introduced his new friend to his clever sisters and Henrietta first forged a rapport with Maria, the eldest.[8] But her friendship with Christina was to be the most enduring of all her relationships with the Rossettis. Years later in March 1882, Christina emphatically recommended Henrietta to John Ingram as a prospective biographer for his series of lives of eminent women. Although Christina claimed her friend was an accomplished writer who adorned a brilliant circle,[9] Henrietta declined the challenge, as earlier she had declined William's offer of marriage.

However, at its height, the romance nourished William. Unlike some of the other Pre-Raphaelite Brothers, he always enjoyed socializing with academic women. Between 1853 and 1855 he noted he had received twenty-six letters[10] from Henrietta as their relationship developed, and in January 1856 they became officially engaged. Summer holidays were spent together at Freshwater Bay and Yarmouth on the Isle of Wight, chaperoned by Henrietta's mother. William wrote vivacious letters home to his mother, studded with impromptu sketches, conveying genuine happiness.[11] He was exuberant, secure in their mutual relationship. They shared cliff walks and nature's elemental effects such as 'sea-mist combined with sun-light' that seemed more uplifting than ever before.[12] But on at least one occasion after his official engagement, William took Holman Hunt's seductive model Annie Miller out boating, 'forgetful it seems of Miss Rintoul!'[13] Annie's physique, class, availability and sexual energy made a dynamic contrast with Henrietta's emotional timidity and cerebral repression of the body. During summer 1858, he spent each day of his holiday from 9.00 a.m. until 10.30 p.m. walking and talking with his beloved, always chaperoned by Henrietta's limpet-like mother. But this year he noticed the beach was 'almost all stony'. Did William subconsciously recognize the impasse they had already reached? 'We have remained here quite stationary as yet & there is no *definite* proposal at present to move onwards', he told his own Mamma.[14] Yet, a year later in September 1859 he again joined the Rintouls on holiday in Eastbourne where he took lodgings between the downs and the sea.

The episode with Annie Miller may provide a clue to the otherwise mysterious ending of a sustained courtship. The Rintoul relationship had been as protracted as Gabriel's engagement to Lizzie Siddal, which was founded almost upon impossibility. Henrietta continually played for time, and postponed naming a date for her marriage to William. She endlessly invoked responsibility to elderly parents as her reason for delay. When both her parents died she still could not find the resolve to commit to William. Family legend whispered that she asked for a marriage without sex, which William rejected. Whatever failed between them, it was undoubtedly too painful for words. When the engagement was finally broken off in 1860, they returned each other's letters and probably burnt them. It is characteristically maddening of William, passionate archivist of other people's lives, that at the most interesting crisis points in his own he leaves very little personal trace. The diaries are suspended. The letters vanish.

Christina Rossetti was the only witness to record Henrietta's distress. On 29 November 1860 she visited Henrietta and had never seen 'anything like her misery', as she told William the next day. 'She held me fast kissing me and crying, and I could feel how thin she is and how she trembled in my arm. It seemed some relief to her to tell me a great deal about what is past and what now is: poor dear, I pity her beyond what words can express, and would give much to comfort her effectually; but that is indeed not in my power.' Christina's loyalties were uncomfortably divided, and although she always remained friendly with Henrietta, in the final analysis she supported her brother. It is clear that Christina understood the irreconcilable physical objection which divided the couple. 'If her happiness and yours were compatible, I would make a sacrifice to secure hers: but if otherwise, she cannot be dust in the balance with me, weighed against my most dear brother, whom

I love better than any man in the world and who has bought my gratitude by lifelong kindness.' Desperately trying to compensate William for the loss of Henrietta, Christina ended, 'I wish it were something better, but don't despise the love even a sister has to offer'.[15]

1860 was a difficult year for William. His engagement to Henrietta was over but Gabriel finally married his fiancée Lizzie Siddal on 23 May. Two years later in July 1862, William holidayed in Venice with William Bell Scott and out of habit or kindness wrote innocuous letters home to Henrietta, which were not intended to revive the relationship. By coincidence, 1862 was the date of William's first concerned mention of nineteen-year-old Lucy Madox Brown, 'poor Girl—' in a letter to his mother.[16] Prophetically it was a reference to ill-health, congestion of the lung.

By January 1865, five years after his engagement to Henrietta had ended, William had not forgotten her. Although there is no record that they ever met again by choice after 1860, he undoubtedly still identified his intellectual life with interests they used to share. As he prepared his translation of Dante's *Inferno* for publication, which had been written while he was engaged to Henrietta, William confided in Christina. Without a trace of malice he asked her to find out whether Henrietta would accept the dedication he had always promised to attach to his *Hell*. Henrietta had been away in Russia and Christina had not heard from her for months. She wondered whether Henrietta might prefer to drop the whole Rossetti family. Christina guessed Henrietta was still far from indifferent to William and although she could not pretend to analyse her friend's true feeling she guessed it was 'a very human bitter-sweet mixture'.[17] A fortnight later Christina reported Henrietta's choked response. 'So long as its fulfillment on your side is not under any sense of compulsion, she does not on hers (wish to) go back from the old promise: but empowers me to accept in her name the Dedication.'[18] So a brief dedication 'To H. R.' prefaced the translation, as if William dared not add any term of endearment. Thus, simply, he endorsed past love.

Henrietta was an early amateur photographer who photographed both William and Christina in the mid-1850s. Half a century later William remembered their composition precisely.[19] One small image of Henrietta herself survives (fig. 105). Gaze averted, she is heavily ringleted, pallid, inward. She presents an even more withdrawn personality than the famous ringleted photograph of Elizabeth Barrett Browning.[20] William's second daughter Helen Rossetti Angeli had nothing but contempt for 'that tedious Henrietta Rintoul' who had damaged her father, she believed, by trapping him in an engagement she never intended to consummate in marriage. 'In the end my father was very firm that he would have no nonsense of "sisterly love" and that all relations between them must *stop*.'[21] Helen Rossetti Angeli's brisk comments came from another perspective and another age. William himself always remained silent and discreet about Henrietta. She never married.

105. Photograph of Henrietta Rintoul. Fredeman Family Collection.

When she died on 15 November 1904, William was in Rome with his daughters and news did not reach him until ten days later. His diary entry, recalling his earlier Dedication, cryptically records just 'H.R.'[22] On 22 March 1905, Henrietta's executrix arranged to return a Chinese vase and a horn spoon that William may have given Henrietta years before but he was not specifically named in her will. [23]

By the early 1870s, Madox Brown's imposing house at 37 Fitzroy Square, 'big enough for a castle',[24] was a hub of artistic and intellectual life where Lucy and William constantly met at invigorating and sometimes bizarre social occasions. 'Dined at Madox Brown's', recorded watercolour artist George Price Boyce in his diary for 17 May 1872. 'Besides himself and wife and 2 daughters and Nolly there were Wm. Rossetti, Swinburne (who got drunk), M. Andrieux [sic], a Communist and a great egotist, and Hy. Wallis.'[25]

Irish politician and author Justin McCarthy remembered heady days in a Fitzroy Square Bohemia with Madox Brown at its heart. 'His home was a kind of open house for all who had any interest in art or, indeed, in anything that concerned the welfare of humanity.' Here McCarthy met Swinburne for the first time, Edwin Long, a painter who died young, novelist Mrs Lynn Linton and long, lanky William J. Stillman, the American artist and journalist. Gradually an informal debating society evolved. The object was to have a talk followed by discussion, 'just formal enough not to be careless and slipshod, and yet not so formal as to deter diffident people from getting up and expressing their ideas...we did not encourage long speeches, and we did not encourage any attempt at display; but we desired as far as was possible to get the opinions of everybody, and to prevail even upon the least practised speakers to get up and give us their thoughts'. McCarthy remembered many animated debates and 'bright extemporaneous speeches. Kegan Paul, the author and publisher, often took part' as did Forbes Robertson who later triumphed on the stage as Hamlet. Many women including the artistic Madox Brown sisters and poets Mathilde Blind and Mary Robinson attended these evening debates, but McCarthy could not recall that they ever spoke up in the open debates. It seems surprising that Lucy didn't 'speak up' as she relished conversation and had a melodious speaking voice.[26] Gabriel, too, enjoyed Lucy's talk, 'sensible, practical, and coloured by high thought and sympathy in the pictorial and the poetic arts'.[27] Perhaps McCarthy simply forgot the female contributions.

As well as holding debates, the Madox Browns threw large and brilliant parties. Prominent guests came from the worlds of art, literature and politics, personalities who 'were in the playbill' such as Sir Charles Dilke, Lord O'Hagan, several *Times* leader writers, Edmund Gosse, Professor Minto, William Allingham, poet Arthur O'Shaughnessy, and Henry Kingsley. 'Those were bright gatherings; and those were genial times.'

37 Fitzroy Square, with its Grecian urn above the front door, in the west-central heart of the metropolis, was once well known to Thackeray who used it as the fictional home for Colonel Newcome in *The Newcomes*, published 1853–5. By 1874, when Lucy married from the house, it was an aesthetic paradise, but Dr Marshall's snobbish daughter Jeannette thought it distinctly peculiar. 'The drawing room (I suppose) is carpeted with cocoa-nut matting, like our kitchen, with common gas burners, & the most extraordinary pictures on the walls; cane-bottomed chairs & a kind of divan in the centre' which she mockingly dubbed the 'woolsack'.[28]

From basement to attic at Fitzroy Square there were twenty rooms on six floors with two stone staircases, serviced by Charlotte Kirby the cook, a housemaid, and at one time a very pretty lady's maid – who spent most of her time posing for pictures. Heavy coal-scuttles to feed the fires on each of the five principal floors of the house, cans of hot water, paraffin lamps and trays of food for frequent invalids had to be laboriously dragged up and down stairs. The servants' day always began with the fireplaces, cleaning out cinders, black-leading bars and grate, and hearth-stoning the flags. At least once a week Charlotte scrubbed down the main staircase, the fine entrance hall and the vast floors on her hands and knees. Immaculate hearth-stoning of door-knocker, doorsteps and flagstones was another back-breaking but sacred domestic ritual.[29]

Lucy absorbed her father's attitude towards servants, a fusion of democratic principles with autocratic practice. So although she would pay their medical expenses and call servants by their first names, just like Virginia Woolf in a later generation, she upbraided them for their shortcomings, was unsentimental about 'letting them go' and constantly lamented the 'servant problem'. This was a persistent theme throughout Lucy's twenty years of married life with William. Lucy often suspected servants of cheating her or stealing from her, whereas William, although he often found them exasperating, took a more amused view.

Madox Brown's home was the nucleus and focus of the whole undefined organization. When he left London towards the end of the 1870s to paint his great series of murals for Manchester Town Hall, the Fitzrovian centre of this ad-hoc Bohemia could no longer hold. People migrated to the West End. The debating parties gradually broke up and eventually became only a memory. A quarter of a century later, Justin McCarthy could still remember 'bright things that were said, odd paradoxes that were started, and sparkling sarcasms that were tossed about in those nights of extemporaneous and unambitious discussion which began in the early seventies and ceased to flourish long before the seventies had drawn to their close.'[30]

This charged and exciting atmosphere was the backdrop to Lucy and William's early familiarity. They were simply part of each other's lives without even realizing it, although looking back, William believed that for several years before 1873 he had harboured a 'warmly affectionate feeling for Lucy Brown. She was the mainstay of her father's house; I always saw her sweet, gentle, and sensible.'[31] If Brown's home had been the hub of Fitzrovian social life, William perceived Lucy as the centre of that home. She appealed to him for many different reasons. He admired her 'ability of no common order as a painter', and her radical, libertarian views on politics and religion which closely matched his own. Although neither were atheists, both were confirmed agnostics, anti-monarchists and feminists. Physically, Lucy had a delicate, madonna-like prettiness and a taste for unusual dress and ethnic jewellery that accentuated her slender outline.

In spite of her obvious allure, little documentary evidence remains to record romantic entanglements during Lucy's girlhood, apart from a folder of unrequited love poetry in her hand, addressed to un-named objects of desire, such as this Valentine:

> Oh love! who from my youth up I have sought –
> Whose light hath beamed upon me from thine eyes
> Oh sweet one whom I dare not yet approach
> And yet can stay away from in no wise,
> Oh let me for this one time call thee mine,
> Oh let me say 'I love thee – in this Valentine.'[32]

Unsatisfactory love longings kept Lucy up all night, thinking elegiac thoughts, until with the sunrise she wrote a sonnet 'After sitting up till 6'o'clock.' There were assignations and declarations, 'my love held me by the hand,' and 'words of love by him were said' but the thread never led anywhere:

How long oh time! Am I to wait
Since joy of love have passed me by?
How long is now my weary fate
To hold the thread so patiently?[33]

In spite of, or perhaps because of, the insecure tone of her interior life, within the social whirl of her father's household, Lucy had acquired a certain outer confidence, a presence that could be formidable. Fourteen years her senior, and well established both in his full-time position at the Inland Revenue and as a prominent art critic, William was not disconcerted; he became increasingly intrigued. He was, however, recovering from the searing events of his brother's nervous breakdown in 1872 and felt most at ease within a family context. The Madox Browns, particularly through Ford's deep friendship with Gabriel, were almost family. Lucy, too, was in a period of recovery. During the early 1870s she had been pursued by the over-rated and now forgotten poet John Payne whom she was said (by his adulatory biographer) to have held in 'genuine regard'. However, it is extremely unlikely that Lucy entertained a single romantic thought about this misogynous egotist. When she married honourable William Rossetti instead, Payne's friends sneered she had exchanged 'a tongue of flame for an icicle'. Wounded, Payne gave out that his feelings for Lucy had been only a 'brief intoxication'. He penned a few bitter epigrams at the expense of William and women in general (most of whom he thought could be improved with a touch of the stick) before he forgot all about it.[34]

In the interim Lucy had lost the everyday support of her two most constant female studio companions. She had lost them to marriage - and they were both younger than Lucy. Marie Spartali had become William J. Stillman's second wife in 1871. On 3 September 1872, Cathy Madox Brown had married Dr Franz Hüffer. Dr Hake gossiped to William Bell Scott: 'The Bruno-Hüfferian conjunction – have you heard? – comes off on the third per registrar – the altar being out of date...Hüffer has taken a house at Merton.'[35] Cathy's departure increased Lucy's sense of isolation and during the winter of 1872/3 she was far from well, suffering her usual bronchial problems.

These two factors prompted Madox Brown, who was incurably romantic, to devise a plot. Ever since his broken engagement to Henrietta Rintoul in 1860, William had protected himself within the untouchable aura of a confirmed bachelor. More recently, he had suffered profoundly during Gabriel's breakdown and recovery in 1872. Madox Brown was sensitive equally to the needs and longings of his daughter and of his old friend. So when he heard that a touring party to Italy consisting of William Michael Rossetti, William Bell Scott, with his established companion Alice Boyd as well as his wife Letitia Scott was due to leave on 26 May 1873, Brown encouraged Lucy, now twenty-nine, to join the group. At home, Cathy was just pregnant with her first child, the future novelist Ford Madox Ford, to be born on 17

December 1873. Cathy's news, although barely public, was probably shared with Lucy on the eve of her departure and had its effect on her mood. For his part, William openly told his mother how much he wanted Lucy Madox Brown to join the party to Italy.[36] The boat-train was due to leave Victoria Station at 7.40 a.m. William arranged to collect Lucy from Fitzroy Square at 6.50 a.m. and asked her, as he was to take charge of all the party's luggage, to label hers:[37]

W.M. Rossetti
Passenger to
Paris & Rome
———————
L.B.

Bell Scott's passport survives, showing their exact route.[38] They travelled outward via Paris, Macon, Chambery, Mont Ceni, Turin, Genoa, Spezzia [*sic*] and Pisa to Rome. During the Italian holiday Lucy and William shared not only their passionate, democratic views but also a heightened response to the art everywhere around them. In the Roman summer she visited a photographer's studio for a *carte-de-visite* likeness taken by L. Suscipj (see fig. 20). Suffused with quiet happiness, Lucy looked noticeably younger than her nearly thirty years. 'We are all making ourselves as amiable to each other as our respective dispositions allow', William wrote to amuse his mother on 10 June 1873, enclosing a tabulated list of ailments suffered by each member of the party. He was already mildly alarmed by Lucy's tendency to cough and droop but in spite of this she rallied to admire 'a glorious moonlight view of the Colosseum' and, as he reported with quiet satisfaction to Mamma, seemed 'to be enjoying herself very greatly indeed – more than anyone else, with the possible exception of myself.'[39]

Drawn together by a shared admiration for Shelley, his great libertarian hero, and in the liberating freedom of holidaying abroad, William soon began to feel that Lucy was 'too dear to me to allow of my ever parting from her again.'[40] He saw no reason to delay a declaration but he nearly missed the moment. They had left Rome on an evocative return journey via Assisi, Florence, Bologna, Venice, Verona, Milan, Como, Bellinzona, the St Gotthard Pass to Basle, Langres, Paris and eventually the Channel, crossing at Calais. He managed to speak to Lucy on the necessary subject in Basle, Switzerland, when the party was nearly over.

They became engaged on 1 July 1873, which Lucy remembered years later as that 'strange happy sleepless night' when she first signed herself 'Your own Lucy'. Although the courtship was conducted with propriety within the unusual freedom of a group of Bohemian Victorians travelling abroad, Lucy's language suggests an eroticism that the holiday had already stirred in her and that marriage would fully arouse.

When William arrived home he observed the proper formalities even though, as his future father-in-law pointed out, both Lucy and he were mature adults well able to make their own decisions. Madox Brown freely gave his affectionate and unsurprised consent and privately told Lucy:

> W.R. is one of the men I most esteem…and as we all know quite incapable of allowing anyone who is near him to be unhappy – he is moreover of congenial tone of mind and occupations to you – how then could I do otherwise than cordially approve if you both love each other and wish to be united – if this is giving my consent you have it, but you know that I consider you quite wise enough to decide for yourself.[41]

Brown guessed that the newly-weds 'might for the present all live together in Euston Square' but he instantly reassured Lucy that she could 'come and paint at the studio as usual.'[43]

William next informed his dearest Mamma of his intentions.

> You know the extreme regard in which I (as also you and all of us) have always held Lucy Brown…It was yesterday week that I explained myself to her distinctly at Basle, and she avowed that she returns my love, and would willingly accept me…Lucy and I are therefore now engaged to marry: she speaks of a delay of a year or so, which to me appears more than wanted, but about this we shall see.

William was anxious not to repeat the long years of game-playing he had complied with during his engagement to Henrietta. In the event, Lucy kept him waiting just nine months, a healthy compromise. 'Dearest Mamma,' continued William, 'I am practically quite certain that you not only acquiesce with maternal affection in this resolve, but highly approve and rejoice in it.' He pressed home his advantage, putting words into his mother's mouth that he sensed he might not otherwise hear from her. 'I am pretty sure that our dearest sweetest Lucy would have been the wife of your choice for me, had you had to select one. To me she has long been the woman among women.' He swiftly moved on to reassure his mother that everything would remain the same. An Englishman Italianate, William subscribed subconsciously to the Latin conventions of family life. 'I told Lucy from the first that I should continue living with you and my sisters: to me any other course would be out of the question. If you had heard how warmly she confirmed my resolution, you would not have…the slightest doubt that she really approves and likes this arrangement.' But his resolute, affirmative language was undermined by a subtext of negative terms, 'out of the question' and 'slightest doubt'. While appearing to pay homage to his Italian roots, William was a modern, even a feminist man, as sympathetic to Lucy's career as he was to his sisters' vocations. 'We must enable her to use one room or other as a studio.'[43]

106. Dante Gabriel Rossetti, *Eliza Polidori*, 1858. Pencil, 229 × 178 mm, Surtees 411. Reproduced with kind permission of Christopher Powney.

William still had the complexities of maternal approval at the back of his mind just before his wedding eight months later. Thanking Mrs Heimann for her present of a teapot 'with a capital handle', he added wryly how glad he was that her son Charles had found 'a bride so much to your taste and (what is still more important) to his own.'[44]

The only person in the immediate Rossetti family who had shrewdly forecast the engagement was William's unconventional and alarming aunt Eliza, the youngest of the Polidori sisters, who had nursed with Florence Nightingale in the Crimea in 1854.[45] She smelt of pepper and was 'only partially amiable'. Her great-niece Helen Rossetti Angeli said she had 'the features and complexion of a Red Indian' and forced little girls to eat tapioca. She was notorious in the family for wearing hopelessly out of date coal-scuttle bonnets, green eye-shades or caps with flaps over the ears which gave her 'an uncompromising aspect' (fig. 106).[46]

Frances wrote to her sister Eliza on 10 July 1873 from Kelmscott where she and Christina were staying with Gabriel. 'Perhaps you have heard of your surmise being realised by William proposing to, & being accepted by Lucy Brown…I am very pleased that William's choice has fallen on so good tempered & estimable a woman as Lucy…You & I will have a talk about it when we meet'.[47]

Some cynics in the Rossetti–Brown circle were unsurprised by the post-holiday announcement of an engagement. William Bell Scott and others suspected Brown's hand in the affair. 'You see how my anticipations and surmises about old Brown's intentions in sending Lucy with us have been exactly fulfilled', he wrote to Alice Boyd on 11 July 1873. 'The investment has been a good one. The old fox is really an able diplomat. The last ruse of going out of town and so leaving Lucy almost alone on returning home completed the trick'.[48] A week later, Madox Brown denied the accusation of match-making. 'He had no idea of William assuming the position of a Lover, of course not'. However, Brown's protestations failed to convince Bell Scott, who 'did not let him carry away the notion that I was so green as to believe that'.[49]

Lucy's 'loving sister Pussy Cat' (Cathy) heard the news from their father and wrote to congratulate Lucy in aggrieved tones – why hadn't Lucy told her the news direct? Pregnant and moody, Cathy concluded her letter more graciously, 'I do so hope you will have a happy life' and promised that Franz would compose a chorus for all the guests to sing at the wedding breakfast.[50] Other relations and friends sent congratulations, aunt Helen Bromley, Mathilde Blind and Lucy's excited, romantic cousin Lizzie Cooper.[51] In contrast, Gabriel composed a mischievous private doggerel that mimicked William's habit of grave understatement:

> *Monody*
> I can no more defer it
>   Conclusions I must tell, –
> She's not devoid of merit
>   And I love her pretty well.
>
> My name begins with W.
>   And hers begins with L., –
> With details I'll not trouble you,
>   But I love her pretty well.
>
> Perhaps to wait were better, –
>   A thought I would repel,
> Indeed it makes no matter,
>   And I love her pretty well.

William Bell Scott crowed to Edmund Gosse 'it is so tremendously like W.M.R.'[52] – who was notorious in their circle for commending any new art work with the words, 'It's not without its merit and I like it pretty well'.

Nevertheless, Gabriel told William 'how heartily I rejoice in your engagement to Lucy. I really believe there is not in the whole of our circle a woman on whose excellence all of us could place such perfect reliance, all of whom we should feel so sure that she would make you happy…Will you give Lucy my sincere love, and say I wish I were worthier to be her brother and yours?' He also managed to slip in some heartening allusions to family approval. 'My mother has been thoroughly enjoying herself here, I'm sure; and it is curious that both she and Christina have happened more than once to speak very strongly in Lucy's praise, and express their love for her very warmly…yesterday in the boat my Mother was saying…that she valued Lucy more than any woman she knew.'[53]

On the same day 10 July 1873, Christina wrote to her 'very dear William' to tell him he had 'brought a fresh spring of happiness and interest into our family, and the kindness with which your letter alludes to me in one general sentence is warm in my heart. Who shall wish you well except the sister whom you have cared for all her life? If dear Lucy and you are as happy as I would (if I could) make you, earth will be the foretaste and stepping stone to heaven.' It seemed entirely natural to William that Christina would relate his present happiness to an afterlife in which he had no belief. It was an obtrusive piety that, all too soon, Lucy would find grating. At this early stage Christina was generous about Lucy. 'Her sweetness, amiability and talent make her a grace and honour to us – but I need not state this to *you*...I had a little friendly chat with Mrs Brown [Emma Madox Brown, Lucy's step-mother] this morning, and find her and hers as full of welcome as we are. I have ventured to write affectionately to Lucy',[54] which she did most gracefully: 'I should like to be a dozen years younger, and worthier every way of becoming your sister; but, such as I am, be sure of my loving welcome to you as my dear sister and friend. I hope William will be all you desire; and, as I know what he has been to me, a most loving and generous brother, I am not afraid of his being less than a devoted husband to you. May love, peace, and happiness, be yours and his together in this world, and together much more in the next; and, when earth is an anteroom to heaven (may it be so, of God's mercy to us all), earth itself is full of beauty and goodness.'[55]

William and Lucy's wedding plans, however, were firmly rooted in this world rather than the next. They were already plotting an Italian honeymoon for the whole of April and part of May 1874, including Naples, Rome and Florence on their itinerary. Both Madox Brown and Emma had been unwell during the winter of 1873/4, Brown with excruciating gout, and they longed to throw one of their old style parties. They planned a fashionable, pre-wedding evening party, starting at 9 p.m. on the continental model, at 37 Fitzroy Square on 30 March. Gabriel's jangled nerves were not up to the occasion as he explained to William, 'the fact is that, at such a gathering as you indicate, every bore I know and don't know would swoop down on me after these two years' absence, and I am not equal to it, now that solitude is the habit of my life.' Gabriel shrank from the event with spoken and unspoken objections. He cited Swinburne's abominable ways as a particular disincentive. Brown tried to wheedle, and then bully both Gabriel and Morris into attending but only added his personal grievance to already strained relations. 'Morris I certainly regard with great affection but what sort of an *old friend* is it who can't bring himself to say a few civil words when one's son brings out such a book as mine has',[56] smarted Brown, quick to perceive a slight to precocious eighteen-year-old Nolly's publication of his novel, *Gabriel*

Denver, in 1873. Neither Morris nor Gabriel attended the evening party on 30 March 1874. Holman Hunt and George Price Boyce did attend and met a great number of friends old and new.[57]

Gabriel jibbed, too, at the prospect of the private family wedding fixed for the next morning, but in spite of expressing his qualms in strongly negative language, he promised to attend. 'I cannot say that a breakfast of unknown relations smiles on me either, any more than on you; but that is unavoidable, so there's an end.'[58] His dread of the wedding was compounded by the thought of coming face to face with William Morris. Janey Morris also declined the evening party, probably from similar scruples, but found Morris and herself committed to the 'extra quiet wedding-breakfast' following a brief civil ceremony, specifically chosen because of the bride and groom's secular principles. Morris rumbled in private: 'Sad grumbling, but do you know I have got to go to a wedding next Tuesday; to wit Lucy Brown and William Rossetti and it enrages me that I lack courage to say "I don't care for either of you and you neither of you care for me and I won't waste a day out of my precious life in grinning a company grin at you two old boobies." '[59] In his autobiography William Rossetti did not flinch from quoting Morris's offensive remarks about himself and Lucy – although he firmly cut the quotation before the 'old boobies'. There had been happier relations in the past, when Lucy had spent her twenty-sixth birthday with the Morrises, holidaying together in Calais.[60] 'That Morris did not care for either of us', wrote William, 'cannot now be helped; he was mistaken in thinking that I did not, in all reasonable measure, care for *him*. But indeed I had never seen ground for supposing that Morris regarded me with anything that could be called predilection', explained William frankly. 'It was Madox Brown (not myself, averse as I am from everything of the sort, and most prompt to believe in the aversion of others) who bespoke Morris and his wife to the wedding-breakfast'.[61] In his own mind William tried to deflect Morris's animosity with humour, commenting awkwardly that 'the author of *The Earthly Paradise* was the least paradisal of men.'[62]

In spite of, or perhaps because of, the humiliating embarrassment Morris dreaded at the Rossetti–Brown wedding, when he would have to smile at Gabriel – his wife's lover – he gave William and Lucy a tersely inscribed but perfect copy of a rare antiquarian book. It was Schedel's *Chronicum Nurembergensis* (*Chronicle of Nuremberg*) – a history of the world dated 1493, containing over 2,250 'very quaint and spirited woodcuts of portraits (including Pope Joan, unmutilated), cities, historical events, etc. (many very large), by Michael Wolgemut (Master of Albert Dürer).'

On 31 March 1874 at St Pancras Register Office (where Cathy Brown and Frank Hueffer had married in September 1872, and where Virginia Stephen and Leonard Woolf would marry in 1912) Lucy's father and William's mother were witnesses at the brief ceremony. Back in Fitzroy Square at the wedding

107. Syrian chest, wedding present to William and Lucy from Holman Hunt (40.6 cm high, 61 cm wide, 34.3 cm deep). Private collection.

breakfast, wary guests included both uneasy factions – William and Janey Morris, Gabriel and Christina Rossetti. There is no record that Lucy's old tutor, Maria Rossetti, was present at the non-religious ceremony – perhaps because the rules of her All Saints Sisterhood precluded it – although before her novitiate she had attended Cathy's secular wedding.

Lucy and William's wedding presents accurately reflected the bride and groom's intellectual and aesthetic tastes as well as the current craze for Japonisme. George Price Boyce presented '7 pieces of Nankin and Japanese black and white china, etc.'[63] Literary friends Mathilde Blind and Lowes Dickinson sent presents and congratulations, declaring no one more deserved a happy future.[64] Photographs, watercolours and engravings came from Gabriel's studio assistant Henry Treffry Dunn,[65] Mrs Harrison[66] and Lawrence Alma-Tadema.[67] James Leathart, the Newcastle industrialist and Gabriel's patron, sent a 'handsome silver boat dish'[68] and Augusta Webster presented one of her own books.[69] Artist Arthur Hughes gave plates for serving almonds and raisins, and Edmund Gosse, the literary critic and Scandinavian specialist, sent a miniature set of Danish cups and saucers. Four days before the wedding he wrote to Lucy from the British Museum, acknowledging her impeccable aesthetic credentials: 'It is difficult to think of anything that you have not already, you who live in the midst of beautiful things. I am forced back upon my foster-country. Can you ever drink "aesthetic tea" out of the tiny Danish service that accompanies this? It has come from Copenhagen.'[70] Swinburne cracked a convoluted and obscure joke about the benediction of Urizen in his wedding message. It amused the intellectual Lucy whose 'glee was touching', reported her happy fiancé.[71] Holman Hunt presented one of the most exotic gifts, a magnificent ornamental chest, probably Syrian, which he had brought back from the East (fig. 107).[72] Pasted inside the lid, William's careful, archival note still survives, confirming the donor and the occasion.

Her new brother-in-law Gabriel offered Lucy a unique wedding present – her portrait (see fig. 22), for which she posed during summer 1874, giving him a final sitting in early August, a few days before miscarrying her honeymoon baby.

After their wedding Lucy and William left from Victoria station on a honeymoon that partly retraced their Italian footsteps of the previous year.[73] The next day William wrote to his mother from the Fountain Inn, Canterbury, en route to Dover and the Channel crossing. 'I have not much to mention beyond what you will readily believe – my entire happiness.'[74] The frigidity of Henrietta Rintoul was buried in his past. He knew himself loving and beloved. They reached Paris by Thursday afternoon when Lucy had a small but characteristic 'turn-up with the chambermaid.'[75] Over a cold, wet Easter weekend many Parisian attractions were shut but they enjoyed excellent French food, went to a morning performance of Molière, visited the Jardin d'Acclimatation and the Louvre, and Lucy shopped for chic baby clothes in the rue de Rivoli for Cathy's firstborn. By Monday Lucy had one of her recurrent colds but they were up before 5.00 a.m. to catch the train to Lyons. Delayed in Marseilles, both Lucy and William admired paintings by Henri Regnault in the art gallery. Regnault's exotic politico-historical pictures made tacit reference to dictators and oppression everywhere and struck a thrill of recognition in Lucy's mind. Only a year before she had painted *Margaret Roper*, her own most feminist picture on the theme of tragic injustice under the Tudor dictator, Henry VIII (see fig. 89).

From Marseilles, they sailed to Naples on Sunday, 12 April. Lucy was limp and seasick for the two days' voyage but gradually recovered to make, like most tourists, the 'usual glorious' excursions to Pompeii, Capri, Paestum, Salerno, Ravello and Amalfi. They arrived in Rome by train on 28 April where they stayed at Hotel d'Amérique, the same hotel as the previous year. Lucy still had a sore throat and flu-like symptoms but gallantly sat for a touching honeymoon photograph, the only surviving picture to show Lucy and William together (see fig. 21). Indulging his bride's love of art and taste for the morbid, William bought Lucy photographs of Italian art works and 'sepulchral slabs'.[76] Madox Brown sent 'all our best loves to William' and hoped the newly married couple would 'both be as happy as possible'.

Both partners relished the new freedom of the honeymoon. William told Lucy's teenage brother rather solemnly, 'I am sure no man can be happier than I am in the society & love of his wife'[77] and assured his mother, 'We are both most happy. I am, and Lucy tells me she is, and all appearances confirm the assertion.'[78] From Kelmscott, Gabriel joked to Madox Brown that 'William's naïf description of his bliss should bear fruit in nine months'.[79] It was marred only by premonitions of Lucy's tubercular illness. With painful memories of the frail constitution of his own wife, Lizzie Siddal, Gabriel speculated that Lucy's fragility was organic, her persistent colds an omen of future anxiety and he feared for William's prolonged happiness. 'No man deserves happiness more, or is better adapted to give and receive it',[80] thought Gabriel, rejoicing that at last marriage had revitalized his brother's 'somewhat fossilized habit of life'.[81]

Before setting off homewards, in Florence the couple visited William's cousin, Teodorico Pietrocola-Rossetti and his wife Isabella, who treated Lucy with homeopathic remedies. She had been suffering for days with aching limbs and an even worse sore throat. After dinner, she could scarcely walk back to their hotel and William had to find a cab over the Ponte S. Trinita.

Lucy and William returned to England on 13 May 1874. They settled with Frances and Christina Rossetti at 56 Euston Square, later renamed 5 Endsleigh Gardens in January 1880 after the notorious 'Euston Square Murder', when neighbours thought gentility would be restored by a change of address. Nasturtiums and sunflowers bloomed in the communal garden square. But growing up as a child there in the 1880s, Lucy and William's daughter Olive remembered the whole neighbourhood marked by a dingy 'and depressing respectability'.[82] William had taken a twenty-one-year lease on this Cubitt-built, end of terrace town house from 24 June 1867 at an annual rent of £125,[83] plus rates, taxes and £3 fire insurance. It was a modern, spacious, corner house[84] comprising sixteen to eighteen rooms from basement to attics.[85] Gas for lighting, although not for heating, was laid on, and an elaborate bell system for summoning servants installed. There were three water-closets, two with mahogany seats for the family, and one with a painted seat in the basement for servants.

The kitchen (which Lucy never entered, according to her daughter Helen) was equipped with a five-foot range with oven and boiler, swing trivet, roasting crane, spit rack, water supply from a cistern and a ten-foot dresser with drawers and shelves. Adjoining was a scullery, larder, pantry and wine cellar. More labour-intensive devices including a 41-inch range with ironing stove and a nine-foot range of presses, presumably for wringing wet laundry, were kept in the housekeeper's room. The yard outside housed a lockable meat safe, the knife house and 'dust hole' for dustbins.

Above stairs, on the ground floor were a lobby, two dining-rooms, a third room and a lavatory; above were two balconied drawing-rooms divided by folding doors, two bedrooms, a dressing-room, bathroom and lavatory; three further bedrooms on the next floor and the final (fifth) servants' floor housed cupboards, a lead cistern, skylight with iron guard bars and the sprung bell system. Register or Romford stoves for burning coal were installed in all the main rooms, some with black marble chimney-pieces and stone hearths. The fitments were mainly brass, oak and mahogany and the lease specified 'about 102 feet of picture rods and forty-one wall hooks' – a fair start for William's expanding art collection.[86]

Over the fifteen years, from 1874 to 1890, of Lucy and William's joint occupation, the house became crammed with furniture, books, pictures, china, bric-a-brac and 'lumber of all possible descriptions' including, after Gabriel's death in 1882, all the 'detritus from Cheyne Walk that had been considered unfit for the sale and had been spared by ghouls and vampires.' All the heavy work was done by the servants, the Barneses. 'Nominally the house was run with two servants (Heaven help them!) – a cook and a housekeeper', recalled Helen Rossetti Angeli. 'But those "two servants" were a fiction: they throve and multiplied like black beetles in the lower depths.' The Barnes tribe was augmented by Uncle Barnes, a carpenter who taught young Arthur Rossetti woodwork. 'Father Barnes', although a skilled craftsman, a furniture gilder, posed a problem. He was often in the house but unable to work as rough labour would spoil his perfect gilder's hands. 'Gilded furniture had gone out of fashion some 50 years earlier with the Regency', and demand for Father Barnes's skills had dried up. He had been unemployed for nearly two decades, 'jealously preserving his hands for a revival.' Neither Lucy nor her father were able to induce him to do any picture-framing although he constantly assured them 'he was ready at any moment to re-gild the sofa.'[87]

On their newly-wed return to 56 Euston Square in mid-May 1874, rooms on an upper floor were assigned to Lucy and William. Gabriel pressed them with furniture from Chelsea and entertained them there together with the Browns and Watts.[88] Lucy was just pregnant but told no one in the house except William. Everyone tried to make a success of communal living but the atmosphere soon became unbearably strained. With his habitual gift for understatement, William noted that domestic harmony 'was not unflawed, and was sometimes rather jarringly interrupted.'[89] The real sticking point was the relationship between Christina and Lucy. They held diametrically opposed views on religion and on Christina's side there was aversion, compounded by rigorously controlled jealousy. She worked so hard over the years to love Lucy and Lucy shuddered at it. It was bitter to be loved only because she was married to William, that precious 'last fragment' of Christina's 'original nearest and dearest' for whose sake 'his wife and children occupy affectionate niches (what a phrase!), as indeed they may well do for their own', the poet wrote self-consciously to a friend much later.[90] Christina and Lucy were better on paper and apart. Once the experiment in communal living had been abandoned, they exchanged letters which kept up the fiction of mutual affection and united them in genuine, fierce love of William and Lucy's children.

Christina unburdened herself at length to her friend Caroline Gemmer who had obviously dared to inquire on the subject of Lucy.

> I will not suspect your question of being less than a kind one! And I select to answer it!! Lucy & I knew each other many years before I foresaw our

present close connexion, (which foresight indeed dawned upon me only along with *the* proposal), – I her from a child, & she me from a young woman, for there are many years between us, – & thus we in great measure knew or might have known each other beforehand. I do not suppose we are altogether congenial, but we do very well together: she is clever in her way, & I think she would (oh vanity!) say as much for me in mine; & her way being art, & mine literature, our fields are all our own.

The poet's retiring soul and poor health were at odds with Lucy's active taste for social life. Although 'still only a bride,' Christina continued, 'she is quite at her ease in housekeeping & in receiving friends, & thus no trouble devolves on myself. One thing I thoroughly enjoy, that my Mother & I can now go about just as we please at our own sweet wills, without any consciousness of man resourceless or shirt-buttonless left in the lurch!' Christina claimed bravely,

we are all very independent of each other, & this is quite comfortable to me. My account does not read brilliantly, yet compared with many a possibility it is even excellent: & perhaps a year hence I may look back at this experimental stage, & own that it paved the way to much brighter things, *if* only *I* exert myself to be homelike & eligible: I know of plenty of faults on my own side to account for a standard of ideal perfection not yet having been attained.[91]

Christina welcomed the opening given her by Caroline Gemmer's question. It allowed her a safe place to confront her own tangle of emotions about the new Mrs Rossetti. One of the problems was undoubtedly the difference in their ages; Lucy had been a paying-guest and schoolgirl in the Rossetti household, a very junior member. Now, Christina felt that their positions were subtly reversed. She was suddenly, firmly the established old maid, no longer the first woman her brother turned to either for mental resources or mundane buttons. Christina admitted that she and Lucy were not 'altogether congenial'. There was something in her that recoiled from Lucy personally. Lucy's intelligence was exacting but it was not instinctive like Christina's. Instead of being a bond, it was a barrier between them. Christina was relieved that at least Lucy would not be pitted against her in her own field of literature. She would be contained, if not safely, in the studio. Outside it, Lucy who had been used to running her father's household, was irritatingly confident about running the Rossettis' and glibly imported her own circle of friends into the sober days at Euston Square. Christina and her mother tactfully kept out of the way. Lucy felt that her friends were being ostracized. Misunderstandings multiplied. Lucy later confessed she had 'a capacity for inspiring dislike!'[92] Christina was conscious that the experiment in collective living was not going 'brilliantly'. The standard of 'ideal perfection' she yearned for in her relations with her sister-in-law seemed unattainable, although she put as bright a face upon it as she could. The pathos and bravado in Christina's account is painful witness to embarrassing emotions on both sides.

Some responsibility for the simmering tensions lay with William himself, as he later admitted. In the end there could be only one possible resolution – judicious separation, in his diplomatic phrase. 'No two persons could be less encroaching or less interfering, or more observant of the rightful rule that the wife is the mistress of the house, than my mother and sister...it was obviously a great grief to my relatives to find that Lucy...was as far from orthodoxy as myself.' Although his elder sister Maria had decided to become an Anglican nun and enter the All Saints Sisterhood before Lucy arrived, High Anglicanism was in the very air breathed by William's elderly mother and his younger sister Christina, now forty-three.

> After giving a fair, or indeed a prolonged, trial to the experiment of the joint household, we decided to separate. My mother and Christina, along with my two aunts, took a house for themselves, 30 Torrington Square, at Michaelmas 1876; while I, with my wife and the daughter born to us in 1875, remained in Endsleigh Gardens...The separation was highly painful to my mother, and only a little less so to myself...There appears to be a general rule, suitable at any rate to English people: it is not well for a wife to be housed with her mother-in-law, nor yet for a husband with his.[93]

The inevitable chafing between the generations was exacerbated by totally differing views on religion, as William conceded. But William was also to blame for creating this impossible situation, driven by his sentimental optimism.

In marrying Lucy, William allied himself with a mature woman with a career. She was not a conventional Victorian mouse-wife but a woman with a formed and independent personality. When Lucy married William, she had no intention of giving up her profession as an artist. William admired her work and knew she was 'ambitious of excelling, and not indifferent to fame'. Conscious of her intellectualized and 'exalted idea of art and its potencies', he never trivialized her artistic ambitions and it became a matter of genuine regret to him that marriage and domestic responsibility effectively curtailed her career. 'After our marriage she tried more than once to set resolutely to work again; but the cares of a growing family, delicate health, and the thousand constant interruptions...always impeded her, and very much to her disappointment and vexation, she did not succeed in producing any more work adapted for exhibition.'[94]

Mutually appreciative, Lucy encouraged William's literary career. 'Make your lectures [on Shelley] a success' she urged him when he went to Newcastle in January 1876, 'but they are sure to be. I believe in you.'[95] At the Leatharts' Newcastle dinner party, Mrs Watson asked him if Lucy looked like her very pretty sister Cathy Hueffer? William replied that Lucy was much the prettier and had 'vastly more expression'.[96] He reported to Lucy that the

Leathart baby, a boy, was far inferior in scale, rotundity and intelligence to their own Olivia.[97] Lucy was nervous at home without him, imagining burglars in the night. He continually tried to soothe her hyper-anxiety. 'Dearest, dear Lucy, you must not make yourself nervous and dispirited. Solace & amuse yourself with the kid, & be certain – as indeed you *are* of my unfailing love.'[98] Spoken or unspoken, written or unwritten, he wanted her to feed off the depth of his love.

Lucy's health, or lack of it, was the sad reason that such full and detailed evidence survives to document the marriage. Marriages are rarely witnessed by hundreds of surviving letters unless the partners are separated geographically. The only palliative doctors could offer Lucy was climatic, to seek the South, first the south coasts of England or the Isle of Wight, and later French and Italian Riviera resorts. Lengthy separation was made bearable by William and Lucy's '*diurnal correspondence* system'[99] revealing their inter-dependent and oscillating relationship. Even though Lucy was slightly in awe of her middle-aged husband in the early years, she became skilled at exerting her needs and her personality. In spite of her own admitted 'general remissness' as a letter writer, Lucy wrote regularly, compulsively to William, sympathizing with his constraints of office life and longing that he could be instead, as on this occasion in August 1878, here 'my darling' in Charmouth, Dorset, though ruefully fearing 'you often find me far from your taste. I wish I could always be charming to you.'[100]

After suffering a miscarriage in August 1874, Lucy gave birth to her first child, a daughter, Olivia Frances Madox on 20 September 1875 (fig. 108). Consciously or subconsciously, her parents named her after her young dead uncle, Oliver Madox Brown. Cathy named her second son Oliver (born in 1877) for the same reason. Both sisters were keen to please their father Madox Brown. Lucy recovered well from her confinement and one of Olivia's earliest admirers was Swinburne. William thanked him for his attentive letter sent swiftly after the birth and told him, 'Lucy took such excessive delight in its references to the baby that she has kept it by her all this interval...we shall of course be extremely pleased to reveal the baby to you at your convenience; and Lucy confesses to a lurking hope and ardent wish that you may yet write a verse or two to welcome the bantling'.[101] Swinburne was a famous admirer of babies and Lucy's wish was immediately fulfilled. Four days after William had floated the idea on 15 October, Swinburne sent *A Birth Song* to Olivia's parents, later published in the *Athenaeum*. It told how, after the previous autumn's grief when Oliver's death 'fell colder than a tear', the arrival of the 'sweet small olive-shoot' before the end of this year's harvest, had re-quickened 'high hopes and hearts'.[102] 'How many births, I wonder, have been at the instant celebrated with anything approximating to it, since the beginning of the world?' William enthused to the poet.[103] To mark the first anniversary of Nolly's death on 5 November, Lucy and William spent a few subdued days

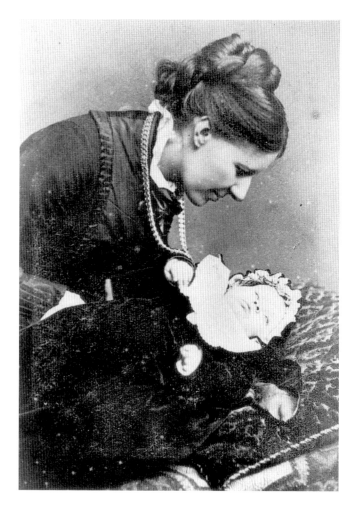

108. Lucy with her first child, Olivia, photograph sent to Swinburne, 9 April 1876. Cathy Hueffer's photograph album, STH/BH/2/3-6. The Stow Hill Collection, HLRO, and the Hon. Oliver Soskice.

with Brown and Emma. Remembering him made their baby more precious. Four other children followed, (Gabriel) Arthur on 28 February 1877, Helen on 10 November 1879, and finally twins Mary and Michael on 22 April 1881 – 'a serious look-out'– as William sighed to his diary.[104] With each successive birth, Lucy displayed an unexpected, boundless zeal for her late-found maternity.

As was customary for Victorian middle-class wives, Lucy spent long summer holidays at the seaside. Usually William could only get away from Somerset House for a fortnight but he often made a dash by train at weekends. 'My own darling,' wrote Lucy from Ventnor, Isle of Wight, on 12 September 1876:

you are so welcome to me in your letters which arrive before I am up...Olive has the envelope and kisses it instead of Papa whom she always looks for. Last night she was very wakeful with her teeth, moaning for hours and making me feel most wretched...We are going to Shanklin this afternoon, to call on Mrs Spartali and the John Marshalls, whom Marie [Stillman, née Spartali] thinks of asking to lunch tomorrow...I hope you found Gabriel well last night – I'm feeling so sick and tired darling, I suppose with being so much up in the night...so if this is short dear Ffof, do not think I love you less – all the more if possible – your own Lucy.[105]

She was just over three months pregnant with Arthur, which made attending to fretful one-year-old Olive even harder. Three days later the strain of separation deepened:

I fear that not having me by, to talk nonsense to my dear Ffof, is bad for you, for tho' I am what you call timorous, I recover myself sooner, and try always to foresee the best. How I wish I were with you and you with me – it would be difficult the one without the other but I mean the wish...Tell me if you would like me to come home sooner.[106]

She called him affectionately *Fofus, Ffof* or *Foffus*, meaning approximately 'funny, fussy old fogey'.[107] Nearly a decade later when he was supplying lists of quotations to illustrate definitions of words for the new *Oxford English Dictionary*, William teased Lucy with a semantic explanation: 'You and I have sometimes joked about the name Fofus – whether any mortal was ever called so etc. It is curious that, in now reading the letters of Horace Walpole...I find the word Phobus applied in much the same sense which Fofus conveys to us – obviously not very far distant from "old fogey".'[108] Sometimes he even embellished his signature as *Fofeticus Ineptus* or wrote it with a flourish in Greek letters: Φοφος or even Φοφη μου σας ἀγαπω – (O Fofus of mine I love you).[109]

Underlying the playfulness between husband and wife were earnest and repeated declarations of love on both sides. In April 1876 Lucy sent her 'Dearest Love a few lines to say how much I love you'. She marvelled at the perfect reciprocity of their feelings, found his sweet letters 'like a gleam of sunshine on this unclouded day'[110] and longed for him to leave his office routine to join her and baby Olive on the beach at Broadstairs.[111] She was avidly reading George Eliot and working every day on a sketch of the seaside resort with its Dickens' associations (see fig. 94). She teased him that love letters from admirers might be piling up for him in her absence, although he reassured her that Fofus was no 'gay Lothario'. Above all, she needed his physical presence. He too longed to be with his 'dear love' to 'give you a blow', which really seemed to improve her health and sick headaches.[112] His daily letters were a tangible substitute, as refreshing as 'blows'.[113] 'I wish so you were here but only lovingly darling – to give me a "blow" for one thing',[114] she wrote, in their private code for making love or an orgasm.[115] He teased her:

Who gave me a refreshing blow
Tho' I repeatedly said No?
My Fofus.[116]

'Oh my darling I did want you so much to give many *proper* kisses to – ';[117] 'My poor Ffof, I do so want to kiss you'.[118]

Lucy's need for sex may have been related to what she believed was its therapeutic function. Nineteenth-century doctors not only advised lovemaking for patients with a tendency to consumption, but the contemporary received wisdom about tuberculars was that they experienced heightened erotic cravings. Without a doubt the physical side of the relationship was passionate and satisfying until the final stages of Lucy's illness. For historians conditioned to believe stereotypes of prim Victorian behaviour, it is fascinating to find a couple writing so openly and intimately to one another, but as quasi-Bohemians William and Lucy were somewhat outside the constraints of conventional middle-class mores. Lucy also informed William about menstruation, when she often stayed in bed. 'My next period will recur in about a week or a day or two more – I must be particularly careful this time not to move till it is over.'[119] Although Helen Rossetti Angeli remembered a conspiracy of reticence on the body during childhood, her elderly father discussed breast-feeding and nipple shields (that Mamma had sometimes needed) with her in 1905.[120]

In her letters Lucy fretted that 'poor Ffof' would not only disapprove of her slapdash handwriting but her idiosyncratic spelling and lack of punctuation would not meet his own high literary standards. She warned him 'I always write my worst to those I love the best.'[121] Her assertiveness concealed a fear that William, the literary man, might discover her imagined inadequacy. 'It is a good thing I am what I am to you or how intensely stupid' he would find her letters.[122] She channelled their late-found mutual love into a fervent commitment to all their children, especially, after her miscarriage, their precious first-born daughter Olivia. 'Our little Olive will be one year old tomorrow – Oh darling I hope we may both see our baby's baby at least the same age.'[123] With her uncertain health, Lucy's nervous premonition was destined to be fulfilled. She died when Olive was only eighteen.

Lucy's edgy personality, her perversity, her irritability is evident from the earliest days of the marriage but intensified later in the active stages of consumption. A distinctly querulous note is sounded in her declarations of supplicating love from Dorset in summer 1878 for 'poor Ffofus' whom she chides 'is always too tired or sedate to take a walk with his wife in London. Does he remember how she upset his equanimity by an occasional suggestion that way? - fondest love dearest - Your own wife (whether you like it or no) Lucy'.[124] William wrote daily from his busy London life, spicing affection with humour (fig. 109). He missed his little family.

109. William Michael Rossetti's sketch of his two eldest children, Olive (nearly 3 years) and Arthur (18 months), at the end of a letter to Lucy, 7 August 1878, 8 p.m. Pen and ink, 178 × 121 mm. University of British Columbia Library, Rare Books and Special Collections, Angeli-Dennis Collection 7-8.

Lucy wished she were kissing William instead of scribbling. 'I shall do a little more work again at my pictures...Olive and Arty are the prettiest children in the place everyone says...You cannot think how I long to kiss you'.[125] She played with the word 'darling' and used it against him in mock rebuke. 'My own Darling, I like your sweet letter calling me darling, being a rather unusual word of yours makes it perhaps all the dearer when it comes.' She was not above using the children to insinuate herself into his favour. 'Olive woke up in my bed this morning saying in innocence I do want to go back to London [.] Why? I said – to kiss my dear Papa – there dear is love that I have brought you – do you love me for it?'[126] Summer holidays stretched out too long, due to middle-class conventions in the early days, but all too soon for health reasons. 'Dearest Love, Only one day more and then I shall see you - I love your sweet letters as I do you.' [127] Back in London they attended a huge, fashionable *Soirée Musicale* at Dr Marshall's to hear extracts from Mozart, Handel, Verdi and Meyerbeer in the company of guests with the best aesthetic credentials, the Burne-Joneses, Holman Hunts, Alma-Tademas, Spartalis and Hueffers. Supper was served at 1 a.m. and delicious ices in the interval. It was the sort of occasion Lucy relished and William attended for Lucy's sake.[128]

Affection was still uppermost two years later in 1880. He was still her 'dearest love' but her tone fluctuated uneasily between archness and astringency. Lucy teased William: 'I was reading last evening "Advice to Husbands" in that book of *Domestic Economy* which you studied; it says – "Do not be stern & silent in your own house & remarkable for amiability elsewhere," "Remember that your wife has as much need of recreation as yourself, & devote a good portion of your leisure hours to such society and amusements as she may join. By so doing you will secure her smiles and increase her affection."' She concluded sweetly, 'you know you have plenty of smiles and always love my own from your loving wife Lucy'.[129]

The two partners' wildly contrasting temperaments gave the relationship its dynamism from the very beginning. Gabriel told Frances Rossetti that 'of several lovers' tiffs during the courtship, only one seemed at all serious; and that was on one occasion when the question arose as to whether William loved Lucy better than *any one* else' and William obtusely but loyally refused to say he loved his bride-to-be more than his mother.[130] During marriage, the balance of power constantly shifted from one partner to the other. Sometimes Lucy seemed almost afraid of the husband fourteen years her senior; at other times William was distinctly wary of Lucy's moods, although his avowals of love never diminished. 'Don't get out of spirits, Lucy dear: I shall soon see you again. With all love, Your own W.M.R. (P S) Kiss to kid'.[131]

Even when they were both at home in London, their relationship was conducted partly by post. William and Lucy could have a row in the morning, negotiations could move swiftly between Somerset House and Bloomsbury by lunchtime, and resolution or apology could close the matter by teatime, before William was home from the office. William knew he was as guilty as Lucy of 'more than needed wrangling'. But in its best years and even beyond, his marriage sustained him, as he tried to express in a sonnet written on their seventh wedding anniversary, 31 March 1881:

> *To Lucy*
> Lucy this day since seven years past & gone
>   Joined thee and me in generous matrimony
>   And now how near our eyes & hearts we see
> Three children play, two daughters & a son.
> Our seven companioned years have wiled us on
>   Close linked in love's supreme affinity:
>   Life of my life & lifelong memory
> Friend, lover, wife, my Lucy wooed and won. [132]

At crisis moments in his life, when William had no heart to keep his daily diary, he always continued to write to Lucy. As Gabriel lay dying at Birchington in April 1882, he wrote several times a day, reiterating his love and his neediness: 'Yours, dearest, in woe as in weal', 'Dearest Dear – in whom I take refuge in all my troubles', 'with entire love', 'I write to you before anyone else.'[133] 'I miss you very much, and look with some dismay to weeks passing and no one to say a good-natured (when it *is* good-natured) word to me: but never mind, as it is quite needful you should be out of town. *Tell me at once, and frequently in future letters, how your finger is.* Kisses to dear little kids – and many more to poor Lu from her Fofus.'[134] Solicitous and affectionate, he knew he could also be gouty and disagreeable. 'My temper is pretty well known (except by you) to be a good one'.[135] In the aftermath of Gabriel's death in summer 1882, when he was trying to disperse bequests to old friends and fearful the estate would not be sufficient to pay off all debts, he wrote sharply to Lucy, who was sending directives from Southend. 'I like your opinion & advice on all these matters: only I very much dislike that you shd. *assume* that I am a patent fool & squanderer in the matter'.[136]

But he was always interested in what interested her: art, education, and women's rights. Both William and Lucy were feminists who attended Women's Suffrage meetings together, but it was William who addressed a large gathering at Mrs Hancock's on 1 March 1879.[137] A year later he seconded a resolution to form the Somerville Club for women in London, which Lucy decided to join.[138] Together with Mathilde Blind, they all went to a crowded Women's Rights demonstration in favour of female suffrage at St James's Hall on 6 May 1880. They heard two eloquent speakers, Miss Craigen and Miss Helen Taylor, as well as Miss Rhoda Garrett. Only women were allowed to address the meeting and men were confined to certain areas of the hall. On 17 August 1882 at noon precisely, writing from Somerset House, William dashed off the news he knew would elate 'Dearie Lu' that 'the Married Women's Property Bill has now actually passed into law!'[139] The most pacific of men, William subsequently supported militant suffragette action. 'Be sure that if they had restricted themselves for ever to "drawing-room meetings" and peaceful talk no one would ever have paid any attention to them', he told his daughter Helen.[140]

As well as feminist ideals that took them out together, Lucy and William enjoyed theatre, opera and concerts. Their tastes were classical and highbrow. In May 1877 they saw Wagner at the first of a series of concerts he gave at the Albert Hall that year to raise money for the Bayreuth Theatre. Frank Hueffer, Cathy's husband, often sent them tickets for musical events and on 19 April 1880, he got them a box at Covent Garden where they heard Massenet's *Il Re di Lahore*, 'good scenic sort of music', thought William, but 'not very memorable'.[141] Later that year they took Olive, aged five, to her first opera, *Aida*, at Her Majesty's Theatre. They heard *Maritana* by the Irish composer Vincent Wallace a week later. In January 1881, the balcony was so crowded that Lucy, who was pregnant, had to leave halfway through Berlioz's *Damnation of Faust*. William found the music 'brilliant, *saisissant*, but arduous'.[142] Olive 'to her vast delight' accompanied her parents to see Henry Irving ('dry and reserved') and Ellen Terry ('bright and genial') as Benedick and Beatrice in *Much Ado about Nothing* on 13 October 1882. Lucy also enjoyed, when she was fit, outings with William to the Zoological Gardens or to Kew.

Shared interests united them but subtle differences in attitudes to society divided them. William refused to kowtow to any authority figure even if he was his ultimate superior as Chairman of the Board of Inland Revenue.

William had been only 'moderately amiable' on their journey to Chester in November 1883, Lucy remarked to her father, but had 'thawed' in response to the 'quaintness and beauty' of the black and white town. They roamed through the cathedral cloisters and were just about to hail a cab when they happened to meet Algernon West[143] 'who had just run over from Hawarden where he was staying with Gladstone'. (West was the man who had failed to support William's bid for promotion to the Secretaryship two years previously.) He graciously asked to be presented to Lucy, and inquired whether William could spare him five minutes? Grudgingly William awarded him about two, as he was keen to get over to Easton Hall to see the stained glass by Shields. Lucy fumed at William's failure to ingratiate himself with the man who had been 'the companion of Gladstone & Tennyson at Copenhagen hob-nobbing with kings & Czars', especially 'considering how much our fate lies in his hands'. Such a VIP 'surely ought to have commanded an audience!'[144]

As an anti-monarchist William was indifferent to ceremony. On Queen Victoria's Golden Jubilee, Tuesday, 21 June 1887, which was a public holiday, he refused tickets for the formal rituals in Westminster Abbey 'on the ground of the trouble & expense of donning court-costume' but took ten-year-old Arthur for an evening stroll through London to see Regent Street, Piccadilly, Bond Street and Oxford Street garishly illuminated in a 'blaze of light & throng of people', he supposed 'beyond anything I had seen before – or shall see again'.[145]

Recalling wonderful parties in the Fitzroy Square days before she married, Lucy relished social occasions whereas William endured them for her sake. Lucy enjoyed playing 'the amiable hostess' with 'the everlasting fan in hand, and an old lace front to her very light dress, quite charming', Bell Scott reported to Alice Boyd, subduing his old repugnance for the Madox Brown women.[146] Menus at Lucy's 'at homes' included lavish as well as more modest dishes, 'turkey, 2 pigeon pies, lobster salads, jellies, tipsy cake, stewed pears, chocolate cakes, pretty cakes, custards, oranges, grapes, apples, pears, figs and almonds'.[147] William's shyness made him seem stodgy and pompous in company, as Violet Paget[148] reported to her mother when she first came to London in 1881, although she soon amended her opinion when she realized that William Rossetti and Oscar Wilde were the only two London critics who had heard of her literary reputation (fig. 110). William considered Violet, 'more than moderately ugly, but of course seems clever'.[149]

As a young celebrity, Violet constantly met the Rossettis at tea-parties and dinners during the early 1880s in literary-artistic circles adorned by the Alma-Tademas, Gosses, Spartalis and the Stillmans. She dined with Lucy and William at Endsleigh Gardens in June 1882 and, in her famously tactless way, was horrified. 'Oh what a grimy, dingy, filthy aesthetic house! I shuddered to sit down in my white frock. They were *very* friendly', she conceded. Talk ranged from Keats and Browning to 'a grand discussion about thrashing brats'. Marie

110. John Singer Sargent, *Vernon Lee* (pseudonym of writer Violet Paget 1856–1935), 1881. Oil on canvas, 53.7 × 43.2 cm. © Tate, London 2003.

Spartali Stillman, still a vision of loveliness, declared herself in favour while Lucy was fervently against. The Rossetti children would be much the better for the occasional smack, Violet added tartly.[150] Violet liked Lucy, although by the early 1880s she was no longer fresh and youthful but 'a plain, Italian looking, extremely engaging woman'. At the Grosvenor Gallery Violet enjoyed the people rather more than the pictures, 'Quite the nicest person is Mrs. Wm. Rossetti; I like her extremely'.[151] Lucy's unusual combination of vivacity spiked with 'brilliant' intellectual conversation based on her extensive 'scholastic and classical knowledge'[152] intrigued the aspiring and forthright author.

The home atmosphere both parents created for their children was a direct outcome of their love for each other, passionately protective on Lucy's side, liberal, playful and relaxed on William's. When apart, 'Old Fofus' wrote in large handwriting to the youngest, Mary: 'as Miss Marykin is not able, she will *hear* the letter read by her dear kind Mamma, who is always thinking what she can do for one or other of her ducklings' (fig. 111).[153] Although childhood memories were punctuated with constant illnesses, both their own and Lucy's, the Rossetti children never forgot the thrill, wonder and romance that their parents wove into their lives. Frequent domestic crises, confusions and upheavals distressed the adults but created excitement for bright and secure children. Fifty years before, Frances and Gabriele Rossetti had never banished William and his siblings to a separate nursery at the top of the house. Lucy and William followed their enlightened lead but unlike Gabriel and William, who were sent to school, all the latter-day Rossetti children were educated at home in a designated schoolroom, mainly by Lucy with dedicated zeal.

Her half-niece Juliet Soskice, née Hueffer, lived with the Rossettis for a while after the death of her father, Frank in 1889. She remembered how Aunt

Lucy used to sweep into the schoolroom early in the morning in her dress-ing-gown, listen for a minute, then 'whirl the governess out of her chair and give us the lessons herself. She knew how to hit on the parts we knew least. Her voice went very high and very low, and she explained beautifully'. Nine-year-old Juliet composed poems by night. Early in the morning, she rushed into her aunt's bedroom, sat 'beside the dressing-table while she was twisting her hair up, in her petticoat-bodice in front of the glass', and recited the poem before it was written down. Uncle William still in bed wearing 'his nice white nightcap', would listen, laugh and say 'Bravo, bravo, my little girl!' 'And Aunt Lucy used to leave go of her hair and stoop down and kiss me and tell me what she thought about it. She always said at the end, "Write about every-thing that interests you, little dear, and if you can't write it in poetry, write it in prose". And I did'.[154] Lucy's educational methods blended imagination with exactitude. Even the dedicated scholar, Charles Bagot Cayley, was non-plussed when he heard two-year-old Mary reciting the Greek alphabet.[155] But Lucy also made sure her children learnt to swim. She encouraged them to write plays about Greek heroes, which they staged at home with scenery she painted and monsters she constructed. Mademoiselle Combrisson came to teach French when Olive was nine (fig. 112), Arthur seven, Helen five and Mary only three. She stayed about two years and as a result they all spoke French fluently.

'France hardly less than Italy was a tradition in our family and we all grew up in it. We talked French constantly and battened on Victor Hugo', remem-bered Helen. Olive was addicted to the French Revolution, both for its inspiring socialism and for its Frenchness. Their grandfather Madox Brown as well as their mother Lucy had both been born in France and loved the country. William and Lucy had many French friends and felt affinity for French cultural life. Later they engaged Mademoiselle Heymann from Alsace

111. Ford Madox Brown, *Mary Elizabeth Madox Rossetti*, January 1885. Chalk, 480 × 460 mm. Wightwick Manor, National Trust.

MARY ELIZABETH MADOX ROSSETTI   dB Jan 85

112. Lisa
Stillman, *Olivia
Frances Madox
Rossetti*, aged nine
or ten, 1885.
Pastel, 740 × 465
mm. Private
collection.

who had lost her father and brothers in the Franco–Prussian War to teach the
children some German. Strangely enough, they were not formally taught
Italian, except in San Remo in 1886/7 when Signorina Carsini gave lessons
to Olive and Arthur. Helen felt that Italy simply seemed remote and far-off
in her childhood, although they all knew of the Rossettis' Italian origins and
of long-dead grandfather Gabriele's Italian relations from Vasto in the
Abruzzi. Occasionally cases of Italian confectionery arrived, 'very thrilling
and delectable with a strong flavour of roses and cinnamon.' Helen's first
treasured book was a child's *History of Rome*, which she constantly reread. As
a child she vowed that when she grew up she would 'nationalise [her]self
Italian and enrol as a Socialist', and as she later reflected, she somehow carried out both resolves.[156]

Lucy lavished as much energy (and expense, in William's view) on children's parties as she did on adult ones. One hour's entertainment from a magician with a performing dog at Olive's fifth birthday party in 1880 cost two guineas, 'higher than I expected', groaned William.[157] 'Arty, Nelly, Maizie & Poppy[158] were all as happy & as good as gold' when Lucy threw a party on the grown-up scale for them in 1884, including a sit-down supper, dancing and a conjurer, for sixty or seventy children, aged from three to eight. One small boy, Arnold Ward, proposed to Olive who returned an 'amusing and characteristic' answer.[159]

In the early 1960s, aged eighty-three, Helen Rossetti Angeli looked back on a Victorian childhood, a gaslit world peopled with muffin men and milkmaids carrying milk through the streets on yokes and itinerant charwomen who came to clean the doorsteps. Lucy always made the children put their own Christmas presents out on the doorstep for poor children. She had a practical as well as an idealistic response to London poverty. Once in the Tottenham Court Road a man asked her for 'a penny to buy some food'. Trailing all the children behind her, Lucy immediately bought him a white bread roll and a hunk of cheese. 'You might have stood a pat of butter, Madam', he said quietly, 'and she looked at him and went back into the shop and paid the shopman to cut the roll and spread some butter on it. Then the man began to eat it at once. We thought she would have been angry, but she was not, only thoughtful'.[160]

The young Rossettis knew they were different from other Victorian families. 'There was no interference with our reading, or thinking, or way of life…We were always with the family; as soon as we became capable of behaving at table, we were always at table with our elders.' William consistently treated them as reasoning human beings, never patronized or talked down to them. 'We were allowed to read what we wanted; there was no bowdlerizing.'[161] They never had strict nurses or Victorian rules about being seen but not heard. On the contrary, they were encouraged to think independently and speak up for themselves. They were all amazingly precocious – Olive and Arthur read Shakespeare from about the age of four – and flourished in an ambience of great liberty with their father. Christina complained the children were 'all too free and easy with Papa, because we used to call him by a fancy name [Fofus]…He didn't demand any ceremony at all, but one respected him and obeyed him.'

As very young teenagers, the Rossetti children became Anarchists and used to stay out at activist meetings sometimes until the small hours. William encouraged them: 'Vive Kropotkin! Honneur a Louise Michel! Bravi Malatesta e Merlino!'[162] By the 1890s, Lucy was almost a total invalid and although 'she didn't quite approve of these things', at any rate she didn't interfere. 'She knew we went. We knew some very fine Anarchists: Kropotkin,[163] and Louise Michel,[164] and others.' On one occasion they didn't get home

113. Michael Rossetti. Cathy Hueffer's photograph album, STH/BH/2/3-6. The Stow Hill Collection, HLRO, and the Hon. Oliver Soskice.

until 2 a.m. having 'prolonged proceedings in a fried fish shop'. They had pre-arranged for one of the servants to unlock the door but

> unfortunately, my poor mother, who was in bed upstairs, got scent that we weren't in. And when we got to the door and gave a feeble ring or knock, she was there, very indignant. And she called my father out to give us a lecture. Poor Papa! I remember his reaction. He said 'Why didn't you ask me for the latch-key? It would have saved all this trouble!'[165]

Looking back, Helen considered that Lucy's obsessional over-anxiety was rooted in her chronic tubercular disease. 'One of the noblest of women and the most perfect of mothers,' she became more or less an invalid following bronchial pneumonia early in 1885 when Helen was six.

> I fancy she never quite got over her rapid succession of confinements and an earlier miscarriage. She certainly never recovered from the grief and agony of baby Michael's death – Mary's twin brother – in 1883. Michael was a beautiful and adored child and died of meningitis before he was 2. My poor mother nursed him to the end and did a lovely drawing of him in death.[166]

Swinburne had celebrated the birth of the Rossetti twins with a poem *O Gemini!* on 28 April 1881. Now he mourned Michael (fig. 113), 'A human flower of faultless frame', in another poem, *A Baby's Death*, in January 1883. The poem was deeply painful for Lucy as she explained when thanking Swinburne 'for giving such a tribute to my sweet child'. She could not share the sentiment Swinburne expressed to console her, even if he did not subscribe to it himself, that Michael's 'little soul' had taken wing for heaven. 'I wonder if I could literally feel as you write, if I should feel the pain less of being without him – but at present the loss seems too crushing – So much hope seemed justified in Michael. I wish you had seen him again'.[167] Marie Spartali Stillman tried to remember times they had laughed together as students in Madox Brown's studio but, writing from Florence, told her 'dear dear friend' that 'I do not know what to say to you because I know the pain & that time even cannot heal it'.[168]

Even when Lucy's life became a litany of debilitating illnesses from the mid-1880s, she never neglected her children and still remained 'keenly intellectually alive and passionately interested in the arts.' But, recalled Helen, her constant suffering

> told terribly on her nervous system and she became very neurasthenic – tho' the word was not used in those days – and got somehow estranged in feeling from our Father. I remember all this as very painful. She was irritable and excitable and something in their temperaments clashed – his invariable calm grated on her more excitable nature. He suffered greatly and so did she. The whole trouble was pathological, no doubt, but it was very distressing and I felt it all most keenly on my Father's account.[169]

They spent their twelfth wedding anniversary, 31 March 1886, apart. William's mother Frances Rossetti was slowly dying in London after a fall. Lucy was in Ventnor desperately trying to avoid a recurrence of the bronchial pneumonia that had nearly killed her the previous year. William sent 'My bride this day 12 years' a detailed questionnaire on her health, assuring her it came 'with the same love as on 31 March 1874'.[170] For her part, out of 'the intense love I feel always in the depths of my heart for you', Lucy offered William £200 or £300 from her own savings to send him on a holiday of his dreams to Egypt and Japan in 1888.[171] Because of 'distance, time & cost' William met Lucy's offer with 'a resolute negative'.[172] It had been more than a financial sacrifice for her to offer for she dreaded being apart from him. Physical frailty made her dependent, but she longed to prove her altruism and her love.

Illness or fear of illness constantly sapped both partners; by sheer effort of will, however, Lucy not only retained her grip over the children's upbringing and education but managed to exert herself socially by entertaining and travelling, and creatively by drawing, painting and writing. William kept up his routine at Somerset House – indeed he had no option – as well as a punishing evening and weekend schedule of writing and reviewing. Perhaps Lucy felt there was little time left over for her. Her necessary effort of will hardened into an illness-driven self-absorption that increasingly sidelined William. After coughing up blood in August 1890, a brief remission fired her determination to move house from Endsleigh Gardens to the more elevated, less foggy and coal-dust polluted position of St Edmund's Terrace beside Primrose Hill.

September was the hottest month that year. First Lucy decided to buy No. 4, but after another turn of the kaleidoscope, when that fell through, she set her heart on No. 3. Negotiating with vendors sent her whirling from agitation to despair. She was up all night rummaging through drawers in Endsleigh Gardens preventing William from sleeping either. He tried to live in his other world of poetry and politics, discussed Blake with the young W.B. Yeats, went to hear the inspiring French revolutionary Louise Michel, and proof-read his latest article on Browning. The whole family had to decamp to Christina's at 30 Torrington Square while the old house was renovated for the incoming tenant. At the same time Emma Madox Brown, Lucy's stepmother, was declining and eventually died on 10 October. William was surprised when she expressed a wish to see him during her final days, but he went immediately and found her 'not seriously changed in appearance'.[173] Her face had looked out from some of Madox Brown's most resonant Pre-Raphaelite pictures including *Pretty Baa-lambs* (1851) and *The Last of England* (1852).

Meanwhile, Lucy excitedly negotiated a contract with the Nineteenth Century Building Society, whereby after a few years' rent (actually paid by William) she would become the owner of the leasehold. At Christina's, Lucy suffered an attack of 'colic', either tubercular or psychosomatic in origin, but managed to summon strength from somewhere to organize this 'most formidable upheaval and exodus', and crammed the contents of Endsleigh Gardens into the thirteen smaller rooms at St Edmund's Terrace.[174] Loath to leave the old house where he had spent a third of his life, William worried too about heavy removal expenses, but eventually on 25 October 1890 they were established in their new home.

During these last years of the marriage, from approximately 1889 to 1894 when Lucy was increasingly looking into the void of terminal illness, she found an unexpected new confidant. He was William Money Hardinge (1854–1916), at first sight a bizarre choice.[175] Hardinge was notorious, at least in Oxford, as the 'Balliol bugger' whose passionate behaviour, adoring correspondence, and homoerotic sonnets compromised Walter Pater so injuriously in 1874 that Benjamin Jowett (Master of Balliol College, Oxford) baulked his promotion to a proctorship.[176] Aged nineteen, Hardinge was temporarily sent down, but was a good enough poet to win the prestigious Newdigate Prize two years later for *Troy*, whose Homeric landscape allowed him to celebrate a time 'when/Men walked as gods, and gods befriended men'.[177] Edward Elgar even set one of his translated Greek lyrics to music 'It's oh! To be a wild wind – when my lady's in the sun.' Friend of Ruskin, Hardinge also wrote a 'distraught' letter to that debonair and ambiguous figure, Morton Fullerton, later the lover of Edith Wharton.[178] Tangentially, Hardinge's romantic homosexuality and 'aestheticism' impinged on the lives of several eminent Victorians.

His pervasive reputation lingers on. Tom Stoppard introduced him as a bit player into his play about A.E. Housman, *The Invention of Love* in 1997, when the Student charms the Aesthete (twice) with his adulation: 'No one has written the poetry I wish to write, Mr Pater, but you have already written the prose.'[179] Although Hardinge's literary ambitions lay in poetry, he became a novelist in the 1880s, publishing *Clifford Gray: A Romance of Modern Life* (1881), *Eugenia: an Episode* (1883), *The Willow-Garth* (1886), and *Out of the Fog* (1888). These were all romantic love stories and, naturally enough in the climate of the times, heterosexual.

He also wrote articles for the *Magazine of Art* and *Temple Bar*, and one of these brought him into contact with William. On 20 June 1890 Hardinge sought William's advice on an article he was preparing on Gabriel, *A Note on the Louvre-sonnets of Rossetti*, which William found 'discerning'.[180] After that he visited the Rossettis often, both at Endsleigh Gardens and at St Edmund's Terrace. He immediately established a rapport with Lucy and in their hours together she 'was readier in confiding to him than to almost any one else any projects or performances of her own in art or in literature'.[181] William reported the relationship without an ounce of jealousy, probably aware of Hardinge's sexual reputation. Noted for her 'very liberal' views, Lucy was unlikely to have found Hardinge's past an impediment to their intimate friendship.[182] In fact, she may have found it liberating. Marie Spartali Stillman and Lucy frankly discussed a lesbian attachment that Violet Paget had for their mutual friend, the poet Mary Robinson.[183] Such matters were not unspeakable in private, Rossetti circles. Indeed younger women often found Lucy appealing. Violet had liked Lucy 'extremely' and Olive Garnett's spontaneous affection made her blush.[184]

With William Money Hardinge a dozen years her junior, Lucy felt free to transcend mundane reality. She could discuss matters of the intellect and know he would understand and respond. 'The idea has always seemed to me one of the only means of going a little beyond oneself – so desirable', she told him.

> My conversations have generally had to be imaginary, but I have had pleasure from dreams, and somehow I seem to have lived in a dream for some time. I scarcely know what is dream and what is life, but the heroes of romance and chivalry have in some way come into this dream and appeared to have *a* reality…Curiously, work-a-day life has been easier while dreaming.

Was cultivated and slightly dangerous Hardinge, now in his late thirties, a chivalric hero for sick Lucy, come to rescue her from monstrous fate? Or did she simply find it easier to unburden herself to the kindness of a stranger?

Hardinge was also an effective translator, mainly of French and classical Greek poetry, which he had published in *Nineteenth Century*, and this capacity drew him closer to Lucy. Incarcerated at home for weeks on end, especially during dark winter days, she frantically exercised her brain, if not her wasted body. Secretly Lucy set herself to translate some of Petrarch's poems. 'I think the occupation has *helped* to keep me alive during the winter: does not it sound a little like the Thousand and One Nights – a thing to live by a little longer?' she asked Hardinge, again tacitly linking him to legendary story and imbuing him with mythical powers to prolong life.

She sent her translations off for his critical advice. Initially he was embarrassed because 'the things would not do at all, and as an honest friend, I had to tell her so'. Fearing a painful scene, he was enchanted when Lucy clear-sightedly accepted his judgement and threw her little manuscript book straight into the fire. Later she felt by letting him see her translations she had exposed her inner soul to him and 'committed a kind of moral suicide, for I valued your friendship. Now you will see me as others see me…This letter is like a long journey after a happy time which one would not wish to end as it seems part of the time. I felt I should get truth from you; – if only all could be truth!' He offered her unique consolation and a semi-romantic connectedness. Lucy felt the *tendresse* and she inspired it. Above all, because he was partly a stranger, she could open her heart to him about art, how it lifted her sore spirit 'out of the common life' and moved her to thoughts of eternity. 'The creative, intellectual, and moral qualities must have continuation, though the more earthly are of the nature of dust'. The bond was mutual. They continued to correspond until the final weeks of her illness in February 1894.

After dealing with the translations, they moved on to discuss her real forte – painting. Hardinge felt 'it was like coming out of some hazardous cutting into clear sunlight, and an open road'. Lucy's exquisite picture *Romeo in the Tomb of Juliet* (see fig. 82) was displayed on an easel in the front drawing-room where the north light was still clear. 'Here was a rendering, here a translation indeed!' The picture, in Hardinge's words 'speaks for itself, as perfectly poetical, perfectly new'. Lucy turned to the spectator, ' "I don't believe I could paint like that now," she said. "I've been wondering: is it really good?" '. On this point Hardinge could be triumphantly affirmative. They chatted about the possibility of a public gallery buying the picture, but as dusk gathered and Lucy sank further into her armchair by the long windows, he was struck by 'the queer removedness of her manner. "But I would not sell it now," she said, "at any price; I have made other plans for that picture." '[185]

In fact Lucy was planning her will, specifically bequeathing her picture of *Romeo and Juliet* to William Money Hardinge for his lifetime – and after his death to her youngest daughter, Mary. The action touched Hardinge deeply and his novelist's pen instantly imagined Lucy's inner dialogue: 'He shall have the picture always before him, to show that I could do something great, something better than the Petrarch translations…as a memorial of today.'[186] Lucy's consumption was now rampant. Weak and emaciated, she struggled out with Olive on 2 March to the Trafalgar Square Theatre, to see the Elizabeth Robins production of Ibsen's new play *The Master Builder*, which she found 'fine and impressive'.[187] Henry James had reviewed the play a fortnight before and rated Ibsen 'a master', who though 'strangely inscrutable', nevertheless 'gives us the sense of life' – exactly what Lucy craved.[188] But on 10 April 1893, she was prostrated with 'a terrible attack of congestion of the lungs, which came very near to a fatal ending'.[189] William was desperately worried, too, about Christina whose breast cancer had recurred, complicated by her old heart trouble. Weighed down by grief and dread, he suspended his daily diary.

Hauling herself back from death, and without telling William, Lucy instructed Hilton Percy Barraud, a City solicitor, on 21 April 1893, to draw up her final testament, excluding her husband from any part of her estate. She left practically all her property, including the leasehold of 3 St Edmund's Terrace, in trust to her children, appointing Madox Brown and Barraud as joint trustees. Seventy years later her daughter Helen was still seeking to understand what she and all the family had found an extraordinary will. 'The terms of this regrettable Will were due to the extreme state of nervous exhaustion (neurasthenia?) and ill health in which my poor mother was at the time…There was no valid reason for ignoring her husband's feelings or interests, but she was desperately ill and suffering and unfortunately she listened to foolish counsel'.[190]

Just back from San Remo following Lucy's death on 12 April 1894, William confided to Christina that his position was now 'a matter of some embarrassment and speculation to myself, as I seem to have no personal right in the house – not even to live there, were Barraud to decree otherwise (not that this can be in any way expected). Business-worries thus crowd round me, to whom grief had seemed to be enough.'[191] Facing imminent retirement in September 1894, William could also foresee a one-third reduction in his annual income. In his autobiography twelve years later he took a more detached view of Lucy's final instructions, ascribing the main problems to 'difficulties consequent upon the trusteeship of the will', but he did not disguise the legal hoops he had to go through when, in 1902, he bought back the lease of the house from his own children.

Lucy herself felt some twinges about the will because the day after she signed it, she added a codicil in which she left William the portrait Gabriel had made of her in happier days (see fig. 22). The codicil also left a small weekly income to a relation, Tristram Madox, and to the old family servant Charlotte Kirby. But it might seem, that in a flash of bitter resentment against the partner she knew would survive her, Lucy had assigned William to footnote status.

However, Lucy's will is open to another equally plausible interpretation. At the time she instructed Barraud, she knew her condition was incurable but she and William kept up the fiction of hope in their daily conversations. By not naming the disease, they kept it at bay. At the time William's emotions were only perilously in check, reflected in Olive Garnett's observations, and the gap in his diary from mid-March until mid-June 1893. He usually only suspended this therapeutic exercise at times of personal crisis. Deliberately avoiding the Rossetti family lawyer Sharon Grote Turner, Lucy consulted Hilton Percy Barraud privately and probably at home, in order to spare William the knowledge she was preparing for death. The will Barraud drew up was unsurprising. He may well have asked her to consider the children's position if their father were to die soon or re-marry. Mrs Rossetti's primary concern was the protection of her children, all still minors ranging in age from ten to seventeen. Lucy knew William had income and assets of his own. It might have been kinder to have inserted a clause explaining 'I have made no provision for William because…' but such an explanatory clause may have been unusual in 1893, and anyway deemed redundant.

Lucy's personal assets were shares given to her by her father, pictures she owned and the leasehold of the house at St Edmund's Terrace, amounting to a probate value of £3,064 19s 1d.[192] It is fairly common practice today for wives to try to ensure that what is their own share of an estate is passed intact to their children. Any future marriage by a surviving husband alters the financial position of his children by a previous marriage. Lucy sought to protect Olive, Arthur, Helen and Mary from the consequences of any new relationship in William's life following her death. She also assured them of a roof over their heads and a small independent income. Indeed she may have seen this as a way of liberating William from a sense of over-burdening responsibility to the children. Choosing her elderly father and the solicitor as joint trustees and omitting William was probably the aspect of the will he found most hurtful. Lucy's father predeceased her and William subsequently renegotiated the terms of the will to become a trustee in 1898.

The language of the will is the standard, non-emotive, legal language of such documents of the day (and today). It is Barraud's language, not Lucy's, reflecting the fact that all wills become public documents after probate and are not private love letters.

Under this alternative interpretation of the will, the day after making it, Lucy had second thoughts, concerned that she had not even mentioned William's name and had forgotten to make some provision for a Madox relation and a devoted servant, Charlotte Kirby. She summoned the lawyer back and added a codicil, bequeathing William 'from his faithful wife' the tender portrait Gabriel had made of her in all the glow of early marriage. She had not forgotten him; she had left him an enduring image of her best self.

When Lucy consulted Barraud she had been close to death only days before. When thoroughly healthy people consult lawyers to make their wills, many exhibit signs of stress, forget things and often add codicils almost immediately. Lucy on the contrary was desperately ill. The will had a lurching immediacy for her – it was a realistic concession to death and she was tired to death when she made it. It may not have been a perfect will, but it was not a badly drafted will, nor a bad will *per se*. The fact that Lucy screwed her courage to the sticking point to formulate her last testament was an expression of her long-held feminist principles, principles William shared and supported. It was also an attempt to project her identity and her resolution beyond the grave. In many ways her children were surrogates for the pictures she never had time to paint, Lucy's hooks into futurity and in this will she tried to provide for their security.

After her death nearly a year later, the fact that Lucy had made a will at all was a complete surprise to William, let alone its careful dispositions. Any surprise after a death is particularly painful for the survivor and tends to erode at least temporarily, and perhaps alter forever, the perception of the partnership. The fact remains that Helen found it a 'regrettable' will which she ascribed to Lucy's 'neurasthenia' or nervous debility in the face of terminal illness. The 'foolish counsel' Helen blames is most likely to have come from Barraud striving to interpret what he understood to be Lucy's intentions. Helen was only fourteen and a half when her mother died; the illness had enraged all the Rossetti children and driven them to suicidal thoughts. Helen may have displaced her anger from Lucy for leaving, to Lucy for leaving a will whose vigilant maternal concerns caused immediate consternation rather than reassurance.

William remained unfaltering and gracious. He supplied information for Hardinge's accolade to Lucy, even proof-reading it before it appeared in the *Magazine of Art* in 1895, and returned to her grave in San Remo on several occasions between 1895 and 1907. Three days after her death on 12 April 1894 Holman Hunt poignantly recalled the unmistakeably liquid tones of Lucy's laugh as a girl.[193]

Radicals

WILLIAM'S *Democratic Sonnets*

Hogarth considered painters and connoisseurs to be the only competent judges of art. A true connoisseur accrues and expands specialized knowledge, usually but not exclusively in the fine arts, and like a collector, exercises the faculty of choosing, selecting and evaluating. In so doing, he or she may create fashion and form public taste. 'Connoisseur' implies scholarly expertise independent of the academy, but without any suggestion of English amateurism. A true connoisseur transcends narrow, national boundaries and is a cosmopolitan of the mind.

William was certainly the most cosmopolitan of all the Rossetti siblings, probably the most cosmopolitan of all the Pre-Raphaelites. His role as art critic and connoisseur, as well as his political commitments and three-quarters Italian inheritance opened up the world to him. When Ruskin recommended William Rossetti as the London arts correspondent for the New York *Crayon*, William Stillman – its enthusiastic young American editor – accepted with alacrity. 'Mantz was our French Correspondent, and William Rossetti our English', he crowed, enjoying the *frisson* of employing a French reporter with a German name and an English reviewer with an Italian one.[1]

From their youngest days all the Rossetti children had been conscious of their double cultural loyalties, speaking Italian with their father and English with their mother. Not Dante or Shakespeare but Dante and Shakespeare were their cultural heroes. The Anglo-Italian nature of the family was reinforced by its context within a wider cosmopolitan community where exotic dissidents and émigrés gravitated to Gabriele Rossetti, a lodestar patriot in exile. The family was in a paradoxical position, both integrated into and alien from English society so that visitors like young Holman Hunt felt an outsider listening to tragic passions he had never heard before – except on the stage – aired in the cosmopolitan buzz of the Rossetti home.

The father arose to receive me from a group of foreigners around the fire, all escaped revolutionists from the Continent…The conversation was in Italian, but occasionally merged into French…objects of the severest denunciations were Bomba, Pio Nono, and Metternich…Count Rosso and his memory; with these execrated names were uttered in different tones those of Mazzini, Garibaldi, and Louis Napoleon who had once been a visitor.[2]

Hunt's choice of language in the surrounding passage from his autobiography – 'refugees', 'excitement', 'gesticulate', 'sighs and groans', 'distress', 'alien company' – suggests how exotic, how non-British the Rossetti family was perceived to be within London society during the late 1840s and early 1850s. Adding to this sense of being outside conventional society, Gabriele's English friends were all Freemasons, according to Olivia Rossetti Agresti, his granddaughter. William told her 'that in his early years Masons were constantly calling at the very modest Rossetti home, coming for financial or other aid.'[3]

Years later Gabriel's doctor, Thomas Gordon Hake, ascribed his patient's genius to a cosmopolitan genetic inheritance, but also alluded to the Rossetti status as outsiders. 'The family, one and all, are almost purely Italian. The father, a poet, was a Neapolitan; the mother was a Tuscan, with some Scotch blood. Rossetti may be regarded, not as English, but as one of those powerful leavens with which the genius of one country sometimes ferments that of another, to give it a new vitality'.[4] Dr Hake interpreted Italian-British duality as positive and creative but Olive Rossetti Agresti, William and Lucy's eldest daughter, felt this same duality was responsible for a destructive and unresolved tension in the temperament of her aunt, Christina Rossetti. 'The fire was there, the passionate heart was there…the deep and tender family affections so characteristic of her Italian ancestry were there, but all under strict control, all mastered and repressed by the puritanical conventional strain inherited from the quarter of English blood that came to her from the Pierces [her maternal grandparents] whom my father remembered as severe and strict protestants of the Hell fire variety'.[5]

Dante Gabriel Rossetti exhibited a dichotomy. At a profound internal level his work, especially his translations of Dante, *The Early Italian Poets together with Dante's Vita Nuova* (1861) grew out of his beloved Italian literary heritage, yet as Jan Marsh pointed out in her biography (1999) this most apparently Italianate and dynamic of the four siblings was the precise opposite of a cosmopolitan, externally at least almost a xenophobe. Even allowing for a possible redeeming tone of irony in the speaking voice, now lost, he 'consistently rubbished France and Belgium for being foreign like any ignorant Briton'.[6] 'Being abroad', which was only twice in his life, 'always roused the bulldog' in Gabriel, noted Marsh. William, too, was forced to concede a disturbing counter-side to Gabriel's nationalism. 'My brother was in many respects an Englishman in grain, – and even a prejudiced Englishman quite ready – too ready, I always thought – to abuse foreigners'.[7] 'He liked England and the English better than any other country and nation; and he never crossed the sea without severe discomfort, or contemplated the crossing of it without revulsion'.[8] Yet the paradox remained. William himself always regarded his brother 'spite of some ultra-John-Bullish opinions and ways – as more an Italian than an Englishman – Italian in temper of mind, in the quasi-restriction of his interest to the beautiful and the passionate…And yet he was mentally very far from being like his Italian father, and was wholly unlike his Italian grandfather [Gaetano Polidori]'.[9]

Cosmopolitanism is free from such concepts of bipolar national oppositions, as it is also free of any gender implications. A cosmopolitan is an 'inclusivist', a citizen of the world, equally at home in regions other than his or her native land, not indifferent to constitutions, religions, politics and beliefs but tolerant of other people's rights to hold differing positions. Whereas most of the Rossetti family of their generation, today might have been Eurosceptics, William and later Lucy were both Europhiles, 'before the word had been invented', as William said of his agnosticism.[10]

William's cultural and national identity was an inevitable tension between emotional loyalties but one he resolved with grace throughout his long life. The blood in his veins, as he proudly told Walt Whitman, was three-quarters Italian.[11] In his youth, William looked Italianate and moody enough to have been continually in demand as a model for Pre-Raphaelite paintings[12] but his temperament was reserved, stoical, and externally at least, stereotypically English, more attributable to the two pints of British blood inherited from his mother's mother, Anna Pierce. For William the political landscape was always wider than little England. He took an informed and radical interest in world events, which he shared with Lucy, as in this letter to her on 12 September 1876 on the 'Turco-European' question:

> I believe we may yet see the Turk chained & gagged in his own back yard, & his subjects kicking their heels about while he impotently scowls. England, I think, will be compelled to move – the government set on by the people (almost always better than their rulers) horrified at the loathsome Bulgarian business, & England will move other European powers – & they will checkmate Turkey.[13]

In 1878 when William was nearly fifty, W.S. Gilbert wrote a notorious, triumphalist chorus for the crew of *H.M.S. Pinafore*:

> For he might have been a Roosian,
> A French or Turk, or Prussian,
> Or perhaps Ital-ian!
> But in spite of all temptations
> To belong to other nations,
> He remains an Englishman!
> He remains an Englishman!

Although William fiercely identified with Italy in her struggle for unity and independence, counted Garibaldi as his 'greatest and most flawless personal hero'[14] and loved the land of his ancestors, which he regarded, as he told the Italian ambassador, as being his 'native country almost in equal degree with England',[15] he thought of himself as English. His natural sphere of operation was always England. In particular he was a Londoner and never lived any-where else. From this secure base his political and social interests enlarged to transcend mere national issues. His lifelong cultural and intellectual commit-ments were English, Italian, American, French, Eastern European, Oriental, Antipodean and ultimately global.

Many of these allegiances are indicated in brief by his fifty *Democratic Sonnets*, mostly written in 1881, not published until 1907 when they had lost their fiery topicality. Addressing a whole gamut of international issues they offer a distillation of his macro-perspective. The *Democratic Sonnets* are signifi-cant for their politics, not for their poetry. William's draft survives of the titles he originally projected in 1881 and indicates the international scope of his political interests, dealing with public events and personalities of his own time. He arranged his subjects in national sections, in broadly chronological order, ranging from the reburial of Napoleon in 1841 to affairs in the Transvaal and Ireland in 1881. He wrote in a great spate, often a sonnet a day. Travelling back from Manchester on 9 February 1881, he 'composed in the train a sonnet on Free Trade', the eleventh he had written since leaving London on 28 January. 'I find the work comes much more readily to me than I had counted on', he wrote buoyantly in his diary, contemplating the out-come 'with satisfaction & some degree of confidence.'[16]

However, Lucy began to feel a few qualms – which she did not hesitate to voice. William countered at once: 'I don't see why the Fenian Sonnet shd. be "dangerous". Do you think Fofus is to be strung up at the sentence of a Drumhead Court-martial, imprisoned under the Lord Lieutenant's warrant till Sept. /81, or what else is to befall him? I don't think there is one word in the sonnet wh. Gladstone, Bright, [e]tc, have not proclaimed & reproclaimed as true'.[17] Gabriel would not be reconciled to those sonnets which had 'an infu-sion of the grotesque or sarcastic', William admitted, but told Lucy, 'I feel that, if I do the thing at all, I must do it in my own way & not other people's way'.[18]

Gabriel who had initially encouraged William's poetic project now realized he had ignited a potentially fatal fuse. 'Several of William's truest friends, no less than myself, are greatly alarmed at the tone taken in some of his Sonnets respecting "Tyrannicide", "Fenianism", and other incendiary subjects,' he wrote on 12 April 1881 to the heavily pregnant Lucy, ten days before the birth of her twins. 'The very title *Democratic Sonnets* seems to me most objection-able when coming from one who depends on the government for his bread.'[19] It was one of the curious but resolved paradoxes in William's career that he could spend every day of his working life at the government offices of the Inland Revenue, while at the same time holding radical political views. So he replied to Gabriel the next day:

> This is a country in which political and religious opinions are free, and in this very Office men of all shades of opinion are to be found. The present government is by no means a Tory or anti-democratic one. It contains (not

to speak of such men as Gladstone, Forster, and Fawcett) 3 of the most determined democrats and anti-aristocrats in the country – Bright, Chamberlain, and the avowed republican Dilke. Democracy is not inconsistent with the English Monarchy: it co-exists with that at the present moment to a large extent, and is certain to advance further and further. However, I am not wedded to the mere title *Democratic Sonnets*, and if I see cause (which at present I don't) I will substitute another…Any idea of my undertaking to write verse about the public events of my own time, and yet failing to show that I sympathize with foreign republics, and detest oppression, retrogression, and obscurantism, whether abroad or at home, must be nugatory. To set me going is to set me going on my own path.

William considered he had written stronger stuff before than anything he had put into the sonnets, for instance on Robespierre and the execution of Charles I in his *Lives of the Poets* in 1878 but 'nobody ever, official or reviewers so far as I know, raised any question about them.'[20]

Gabriel retired from the fray but not without some parting shots. 'I have said my say, which I felt to be my duty'.[21] His motives were complex – embarrassment perhaps about the quality of the sonnets as well as their political content. Eventually William's hectic spate of poetic activity ground to a standstill. Over a quarter of a century later at the invitation of his 'half-nephew', young Ford Madox [Ford] Hueffer, William's sonnets were finally published in two volumes, at the democratic price of one shilling each, on 20 February 1907 in the Contemporary Poets series. If they had appeared when they were written in the early 1880s, Gabriel was right in thinking they could have caused a sensation and William's *Democratic Sonnets* might have been truly contemporary. By 1907 much of their political gunfire had been defused. The world had moved on and was already arming for the Great War which was to cause William deep dismay throughout the last years of his life. But the *Democratic Sonnets* remain his political manifesto, raging at an apathetic world, against the old orders, tyranny and oppression. Yet his global agenda of human rights for all is compressed into one of the most traditional and concentrated of poetic forms – the sonnet and the sonnet sequence.

The sonnets all address political subjects across a multi-national spectrum, interspersed with literary personalities of liberal, left-wing allegiance. Sonnet groups deal with Great Britain and Ireland, France, Italy, Germany, Austria and Hungary, Russia, and America. Designed originally on a more heroic scale as a series of one hundred sonnets, the published sequence shrank to just fifty.

Why did William choose the sonnet form? The traditional format of the sonnet could hardly be said to match his radical politics. But he deliberately chose the European, Petrarchan pattern, rather than the more robust, home-grown Shakespearean model. He wanted to utilize the sonnet's unique power, aiming at the control and concentration possible in its fourteen short lines and unforgiving metrics. Its formal discipline was a metaphor for the discipline of a revolutionary and William had been aware of its potential since boyhood when he, Gabriel, and sometimes Christina, wrote *bouts-rimés* sonnets to order, to pre-set rhyme schemes and against the clock.

The *Democratic Sonnets* are agitprop poems against injustice, employing stark contrasts and swingeing social sarcasm. Bitter sonnets address the American Civil War, the Irish famine, the Crimean and Boer wars, the freeing of serfs in Russia, the unification of Italy, the Paris Commune, the Fenians, as well as affairs in Poland, Austria and Hungary. This is poetry as polemic, more usually found in prose. William is at his best in the sonnets that condemn inequities meted out in Ireland or denounce slavery. He inveighs against apathy in England towards events during the American Civil War in 'England and America, 1861–1865':

> Mourn, England. – 'Wherefore mourn? Because my sons
> Across the Atlantic wring each other's throats,
> And corpses reckon thick as simmering motes
> In dusty sunbeams, and the roar of guns
> Drowns the bride's kiss'…
>
>   – England, mourn –
> Mourn for thyself if thou wilt not for these.
> Thou stood'st erect, the champion of the slave:
> And now thou floutest at the man who frees
> The black and fettered limbs, while blessings rave,
> Rave mid thy cheers, for slavery's cause outworn.[22]

Always a socialist and 'a democratic republican' William abhorred war and jingoism.[23] During the American Civil War his libertarian anti-slavery principles in England made him often feel 'singular and solitary in a roomful of company'.[24] At a dinner in 1866, William rebuked Whistler for giving an offensive impersonation of a fellow passenger on board ship home from Valparaiso. Whistler apparently had 'set himself to snub & insult a negro gentleman (he calls him the Marquis de Marmalade)', knocked his head against the ship's boiler and kicked him all through the ladies' cabin, 'and this merely, it seems, because the poor man is a negro (his humorous account of the circumstances exhibited the most naïve & inveterate prejudice)', commented William.[25] He unhesitatingly asserted a whole range of liberal, minority views on racism, imperialism, republicanism and women's suffrage.

The *Democratic Sonnets* are arranged on the page to graphically underscore William's theme, the conflict between oppression and freedom throughout the contemporary world. So a sonnet about outrageous treatment of the Irish is juxtaposed with one about Dickens, 'Friend of the friendless…Illuminator of the darkest slum'. A deposed despot Louis Philippe, 'denounced from land to land', is set adjacent to William's political ideal – 'The Republic, 1848':

Republic, field unlimited of man,
Equal, free-pasturing, and generous;
Home of the homeless and calamitous;
World-wide embrace unknowing of caste or clan.[26]

William loathed tyrants, slavery, war and starvation. His ideals were those of Shelley and Whitman. Hence he passionately supported the 1871 Paris Commune, lashing at the festering carcass of imperialism:

Shall the Republic be once more betrayed?
                    ...shall the Corsican's
Unlineal nephew foist again on France
His festered carcass, or his changeling's grade
Of empire purple-born? Rather than this,
Parisians, Paris shall herself become
Her own Republic. Here shall Freedom's cry
At least shout forth, and roar the recreants dumb.
Soar, Paris, if our France be Europe's hiss!
Here live we free, or free with Paris die![27]

This sonnet brings the first volume to a crescendo of political outrage. William's cry from the heart is intensified by questions, exclamations, verbal repetitions and rhetorical devices which lead dramatically, and melodramatically, to the triumphant rise and fall of the final line where even martyrdom is exultant: 'Here live we free, or free with Paris die!'

The theme of martyrdom is continued in the second volume but William's heroes are patriots, not religious zealots, who are prepared to die for their cause all over Europe and the New World. Sometimes he alters the format of juxtaposing two contrasting sonnets on opposite pages, and instead places two sonnets side by side for intensification. For instance, he locates 'The Red Shirt, 1860–1867' adjacent to 'Cavour, 1861'. In the first he plays without restraint on the effects of dripping blood suggested by Mazzini's Red Shirts. Time itself is stained with the blood of Italy's martyred sons; the nineteenth-century careers 'crimsoned in streaks to meet eternity'. Redness drenches the sonnet, suggesting both the patriot's cause and his final payment:

Oh red the shirt on which a redder trace
Of blood attests the patriot or his doom.

In the companion sonnet on Cavour, William uses images of plunging and rising, to suggest the dual necessities of thought and action. Italy needs Cavour her statesman, her thinker, just as much as she needs her more physically proactive leaders, Mazzini and Garibaldi. Cavour's skills are cerebral and strategic, to 'accommodate, retard, force onward, lure'. It is appropriate then, and spatially effective in this sonnet, for Italy to 'kneel to Mazzini and Garibaldi' – but rise to Cavour her statesman. The sonnet to Garibaldi,

William's 'Hero of the World', ends the Italian and most substantial section of the second volume,

> Men, who hail his light afar,
> Name 'Garibaldi,' and then hold their peace.[28]

In the German section that follows, William's literary hero is the poet Heine because of his association with 'bright revolt'. Under the Austro-Hungarian heading he launches a bitter attack on Metternich, 'the despot's prop, the people's adversary', contorting his lines to react to the physical impact of stagger and stench, 'the garotte of tyranny', the 'kick which vibrates worldwide'. William invites Metternich, a 'name of nameless stench to Italy' to 'rot from off the earth'. He despises Metternich's 'impassive mask' and smooth diplomacy and denounces Haynau who implemented barbaric reprisals against insurgents in Hungary:

> He bared the backs of women, and he whipped
> Their naked flesh: women, Hungarians born,
> Whose crime was thrilling with their country torn
> By dual beak of Austria's eagle.[29]

In a play on words William conflates Haynau's very name into a ravening hyena. In sections on Russia and America he raises the emotional register yet again to attack serfdom and slavery. Loathing kings, tsars and Caesars, William concedes in choked onomatopoeic language, that twenty-three million Russians 'the age-long-cankering collar quitted', when serfdom was abolished under Tsar Alexander II. Similarly in the American section, his most heartfelt emotion is for 'The Slaves Freed, 1865':

> Black skin and darkened mind; sinews and thews
> Born to be worked and sold and worked again…
> Pulpit and law-court lash the negro down.[30]

William's heroes were the iconic John Brown, a martyr on the scale of Jesus Christ, and Abraham Lincoln who signed the momentous edict of emancipation in 1865. When Booth's bullet assassinates Lincoln, 'America/Groans' with the author of *Democratic Sonnets*. In his final pair of sonnets, William surveys 'the Past' and tries to see 'a purpose in the ages', to suggest that 'through the old order gleams the new'. His imagery drawn from gradations of light is only partially optimistic, more suggestive of how little convinced this angry old man remained about the perfectibility of humankind worldwide.

Lucy's *Mrs Shelley*[31]

'You will find your life quite changed if you write', Lucy's father told her, 'and once you have published this book all sorts of things might be done', adding mysteriously 'and we might be revenged on some of the mean fools who ruin us'.[32] Revenge would seem an unlikely motive for Lucy's biography of Mary Shelley but the acerbity of Brown's world-view was an intrinsic component of his daughter's nature, too.

Her career as an artist had been effectively curtailed by late marriage and a succession of pregnancies. Lucy found deep fulfilment in her children; their upbringing and education became her surrogate career. In spite of her illness and a cacophony of domestic demands, she still yearned for intellectual pursuits and for recognition in the intellectual world. Painting took up physical time, space and effort which she found increasingly difficult to award herself. So when John Ingram, editor of the Eminent Women series, asked William in January 1886[33] if he knew anyone qualified to write the life of Mary Shelley, William proposed Lucy.

Lucy was wintering with the children at the Clarendon Boarding House, on the hill above Ventnor, Isle of Wight. She had coughed up blood during a devastating attack of bronchial pneumonia the previous winter and her doctors, Gill and Wilson Fox, gave her no option but to leave London before Christmas 1885. In Ventnor she struggled with the children's illnesses and her own frailty. William brought down several American medicines, Himrod's powder and a liquid called 'Piso's Cure for Consumption and Bronchitis' but wracking coughing fits persisted, especially at night. Ingram's offer set her a new challenge and a new perspective. Summoning all her self-will and determined to find a new outlet for her latent creativity, Lucy began reading and research immediately.

The Eminent Women series was a companion to W.H. Allen's Statesmen series. Both aimed to produce succinct biographical studies of famous figures in affordable, pocket editions. 'Eminent Women' came out at 3s 6d each (with cheaper limp cloth versions at 1s 6d). *Mrs Shelley* would be twentieth in the eclectic series, which already included lives of Mary Wollstonecraft, George Sand, Madame de Staël, Elizabeth Barrett Browning, Harriet Martineau, the actress Rachel, Mrs Siddons and Elizabeth Fry. Mathilde Blind had written biographies of George Eliot and Madame Roland, Anne Gilchrist had contributed Mary Lamb, Charlotte Yonge had written on Hannah More and Vernon Lee on the Countess of Albany. Lucy's friend, the poet Mary Robinson, had written two lives, Emily Brontë in 1883, and Margaret of Angoulême, Queen of Navarre due out in 1886. Lucy did not fail to realise that she would be in good company – a position she always relished. Ingram accepted William's recommendation with alacrity and offered Lucy an honorarium of £50[34] in February 1886.[35]

William regarded his literary work on Shelley, the *Memoir* (1870, 1878 and 1886), successive editions of the *Works* (1870, 1878, 1894), as well as many other selections, articles and lectures, almost in the nature of a sacred trust. In writing the life of Mary Shelley, Lucy would no longer be a mere supporter of William's greatest literary enthusiasm. She would make Mary her special subject. Mary Shelley was not just a romantic icon; she was a personality with whom Lucy could identify. As her research progressed, she admired Mary's intellectual grit more and more and, at a subliminal level, recognized a temperament similar to her own that veered from volatile to depressive.

Shelley's poetry, his ideals, politics and atheism, all enmeshed with his tragic and romantic death in Italy, had been emotional elements in the friendship that 'melted into love' between William and Lucy.[36] In Rome in 1873, during her newly acknowledged happiness, Lucy had gathered leaves (whose brittle fronds still survive) from around the graves of the English poets Keats and Shelley.

She was drawn to Mary Shelley as a biographical subject both by chance and for other, subtler reasons. When people enquired why Gertrude Stein had written *The Autobiography of Alice B. Toklas*, she said frankly that publishers had asked her to write it. Lucy wrote in response to an invitation, the project arrived on her doorstep. As soon as she had agreed to it, she became aware of its perfect symmetry.

Lucy noticed many coincidental similarities between Mary's life and her own. Both were daughters of famous, gifted and creative parents and grew up stimulated by, or burdened with, intellectual aspiration. Mary Shelley was the daughter of feminist pioneer, Mary Wollstonecraft, and William Godwin, eccentric philosopher. Lucy Rossetti was the daughter of celebrated artist Ford Madox Brown although his wife Elisabeth Bromley had died too soon to make her mark. From the intelligentsia, both families were slightly outside the conventions of middle-class life. Mary and Lucy both lost their mothers in infancy – a first emotional, possibly guilt-inducing loss of the 'watchful love of an intelligent mother'[37] that Lucy always mourned. As a result, both Mary and Lucy would contend with 'respectable but shallow-minded' stepmothers, although Mrs Clairmont who married William Godwin in 1801 was 'not ignorant',[38] and Ford Madox Brown's second wife, Emma Hill, read and enjoyed authors such as Tolstoy. Lucy had half-siblings and Mary acquired step-siblings and later a half-brother. Both women married men with 'names'. Both were intellectuals who had careers of their own and admired 'what was noble and advanced in idea'.[39]

Lucy lived by her advanced ideals of education and feminism. Early in the biography, she set out the major feminist principles that Mary Wollstonecraft, Mary Shelley's mother, had formulated in her *Vindication of the Rights of Woman* (1792) and summarized how far each had been fulfilled by the late 1880s. Lucy's sympathy with Wollstonecraft's pioneering demands is implicit in her précis:

> She wished women to have education equal to that of men, and this has now to a great extent been accorded.
>
> That trades, professions, and other pursuits should be open to women. This wish is now in progress of fulfilment.
>
> That married women should own their own property as in other

European countries. Recent laws have granted this right.

That they should have more facilities for divorce from husbands guilty of immoral conduct. This has been partially granted, though much still remains to be effected.

That, in the case of separation, the custody of children should belong equally to both parents.

That a man should be legally responsible for his illegitimate children. That he should be bound to maintain the woman he has wronged.

Mary Wollstonecraft also thought that women should have representatives in Parliament to uphold their interests...[40]

During the writing of the book Lucy was a signatory in 1889, as 'Mrs Madox Rossetti – historical painter', to a Declaration in Favour of Women's Suffrage,[41] issued to counter an Anti-Suffrage Petition signed, notoriously, by Mrs Humphry Ward. Lucy clearly endorsed Wollstonecraft's social and political philosophy, and especially her views on education. She decried the 'frivolous fashionable' trivialities that passed for education for so many Victorian women of her time and class, and refuted popular beliefs that a rigorous, classical education would compromise women's femininity. 'To make a woman a reasoning being, by means of Euclid if necessary, need not preclude her from being a charming woman also, as proved by...Mary Wollstonecraft herself'. Better education for women would raise the intellectual and moral status of both sexes, believed Lucy. Recalling her own specialized education which combined academic with artistic training, she thought idealistically, that a new woman 'who can appreciate the great reflex of nature as transmitted through the human mind in the glorious art of the world, may really be raised to the ideal state where the sacrilege of love will be unknown'.[42]

Lucy's passion for educating women, as well as her reputation as a formidable conversationalist, were so well known that (without her knowledge) in January 1879 women students at University College, London put her name forward as president of their newly formed debating society.[43] The more public figure of Elizabeth Garrett Anderson narrowly won the vote but the proposal was indicative of Lucy's status among feminist intellectuals, even though she had exhibited hardly any work since marrying in 1874.

Mary Wollstonecraft's feminist vision with its 'repugnance to the laws made by men',[44] was absorbed by osmosis into Lucy's presentation of Wollstonecraft's daughter. It was almost as if the two Marys, mother and daughter, coalesced for her. Work was a direct outcome of Wollstonecraft's agenda and in her portrait of Mary Shelley, Lucy repeatedly refers to the concept of work as 'the great resource'.[45] In the years after Shelley's death, creative work was an important component of Mary's livelihood, as it was for Lucy in the years before her marriage. Even more crucially, Lucy considered that her art, her professional work had given her a sense of identity. As she grew older it also provided solace and fulfilment, as she observed that it did for Mary Shelley.

Lucy thought carefully about the function of a biographer and the problems of trying to convey the authentic essence of a character. While studying the personality of William Godwin, Mary's father, she told William about the difficulties she encountered in trying to collate all the different sources about the philosopher, 'but I think the more details one has the less one sometimes seems to know a character or rather one is apt to lose a broad view.'[46] Godwin's unpredictable character and awkward irritability made her realize that in biography as in life, 'unfortunately, characters cannot always be made the consistent beings they frequently become in romances.'[47] She felt a duty to tell the biographical truth as she found it. Rejecting 'romance', her prose is pacy and free of purple passages, her vocabulary unpretentious and her sentence structure controlled, short and simple, quite unlike the breathless onrush of sentences and maverick lack of punctuation in her private letters.

Lucy not only shared intellectual interests and aspirations with Mary. She also shared a temperamental affinity, an unassailable reserve in reaction to some of life's most poignant experiences. Both women lost children, both suffered miscarriages. Lucy slips into the vivid present tense to describe the cot death of Mary's first baby, threading Mary's own journal into the biographer's terse commentary: ' "Find my baby dead. Send for Hogg. Talk. A miserable day." Mary thinks, and talks, and dreams of her little baby, and finds reading the best palliative to her grief'.[48]

In February 1815 Mary was a teenage mother, her baby daughter illegitimate. Lucy was a mature mother of nearly forty in 1883, secure in a middle-class marriage when Michael, her youngest child, died aged nineteen months. Losing a child made those differences irrelevant. Lucy understood exactly why intellectual Mary resumed her demanding reading programme as an antidote to grief. Mary's annual reading lists were marvels of eclectic scholarship and generally far longer than Shelley's. With similar motives, immediately after nursing her dying child in her arms, Lucy turned to the art form that sustained her and made a picture of baby Michael in death. With her own intimate knowledge of the agony of watching a child die, Lucy empathized with Mary's feelings as another daughter, little Clara, slipped away while on a desperate journey to get medical aid. 'Mary had to endure that terrible tension of mind, with her dying child in her arms, driving to Venice, the time remembered by her so well when, on the same route, nearly a quarter of a century later, each turn in the road and the very trees seemed as the most familiar objects of her daily life; for had they not been impressed on her mental vision by the strength of despair?'[49] Under extreme mental tension, mundane objects often become indelible. For Mary these were the trees and the turns in the road to Venice; for Lucy they were the fresh snowdrops she drew around her own dead baby Michael in 1883.

In a sense, Lucy wrote this biography for William, to participate in his literary life. She noted the parallel that Mary wrote *Frankenstein* for Shelley and looked forward to reading the chapters to him one by one.[50] Lucy wrote her chapters for William who looked forward to hearing her read them aloud when he joined her in Biarritz in March 1889. Lucy considered Mary the ideal wife for Shelley, someone who could match him intellectually. 'Mary had the years of pleasure, which are inestimable to those who can appreciate them, of contact with a great mind; but few among poets' wives have had the gifts which allow them fully to participate in such pleasures.'[51] Lucy prized marital fidelity above all virtues and even described herself in her will as William's 'faithful wife'. She saw Mary as 'a true wife willing to follow [Shelley] through weal or woe',[52] a sisterly conception different from William's view of Mary Shelley.

William recognized Mary's creative powers and mental capacity but he questioned, from his masculine perspective, whether her temperament was an ideal one to partner Shelley's. While conceding that Mary sincerely loved Shelley, and he her, William found 'serious divergences between them, both of character and inclination…Mary disquieted him by jealousies…and by infirmities of temper, and was not always heedful of his personal comfort…after the first few years, Shelley found in his union with Mary not much more genuine unalloyed satisfaction of soul and heart than Harriet would have been willing and capable to afford him.'[53] William was no sexist. Like Lucy he believed in women's rights, attended meetings and stood up on platforms to say so. The organizers of the National Society for Women's Suffrage sought his advice for names of sympathizers, which he provided.[54] But he could not empathize with Mary Shelley as Lucy did.

Aiming, as always, at critical impartiality, William was cool about Lucy's achievement in turning from the brush to the pen. 'My wife treated Mrs Shelley in a spirit of candour, sympathy, and intelligence. Some valuable unpublished materials were placed at her disposal…and she produced, I conceive, a very readable book.' Lucy had 'good innate gifts,' but the biography was not a work 'of highly trained literary accomplishment', he wrote with unexpected severity.[55] Had Lucy ultimately encroached too far into his own province of literary biography, or did he really find her literary style unpolished?

William privately criticized Lucy's efforts in his diary on three counts. First, she would not accept his advice about structuring her biography and spent too much time, he considered, on 'preliminary matter' before getting to the heart of her story.[56] Secondly, when he read the manuscript, he objected to a 'tendency to run clauses together, producing lengthy & loose-knit sentences'[57] – rather like her letter-writing style – but many of his stylistic emendations she accepted. The real sticking point was that on William's own special subject of Shelley, Lucy expressed independent views that were not 'exactly mine', particularly on Shelley's cavalier abandonment of his first wife. Even William's friends found the way he treated Shelley's desertion of Harriet in his *Memoir*, 'somewhat cool and indicative of how a highly educated and humane man is influenced by Liberal doctrines', as John Lucas Tupper observed to Holman Hunt.[58] But summoning his usual fair-mindedness, William affirmed 'but of course it is desirable & requisite that [Lucy] should express her own [views], whatever they may be'.[59]

Lucy knew the task of tackling Mary Shelley's complex life would be difficult.[60] She was also provoked, but not deflected, when she heard in July 1887 that Mrs Julian Marshall was writing a biography of Mary, authorized by Sir Percy and Jane, Lady Shelley. Florence Marshall's two volumes came out in 1889, ahead of Lucy's, and benefited from using many hitherto unpublished letters. However, Marshall had been constrained by her rights of access. Her work was a hagiography. In November, William dissected it at length for the *Athenaeum*[61] where he highlighted the author's outright errors, her inadequacy as a literary critic and her biographic failure to recreate Mary's challenging character other than in terms of unconvincing saintliness. 'No new light is thrown,' he wrote, surreptitiously preparing the public for another *Life*. Marshall's insipid view was that 'the true success of Mary Shelley's life was not…the intellectual triumph, of which, during her youth, she had loved to dream…but the moral success of beauty of character.'[62] By contrast Lucy, who intuitively understood her subject's blend of emotional reserve and emotional depth, chose to present Mary as a creative artist and discussed her literary works with far greater insight than Mrs Marshall.

Lucy genuinely aimed to render Mary's character as truthfully as possible. Just after publication in April 1890, she thanked John Cordy Jeaffreson who had helped with research. 'I am indeed gratified if my little book meets with your approbation.' She told him how much she had enjoyed writing it and was sure she could survive the critics, 'if you and a few others like my attempt at adding to truth.'[63] Lucy had favourable reviews in *The Times*, the *World*, *The Graphic* and the *Whitehall*. She was able to laugh off less positive reviews. 'The article in the *St James* [*Gazette*] is just what I should have expected from a paper which Gosse has to do with. The only fairness it seems to me comes from perfect strangers.'[64] But she could not enjoy success since she was socially ostracized, in quarantine, nursing Arthur and Mary with measles. 'I have had I think many nice notices, but it's a dull way of becoming famous!! shut up in a room!'[65]

In her effort to present her heroine with both objectivity and sympathy, Lucy submerged her own personality, so much so that one of her best reviews, in the *Bradford Observer*, commented accurately on her 'almost oriental passionless way', which pleased her. The reviewer noted the converse implicit in Lucy's cool style, which pleased her even more, 'extremes meet and [she] could show "righteous indignation" against low cowards if necessary.'[66] Indignation was an essential feature of Lucy's personality, as it was of her father's, but she tried to temper this characteristic tone in her biography.

Well aware of the demands of scholarship, she cited sources, quoted documents, journals, diaries, letters, referred to earlier research and generally refused to speculate. 'It is scarcely the province of a biographer to say what might have taken place under other circumstances.'[67] However, her biographical style was not as prim as this might suggest. She varied her tenses and her narrative techniques, sometimes paraphrasing Mary's letters to suggest urgent stream-of-consciousness:

> Shelley is house-hunting in South Devon. Although she wishes to have a home of her own, she dreads the time it will take Shelley to find it. He ought to be with her the next day, the anniversary of their journey to Dover; without him it will be insupportable. And then the 4th of August will be his birthday, when they must be together. They might go to Tintern Abbey. If Shelley does not come to her, or give her leave to join him, she will leave in the morning and be with him before night to give him her present with her own hand. And then, is not Claire in North Devon? If Shelley has let her know where he is, is she not sure to join him if she thinks he is alone? Insufferable thought![68]

Although Lucy suppresses her own persona, and never uses the first person singular except in her short preface, her authorial voice is clearly to be heard. She is alternately 'we', 'one' and 'the present writer'.[69] She is aware of her audience and invites us in to sympathize with 'our heroine'. She asks us to fly back into the past with her. 'Picture these four young imaginative beings.'[70] She involves us with teasing, rhetorical questions. 'What prudent parents would have countenanced such a visitor [as Shelley]?'[71] A sharp Lucian wit, usually with a socio-political subtext, bubbles to the surface. Those who can afford to buy books in three guinea volumes 'are not usually inclined to overthrow the existing order of things',[72] she comments wryly. Shelley's aristocratic mother 'thought more of him bringing home a well-filled game bag...than of trying to understand what he was thinking.'[73] As always, the role of an intelligent mother was one of her priorities.

Her other major priority – visual art and its role in human development – she infiltrated into the narrative at several key points. She considered Shelley's education deficient in fine art, although he eventually expressed his imagination in poetry. She deplored the neglect of art as a 'legitimate outlet for imagination...in a country like ours...where the hereditary owners of hoarded wealth rest content, as a rule, with the canvases acquired by some ancestor on a grand tour at a date when Puritan England had already obliterated perception'.[74] Mary's drawing lessons had been equally inadequate, another example of 'that terrible way of teaching Art, by accustoming its students to hideousness and vulgarity'.[75] No wonder Mary did not meet Lucy's high standards of art appreciation when she travelled in Europe. Mary may have been impressed by famous works of art but her remarks 'though those of a clever woman'[76] did not show a genuine love of plastic art or an understanding of the emotion that drives it.

The problem as Lucy saw it, was that literary art does not necessarily understand pictorial art. Words for her could not explain the mystery of art, a covert attack on the art criticism that had been an integral part of William's literary life. As an artist, Lucy wanted bookish Mary off her territory, but failed to see the irony that in writing the biography at all she was a trespasser in Mary's province. But she conceded that sometimes Mary's art appreciation rose from being merely clever to become eloquent. In Lucy's exalted opinion, visual art can express without words 'religious sentiment and divine ecstasy' as well as 'the grand feelings of humanity, the love which is faithful to death, the emotions such as Shakespeare describes'.[77] Art was Lucy's religion, her ideal, and a way of living better. It was also a consolation for what she saw as 'the battle of life'.[78]

In Lucy's mind, art was linked with Italy and she shared with Mary an intense visual appreciation of that country. Most of Mary's most searing life experiences had taken place in Italy and for Lucy, too, it was inextricably meshed with love and death. She and William found love visiting Naples, Rome and Florence but in later years disease made Italy a place both of Lucy's release and her exile. From her own experiences, Lucy should have been able to convey Mary's response to Italian beauty, as here in Sorrento:

> She feels herself to be in Paradise; and who that has been in that wonderful country would not sympathise with her enthusiasm! To be carried up the heights to Ravello, and to see the glorious panorama around, she considered, surpassed all her previous most noble experiences. Ravello, with its magnificent cathedral covered with mosaics, is indeed a sight to have seen; the road to Amalfi, the ruinous paper mills in the ravine, the glorious picturesqueness.[79]

Confined to words, Lucy resorted to imprecise generalizing. Her evocation of the Neapolitan coastline is deeply felt but oddly bleached of colour, lacking scale and detail, as if the artist in her could only convey light and perspective with a brush. She does not make the reader see. Mary, on the other hand, especially in *Frankenstein* (1818), is skilled at visual effects of landscape and seascape, in her element describing the elements, 'mountain cataracts, Alpine storms, water lashed into waves and foam by the wind', as Lucy accurately noted.[80]

Lucy wrote a substantial part of the biography during the winter of 1888/9 when she was in illness-imposed exile in the Pyrenees. In Pau she watched light changing on the threatening chain of north-facing peaks that line the horizon. Lucy used her own fretful experience to empathize with Mary's 'passing depression…that often comes when shut in by mountains away from home'.[81] When she decamped to Biarritz where the blue Pyrenees meet the distant waterline, Lucy heard the tide surging and sighing incessantly on the beach. She only had to look at the Atlantic outside her window on the rue des Falaises in Biarritz to word-paint the electric storms Mary saw in Switzerland in 1816, 'lighting up lake and pine forests with the most vivid brilliancy, and then nothing but blackness with rolling thunder'.[82] Watching a thirty-hour hurricane at Biarritz informed her physical description of the storm that killed Shelley. 'For a time the sea seemed solidified and appeared as of lead, with an oily scum; the wind did not ruffle it. Then sounds of thunder, wind, and rain filled the air; these lasted with fury for twenty minutes; then a lull, and anxious looks among the boats which had rushed into the harbour for Shelley's bark. No glass could find it on the horizon.'[83] This is one of Lucy's most effective sections of narrative, tense, precise and evocative. It does, however, contain 'bark', one of the poetic archaisms that disrupt the naturalness of her style from time to time, but none of her grand generalizations such as 'relentless destiny' and 'the altar of fate' which occasionally jar the reader.[84]

In spite of inexperience as a writer or as a literary critic, Lucy knew it was Mary's literary work, not merely her association with Shelley, that gave the '*raison d'être* for this biography'.[85] Mary's life was romantic, tragic and haunting, but its main significance lay in the originality of her writing, especially *Frankenstein*. Lucy countered her father's over-literal dismissal of Mary's now legendary novel. 'It becomes as great rubbish & nonsense as ever I read – & I must say that it lowers not only Mary in my estimation but positively Shelley himself that he could allow her to publish such stuff. The fiend's going off to consume himself on a lofty pyre for no reason & *in the middle of the sea* is too absurd', Madox Brown wrote to his daughter.[86] Lucy's analysis and pertinent commentary shows how conscious she is of Mary's achievement in *Frankenstein*. However, she is prepared to criticize Mary's awkward 'framed' structure, 'which might with advantage have been avoided',[87] although some of her other criticisms, like Brown's, are perhaps too literal for a surreal work like *Frankenstein*. Lucy pointedly but inappropriately criticized the long letters 'quoted by Frankenstein to his friend while dying…which he could not have carried with him on his deadly pursuit'.[88] Family dynamics also inspired Lucy to draw an uneven parallel between her half-brother Oliver Madox Brown's *jeu d'esprit*, *Gabriel Denver* (1873) and Mary Shelley's *tour de force*, *Frankenstein*.[89]

Where evidence exists, Lucy links specific events in Mary's life to key points in the narrative, such as Frankenstein's horror at the thing he has galvanized into life. 'He runs forth into the street, and here, in Mary's first work, we have a reminiscence of her own infant days, when she and Claire hid themselves under the sofa to hear Coleridge read his poem, for the following stanza from the *Ancient Mariner* might seem almost the key-note of *Frankenstein*:-

> Like one who on a lonely road,
>   Doth walk in fear and dread,
> And having once turned round, walks on,
>   And turns no more his head,
> Because he knows a fearful fiend
>   Doth close behind him tread.'[90]

When the monster demands a mate from his maker, Frankenstein decides to set up his gruesome laboratory on a remote island of the Orkneys. To reach his destination, he first 'descends the Rhine, which is described with the knowledge gained in Mary's own journey, and the same route is pursued which she, Shelley, and Claire had taken through Holland, embarking for England from Rotterdam, and thence reaching the Thames.'[91] Lucy notes exactly where Mary seams her own life into the tale.

Her treatment of *Frankenstein* is the most discerning of all her considerations of Mary's works, although she calls *Valperga* (1823) 'a decided advance upon *Frankenstein*',[92] and treats a late work *Falkner* (1837) appreciatively but at inordinate length. Lucy read enough contemporary novels from Mudie's library (she consumed *Daniel Deronda* on its first book publication in 1876) to scent the demise of traditional three-volume novels like *Falkner* whose bulky format 'seems to detract from the strength of the work'.[93] She was astute on Mary's ambitious book, *The Last Man* (1826), set in the year 2073 and filled with the writer's biographical reminiscences. Although Mary's writing could be stilted, Lucy recognized that this 'highly imaginative work' contained 'some of the author's most powerful ideas'.[94] She also admired the readability of Mary's series of short biographies, *Lives of the Most Eminent Literary and Scientific Men of Italy, Spain and Portugal* (2 vols 1835 and 1837) and praised her for 'freedom from affectation, and a genuine love of her subject'.[95] Discussing Mary's *Rambles in Germany and Italy* (1844), she recognized their autobiographical substrata.

By now Lucy knew from experience some of the problems faced by a biographer. Like Mary, she showed considerable 'freedom from affectation' and her love of her subject is palpable. But does she make Mary live and breathe for us, as Frankenstein made his monster live? Lucy cared about truth, refused to indulge in speculation, absorbed countless facts about Mary and transformed them with economy and grace into a unified conception. But even the artist in Lucy could not fully reveal the inner workings of her subject's literary imagination.

The essence of Mary's character has remained elusive and unknowable – even to the most conscientious and ingenious biographers. As a subject, Mary resisted most biographers' honourable endeavours to conduct Frankenstein's experiment and breathe life into dead parts. But *Mrs Shelley* was an important outcome of Lucy's thwarted artistic vision.

Finishing the biography gave Lucy an appetite for more literary work. In November 1889 she conceived a plan for a hugely ambitious project 'The Art of Painting as Practised in the Nineteenth Century'. William did not believe it was feasible but they spent an evening in earnest discussion together, poring over his collection of relevant art books.

9

The Patient

Lucy's grave is in La Foce international cemetery in San Remo, Liguria, Italy. William, Olive, Arthur, Helen and Mary laid her wasted body there two days after her death on 12 April 1894.[1] Her struggle with tuberculosis was finally over. Today the cemetery is an elemental place, caught between sun and sea. Surprisingly, it is not a dead place but full of vitality, where people come and go, brushing dust and leaves from the graves, sluicing them down with buckets of water, sweeping, talking, meeting. Death in this beautiful place is not sad but natural, restful, a fact of life. Lucy lies besides the 'murmurous Mediterranean' that she had crossed with William on their honeymoon journey of 1874 and William would hear on his several return visits to La Foce. From Lucy's grave he could look out across the whole cemetery, its shady walks marked by tall cypresses, serene colonnades of peace and dignity.

Wandering among the 'streets' of this intimate graveyard is a cosmopolitan experience. San Remo was created as a winter resort in the second half of the nineteenth century and owed its livelihood to the febrile foreigners who sustained it. In death, the San Remese repaid the debt and housed them in an international graveyard. Buried together are Americans, Canadians, Germans, Russians, French, Scots, English, Catholics, Protestants and Jews, believers and unbelievers alike. The elderly lie side by side with babies of a few months old. The middle-aged jostle the young. Edward Lear's grave is just a few steps from Lucy Rossetti's. Lear died on 29 January 1888 in the place he had loved and painted, and William permanently regretted he had failed to look up his old friend when he joined Lucy for a few weeks in the earthquake year of 1887. Today the Comune di Sanremo honours the graves of both Edward Lear and Lucy Rossetti with brilliant yellow chrysanthemums on saints' days and holidays. La Foce promotes a sense of removal from worldly pressures. It seems unpretentious and appropriate that William preferred Lucy to remain in this place of grace instead of hauling her body home to England at considerable expense – it would have cost at least £200 in 1894. Some graves are floridly embellished with religious insignia and elaborate sentiments. By complete contrast, and in testament to her long-held agnosticism, a simple slab of grey-veined marble with no religious or Christian symbolism identifies Lucy's

114. William
Michael Rossetti
at Lucy's grave, La
Foce cemetery,
San Remo, 1907.
Photograph by J.
Scotto, Via
Vittorio Emanuele
15, San Remo.
Inscribed by
William Michael
Rossetti, 'of my
dear Lucy's
Tombstone with
myself taken on
my 78th birthday
25 September
1907'. Private
collection.

tomb (fig. 114). She had always felt 'if there is one thing with me to add to the horror of death and interment it is the ostrich plumes and unnecessary trappings mais qu'import[e]?'[2] The inscription began to dissolve away in the first few years after her burial. Today it is only just discernible with tracing paper and the aid of old photographs:

LUCY MADOX ROSSETTI
PAINTER AND AUTHORESS
THE BELOVED DAUGHTER OF
FORD MADOX BROWN
THE BELOVED WIFE OF
WILLIAM MICHAEL ROSSETTI
BORN IN PARIS 19 JULY 1843
DIED IN SAN REMO 12 APRIL 1894
INTEGRA VITA SCELERISQUE PURA

William adapted the last line from one of Horace's Odes, meaning 'of unblemished life and spotless record'.[3]

Did he believe it, or want to believe it? Years of ill health had aggravated Lucy's personality while William had made valiant efforts to understand the pressure of stress on her erratic psyche. As consumption continued to consume her from within, William noted the distressing accompaniment of what he called 'brain-exhaustion'. Although tuberculosis is popularly associated with the lungs, it may attack other organs of the body, including the brain. But William's analysis suggests Lucy's hostility was rooted in understandable depression, rather than dementia, and he dates its onset specifically from November 1892, eighteen months before her death.

> It did not in any way weaken my wife's readiness or keenness of perception, or her power of estimating things by an intellectual standard; but it gave a swerve to her feelings, and to her construction of persons and occurrences, and made her look at all sorts of matters with a resentful bias. Mentally, it was the same kind of thing as if she had gazed with the physical eyes through blackened spectacles.[4]

Felicita Jurlaro, who wrote a book on Christina Rossetti, recalled that Lucy's daughter, Olive Rossetti Agresti, told her unequivocally that at the end Lucy 'became insane'.[5] Olive was only eighteen during Lucy's final illness. All the children had faced trying sojourns in seaside places, in decaying houses with dying people, as Olive bitterly told her friends.[6] Lucy became habituated to dependence on her eldest daughter who was condemned to watch first-hand the consuming, emaciating effects of the disease on body and mind. Olive's judgement is likely to be close to the truth as she perceived it then and remembered it later. However, rather than clinical dementia it is more plausible that Lucy suffered from a logical depressive state with extreme agitation. Psychotic symptoms may have been produced or exacerbated by medications she was prescribed, which probably included highly toxic ingredients – nineteenth-century cough linctus commonly contained opium. The fact that Lucy remained intellectually and creatively active until the very final stages of her illness is in itself evidence against 'insanity'.

Although *mycobacterium tuberculosis* might have spread to the brain, it is impossible to diagnose in retrospect. It is unlikely that Lucy had tuberculosis of the brain, as it would have killed her much more quickly. Facing any terminal illness is traumatic and in the later 'galloping' stages of consumption Lucy would have been constantly feverish, constantly frightened, anxious and irritable, symptoms which observers might have ascribed to mental instability.

There was no cure for tuberculosis before 1952. Today, in overcrowded living conditions – particularly in the sub-Saharan continent, the old Soviet Union, parts of South America, the Indian sub-continent and the Philippines

– the bacterial infection of tuberculosis especially in connection with HIV, is challenging the cocktail of four antibiotics, isoniazid, ethambutol, pyrazinamide, rifampicin, that was used so successfully in the second half of the twentieth century. But even in the developed world, tuberculosis is making a significant return - over six thousand new cases are currently being notified in the United Kingdom every year. Exacerbated by poor housing and hygiene, malnutrition and stress, more than eight million people a year now contract the disease worldwide and a quarter of that number die. It is estimated that by 2050 there will be five million deaths each year from TB. Now, as then, the disease can be contracted from the breath, from a skin lesion or from the sputum (hence the otherwise opaque injunction – 'no spitting' – on continental trains.)

Tuberculosis has always been with us; it was known in ancient civilizations to the Aztecs, Incas and Egyptians. The symptomatology and pathology of the disease was highly developed as early as Hippocrates. He described the typical physique of sufferers who classically exhibited chests like two boards, shoulder blades like wings, and a prominent larynx. He added that their chests were tender, spongy or weak. Lucy exhibited a similar feminine physique – narrow shoulders and chest, soft hair and a luminescent complexion – which the nineteenth century also associated with consumption, and which would have been recognizable to Hippocrates.

Pulmonary tuberculosis (Lucy's illness) presents a persistent, productive cough with associated symptoms of lassitude, fever, chest pains, night sweats, weight loss, no appetite and haemoptysis (coughing up blood). It does not occur spontaneously or suddenly but is a developmental disease, dating from a primary infection by the bacillus, often unremarked in childhood, followed by a period of 'indolence' or resistance as the body fights back. The adult disease is thought to result from reactivation of lesions quiescent since the primary infection.[7]

The nineteenth-century mythology of tuberculosis was paradoxically both negative and positive. It was associated in the public mind with sensitive, spiritual or extremely creative people, a myth reinforced by the tubercular deaths of romantic figures such as Schiller, Keats, Paganini, the Brontës, Chopin, Emily Patmore, Marie Bashkirtseff, Robert Louis Stevenson, St Thérèse of Lisieux, Beardsley and Chekhov. Women were thought to be more susceptible to the disease, although many men contracted it. The disease gave the sufferer at times a terrible beauty, illuminating the skin alternately with an alabaster pallor or a deceptively rosy glow. This delicate tubercular suffusion may have given Gabriel's 1874 pastel portrait of Lucy its special bloom (see fig. 22).

'Tuberculosis' and 'consumption' were words that William and Lucy strenuously avoided. She had a bad cold, an annoying cough, 'wheezing', even bronchitis (although William warned Madox Brown not to mention the word 'pneumonia' during her critical illness in February 1885), but her lungs, they assured themselves, were not affected. It was as if by not naming it, the disease did not exist, a strategy for (ef)facing illness by denial that is well recognized. Although patients could spontaneously recover, the standard treatments for tuberculosis were ineffective at worst, and palliative at best. In autumn 1889, Lucy lined her London bedroom with slabs of virgin cork and managed to convince herself that she felt the benefit. She even wrote to Tennyson, the Poet Laureate, to recommend the cure but eventually was forced to admit bleakly that the cork had no effect. Today doctors dismiss the cork treatment and suggest it could only have alleviated Lucy's symptoms psychologically.

During the nineteenth century, it was doctors' standard practice to advise middle-class patients to flee from English winters and to head south. Fashionable hotels, hospitals and sanatoriums sprang up for tubercular patients on the south coasts of England, the Isle of Wight, and along the 130-mile stretch of the Franco-Italian Riviera. By seeking salvation in the sun, Lucy both exiled and empowered herself. But she does not fit glibly into latter-day stereotypes of sick Victorian women who used disease as an alibi. Illness did not free her from domestic responsibility in order to pursue artistic work, as it did for Elizabeth Barrett Browning, or to go off exploring in the spirit of Isabella Bird. With four mettlesome children Lucy could not exploit her infirmity like Alice James. She was trapped in a geographical double bind. London represented for her the focus of artistic and intellectual life, but it also meant choking, smoggy winters, coal-dust particles in the city air that irritated her lungs, and doctors who only allowed her to go out briefly between midday and two in the afternoon. Continental travel with some or all of her children, gave her self-determination, a sense of independence, even a tentative return to artistic practice. But she felt cut off, sidelined, subtly oppressed by a male conspiracy of husband and doctors. There were no major art galleries in San Remo, she complained to William. Bubbling between the lines of her letters home was a persistent sense of isolation and deprivation. On the other hand, the benefits of continental wandering were equally apparent. Lucy and her children became Europeans and cosmopolitans. They spoke the languages; they made new friends; their horizons expanded.

Looked at objectively, or with hindsight, neither Lucy's genetic inheritance nor her health profile was encouraging. She never knew her paternal grandmother, Caroline Madox Brown, or her paternal aunt, Lyly Brown, who both died of consumption, aged forty-seven and twenty-two respectively, before she was born. When Lucy was less than three years old her mother, Elisabeth Bromley, also died of consumption in her mid-twenties. Lucy was not her first

115. Ford Madox Brown, *Arthur Gabriel Madox Brown*, 1857. Watercolour, 114 × 89 mm. Private collection.

baby – Elisabeth had bitterly mourned a son she had lost at just five days old. After her mother's death, on their way home from Italy via Paris, Madox Brown placed Lucy with 'Aunt' (by marriage) Helen Bromley and her young family at Melliker Farm, in Kent. It is possible that Lucy was first infected with bovine TB by drinking unpasteurized milk on the farm. In early child-hood Lucy was mostly well, although her father recorded bad colds and ear-ache. Just before her sixth birthday he noted that Lucy had 'Hooping cough'.[8]

During the early 1850s, as cholera raged furiously in London, Lucy flour-ished in the beneficent Kent countryside. While her father was establishing a new family with his second wife in London, Lucy, in Gravesend, remained healthy. But her elder cousin, Aunt Helen's beloved daughter, another Helen, was conspicuously delicate. She died of consumption, aged only seventeen, also perhaps from a primary infection contracted on the farm. In September 1856, Lucy's second half-brother, Arthur Gabriel (fig. 115), was born but lived only ten months. According to his sister Cathy, he died of tubercular menin-gitis.[9]

There is little indication of Lucy's health as a young woman except the 'bad news about Lucy Brown, poor Girl – congestion of the lung' that William had mentioned to his mother in 1862.[10] A decade later, aged twenty-nine, she suf-fered another, unspecified illness. Either of these two crises may have been the instance of Lucy's primary infection (if she had not been previously infected on the farm) or may indicate reactive phases of the disease. In May 1873 her father encouraged her to join what he recommended to her as a recuperative pleasure tour to Italy; reports from William that Lucy was 'much indisposed' even on holiday distressed her future mother-in-law Frances Rossetti.[11]

On their honeymoon in Italy in April 1874, William could not fail to notice Lucy's bronchial symptoms. In August she miscarried and six weeks later William told Gabriel that Lucy was 'still *far* from strong: at times fairly well, at others much knocked up.'[12] Insomniac, and in a low emotional and physical state, Lucy dosed herself with chloral, the drug that eventually played a notorious part in Gabriel's destruction.[13] Alphonse Daudet described the agonies of sleeping, and then not sleeping, with chloral. 'Bad night, woken with a jolt at three; no actual pain, but highly strung and in fear of pain. I had to take more chloral…Attempt to sleep without chloral. You close your eyes and chasms open to right and left. Five-minute cat-naps filled with harrowing nightmares: skidding and sliding, crashing down, vertigo, the abyss'.[14]

Then only two months after her miscarriage, Lucy received one of the most wounding blows of her life. Her much loved half-brother Nolly died on 5 November 1874 from an insidious blood poisoning infection which at first no one had taken seriously. Still fragile after her miscarriage, Lucy helped nurse Oliver through long agonizing days. He was a marvellous boy, at only nineteen already an artist, poet and novelist, with whom Lucy had always had a genuine rapport. He had been far easier to love than Cathy, her pretty and competitive half-sister. Madox Brown's grief was overpowering and frightening and Lucy spent long days in Fitzroy Square comforting both Emma and her father. It seemed he would never cease to mourn. Lucy's grief was parallel to his and every future loss in her life recalled Nolly, her spectacular golden brother. A few days after Oliver's death, Gabriel commented to Aunt Charlotte Polidori, 'Poor Lucy's health seems still further seriously affected by her pain of mind and exertions as a nurse'.[15]

In December, Gabriel shared his foreboding with his doctor, Thomas Hake, 'Lucy's health seems to me destined to be a permanent cause of anxiety'.[16] But in January 1875 she set off north with William, to support her father who was lecturing in Newcastle and Edinburgh. She probably conceived again on this trip. She felt well enough in mid-summer 1875 to accompany William, Madox Brown and Emma to Belgium and Holland. They stayed at the Hôtel de l'Europe in Antwerp to see the modern wall paintings by Baron Leys at the Hôtel de Ville and Lucy joined in a rigorous programme of sightseeing. They went on to Brussels where Madox Brown was keen to take a Turkish bath. Although Lucy was six months pregnant, her father was determined to find the grave of his sister Lyly Brown who had been buried in Brussels thirty-five years earlier. Mortality was never very far away from their thoughts. Lucy was restless at night and continued to take chloral until the very last stages of pregnancy. When her first child, a daughter, was born on 20 September 1875, after a stressful labour, she was named Olivia after the dead boy Oliver.

Curiously perhaps, for somebody who endured delicate health for so much of her life, Lucy negotiated pregnancy and childbirth with relatively few

116. Ford Madox Brown, *Gabriel Arthur Madox Rossetti as a child*, 1879. Black and red chalks, 521 × 476 mm. Private collection.

problems and managed to breastfeed four of her five children. She recovered well from all her confinements after Olivia but, as was standard middle-class practice of the times, she stayed in bed for weeks afterwards. Then, just over a month after Olivia's birth, Lucy received another shock. Her flirtatious first cousin, near contemporary and close friend, Lizzie Cooper (née Bromley) died suddenly in her early thirties. That this giddy, girly voice could be silenced in her prime, unexpectedly and finally, was a painful jolt to Lucy, nursing her baby. But absorption in Olivia helped to insulate her from Lizzie's too casual departure, which, on 12 November 1875, cruelly coincided with the first anniversary of Nolly's funeral.

For most of her childbearing years from 1875 to 1881, Lucy was not rampantly consumptive. She took an educated but not obsessive interest in health matters. When smallpox was prevalent in 1877, Lucy arranged for William and the family to be revaccinated.[17] He recalled that he had been vaccinated first in infancy and again in 1860. But Lucy's forethought may well have ensured that William did not contract smallpox twenty years later when the disease broke out on board the steamship *Nineveh* which was taking him to Australia. With the birth of her second child, a son, on 28 February 1877, Lucy was in labour for only about four hours and made a rapid recovery. The baby (fig. 116) was named Gabriel Arthur, after Gabriele Rossetti the grandfather he never knew, on whose birthday he was born, but he was always called Arthur, after Lucy's long-dead little half-brother (see fig. 115).

During summer 1877, Arthur was continuously ill for several months. In spite of this Lucy entertained indefatigably at home. This expenditure of energy left her more exhausted than she would care to admit and in January 1878 William arranged for Lucy, two-year-old Olive and a nurse to go to

Eastbourne for a week's recuperation. He confided to his diary that Lucy's health was 'certainly not strong of late, with persistent thinness & want of appetite'.[18] The doctor's bill for medical attendance during 1877 was a substantial £47 5s 0d. Arthur was the one child whom Lucy did not continue to breastfeed. Instead, for some unspecified reason, on 25 May 1877, when Arthur was three months old, she and William engaged a wet-nurse, Mrs Bowen. In spite of her occasional emotional outbursts (understandable, as she had to leave her own infant son who subsequently died), Arthur eventually flourished in her affectionate care. William worried about the effect of weaning when Mrs Bowen's reign ended, exactly one day after Arthur's first birthday.

Throughout 1878 William's diary refers to Lucy's digestive derangements, bad colds and gumboils. She turned the tables on him by secretly discussing his digestive functions with Dr Gill who called on William at the office, against his express wishes. However, William listened politely to Gill's curious advice to follow a regulated diet avoiding eggs, too much fruit or green vegetables, but to take large amounts of rice and cocoa (rather than tea or coffee). During 1879, Lucy's pregnancy, confinement and recovery went smoothly again, resulting in the birth of her third child Helen, on 10 November. On 6 May 1880 William noted the healthy weights of his family: 'Self 11 st. 5, Lucy, 9-10, Olive (aged four and a half) 3-6'.[19] Lucy, at nearly thirty-seven, was clearly not exhibiting the wasting symptoms of advanced consumption.

In September 1880 Lucy conceived her last pregnancy, the twins Mary and Michael. As twins very often are, and as William observed, they were '8 months children'. Just before their birth Lucy suffered 'neuralgic toothache' for which she consulted Jameson, a dentist, and Gill, her own doctor-accoucheur (fig. 117). Their housemaid had died recently in the Fever Hospital and Lucy arranged immediate 'house-disinfection', an entirely sensible course of action. When the twins were born on 22 April 1881, they were both small but viable, first Mary at 10:28 p.m. and then Michael at 10:40 p.m. As usual, Lucy stayed in bed immediately after the birth but within a fortnight she was out of bed for part of each day, although she stayed in her bedroom and did not come downstairs for some weeks. She breast-fed both twins for eleven months. Her 'incessant & laborious attentions to these small incubuses have been most touching', William noted, adding with an ominous hint, 'they don't seem to have lowered her health or strength as yet'. When they were finally weaned on 24 March 1882, he reported 'Lucy in no little pain locally.'[20]

Dr Gill praised Lucy's devotion to the twins and perhaps in a reciprocal gesture for his care, she gave him one of her paintings, *Broadstairs* (see fig. 94), first begun in 1876, 'with herself and her then two children in the foreground and

117. Dr Gill. Cathy Hueffer's photograph album, STH/BH/2/3-6. The Stow Hill Collection, HLRO, and the Hon. Oliver Soskice.

Bleak House prominent in the background'. Dr Gill found Lucy, though 'a lady imbued with artistic charm', always poised for combat. 'One day Mr and Mrs Rossetti called on me, and he in his calm art-critical way began criticizing this picture and said to me "this is one of Cathy's" (Mrs Rossetti's sister). Mrs Rossetti was very angry and as we were only three in the dining room I took up the poker going to the fireplace, and handed it to her saying, "Here you are m'am and I will look out of the window". Mrs Rossetti went home, told the story to her children, and they dubbed that picture "the Poker Picture", and so I hope it will always be called'.[21]

With the domestic help available in her Victorian middle-class household, Lucy in her late thirties threw herself into committed motherhood, coping with the demands of five children under the age of six. But when Madox Brown left London to paint his great series of murals in Manchester Town Hall at the end of the 1870s, her health began to deteriorate. After the traumatic death of her brother-in-law Dante Gabriel Rossetti in 1882, she suffered a persistently infected finger for weeks but managed to take five-mile walks on holiday at Southend. She requested a folding sketching easel from Gabriel's studio effects, signifying not only her boundless admiration for his art but also her own intention to keep practising and please her father.[22] As the 1880s advanced, almost daily letters between Lucy and her father underlined their marked mutual interdependence. On 5 November 1882 she joined Madox Brown and Emma in Manchester for the eighth anniversary of Nolly's death.

The beginning of 1883 was not auspicious. The infant Michael, aged nineteen months, was continually feverish. Michael's grandmother, Frances Rossetti, dictated a terse diary entry to Christina on 24 January 1883:

> Olive and Arthur brought a note from Lucy saying that dear little Michael was dying. Christina went round between 10 and 11, found all in grief, and sat with poor William and Lucy till the baby died just before 1 o'clock. He was suffering from pressure on the brain, which mercifully (we are told) was unaccompanied by consciousness, although his eyes continued open. Mr Gill, who attended him assiduously, brought Dr Roberts to see him in consultation last Thursday, and yesterday William called in Sir William Jenner. Christina returned to Endsleigh Gardens in the afternoon, carrying a heath in bloom to place in the room.[23]

Michael's cause of death was certified as meningitis. He suffered attacks of convulsions and coma, classic symptoms of tubercular meningitis. Lucy internalized her grief but could not disguise that her feelings were 'on the stretch'.[24] She turned to art for therapy and resolution, drawing a pastel portrait of little Michael the day after he died, surrounded by snowdrops.[25] Frances Rossetti noted the effect of this picture on Michael's baby twin Mary, and by transference, on all the adults affected by the child's death:

> Christina called on Lucy, whom she found at home with all her children. Lucy brought in her beautiful drawing of Michael lying dead, to show Christina – at sight of which little Mary became quite excited, scuttling along towards the portrait. It seemed to attract her like a magnet, affectionately and pleasurably. Holding her mother's hand, she walked some distance round the room, accompanying the portrait held high in Lucy's other hand. Then, seated opposite it, she made kisses towards it; once broke into a laugh and uttered inarticulate baby-chatter, pointing and stretching out her little hand in her vain endeavour to touch the drawing.[26]

It is an intense image of Lucy's maternity in action, confronting her child and herself with the reality of their loss but assuaging it with the consolation of art.

Lucy bore her grief with dignity, managed to submerge it to some extent, and was healingly caught up in the quotidian care of her remaining four active young children who were often ill or involved in accidents. But her daughter Helen believed her mother never recovered from Michael's illness and death. Lucy's coughing and wheezing became more frequent and more severe. She fought constant fatigue by frantic involvement with her children. 'I am quite sure people never know the value of strength till they lose it', she told William in August 1884 and by September she warned him that she was going grey.[27] Winter 1885 saw a definite reactivation of her tubercular illness with a near-fatal attack of 'bronchial pneumonia' in February and a relapse in March. Much later, in his autobiography, William called it a 'formidable malady...the evil was never extirpated, nor even thoroughly subdued; it proceeded from stage to stage, and ended in phthisis'.[28]

Still frail, she went to recuperate in Bournemouth in April 1885 but by the end of June, although she and William professed 'much confidence' in Mr Gill, they consulted a second doctor, Wilson Fox. By autumn 1885 William tentatively assessed that Lucy was improving, although she would have to observe 'very strict precautions'. The seasons now dictated Lucy's annual routine. In summer she alternated between her inner London home and English seaside resorts. As chill winds and yellow fogs whirled into Endsleigh Gardens, she and William had to plot her escape.

Feeling abjectly weak she fled London, with the children, for Ventnor, a resort that specialized in clinics and hotels for chest patients on the south coast of the Isle of Wight, from 23 December 1885 until 19 May 1886. Arthur Hill Hassall, a doctor who had suffered from 'fibroid phthisis' of the right lung, finding himself in unexpected remission, determined to do something for other chronic cases. The physician who had attended him in his illness, Sir George Burrows, met Hassall at a medical conference and exclaimed, 'Why, Hassall, what business have you here? You know you ought to have been buried long ago; why were you not?'[29]

From observing his own case, Hassall concluded that tubercular patients did better away from the damp and polluted atmosphere of London, particularly during sunless winter days. His own experiences convinced him that overcrowding in large hospital wards only exacerbated the sufferings of bronchial patients. So he decided to set up the National Hospital for Consumption in Ventnor, Isle of Wight on what he called the 'Separate System' – ensuring that patients were physically separated as far as possible. In effect it was an early sanatorium with patients occupying separate bedrooms in a series of small, warm and well-ventilated houses all facing south. He chose Ventnor because of its unique locality and temperate sheltering climate. Doctors such as Hassall helped establish the growing reputation of the Isle of Wight for medical good practice, which enticed increasing numbers of consumptives, like Lucy, to the island.

William visited intermittently. The children had chickenpox, which increased the strain on Lucy. William privately worried that she was 'distressingly weak' and her bronchial symptoms were 'more troublesome than usual'. Mr Harvey, a medical man on the island, tried to feed her up – standard advice given to consumptives. Her first haemoptysis occurred in Ventnor, coughing up a little blood on 10 March 1886, and three days later she expelled 'a lump of blood' from her mouth, but doctors assured her that it came from the throat, not the lungs. (Lucy had been concerned ten years before when her

118. San Remo railway station in the
nineteenth century, from *Sanremo
com'era* (Sanremo: Famia Sanremasca,
1974).

half-sister Cathy had become progressively thinner and coughed up blood
twice towards the end of 1876. In spite of these early warning symptoms,
Cathy, born in 1850, did not die until 1927.) During March 1886, Lucy was
still bronchial.

On her return to London, it was obvious Lucy's health was still declining
although she threw herself into educational projects for the children, setting
Olive and Arthur to write a 'Handbook for Children to the National Gallery'.
William took a realistic view, 'I am afraid this project will come to little'.[30] By
November 1886, doctors gave Lucy no choice but to leave England to winter
in the south, taking the two elder children, Olive and Arthur. Helen was left
in the care of Aunt Cathy and Mary was dispatched to her grandparents,
Emma and Madox Brown in Manchester.

The rail link to the Riviera had been established for nearly two decades.
Although she booked tickets via Turin, because of local flooding in Italy, Lucy
had to change her route and go via Calais, Marseilles and Nice, 'not nearly so
convenient & much dearer', as she told her father and Mary, her youngest
child, 'Ma petite Maisie bien aimée'.[31] She entered Italy at Ventimiglia, having
mislaid her luggage several times en route, before eventually arriving on 18
November at San Remo's railway station parallel to the sea on the Riviera dei
Fiori (fig. 118).

Exhausted, she collapsed into one of the resort's magnificent hotels, the Royal, with its 'English sanitary apparatus', and temporarily took front rooms facing south at 35 francs per day.[32]

Lovely though San Remo was, with its more than forty species of palm trees, sheltered by mountains and the inky blue Mediterranean, she longed to be with William. But she took solace in an Italian autumn like 'the *most* beautiful English summer', and the old town's pyramidal, medieval world of narrow, shadowed streets bridged by stone arches. Like its climate that was thought to be both tonic and sedative, San Remo, with its flowery balconies, secretive piazzas and ancient churches, offered both visual stimulus and physical repose. Indeed, it might have been a green paradise with its terraced vineyards, citrus, almond, fig, olive, palm and chestnut trees, Lucy thought, if only the whole family could have been together. Within a week, she had to cut costs and move to the more modest Hôtel-Pension Anglo-Américaine, just two minutes from the railway station.

Lucy was a divided person in San Remo, basking in golden days but truculent about being excommunicated from the 'real' world. 'What is all this about Ireland, I suppose it is the upshot of not accepting Gladstone's bill. I am quite out of the world for I see no paper except a five days old Standard.'[33] In moments of grace, when the illness retreated, she recorded small triumphs, 'I scarcely ever cough, have had next to no wheezing' and enjoyed conversations with her *femme de chambre*, a rough looking Swiss woman with a taste for Wagner and Shakespeare.[34] On good days she painted, went on walks with the children, boxed up roses in December to send home for Christmas, planned trips to a chocolate mill, socialized with other guests and went on manic mosquito hunts at dusk. On bad days she stayed in bed with influenza or a swollen hand from mosquito bites, or skirmished over fees with Signor Gandolfo who ran San Remo's largest subscription library.

Characteristic of tubercular condition, she swerved between bipolar bouts of hectic activity and languorous debility. On Christmas Day she wanted to take the children 'à l'église catholique aujourd'hui mais ne puis pas sortir'.[35] Everyone spoke French in San Remo - Lucy worried that William would not think she had improved her Italian.

When William joined her in late January 1887, San Remo seemed a perfect haven but pierced always with a sense of regret, the same 'thrilling, delicious kind of regret' that Nathaniel Hawthorne associated with malaria in Rome, where 'fever walks arm in arm with you, and death awaits you at the end of the dim vista. Thus the scene is like Eden in its loveliness'.[36] San Remo's reputation as an international retreat for northern European invalids, had been growing ever since 1868 when modern villas, pensions and first class hotels set in semi-tropical gardens were built to satisfy the new boom in medical tourism. Initially, Lucy had hankered for the more fashionable French resort of Cannes but William, worried about his limited budget, had persuaded her to try San Remo (which a century later Duncan Fallowell in a Ford Capri found 'lusher, less garish, sexier than Cannes').[37] Although artist Lizzie Siddal and author Mathilde Blind, as well as the glamorous consumptive painter and diarist, Marie Bashkirtseff, had chosen Nice, other people dismissed it as vulgar, 'a great, ugly, modern town, with Parisian shops and a glaring Esplanade along the sea'.[38] By contrast, San Remo's grandeur and elegance made it more like a park with palaces than a conventional seaside resort.[39] It catered for foreigners, Russians, Germans but especially the British, supplying every amenity of home life including three English churches, as well as doctors, dentists, pharmacists, opticians, photographers, omnibuses and carriages servicing an international community.

Many books were published on the health resorts of the French and Italian Rivieras during these years, discussing their climate, medical resources and best routes from northern Europe. Edward Isaac Sparks estimated the cost of living at San Remo was much the same as Mentone and Cannes but considered San Remo enjoyed the most equable climate of the three. The average death rate in San Remo, he reported, was one in fifty, or twenty per thousand, and he claimed that phthisis was 'rare among the inhabitants...it never assumes the acute form, and usually runs a very protracted course'.[40] Doctors compared death-rates from various diseases in London and San Remo in the last quarter of the nineteenth century and claimed that one in five deaths in London was due to pulmonary consumption but only one in sixty-five died of the disease in San Remo.[41] San Remo became so popular that Henry James complained all the *alberghi* were so packed with English and German consumptives that he couldn't get a meal at a decent time.[42] Along the Riviera between Hyères and San Remo there were thirty-nine British doctors – in Rome there were only seven.[43] San Remo reflected its love affair with the British by naming its most impressive hotels, des Iles Britanniques, des Anglais, de la Grande Bretagne, de Londres, the Grand, Royal, Victoria, Bristol, London and the West End. The Reverend Hugh Macmillan enthused about a garden-riviera of eucalyptus, oleander and mimosa that nevertheless had become almost British with great masses of 'rosy, golden, and purple-flowered mesembryanthemums, glowing in the brilliant sunshine, which stream over the garden walls and over the wayside banks almost everywhere' (fig. 119).[44]

Foreign invalids, bronchitic, asthmatic, rheumatic but mostly consumptive, closed their minds to San Remo's Leper Hospital and the fearful disease it housed. They came to San Remo in search of winter warmth, sunlight and pure air – and they found it. They took gentle excursions in the olive groves near the town, by foot or on donkey and, swaddled in travelling rugs, enjoyed breathtaking drives or rail journeys along the Corniche road to Bordighera with its waving palm-trees, or further west to Ventimiglia, Mentone and

119. Edward Lear, *San Remo*, 5 October 1870. Pencil, 362 × 533 mm. Private collection.

Monaco. Patients were encouraged to walk, to take up geology, botany and entomology, or to go rowing, sailing or even seawater bathing. San Remo supported a sub-culture of the ill with its two theatres for opera and concerts, a town band, libraries, a tennis club, parties, picnics and a Circolo Internazionale with rooms for *conversazione*, reading and billiards. Even such un-decadent diversions roused physicians to warn puritanically that the 'pursuit of health and pleasure cannot often be successfully combined'.[45] Doctors also cautioned patients not to undo the good San Remo had done them by leaving before the end of the winter season on 15 May.

San Remo's popularity with doctors and patients only increased after the earthquake of 1887 when the town embarked on a major rebuilding programme. Hygiene was now its priority. A new aqueduct made it one of the first resorts whose hotels had indoor water closets and running water. San Remo was proud of its pure, limpid water piped from clear springs beyond Taggia and numerous drinking fountains all over town. Sealed carts collected rubbish twice a day and streets were hosed down daily. Hotels advertised porcelain spittoons 'in all the rooms, saloons, landings and closets to remove the spittle easily'. On penalty of losing their licences, hotels and lodging houses had to disinfect their premises with super-heated steam apparatus after every tubercular death, lessening the risk of infection.[46] Precautions like these appealed to Lucy when she returned to the town in 1894.

However, San Remo's popularity was not only due to its climatic and curative qualities. It also held the lure of romance ever since first publication in 1855 of Giovanni Ruffini's wildly popular but now nearly forgotten novel, *Dr Antonio*. Written in English, the novel went into dozens of subsequent editions all over Europe and in America. The story featured lovely Lucy Davenne, a young English aristocrat thrown from her carriage while travelling along the Italian Riviera. A broken leg confined her to her sick bed where she was tended by the dashing eponymous doctor.

Ruffini came from Taggia near San Remo and Italian critics likened him to Dickens. In fact, his work does not fit neatly into either Italian or English culture. However, he made reference to stereotypes of British and Italian nationality still prevalent today. His 'Lucy' translated the bays and coves from Bordighera to San Remo into a personal Edenic vision. 'No fancy, not even a poet's, could conjure up, in wildest day-dream, this wondrous beauty', she told her benevolent doctor-mentor.[47] Ruffini painted the natural scene:

> the immensity of sea, smooth as glass, and rich with all the hues of a dove's neck, the bright green, the dark purple, the soft ultramarine...there glancing in the sun like diamonds, here rippling into a lacelike net of snowy foam...On the right, to the westward, the silvery track of the road undulating amid thinly scattered houses, or clusters of orange and palm trees...every shade of green that can gladden the eye, from the pale grey olive to the dark foliaged cypress.[48]

Reading pellucid descriptions like this in dank, smoggy London encouraged many a Lucy to book tickets for the south at once. Although Lucy Davenne's complaint was an injured limb, subtle suggestions in the text, 'shattered health', 'emaciated appearance' and 'frequent fits of coughing', point to her underlying consumptive condition, which would have been undoubtedly, if subliminally, registered by fellow sufferers.

Dr Antonio mentions a previous earthquake in 1844. Early in the morning of 23 February 1887 an alarming earthquake shook San Remo and the whole of the Riviera. The Hôtel-Pension Anglo-Américaine where Lucy and William were in bed together was demolished. The family and all the hotel guests spent the next night in tents in the garden, a great lark for the children but 'a trying ordeal for my wife in her risky state of health'.[49] Although William encouraged her to stay on in San Remo, which had seemed to suit her so well, Lucy, in common with many other health exiles, had lost her nerve about the place. William returned to his London office and Lucy began a slow progress home via Dijon and Paris, through snow and ice, sketching the frozen landscape as she went. She continued the children's education en route, taking them to church in Dijon as part of their comparative studies of religions. In spite of the 'orthodox' sentiments expressed in the sermon, it was a service that 'could come home to any one of my way of thinking showing how the soul becomes purified by suffering & can attain to something higher'.[50] It was a consolation she could accept more easily when she was in remission. From the perspective of distance she looked back at San Remo with affection. 'I had got used to dear San Remo and feeling it did me so much good'.[51]

Reaching London in late April, she left almost immediately for Bournemouth where she planned her biography of Mary Shelley. Once home she threw herself into arranging a Shelleian musical soirée with her friend Mary Carmichael. Sir Hubert Parry conducted the première of his own *Scenes from Prometheus Unbound* 'greatly to the gratification of the audience', considered William, who found it a fine composition.[52] But rising young author Violet Paget found it 'fearful'. 'The room was crammed with chairs so that you couldn't stir, and for an hour & a half a string of songs & choruses to words of Shelley's was performed without one half minute's interruption – about 20 I should think, & one more boring than the other. And the extraordinary frowsty ghosts of the great aesthetic movement that constituted the audience! You *shd* have seen!'[53] On this very warm London evening, Wednesday, 6 July 1887, there were well over 110 guests who included Jacques Darmesteter specially over from Paris, Richard Garnett from the British Museum, the Holman Hunts, as well as poets Mary Robinson and Augusta Webster. Whenever she was well, and even when she was not, Lucy loved to orchestrate social life. The fact that illness made her a social outcast by sending her abroad was particularly grating for Lucy. She sent out copious invitations and specially relished intellectual company. William was not a recluse, but he shrank from organized entertaining and 'at homes' on the scale Lucy enjoyed. Perhaps he recognized that her hectic need for company was a direct outcome of the many fallow months of the year when this was impossible for her.

On 14 July 1887, William, Lucy, the four children and a small crowd of about fifty or sixty others gathered to watch Holman Hunt unveil Madox Brown's fountain-bust memorial to Dante Gabriel Rossetti opposite his house at 16 Cheyne Walk by the Thames. Lucy was the chief subscriber to the fund to raise the statue,[54] driven by a deep need to celebrate the old intimate friendship between Gabriel and Madox Brown – and to cement it even after death. It was another way (apart from marriage) to underline the Brown–Rossetti creative connection. For Lucy, who was no longer artistically productive, it was an association with genius that mattered painfully to her. Her father told Lucy he had made 'a kind of heroic, or poetic likeness; as [Gabriel] looked when thinking; but I am not sure that it looks quite as amiable as I could wish it'.[55] Madox Brown and Emma travelled down from Manchester to stay with Lucy and William that summer, the last before they left Manchester and moved to 1 St Edmund's Terrace, Regent's Park. Lucy's symptoms now included weight loss, chronic fatigue, fevers and night sweats as well as the habitual wracking cough. She took Himrod, a form of chloroform to induce sleep. William worried this would prove noxious in the long-term. Nor did the soporific or sedative effect seem particularly apparent in Lucy's case.[56]

As 1887 progressed, Lucy battled on with her research for the Mary Shelley biography. The interest of the work and her empathy with Mary as a romantic icon energized her, so that after the débâcle on the Riviera earlier in the year, she risked staying in London over the next winter. But she paid the price with another attack of bronchitis in March 1888. From Nice, where spring came early, Mathilde Blind wrote to sympathize with Lucy on 26 March.[57] Lucy's health deteriorated further when she suffered a tormenting 'carbuncle' (a classic tubercular symptom) at the nape of her neck 'quite neglected by the doctor'.[58] Her agony was exacerbated when at the same time she had to nurse adolescent Olive through severe pneumonia. William always remembered how their friend the poet, Mary Robinson, impulsively left London in the throes of her wedding preparations and 'went down for some weeks to Worthing, to give companionship and solace to my wife'.[59] Mary soothed Lucy's unnerved spirit but she couldn't change the English climate.

Pilgrimage to Pau

'Take all my loves, my love, yea take them all'…often passes thro' my head
William Rossetti to Lucy Rossetti, Somerset House 9 Nov. /88 – 12 $\frac{1}{4}$ [60]

Worthing had been tried and failed. Lucy dared not risk another English winter. In mid-autumn, she packed up her books, her watercolours, the four children and their governess Mademoiselle Heymann. Early on Thursday, 8 November 1888, a 'day of hard bleak cold', the little party set out for Pau, a fashionable health resort in the Basses Pyrénées in south-west France.[61] In his office at Somerset House, William worried perpetually about 'Dearest Dear Lu' and the 'poor kiddies'. That evening William took a Turkish bath to ease a strained right arm, but the real strain lay in the mind, which only a telegram from Bordeaux could relieve. '*Touse bien*' was hardly impeccable French, he admonished Lucy, but it served the purpose. They had arrived at Pau's dramatically situated railway station on the evening of 9 November where a letter from Lucy's girlhood friend, Fanny Seddon, asked her to come straight round to the anglophone Hôtel de Londres.

The site of the hotel can be located today at 4, avenue Gaston Phoebus, known as Chemin de Billère until 1897.[62] The substantial, bourgeois Hôtel de Londres, run by Mrs Hall, was a regular five-storey red brick mansion, set off by white filigree *balcons*, located in that area of Pau specially favoured by

120. Victor Galos, *Gélos et la chaîne des Pyrénées c.* 1860. Oil on canvas, 112 × 150 cm. Musée des Beaux-Arts, Pau.

British invalids. Where the British led, in the late nineteenth century, the Americans followed. They all went in search of a cure, real or imagined, in the beneficent effects of Pau's glorious climate, attested in 1837 by a Scot, Dr Alexander Taylor. His book detailing his own recovery at Pau went into several editions, was praised in the *Lancet* and translated into French.[63] As a result, Pau's winter invalid population soared from the 1840s onwards. The English built their own mansions with all the accoutrements of an English lifestyle, gardens, greenhouses, outbuildings and stables. Many of these survive, and a strange sense of Britishness persists to this day in the triangular area bounded by the rue Montpensier, the passage de Ségure (now rue Bourbaki) and the rue des Cultivateurs (now rue Carnot). The year before Lucy arrived, Pau's *Journal des Etrangers* recorded the number of winter visitors as 1,676 French, 1,179 British and 118 Americans. There were also ailing Russians, Germans and other northern Europeans.[64]

As soon as she arrived in Pau (fig. 120), Lucy felt safe and comfortable, 'everything is perfection & kindness. This hotel is most beautifully situated, with fields & hills leading up to the snow & cloud capped range of the Pyrenees, the air is so light & balmy in spite of some rain today that I can feel I have lungs by their power of breathing quite different to what they usually do – & I don't think I have coughed for 36 hours'.[65] Pau was remarkable for its 'stillness of atmosphere...glorified by the Pyrennean panorama'.[66] It was a seductive and uplifting place for an invalid. It had grandeur, a newly restored fourteenth-century château, imposing hotels and chic boutiques as well as a thriving ex-pat community. Today not even the Irish pub, Russian tearooms, Australian bar, insistent music and scooter noise along the boulevard des Pyrénées, nor Miss Eliet's Lingerie van roaring to a halt, can extinguish the stately grace of Pau. The majesty of the north face of the mountain range, with its ever-shifting play of cloud and sunlight, constantly lures the contemplative gaze. Lamartine, the Romantic poet, found Pau 'la plus belle vue de terre comme Naples est la plus belle vue de mer'.

Pau's rarefied atmospheric conditions and dry, fine air exalted Lucy's hopes, in the early days at least. But the strain of the journey took its toll. Two days after arrival, she did not 'quite understand' herself but spent the day in bed.[67] William wondered 'whether nitric acid is a repulsive taste' in his first chasing letter, which recommended this alarming remedy for 'bronchial or pulmonary apparatus'. It was almost as if the body and the illness was a detached entity from Lucy herself. Within a few days William dared to hope, as he told Frederic George Stephens, that Lucy was 'benefiting already' in the crystalline mountain air of Pau.[68] How far did he believe that her condition was anything other than progressively degenerative? If he told himself, his friends and his relations that Lucy was improving, could he make her improve by a sheer effort of will? As ever, the constant stream of letters between wife and husband censored precise medical terms for Lucy's illness – phthisis, consumption or tuberculosis.

Their almost daily letters, supplemented by postcards and telegrams all arrived promptly, in about forty-eight hours or less, far more efficiently than today's international postal service. William's letters were an extension and expansion of his diary. Thinking aloud, he discussed his plans for joining Lucy in Pau, the exact route he would take, the number of days leave he could get from the office, the proposed new taxes on 'Wheel and Van' or 'Horses and Horse-dealers' and his increased workload if they were to be implemented. He told her about bills he would pay on her behalf, 10s 3d to Lewis the bookseller and 12s 6d to Mansell for picture mounting. He joked about the domestic ineptitude of Fofus in the absence of Lucy, losing and finding his pen of 'fofitude' and the daily recalcitrance of the servants, Kate, Agnes and Harriet who conspired to drive him mad. He lamented, 'I am tied to a post or sunk in a hole, & have no means of helping myself, because no time ever, & no daytime at home. Pazienza...'.[69] He told Lucy about his literary work, commissions from Chambers Encyclopaedia, Shelley notes he was compiling to feed into her biography, sometimes his own health (rheumatism and boils) and always made very English observations about the weather.

He reproved her for not pre-paying her postage. If she saved 2½d in Pau, he had to pay double when a letter arrived in London. His letters covertly allude to her assertive character. 'I infer that you gave them as good as you got, Luie', he teased, when she protested about differing standards of service between first and second-class French railway carriages. He knew how to appeal to the snob in her. Dr Stewart 'has just married a sister of the Duke of Norfolk. I presume...that Pau comes into his wedding-trip. He might be worth your bearing in mind – either medically or socially'.[70]

When William spent a weekend in Oxford to attend the Dante Society at Dr Edward Moore's invitation, he deplored Oxford's High Toryism but enjoyed the companionship of scholars. He shared with Lucy a mischievous thought at the prospect of organized religion. 'It will I fear be a practical necessity for me to accompany the family to church: a severe trial for Fofus...Dim visions of saying that my father was a Roman Catholic, & leaving it to be inferred that I also was brought up as one, flit thro' my head...'[71] In the event he got away with simply a university sermon at St Mary's, a convenient compromise without any of the usual accompanying church service. On Sunday, 18 November at 6 p.m., he dined in Queen's College where he talked with mutual animation to the Reverend Archibald Henry Sayce, the great Assyrian scholar. William enjoyed his Oxford weekend, the warm welcome from the Moores, the talk, the shared passion for Dante, the walk out to Iffley's 'fine old yew-shadowed Norman church', and even the dreaminess of travelling back to London in a darkened train that night. Always he wrote his catalogues to Lucy 'with more love than all these dull & plodding details might seem to indicate'.[72]

Meanwhile, at the Hôtel de Londres, Lucy met and made friends with Mrs and Miss Bené who were congenial and supportive. Miss Bené coached Olive in Spanish and made plans with the Rossettis to visit Spain just over the border. When Lucy intruded on hotel space by conducting the children's lessons in the residents' lounge, William gently suggested it might be more considerate if she and Fräulein set up school in an upstairs bedroom. Lucy, who loved company, was also oddly insensitive to it, whereas William, who found socializing a distinct effort, showed far more tact in inter-personal relations. 'Your Hotel seems at present to be a Paradise of Kids: I hope they won't turn it into a Pandemonium of Kids', joked William.[73] Lucy brushed aside the hint.

In negotiation with Robert Micks, his immediate superior at Somerset House, William constantly adjusted the date of his trip to Pau but finally left London by the 8.20 morning train to Dover on Saturday, 1 December 1888, anticipating a family Christmas before returning to the office by 28 December.

He had longed to be with Lucy but his happiness was wordless. As soon as they were reunited he suspended his diary and for obvious reasons there were no letters between them. From the train window speeding home in late December he admired 'the picturesque rocky look of Orthez' with its medieval bridge overlooking the Pau Torrent. Overnight he froze in Paris, but as soon as he reached London he dashed off a brief letter that bore 'no relation to the warmth of love with which it is written'. Back in the tall, empty house at Endsleigh Gardens without Lucy, upsetting dreams disturbed his sleep 'as so often when absent from you', he told her.[74] The separation wrecked Lucy's sleep pattern, too, and William fretted to hear she was in low spirits. 1888 had been a dreary year for both of them, he reflected, and 'it finishes in character: as to myself, I have scarcely ever felt so sunk below my usual equable... level of temperament'.[75]

In Pau, Lucy battled with incessant domestic interruptions while trying to resume work on her Mary Shelley biography. She and William were both better and worse apart. Before the old year was out, she irritated him on two counts, by sending postcards to reduce her postage, and by writing them in German, to ensure her privacy from the eyes of servants. William berated Lu not only for her 'scrappy and scraggy' specimens of German correspondence but also for pretentiousness and opaque references. He preferred her to write in her native tongue. His tone grew scratchy and aggrieved. He complained he had only two clean pocket-handkerchiefs, as if Lucy could remedy this over a distance of 750 miles. William's genuinely considerate nature re-emerged when he sent her £40 and a subscription to the *Pall Mall Gazette*. In truth he was lonely, even though he spent New Year's Eve with Emma and Madox Brown, Cathy and Frank Hueffer and all the family who drank the first toast to Lucy's health. Frank told William he had some trouble in his left arm and shoulder but it was nothing serious. New Year 1889 opened in a swirling, shrouding London fog. William had to call a lantern-man to see him from the end of Endsleigh Gardens to his own front door. Gill the family doctor sent in his annual account, only eleven guineas, noted William with satisfaction.

Flitting to Biarritz

My dearest Foffy, I do wish you were here – I am sure you would like this place
    Lucy in Biarritz to William in London, 15 January 1889 [76]

Dearest Lu...to be with you day and night is my one substantial pleasure
    William in London to Lucy in Biarritz, 23 April 1889, 9.15 p.m.[77]

Lucy was suddenly restless in Pau – or perhaps her fellow hotel guests had made their feelings felt about precocious children. (Olive may have failed to delight them all when she put on a play at Christmas.) Lucy fancied the bracing air of Biarritz might alleviate her wheezing and on 9 January 1889 she and her entourage 'flitted' there, taking spacious, cheap lodgings (only 6 French francs per day, £1 15s 0d a week) at 1, rue des Falaises, 'on a beetling cliff' commanding 'a noble view of the mighty Atlantic'.[78] Lucy in her joy reported to William 'Wir sind in Himmel hier'– we are in heaven here – and for once he let the German pass unreproved.[79]

By favouring Biarritz over Pau, Lucy was just ahead of a tourist trend that would be confirmed within a few weeks when Queen Victoria made the same decision. Pau's heyday with the British went into decline and Biarritz took over as the elegant resort of choice for royalty, celebrity and fashionistas. Foreign visitors headed for Biarritz after Napoleon III built a rose pink palace there for Empress Eugénie, and the Prince of Wales favoured its rocky seashore in 1879. For a few days William rejoiced in Lucy's new happiness and playfully resumed his pet-identity as 'Fofus'. Biarritz and its storms temporarily invigorated Lucy where she drank in 'a sea-spectacle far surpassing anything' she had yet seen.[80]

Lucy's lodgings no longer stand today; the rue des Falaises has become the Perspective de la Côte des Basques, but the view over what is now one of Biarritz's main surfing beaches remains awe-inspiring. The cliffs curve away towards the point where sea meets sky. The Pyrenean mountains straddle the horizon, their craggy shapes oddly mimicking the cloud formations above. Peculiar atmospheric conditions at Biarritz produce dramatic electric storms and ever-changing colours, especially at sunset, from gold to Paine's grey. On squally days Lucy put aside her Mary Shelley manuscript, opened her box of watercolours and watched the play of sky, spume and breakers unfold before her. True to her father's Pre-Raphaelite principles, she made several studies from watery nature, all of which are now sadly unlocated.[81] Here on the edge of the land she slept to the elemental solace of the ceaseless, low rhythm of the surf that vibrated deep within her sore chest. In the mornings she and the children awoke either to opalescent sunlight and spray breaking on the black rocks or to the relentless grey-green storms of the Atlantic.

Lucy and the children enjoyed the freedom of life above the wide, sandy beach in rue des Falaises where the language of the house was Basque, not French. The landlady, Madame Serre, and the young servant-girl Catherine made the family welcome. It is possible that Lucy's *Portrait of a Parisian Landlady*, viewed in the north of England during the 1960s and praised by L.S. Lowry as 'an excellent picture',[82] may instead have been a portrait of the kind-hearted *basquaise*, Madame Serre of Biarritz.

Fofus and Dearest Luie were back in harmony. By mid-January she was newly creative, writing and painting, as well as organizing the children's daily routine. 'I know it must seem to you as to myself that I never do anything and yet it is extraordinary how the time is filled up…I give the children an English Grammer [*sic*] and History lesson and later…I have a reading for Arthur in French and German'.[83] However, her daily schedule exhausted her and the

Biarritz weather turned treacherous. 'My hands are so cold I can scarcely write tho I am beside the fire'.[84]

In London, William was ahead of schedule on his book *Dante Gabriel Rossetti as Designer and Writer*. Work absorbed him and so did left-wing politics. On 17 January 1889 he voted for principles he held dear, and therefore for Bartlett, the Socialist candidate, in elections for the newly constituted London County Council. He had no realistic hope that Bartlett would win, as he told Lucy: 'My Socialist candidate was at the bottom of the poll: just what I expected'.[85] He planned to travel to Biarritz in mid-February and looked forward to hearing Lucy read draft chapters of *Mrs Shelley*. On 16 January Lucy's weather report for Biarritz was 'wunderschön'. William did not fail to notice that, once again, her postcard was 'in German'. Reiterating his preference for English, he gave up, defeated, 'do as you please, Luie'.[86]

The same evening he capitulated on the German question, 19 January, William went round to 90 Brook Green to visit Frank Hueffer, and found him in bed, his face swathed in wrappings and 'beyond a doubt seriously ill'. Frank was suffering from 'a sharp attack of erysipelas' and infected throat brought on by riding on the outside of an omnibus at night, thought Cathy. Although two doctors were attending Frank, Cathy saw no reason for undue alarm, William assured Lucy, adding his own vigilant negative, 'I have concealed nothing from you'.[87] In fact, when William wrote this letter to Lucy on Sunday, 20 January, Frank had already been dead for more than twelve hours. Soon after William's visit, at about 8.30 p.m. he tried to get out of bed and lost consciousness twice, the second time fatally. Frank's eldest son, young Ford Madox Hueffer came round to tell Uncle William the next day.

William's immediate reaction was close to panic. His letter to Lucy on widely black-bordered paper unmistakably shows his handwriting registering physical shock. In a scrawl quite unlike his usual elegant, legible script, he wrote 'Dearest dear Lucy, A frightful calamity – Frank died last night – Saturday', outlined the details and added, 'I dread writing you in the present form or in any other to apprise you of such dreadful news'. Then he steadied himself, 'I have seen [Frank] – he looks calm & stately'.[88]

William was shaken by Frank's death for several reasons. The death certificate gave cause of death as 'Facial erysipelas, 13 days: cardiac syncope'.[89] He had seen Frank only an hour or so before his fatal attack and had failed to realize that death was imminent. It struck him that Frank had been a comparatively young man of only forty-three and William himself would reach the epochal age of sixty later that year. Cathy's courage moved him and he longed to do her service. He instinctively feared that Frank's financial affairs were a mess and indeed this was confirmed almost at once. Dreading the effect of bad news on brittle Lucy, he could not hope to gauge her reaction at such a distance. All these factors compounded his agitation.

William wore himself out writing letters 'on this dreadful subject'[90] and trying to arrange cremation for Frank who had been 'more or less an Agnostic'.[91] However, the cremation apparatus was not in working order and William had to fall back on Parsons, a conventional undertaker. William's stomach rebelled and he was physically ill for a day or two. His general gloom was intensified by 'wretched weather – damp steaming sweltering mists, and reeking mud underfoot'. His suspicions about Frank's provision for Cathy and the children were soon justified. Although Frank had a life policy with the National Provident, no drawer at Brook Green yielded the appropriate document. William concluded that Frank had recently borrowed money against the security of the life policy. Eventually, Frank's bank balance revealed no more than £56. William sent Cathy £30 to cover urgent expenses, tactfully explaining he had never paid her for having Helen to stay while Lucy was in San Remo two years before. Under pressure from her father, Cathy returned the cheque at once.

The immediate problem was the education of Cathy's two boys, Ford and Oliver, at an expensive boarding school in Folkestone. He tried to persuade one or some of Frank's well-to-do German brothers to take responsibility for the fatherless family. When Alexis Hüffer came over for Frank's funeral, William entertained him for dinner and found him affable but evasive on the subject. In all his efforts William was consistently baulked by an outraged Madox Brown who fired off a warning shot to Lucy.

> At the distance you are you cannot advise…William kindly sent off a cheque to Cathy for 30£. But she is not destitute & moreover has me to look to, & of course could not accept the kind gift. Then William said something to Alex Hueffer, who was at the funeral, about the H. family doing something for Cathy. I wish he had not, but I don't think I shall speak to him about it, for it is done & can't be helped.[92]

Madox Brown saw the crisis as his to solve alone. In a state of shock, he failed to imagine the depth of William's fears. William calculated that Cathy's family needed a minimum annual income of £300,[93] which would make severe inroads into his already overstretched budget. He confided to his diary that if Brown were to die, 'I don't know what is to become of Cathy, her 3 children, and also Emma, except that I myself should provide for them – a condition of things very anomalous in itself, and highly irksome, or indeed next to impracticable, for me to meet'.[94]

The day of Frank's funeral, Thursday, 24 January 1889, dawned 'gloomy & squalid damp & chill', but William thought Lucy would be glad to know the grave was very near Nolly's, 'with shadowy trees when they shall come into leaf'.[95] 'There was of course no service', as Madox Brown confirmed to Lucy.[96] Braced by stoic philosophy, 'Men must endure/Their going hence, even as their coming hither', William still found it almost impossible to regard

Frank's abrupt exit with composure. Although unspoken at the time, the words of the Anglican funeral service reverberated through his mind.

'That affair about "my redeemer liveth" is I believe mere mistranslation, fantasy, & ignorance', inveighed William four days after Frank's funeral. 'A Protestant sees the words "My redeemer", & at once says – "Yes, Jesus Christ": a distressing depth of fatuity. The Hebrew original has I believe something to do with "the redeemer of blood" – a matter more related to a family *vendetta* (as I infer) than to Jesus Christ. And all about "in my flesh shall I see God", as if it meant "my soul, apart from or conjoined with my body, will be immortal", is, I believe, an equal & a crass delusion'. Frank's death had not altered William's scepticism on the comforting doctrine of an afterlife. At best it was still an open question. 'Whether the power of human will can prolong into eternity a soul, or spiritual & mental faculty, which, without any or without an adequate power of will, would cease along with the death of the body – this is a vast problem which I find myself totally incompetent to grapple with', he confessed to 'ever dearest Lu'.[97]

Although she admitted to some bouts of crying, Lucy's unexpectedly measured reaction to Frank's death stabilized William, at least partially:

> Frank was one of those one owed so much to, his love of art and devotion to the ideal were so great – but the mortal life has to be lived too, tho' I cannot think that it wholly contains the other. Curiously I have been playing over the duets of Brahms again lately which he first brought us nearly 20 years ago and must have been doing so on Saturday about the hour of his death – and I have been thinking and talking much of him lately not that I ever realized that he was in the slightest danger.[98]

Other people did not have such benign memories of Frank – Vernon Lee found him 'an insolent insupportable huge Oberkellner'[99] and Helen Rossetti Angeli remembered 'his unjustness & harshness with his sons'.[100]

With 'practical fortitude & clear sense' Lucy immediately offered to have young Fordie down to Biarritz to stay with his Rossetti cousins.[101] A schoolboy ticket would cost only about £2 10s 0d and she had found an excellent local tutor who coached for public exams. In the event, Ford did not go, partly because Cathy needed him and partly because he recalled with horror the 'excellent lessons' and 'the full educational fury' of Aunt Lucy, who was determined to turn every young person into a genius.[102] Throughout the following weeks, Lucy repeatedly offered to contribute to Cathy's expenses but Madox Brown resisted her offers as doggedly as he had resisted William's.

Oppressed by Cathy's uncertain future, his daily workload at the office, as well as trying every evening and weekend to finish his book on Gabriel, William had little heart to consider travel: 'I must I think finally relinquish the idea of treating myself to a visit to Biarritz', he wrote, feeling 'particularly drear and helpless', on the day before Frank's funeral.[103] Endurance was the only principle to live by and he was gloomily glad Lucy was reading the children 'one of the great books of the world', the Book of Job. As part of their freethinking educational policy, both William and Lucy considered their children needed a thorough, analytical knowledge of the Bible. But they did not teach any specific religious doctrine 'other than that of duty & goodness'.[104]

William's views on religion were usually tolerant. He never sought to proselytize his own agnosticism, considering that 'a Roman-Catholic may be just as good a man as an "Agnostic"'. As regards his own children he 'would prefer every one of them to be like myself, a free-thinker: but, if some or all of them examine for themselves what Christianity consists of, and finally prefer it to free-thinking, that must be their affair, not mine'.[105]

At a distance he was still in tune with Lucy intellectually and emotionally. When she had bad nights, he did too. He suggested that in his absence she might take Olive or one of the younger girls to sleep in her bed – he would not have given this advice if he had realized her condition was infectious. Although Robert Koch had identified the tubercle bacillus in 1882, it was still unclear, or inadmissible, to the general public exactly how it was transmitted – by droplets spread from an infected person.

As wife and mother, Lucy channelled her creativity into design and dressmaking, conjuring clothes from next to nothing. Now she conjured mourning dress for Frank, and William marvelled, 'you seem to have developed the powers of those beauteous damsels in fairy-tales who take one linen-thread, & spin out therewith a hundred gorgeous court-dresses'.[106] He was busy trying to arrange a Boy Clerkship in the Civil Service for Fordie, as well as finishing his book, visiting Madox Brown to discuss Cathy's affairs, packing up volumes of Gibbon for Olive and searching London for a special tea to send out to Lucy.

By mid-February 1889 William's mood lifted. Working on his book, *Dante Gabriel Rossetti as Designer and Writer*, both spurred and sustained him.[107] He found satisfaction adding its mechanical apparatus, such as tabular lists of Gabriel's art works and writing a preface. In spite of Lucy's report of a thirty-hour hurricane in Biarritz (the guidebook had warned her that the climate was far less reliable than in Pau) his thoughts turned south. Over at Christina's home in Torrington Square, old aunt Eliza Polidori flirted with death but William calmly faced what seemed inevitable. In fact, she did not die until 1893. William even coped with his unreliable servants with fresh equanimity, forgave them for failing to wake him when he was meant to be at the office and presented Agnes with a sovereign when she left. He sent Lucy reports of a new, expensive American medicine (11 shillings a bottle) as he constantly dreaded a recurrence of her bronchial attacks. Too often he heard that she had spent days in bed.

Even though his hopes for any monetary support for Cathy from the Hüffer brothers dwindled, and repeated visits to the dentist's torture-chamber reflected his run down physique, William's spirits rose at the thought of seeing Lucy in Biarritz. His letters now expanded to discuss French politics, the Parnell case and Spanish drama as well as Eliman's embrocation, Cathy's finances and Arthur's birthday. 'Pray keep in good health for my arrival', he begged Lucy on 6 March. He had only a few details to finalize for his book on Gabriel. 'Old-fashioned enough to cling to the dedication-system',[108] he had first thought of honouring Gabriel's closest friends, Madox Brown and Watts-Dunton, but changed his mind and wrote instead:

TO HIS SISTER
CHRISTINA GEORGINA ROSSETTI
AND TO HIS SISTER-IN-LAW
LUCY MADOX ROSSETTI
I DEDICATE
THIS RECORD OF ONE
WHOM WE ALL KNEW AND UNDERSTOOD WELL
AND WHOM TO UNDERSTAND WAS TO LOVE

Quite how Christina and Lucy reacted to being yoked together is unrecorded but William's intention to promote family harmony was clear. On 11 March he delivered his manuscript early to Cassell's, although they showed no inclination to publish before the originally scheduled autumn date. William could now book his travel arrangements. He left London by the early train on Friday, 15 March, arrived in Biarritz at 8 p.m. the next day and stayed for five weeks. Just before he left London, he warned Thomas Wise not to forward to Biarritz any news about the Shelley Society debts that might alarm Lucy and affect her health. 'My wife (with my full assent) opens my letters whenever she feels inclined',[109] William explained. Any negative information might provoke a contretemps.

Queen Victoria had already arrived in Biarritz, with the spring, on 7 March 1889; she stayed until 2 April, becoming 'a familiar sight to the inhabitants, driven about in her donkey-chaise'. In 'grand besoin de repos' she stayed in the imposing Villa du Comte de La Rochefoucauld but when Catherine, Lucy's Basque servant-girl, went to look at her, she 'was both surprised and disappointed to behold a quiet, plump old lady who was not wearing a crown, and who carried a parasol in lieu of a sceptre.'[110] Biarritz took to the Queen and the Queen took to Biarritz. The town gave a concert for her on 16 March with a specially commissioned *Marche Triomphale composeé pour S.M. la Reine d'Angleterre par Ch. Billéma*. Victoria responded by presenting the mayor with a monumental signed photograph of herself which hangs today in the Museé des Archives. William joked to Lucy that the Victoria effect would turn Biarritz 'into a whited sepulchre, but I shall manage to be myself, in my own dear family, there as elsewhere'.[111] Madox Brown was gleeful that the visit of his famously anti-monarchist son-in-law coincided with Victoria's in such a small place as Biarritz. He ribbed Lucy, 'How are you & the Chaplain gelling, & William; & the Queen?'[112]

During this holiday William saw Spain for the first and only time, crossing the border by rail with twelve-year-old Arthur to visit San Sebastian. In April when William had returned to London, Lucy and Olive made the same trip, observing church architecture and a mirage. Reaching home William wrote to Lucy without delay, 'to be with you day & night is my one substantial pleasure'.[113] As the weather grew milder in London, he longed for her to return, advising her to do the journey in easy stages, staying at hotels as she went, as 'a little money spent in that way is better than a great deal in Doctors' bills'.[114] Lucy finally left Biarritz on 5 or 6 May and reached 5 Endsleigh Gardens on Thursday, 9 May 1889. She had been away exactly six months.

THURSDAY 12 APRIL 1894 – 3 A.M.

Early in 1890 Lucy's chest was bad again but in March publication of her biography of Mary Shelley was briefly diversionary. Although she was less well in April, the summer saw a definite remission and the Rossettis took a family holiday in Holland and Belgium. When the wheezing subsided, if only briefly, Lucy saw afresh the visual world that meant so much to her. On the way back from Bruges she complained of pain in the area of her left shoulder blade and once home she consulted Dr Gill who diagnosed 'intercostal rheumatism', probably pleurisy. Then, on 24 August, she coughed up blood 'without any previous warning', for which Gill prescribed ice and some other unspecified medicines. If his diary entry implies she coughed blood significantly for the first time, then either William suppressed his memory of the blood spitting in 1886, or they both exercised selective amnesia to deal with the situation. Lucy remained 'extremely weak' and stayed in bed until she was suddenly galvanized by moving house.[115]

Lucy's stepmother, Emma Madox Brown, died on 11 October 1890 and two weeks later the Rossetti family moved to 3 St Edmund's Terrace, Richard Garnett's old home next door but one to Lucy's father at No. 1. It meant a much longer walk to Somerset House for William (he timed it at 53 minutes precisely) but Lucy thought the elevation of their new home between Regent's Park and Primrose Hill would benefit her health. Proximity to her beloved father helped her weather the severe winter but by early spring 1891, she was suffering from 'bronchial catarrh' and toothache. In August, after staying in Oxford and Stratford (where she met Georgie Burne-Jones by chance in 'Shakespeare's house'), Lucy headed for Bournemouth. After a night of persistent coughing the landlady asked her outright if she was consumptive. 'I indignantly refuted the idea but I have to be constantly careful', she told

William. It was the first time the disease had been named between them in writing but there is a clear implication from Lucy's comment that they both knew the true nature of her disease.[116]

In 1892 William agonized about his sister Christina who underwent an operation for breast cancer on 25 May. On 6 July he noted that Lucy had 'seldom been tolerably well this year'.[117] By November he accepted, if only privately, that Lucy's illness had changed from bronchial pneumonia 'to an incipient form of phthisis', and he conceded inwardly that it had already reached an advanced stage. Her range of doctors now included William Gill, Wilson Fox, Frederick Roberts and Sir John Williams. Her ragged emotions did not diminish her intellectual powers but the force of her angry negativity affected the whole family. However, she could be 'most affectionate' to outsiders and regaled Olive Garnett, the daughter of Dr Richard Garnett of the British Museum and a close friend of the Rossetti children, with the tale of Madox Brown taking all seven of his grandchildren to see *King Lear*, installed in state in two boxes – a gift from Henry Irving. 'Between the acts they all had Neapolitan ices in the Prince's room hung round with pictures. Mr Irving sent his secretary to see how they were getting on and they all enjoyed themselves very much. The anarchists [i.e. the Rossetti children] didn't seem to mind sitting in the royal box', Lucy observed with her usual wit. Olive Garnett was 'so delighted at this that [she] offered [Lucy] a eucalyptus jujube on the spot'.[118]

But on Boxing Day 1892, bronchitis racked her whole body – and everyone who had to listen to her torments. Olive nursed her tirelessly day and night, so that a week later, arrayed in a 'magnificent Liberty silk dressing gown', on a crystalline snowy day, Lucy was able to sit in a chair by the fire to oversee household sewing. 'Even anarchists must have their clothes mended', she told her revolutionary children. In brief remission she glittered and 'looked very handsome indeed'. Under the strain of Lucy's condition – unpredictable but hopeless – young Olive Garnett noted, 'Mr Rossetti was quite gay, and laughed a good deal'.[119]

On 2 April 1893 Olive Garnett found Lucy alone and in confidential mood. 'She showed me her "Romeo & Juliet"…the colour is lovely. What a pity she no longer paints!' Lucy had always enjoyed conversation and now she talked well 'without a trace of irritability' on a range of topics, 'though she was interrupted by several fits of coughing'. Olive felt sorry 'that her gifted mind should apparently produce so little. How charming she can be when she likes.'[120] A fortnight later Lucy suffered a critical relapse, severe haemoptysis, bringing up significant quantities of blood. As before, she and William convinced themselves that it was the first time they had seen this symptom, although it had clearly been ongoing since at least 1886. This time she was unable to move unaided and, with the egotism of suffering, refused to have any nurse other than her children, usually her eldest daughter. Unable to live herself, she clung passionately to Olive's vitality, subconsciously projecting her own tremulous identity onto her child and thence into the future. Achievements meant so much to Lucy and on examination she judged herself inadequate. 'I do trust my children will do something to make up for me', a longing she had clung to ever since the birth of her symbolic eldest daughter.[121]

Poor Mrs Rossetti, thought Olive Garnett on 22 April, the day Lucy signed the codicil to her contentious will,[122] 'is in a fearful state of irritation, hardly responsible I should say, as her temperature is 101° (it was 104°).' William 'looked utterly wretched', and confessed to the dinner table, 'for years I have had this on my mind'. (Also on his mind were the simultaneous critical illnesses of his sister Christina, his father-in-law Ford Madox Brown, and his old aunt Eliza Polidori.) The children were kept running up and down stairs all day, ferrying messages from Lucy's bedroom to those having dinner below and on one occasion William rushed up to extinguish some lilies set alight by a candle.[123]

In the nineteenth century, the terminally ill tubercular patient went through the five stages identified by psychiatrist Elisabeth Kübler-Ross in the twentieth-century. Her work, *Living with Death and Dying* identified first 'Denial and Isolation', then 'Anger', followed by 'Bargaining', 'Depression' and finally 'Acceptance'. Resenting the fact that William, although so many years her senior, would now survive her, Lucy had not reached acceptance in April 1893, when she was so ill that William steeled himself to face the fact that each day might be her last. [124]

She survived the crisis but did not rally, and by June 1893 was 'almost a skeleton, her skin brown & shrunken', her eyes unnaturally large and bright in her gaunt face. She still talked well but Olive Garnett felt she was speaking to a dying woman. The Rossetti children, at breaking point, were smoking and reading articles on suicide. As the terminally ill syphilitic Alphonse Daudet wrote sardonically: 'Pain is always new to the sufferer, but loses its originality for those around'. It is a 'terrible weight on a household' having someone around 'whose illness drags on for years and years'.[125] The Rossetti family atmosphere was like 'a quantity of explosives ready to go off'. William 'hung his head down' and 'literally forced himself to speak & smile'. The only person who seemed at all at ease was Lucy, paralyzed by the fear of death and yet strangely vitalized by it at the same time. Olive Garnett 'fancied she looked at me across the room in an appealing pathetic way, as if soul would speak to soul'. In spite of its appalling physical manifestations, consumption was thought to be a particularly 'soulful' disease.

Then suddenly, in a semblance of social normality, Lucy rose from her bed, dressed and forced William to accompany her to dine with the Holman

Hunts.[126] By July, the sympathetic artist Arthur Hughes was horrified by Lucy's appearance 'so dreadfully thin and hollow-eyed'. He didn't think she could survive another English winter.[127] The same month, punishing herself and those dearest to her, Lucy chose isolation, banned William from their bedroom and took Olive into bed for comfort instead. Since November 1892, William had been cast into depression by Lucy's changed attitude, 'much less cordial in her demeanour' towards him, which he feared would become a matter of 'permanency'. Once so erotically charged, the sexual side of their marriage was over, destroyed by a disease which neither medicine nor love could combat. 'This change in my relations of affection and home life is about the most painful thing that could have occurred to me', William confided to his diary, 'deeply do I feel it, but must bear it as I may'.[128] In symbiosis Madox Brown was fading fast. Did he recall his first wife Elisabeth's dire malady, its link with Italy and the poem he had written nearly half a century before, to Italia 'the land where England's daughters reach to die'?[129] Father and daughter exchanged last farewells. She received almost the last coherent words uttered by the dying man, then on 3 October 1893 Lucy left England for Italy forever with her three frantic daughters who consoled themselves by planning to disseminate anarchism abroad.[130]

Ford Madox Brown died 'of apoplexy' three days after her departure. Lucy learnt the news in carefully worded letters from William which reached her as she 'sat on a bench in front of the lake' at Pallanza on Lake Maggiore in northern Italy, where 'the air, the beauty around at such an awful moment made me quite breakdown...O my beloved father. I can write no more today'. She longed for home, 'you know I never wished to come'.[131]

In Pallanza, reflecting Lucy's distress, it rained as it can only rain in the Italian lakes. She and the three girls (Arthur was at home with William) stayed first at the Hôtel de la Poste, Pallanza (fig. 121) and then rented Villa Cadorno at Castagnola.

Here she experienced the 'flare-up' phenomenon characteristic of the later stages of tuberculosis, when the patient makes a final effort to reassert herself and engage creatively with the world. Thomas Dormandy, in his study of tuberculosis, *The White Death*, links this final flare-up with dramatic construction, specifically in the plays of the tubercular playwright Chekhov. 'In all the Chekhov plays there is an "event" in Act 4...leading to a kind of muted climax. This was true of many tuberculous lives as well. It usually took the form of a last determined and almost always doomed effort to ignore the illness and try to make a come-back into the real world'.[132] Although all her pain had returned, Lucy summoned her remaining strength in a fourth act of her own shadow-play, went boating on the lake with the girls and even travelled to Milan to see the consul in connection with her father's will. At the great

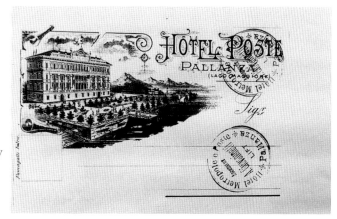

121. Contemporary
envelope showing
Hôtel de la Poste,
Pallanza, Lago
Maggiore.

house on Isola Bella, with acerbic, reverse snobbery Lucy admired the fine old
pictures and magnificent tapestries, the antique chairs with their 'original
beautiful embroideries all uncovered, not like the Queen's at Windsor with
hideous chintzes over them'.[133]

The world was spinning away from her but she was still determined to be
creative, to leave her trace. Impelled by a commission from Longman as well
as her own mortality, she continued to draft instalments of a substantial, projected 500-page biography of her father, based on an article she had written
for the *Magazine of Art* in 1890. But for days on end she had to stay in bed,
wrapped in rugs and shawls. The scenery was very beautiful, she admitted, but
she longed for home and England, commenting unfairly that 'London is very
superior to Pallanza'.[134] Joseph, a devoted servant, prepared *café au lait* and
macaroni to tempt Lucy's failing appetite and at Christmas she was able to try
'a delicious turkey fattened in our own garden and a wonderful Xmas pud-
ding of Olive's making'.[135]

In February 1894 Lucy moved to Genoa where she 'should not have
thought it possible to have broken down so completely'. Dreading yet another
move, she nevertheless determined to reach San Remo in this 'winter of anxiety and misery'.[136] She chose Maurice Bertolini's grand Hotel Victoria with
its hydraulic lift, one of the town's first modern hotels built in 1864, set in lux-
uriant botanic gardens with a majestic Avenue of Palms leading down to the
sea (fig. 122).

The Victoria's architect, Giovenale Gastaldi, had also built Edward Lear's
villas – Emily and Tennyson. Illustrious guests at the Victoria had included
Lord John Russell, Napoleon III with Empress Eugénie, and Tchaikovsky
who found it crowded and expensive in 1877. But Giovanni Ruffini, author
of *Dr Antonio*, extolled the Victoria's seclusion and elegance in his *Sanremo
Revisited*.[137]

Once installed, Lucy continued her fight for breath. The lush natural setting of San Remo may have been consolatory, as it was for a foreign doctor, also terminally ill. 'If it is really not possible to recover, staying in this place can make the end less sad.'[138] Lucy consulted young Dr Ansaldi, perhaps alphabetically top of a list of almost thirty Italian, English, German, Polish and Hungarian physicians in San Remo. Ansaldi had trained in Britain and spoke good English, a comfort for a restless, sick cosmopolitan. He prescribed a diet of beef tea, brandy and milk. Confined to her room, one of her final pleasures was hearing the sweet voice of Signora Giannoli, an Italian vocalist staying at the same hotel.

On 19 March, Olive – at Lucy's dictation – telegraphed William in London, announcing her mother's imminent death and advising him to leave for Italy at once.[139] When he arrived, Lucy lingered for three more weeks, unremittingly consumed from within but enlivened by sheer will and subcutaneous caffeine injections.[140] Tubercular death was not lyrical or operatic, as the nineteenth century had mythologized it in *La Dame aux Camélias* (1852) or *La Traviata* (1853). Instead it was labouring for every single breath, it was 'disintegration, febrilization, dematerialization…the body turning to phlegm and mucus and sputum and, finally, blood…'[141] In the presence of her family and a Rossetti relative, Isabella Cole, Lucy faced this finally with no illusions about the outcome. William noted in a tiny, brown silk pocket book, 'Dear L died Thursday morning 12 April 1894 – 3 a.m. – asked in pain to be turned over on left side – Olive did this and…came the end. Her last words were addressed to Ol – O how I love you dear'.[142] Love was on her lips, if not for William. Conscious to the last, 'her courage never flinched for a moment'.[143] Seven years before, on her first visit to San Remo, Lucy had sent white flowers to the

122. Hotel Victoria, San Remo, in the nineteenth century, from *Sanremo com 'era* (Sanremo: Famia Sanremasca, 1974).

funeral of a young man who had died of consumption at her hotel. After viewing his body, she had written home to William, 'I always think the calm of death so beautiful'.[144]

On 17 April 1894 this was the leading obituary in *The Times*:

Mrs Lucy Rossetti, wife of the author and critic Mr William Michael Rossetti, died at San Remo, Italy, on the 12th inst. She was the eldest daughter of the late distinguished painter Mr Ford Madox Brown. Almost by accident she became herself an artist of merit. She had had little artistic training, when, in 1868, in consequence of the failure of one of her father's assistants, she supplied his place. Her success was so encouraging that she began the systematic study of art under her father's direction. In 1869 she exhibited at the Dudley Gallery a work entitled 'Painting', which met with the approval of the critics. At the same gallery in 1871, she exhibited her most important work, 'Romeo and Juliet', which was warmly praised for its 'dramatic conception, excellent colouring, and poetic feeling.' Among other exhibited works of the artist may be cited:- 'After the Ball', 1870; 'Ferdinand and Miranda playing Chess', 'Cornelius Agrippa showing the Fair Geraldine in a magic mirror to the Earl of Surrey,' and 'Lynmouth' – all exhibited at the Dudley Gallery in 1872; 'Margaret Roper receiving the head of her father, Sir Thomas More, after its exposure on London-Bridge', Manchester, 1875, and 'The Duet', at the Royal Academy, 1877.[145] Miss Brown married Mr W.M. Rossetti in 1874. For some years past she had been in failing health.

Coda

There is a line in Mrs. Browning which reflects too truly the feeling of many of us as we get old – 'All things grow sadder to me, one by one'.
  WMR's MS Diary, 2 March 1894

Close of a year which (spite of painful memories) has been comparatively cheerful to me, owing to perpetual & congenial occupation.
  WMR's MS Diary, 31 December 1895

Lucy died on 12 April 1894, six months almost to the day after the funeral of William's closest friend and father-in-law, Ford Madox Brown. The two men, separated by less than eight years, had enjoyed a 'deeply cherished'[1] friendship over forty-five years in spite of, or perhaps because of, being the temperamental reverse of one another. Peppery, direct, quick to scent offence even when none was intended, Madox Brown unfailingly offered William practical support throughout the many crises in Dante Gabriel's mental health. A highly literary artist, Madox Brown regularly read and commented on William's range of publications. William, though outwardly calm and phlegmatic, was inwardly sensitive and vulnerable. The man of letters always analysed the latest work on his father-in-law's easel and wrote a particularly perceptive account of his output in an article for the Century Guild *Hobby Horse* in 1886.[2]

In spite of differences of taste in art and people (William especially venerated the poet Robert Browning and Japanese art, whereas Madox Brown despised both; Madox Brown had a tendency for feuding and fell out with the Morrises and the Burne-Joneses, but by contrast William was essentially pacific), they were constant visitors in each other's houses, both before and after William's marriage to Madox Brown's daughter Lucy in 1874. They went gallery and zoo visiting together, travelled abroad together, shared projects and interests, encouraged and comforted each other through family crises, illnesses and deaths. At a deep level they were compatible, sharing scepticism and stoicism in the face of life's worst adversities.

Madox Brown's grandson, William's 'half-nephew', young Ford Madox [Ford] Hueffer observed the two old friends, late in their friendship, when the talk by the fireside at St Edmund's Terrace was all of Shelley, Browning, Mazzini and Napoleon III. William's crossed legs would gradually edge closer and closer to the fire-irons until they crashed down into the fender. Ford repeatedly replaced the fire-irons in their stand until Madox Brown finally exploded:

'God damn and blast you, William, can't you be more careful?'
To which his son-in-law, always the most utterly calm of men, would reply:
'Really, Brown, your emotion appears to be excessive. If Fordie would leave the fire-irons lying in the fender there would be no occasion for them to fall.'[3]

They had shared a lifetime of cultural and personal history, entirely at ease with one another.[4]

These family deaths pitched William into one of his wordless black holes, when he refrained even from writing in his diary. The gap was significant – four months from March to July 1894. During that time, he made the decision not to return to the office. He was due to retire in September when he would be sixty-five. The Board was sympathetic and effectively awarded him compassionate leave until his official retirement on 1 September. That summer Christina's illness worsened and William went from Lucy's deathbed to attend to his sister's slow, painful dying.

However, by 22 July, he had set himself a programme of literary work to deal with grief, and give him a purpose. On that day, he began assembling the letters for inclusion in his monumental two-volume tribute to his brother, *Dante Gabriel Rossetti: His Family Letters with a Memoir*. He could involve Christina in reminiscences of their joint childhood and youth and he could lose himself in an arduous research agenda – making a start by reading 260 books. For the first time since he began school at the age of seven, he was his own master - with the novelty of scheduling his working day to suit himself. When he put the final sentence to his *Memoir* of Gabriel, he calculated with schoolboyish exactitude that the writing had 'occupied me 219 days, or 7 lunar months 3 weeks & 2 days'.[5]

In a sense, he was addicted to work. By intuition he knew that 'a life without some sort of definite occupation' might all too easily cast him into negativity. 'To get up in the morning not knowing "what to be at," to dribble through the lagging hours, and then retire to bed without a sense of anything enacted, seems to be a very wretched fate', he believed. For 'a man who retires old from a long career of regular work', it could 'lead to an early collapse of the vital energies, with the coffin closing the scanty perspective'.[6]

Apart from throwing up a bulwark against the depression of bereavement, retirement and old age, William had another factor in mind when he set his vigorous, sometimes manic, programme of mental activity. This was his 'exceedingly slender' belief in any 'probabilities of personal immortality' or an afterlife of any kind.[7] Therefore, if an article, a review, a biography, a translation, an edition, or an autobiography was worth writing, it had to be executed as soon as the idea came to him. 'What a mass of literary work you have been getting through since your retirement', marvelled Harry Buxton Forman, his old competitor in Shelley studies. 'It makes me quite envious'.[8] As dozens of contemporaries and friends died around him, William embarked on each project with zest, in case it might be his last. He had no way of knowing his life would continue for a quarter of a century. 'It may be true that my performances are not important', William conceded to critics who found his rate of production bewildering and his mining of the Rossetti family seam commercially opportunistic. 'They are however carried on with much the same sort of system and assiduity as my office-work used to be. I give to them very nearly as many hours a day as I was wont to give to the office'.[9] At an age when some people might expect their lives to close down, the occupations of William's old age brought him instead a liberation and personal fulfilment he had never previously known.

By 15 August 1894, Christina was in bed. 'I greatly fear [she] will not rise again', William told his diary. His own health was good, although with reason enough in this year of afflictions, he applied to Dr Gill for a tonic. Christina discussed her will, made three years before, of which William was the chief legatee and sole executor. She asked him to make bequests to specific religious houses if he should survive her. He did, of course, survive her, and in spite of his unbelief he was happy to incorporate her final instructions into his own will.[10]

She grew weaker and weaker. He worked harder and harder, and visited Christina daily. By November, Christina was 'dreadfully low', and William could not believe she would live more than another few days. (His half-nephew, Ford Madox [Ford] Hueffer, thought 'Uncle Bill' was close to 'hysterical' but the description was more appropriate to his own psyche than William's.[11] In complete reversal, Ford later called William 'always the most utterly calm of men'.[12]) Christina's religious beliefs were now no comfort but only intensified her gloom. William knew she had 'absolutely nothing to reproach herself with' and was dismayed when she said to him: 'How dreadful to be eternally wicked! For in hell you must be so eternally – not to speak of any question of torments'.[13] But he honoured her beliefs, however self-destructive they appeared to him. He never suggested that she was labouring under what Swinburne reviled as 'the criminal lunacy of theolatry…spiritually infected and envenomed by the infernal and putrefying virus of the Galilean serpent'.[14] On 9 November William was convinced he had spoken to Christina for the last time, but Dr Abbott-Anderson explained her immediate symptoms were due to sulfanella, the soporific she was taking, and warned William she could live for another two months. In William's opinion it was 'cruel to wish for' any extension of her pain which was now acute.[15] On

123. Photograph of William Michael Rossetti at Christina Rossetti's funeral. By kind permission of Tim McGee.

15 November she quietly bade him 'Goodbye, dear William', but continued to suffer. He worked every day on his biography of Gabriel.

On 5 December Christina was sixty-four. On 19 December, seventeen-year-old Arthur caused a flare-up while carrying out a chemical experiment, and injured his eye. William watched over him all night and saw Christina by day. He read letters to her, including one probably from Henrietta Rintoul, his long-ago fiancée, but noted how, 'constantly involved in mental prayer', Christina floated in and out of contact with him. He left her one Friday afternoon, 'kissing her forehead for the last time during her life'.[16] At about 7.20 a.m. the next morning, on Saturday, 29 December 1894, William's 'noble admirable Christina passed away'. The medical certificate gave 'causes of death – primary, scirrhus[17] – secondary, cardiac failure'.[18] New Year's Eve, he commented bleakly, was the 'last day of a very grievous year.'[19]

The funeral filled with 'dignity, grace, & in a way quite consonant to my feelings', took place on 2 January 1895 at Highgate Cemetery. It had snowed during the previous night but the day dawned 'still, fine & sunny' (fig. 123).[20]

Most prominent in the group of family mourners, William with his white beard and skullcap looked like an Old Testament patriarch. He was the sole survivor of the four Rossetti siblings. Christina's death, and her 'memory green to thousands, sacred to me', had brought him to one of the lowest points of his life.[21] He attended her memorial service the following Sunday at Christ Church in Woburn Square, and a few days later her cat, Muff, arrived from 30 Torrington Square.

'Perversely enough perhaps', in view of his long-held agnosticism, William had once owned to Swinburne that he was 'less *dis*inclined to believe [in

ghosts] than many people are'.[22] A year after Lucy's death he recorded without comment in his diary: 'Mrs Belcher[23] told me of her 3 or 4 remarkable
dreams (or quasi-trance-visions) of Lucy'.[24] But neither Lucy's ghost, nor
Christina's, ever appeared to him. In the heat of Rome in May 1902, suffering
from dysentery and a high fever, William dreamed he was composing a poem.
When he awoke, he could recall just two lines:

> Then two great tears came to my lids,
> Like Angels in surprise.[25]

His emotions following the deaths of his wife and sister, within eight months
of each other, were rigidly suppressed, as this fragment testifies. When
Gabriel's death was imminent and inevitable in April 1882, William had told
Lucy, 'it is no use regretting that something which is happening or has happened does happen: one must exert oneself to meet it as best one may for others and oneself, and stand (as Dante says) "tetragono ai colpi di ventura"
[four-square I feel me against all hazard steeled].'[26] Now in the face of not one
but two close family deaths he had to stand firm for his teenage children, of
whom the youngest, Mary, was just thirteen.

William did not minimize Lucy's death. The following summer he took his
two youngest daughters, Helen and Mary, back to San Remo to see 'to dear
Lucy's grave'.[27] He did not hide the awkwardness that her will had caused, for
whatever motives, but discussed it openly with his children over many years
during which he arranged his own joint trusteeship of their financial affairs
and safeguarded their rights to the house. As always, he treated his children as
equals and never patronized them. As their surviving parent, he took sole
responsibility for their ambitions, education, crises, illnesses, accidents, careers
and eventual marriages.

His children brought pleasures as well as responsibilities. He could share
books, plays, exhibitions, politics, chess, pets and discussions with them. He set
himself systematically to reread all of Shakespeare's plays before his 'finale',
particularly enjoying *Julius Caesar*, *Coriolanus* and 'this glorious play' *Richard II*
on the London stage. Lighter entertainments, with one or more of the children, included (less than a fortnight after Christina's death) a pantomime *Dick
Whittington* – a 'very splendid spectacle' with 'Chinese Festivities' at Drury
Lane,[28] and later *The Mikado* at the Savoy Theatre,[29] and Barrie's *The
Admirable Crichton* at the Duke of York's.[30]

As well as his structured rereading of Shakespeare, and his own scheme of
organized study visits to the National Gallery (beginning with the Old
Flemish and German rooms)[31] in which he involved the children, William
took them on equally regular tours of the Zoological Gardens. Animals continued to absorb and charm him, especially, on one occasion, a young zebra, 'a
tall well-grown animal, who seemed as well capable of taking care of himself

as I am – or perhaps a good deal better, he gave a vigorous kick, & behaved in all respects with the greatest aplomb'. Yet William was startled to learn the zebra had been born only that very morning.[32] As an indulgence not just to the children, William kept a small and ever-changing menagerie at home – a domestic version of his brother's more notorious collection in Cheyne Walk years before. At one stage in 1903, he housed four cats, two owls, a bullfinch, a guinea-pig, a hedgehog for keeping down black beetles, and an 'extensive dog', appropriately (for an anti-monarchist) named Cromwell.[33] Most came to early, dramatic ends. Cromwell, a wanderer, was cut in half by a train at Camden Town Station; Jumbo a cat was 'foully done to death' by a passing dog. But William lamented most the gentle owls.

These pleasures, indulgences and pets all took second place to his hectic and self-imposed work schedule. Sometimes he scheduled a whole day for projects such as translating his father's autobiography or writing an article on Lizzie Siddal for the 'new and very sumptuous' art magazine, the *Burlington*.[34] At other times he apportioned strict segments of the day to separate tasks: letter writing – two hours; biography of Gabriel – three hours; editing Christina's poems – one and a quarter hours; arrangement of books (which had come to him from Christina) – one hour.[35] The death of Christina generated his subsequent work on editions of her works, including *New Poems* (1896), *Maude: a Story for Girls* (1897), *Poetical Works with a Memoir* (1904) and her *Family Letters* (1908).

An admirer of Christina's, Mackenzie Bell, wanted to write her biography and naturally applied to William for information. He and the biographer travelled out to Holmer Green, near Great Missenden in Buckinghamshire, a journey which took him back to his childhood, both emotionally and geographically. As urban London children in the 1830s, the young Rossettis had been sent off by stage-coach via Uxbridge, Wycombe and Amersham for country holidays with the Polidoris, their maternal grandparents. William had not been back to the house for sixty years. At first he only vaguely remembered it. But gradually the old memories surfaced, especially when he stood by the pond where he and Gabriel used to catch frogs (fig. 124).

He remembered wasps in the parlour, spiders, earwigs and slugs in the garden, the pig, the pony, the spaniel – as well as the local doctor who had wanted to adopt him. His affectionate grandfather, Gaetano Polidori, had once been secretary to the Italian dramatist Alfieri, but he enjoyed using his hands as much as his brain, 'translating Milton in a forenoon, and fashioning a table in wood-mosaic in the afternoon'.[36] On 30 September 1898, William could almost re-capture the smells of glue and gunpowder of his grandfather's workshop long ago. The agreeable, unpretentious house was still known as 'Polidori House', although local people had forgotten why.[37] William ordered some photographs before he came away.

124. Polidori's
Cottage, Holmer
Green, near Little
Missenden,
Buckinghamshire,
occupied by the
Polidori family
until 1839.
Photographed for
William Michael
Rossetti on 30
September 1898.
Private collection.

When Mackenzie Bell's biography came out, the reviewer in *Literature* accused William of terrorizing Bell and dictating the book to him. Although 'expressly untrue', William decided to treat the slur with contempt and maintain a dignified silence.

Most of his literary projects took him into the Rossettian past and they were a therapeutic way of dealing with it. He had a taste for methodical work and although he sighed over the hard labour of reading proofs and compiling indexes for his books (one index alone had 2,500 entries), he derived satisfaction from completing such tasks, often with the help of Helen or Mary. With his natural inclination for scholarly list making, he enjoyed compiling an invaluable *Bibliography of the Works of Dante Gabriel Rossetti* (1905, 1906), the basis for all later research on Gabriel.[38]

Deaths, not only Gabriel's and Christina's, often prompted his work. Augusta Webster's led to an introduction to a volume of her feminist poetry (1895),[39] Francis Adams's to an introduction of his drama *Tiberius* (1894), John Lucas Tupper's to an edition of his *Poems* (1897). But William did not only live in the past. His manuscripts were now typed by a granddaughter of Charles Dickens, whose effervescent personality more than compensated for her typing errors. He negotiated firmly with publishers in the commercial world of the present day. 'Elvey called, & seemed a little anxious to cut down the dimensions of my Memoir of Gab[riel]. – I at once replied that I mean to regulate this at my own sole discretion, & that, if by chance the copy of the book, as I present it, shd. not suit Ellis & E[lvey], I wd. look-up another Publisher. To this he submitted'.[40] Always courteous but resolute, William nevertheless found that his scope for personal negotiation declined as he grew older. So he put his projects in the hands of William Morris Colles, founding director of the Authors' Syndicate, a modern literary agency. But eventually even his

125. Photograph
of William
Michael Rossetti
in his library at 3
St Edmund's
Terrace, in front
of photographs of
Pre-Raphaelite
pictures, *c.* 1900.
Private collection.

agent had to admit that there was a declining demand for his steady stream of compilations of family letters and Pre-Raphaelite memorabilia (fig. 125).

William applied his usual acumen when negotiating fees for commissions undertaken in his freelance capacity as 'Professional Assistant to the Inland Revenue for Estate-duty on Pictures and Drawings'. Before retiring in 1894, he carried out picture inspections for no extra salary, but after retirement when he continued to work for the Board between 1894–1903, he submitted a modest scale of charges which was agreed with alacrity.

While he was still vigorous during the first half of his retirement, he relished the physical exertion of travelling all over the country to see private art collections, as well as the varied mental stimulus the work provided. His health held up in spite of tinnitus and eventual deafness in one ear. He succumbed to spectacles at last, and recorded many attacks of toothache, gout, sciatica and lumbago. For his arthritic conditions he took Turkish baths, tried a potentially lethal electric bath, took the waters (with no ill effects) at Smedley's Hydropathic Establishment in Matlock, Derbyshire and consulted the ever-stalwart Dr Gill. 'So take from me dear Dr Gill/This record of the good and ill', William wrote in 1900 in a blend of pathos and self-mockery:

> Who tended from dark year to year
> My wife beloved, and lulled my fear
> And more than once prolonged her days
> (But forward Fate still tramps and slays)?
>   My Doctor.
>
> Who did the children's measles rout
> And bleached their scarlet fever out
> And dosed my gouty feet and finger
> And forced 'rheumatics' not to linger?
>   My Doctor.
>
> When drumming on my tympanum
> That insect made a nauseous hum
> Who his existence did bemock
> And made myself a laughing-stock?
>   My Doctor.[41]

'Rossetti came to me last October declaring he had a live insect in his ear, but I said "Wax"', noted Dr Gill.[42] It was Dr Gill's brisk optimism that helped keep William on the road, inspecting and valuing works of art in scores of great houses. He enjoyed his paradoxical role as a socialist mixing with aristocrats but noted, somewhat ruefully, that the more exalted the social status of the people he had to visit, the more charming they were to him. He also inspected collections left by the new industrialists, Lea of Lea & Perrin's Sauce, Colman of Colman's Mustard, his old friends, James Leathart of Newcastle, and banker George Rae of Birkenhead. On 2 November 1900 he went to Farnley Hall, to see 'the famous Fawkes Turners' and was invited to try on a felt hat with an enormous brim that had belonged to one of his greatest heroes, Oliver Cromwell.

On 17 September 1901 William went by train to Glasgow and on to Inveraray Castle to inspect the heirlooms on which the Marquis of Lorne, who had recently become ninth Duke of Argyll, claimed exemption from duty. His wife was one of the most unusual of Queen Victoria's daughters, Princess Louise, a sculptress who was more interested in art and women's issues than in royal panoply. She was the first child of a reigning sovereign to marry a commoner since the sixteenth century. The duke 'was most pleasant & attentive; took me a long walk thro' his grounds up to the lower waterfall' and invited William to dine. He went on to Roseneath Castle where

> Princess Louise was quite equally cordial: showed me the pictures (many of them off the walls, as the whole place is in the hands of masons & restorers); took me out into the grounds to a distance of some ⅔ mile, pointing

out a majestic Irish yew, & plucking rhododendron-roots & heather-root wh. I sent home to be planted. This is the first time she has been at Roseneath C, since a date soon after her marriage. She knew little about the claim of exemption, & said (but with no ill-temper) 'Lorne never tells me anything.' I mentioned to her the news this morning of British reverses in S. Africa (she had not as yet seen the newspaper), & avowed myself totally opposed to the whole affair of the war. She assented so far as to call it 'a cruel blunder'; & says no good will be done so long as Kitchener is in command – he is more an organizer than a strategist.

William enjoyed sharing his liberal political views with the princess (he was pro-Dreyfus as well as pro-Boer) and eliciting her forthright response. 'Her manner is thoroughly frank & straightforward – her utterance emphatic. Her face & person are highly agreeable & somewhat impressive: she is a very good height – contrary to what I had supposed – & the Duke is a very fair middle height'. He liked them both 'extremely well', but 'more espec[iall]y. the Princess'.[43]

These inspiriting visits could not continue forever. A number of commissions were plain dull and he found some dusty collections of old masters 'rubbishy' and their owners philistines. Increasingly, he resented turning out in all weathers on the Board's business, when he might have been making progress writing at home. Aged seventy-four, he wryly confessed to himself how much he disliked 'the notion of running hither & thither, presenting perhaps to impartial eyes the aspect of "a Pantaloon in a Pantomime"', and tendered his final resignation.[44] Although he had supported Herbert Gilchrist's application to succeed him, he was flattered when he received a 'complimentary letter' from the Board informing him that 'Hawes Turner, Keeper & Secr[etar]y of National Gallery, has been appointed my successor as Expert for Works of Art.'[45]

At home, he saw to the introduction of electric lighting and the redecoration of 3 St Edmund's Terrace 'almost totally neglected ever since we entered it in 1890', as he told his valued old friend Frederic George Stephens.[46] He dealt with callers, visitors, claimants like Lizzie Siddal's brothers, charlatans and beggars who all called upon his generosity. Loans to Ford Madox [Ford] Hueffer[47] were frequently commuted into gifts, especially as William, remembering the anguish of Gabriel's breakdowns, was responsive to Ford's state of mind. He wrote in a positive tone to his brilliant half-nephew in 1904. 'There must be tens of thousands of people going about, "from China to Peru," or from Port Arthur to the Dogger Bank, who have had severe nervous breakdowns, and under proper treatment have recovered, and do all their work as well as ever.'[48] William made equally sensitive gifts of emotional as well as financial support to new relations acquired through his children's marriages. And he sent £50 subscription for a memorial to his father in Vasto, the birthplace, although he dreaded an invitation to Southern Italy to be the centre of attention.

He lamented old friends, P.R.B.s and associates, artists, poets, writers, critics, editors, publishers, dealers, collectors, anarchists, as one by one they predeceased him, 'my early and beloved intimate' – Millais,[49] Whistler with whom William had always been 'on the easiest & pleasantest terms' in spite of his 'rather volcanic temperament', Madox Brown, Burne-Jones, Holman Hunt, Morris, Ruskin, Leighton, G.F. Watts, Fairfax Murray, Frederick Sandys, Patmore, Mathilde Blind, Augusta Webster, Swinburne, Meredith, Frederic George Stephens – 'dearly beloved Steph', Stillman, Ellis, Gambart, Rae, Stepniak. His opinions on art reverted to the ideals of radical realism he had first endorsed during meetings of the Pre-Raphaelite Brotherhood half a century before. He privately confessed he found the extreme aestheticism of Burne-Jones, although great in its way, was 'so radically artificial now that one begins to revolt'.[50]

Although William Morris had famously slighted the younger Rossetti brother, at his death, in 1896, William was swift to acknowledge Morris's major contribution to national life:

> I think the loss of M[orris] is the severest that c[oul]d have happened at this date in the region of art-intellect in England. No doubt his work was done, in a certain sense: but his indomitable energy & varied outlook have not appeared to be at all enfeebled by the advances of age, & it looks as if this country wd. suffer in his death a real diminution of power.[51]

Thinking about the deaths of artists he had known for so long led William to ponder the changing language of contemporary art criticism. Writing to Whistler's biographer Joseph Pennell in 1911, he agreed with his correspondent's view on 'the bad condition of British art-criticism at the present day. There is an immense amount of pretentious & fulsome verbiage, & very little solid meaning. In fact (but this may possibly be my own fault) I often don't understand what the [intended writer's] meaning is'.[52] In the tradition of Arnold rather than Pater, he had always rejected élitist jargon and the mystification of art by critics.

But William was not always a liberal; as he grew older, he could show uncharacteristic intransigence. Half a century before, he had fêted Simeon Solomon unreservedly for his 'extraordinary genius in art'.[53] But after Solomon appeared in a police court on homosexual charges in 1873, William, together with the rest of the artistic world (including, vociferously, Swinburne), dropped the brilliant outsider artist, wishing 'never to hear or think any more about him'.[54] Solomon died, a social outcast and an alcoholic, in St Giles Workhouse in 1905. When Everard Meynell, son of the poet Alice Meynell, was researching his entry for Simeon Solomon for the *Dictionary of National Biography*, he found that the artist had long been ostracized by his old friends. In response to Meynell's questionnaire, William wrote that he loathed 'Simeon Solomon and all that relates to his personality', although he had 'no objection to stating (as far as I can) matters of fact to a friend'. By contrast, Georgie Burne-Jones was genuinely sympathetic to the disgraced artist, and glad Everard Meynell had been chosen to write the article 'because you know and care for Mr Solomon's work, which is surely the right key to a man.'[55]

It is difficult to untangle whether William 'loathed' him for being homosexual, or for being a drop-out, or even for being Jewish. He had always noticed that Solomon was 'an unsightly little Israelite'.[56] Madox Brown had made anti-Semitic remarks and Lucy had absorbed her father's prejudices. Ford Madox Ford told an amusing story which purported to reveal Uncle William's anti-homosexuality during the months leading up to Oscar Wilde's trial. In Ford's account, William

> called the male children of his family together and solemnly informed them that if any older man made to us 'proposals or advances of a certain nature', we were morally and legally at liberty to kill him 'with any weapon that offered itself'. The person speaking thus was not merely the brother of Dante Gabriel Rossetti, the Pre-Raphaelite poet, but also Her Majesty's Secretary of the Inland Revenue; one of the most weighty and responsible of Great Britain's permanent officials, and the most reasonable human being ever sent on this earth.[57]

Ford's anecdote revels in the incongruous image of William, of all people, calling on young boys to take up arms. The grown-up Rossetti children always considered their cousin Ford a dreadful liar. But William's attitude to Simeon Solomon was a rare instance of prejudice – an aberration for a man of outstandingly broad tolerance, who owed his career to the good offices of Sir Isaac Goldsmid, encouraged the society of William Money Hardinge, and enjoyed one of the deepest friendships of his life with Swinburne.

William's diary thoughts oscillated between the past and present, counterpointing national events with domestic, and moved without drawing breath between his inner and outer worlds. The externals of quotidian living, public events in art, literature, politics, as well as dramatic and trivial physical ailments, the doings of children, servants and animals absorbed him equally. But the diaries rarely commented directly on his interior life. Omissions, elisions, reticences and long gaps reveal as well as conceal a very private man.

His children absorbed him but their illnesses recalled all too vividly Lucy's disease and death. When Helen seemed to be heading for a similar consumption during her teens, William took her first to Switzerland from January to June 1896 and then on a long sea-voyage to Australia from Christmas Eve 1896 until May 1897. Helen never developed tuberculosis and lived to be nearly ninety. Olive, the eldest, was the first to marry, on 23 December 1897,

126. Photograph of William Michael Rossetti on board the *SS Sumira*, August 1903. Private collection.

in the *Municipio* in Florence, with Antonio Agresti – her 'red romantic' as she called him – in the presence of her father and sister Helen. The following autumn Olive became dangerously ill. She contracted a raging Florentine fever, *tifo*, similar to typhoid, suffered a miscarriage and then an excruciating mouth abscess. For weeks William feared he had lost his clever eldest daughter. He travelled to Florence to be with her for a month and a half and was horrified by her emaciated condition. Olive recovered but never bore a child. Helen married Gastone Angeli at the *Municipio* in Naples on 10 December 1903 in the presence of her father and sister Mary. Mary never married, and suffered from virulent rheumatoid arthritis. She was lively, clever and thoughtful. She had planned to be a doctor but told Dr Gill she considered herself 'the cart-horse' of the family.[58] William agonized about her incurable condition and financed a range of treatments including massage, sulphur baths and later, exotic travel to Algeria and Egypt. While still physically fit, William took Mary on a seventeen-day holiday on the steamship *Sumira* 'right round Great Britain up to the Isle of Orkney' in August 1903 (fig. 126). It was 'a capital vessel, with superior accommodation, excellent fare, good & obliging officers', and father and daughter were popular on board. The other passengers, though 'agreeable', were 'a trifle more hilarious than I desiderate', he told Frederic George Stephens.[59]

Olive and Helen combined to write a novel *A Girl among the Anarchists* (1903) under the pseudonym Isabel Meredith, based on their political and journalistic experiences in the 1890s running an anarchist magazine called the *Torch*. It was an authentic testimony to anarchist times and contained a three-page manifesto to their inter-related ideals of anarchism and free love. In the novel, the *Torch* was translated into the *Tocsin* but the heroine's direction, like the Rossetti children's, was to surrender the editorship and part from anarchism, which they found an increasingly immature movement. Olive and Helen read the opening chapters 'about Anarchists, Socialists, & Faddists' to William when they were in Rome together during May 1902. He commended the 'sprightliness, ease, & directness' of their narrative and assured them the book was well up to standard for publication.[60] He found it easier to be wholly benevolent about his daughters' literary efforts than he had been earlier about Lucy's biography of Mary Shelley. As a work of fiction (although close to their own personal and political experiences) *A Girl among the Anarchists* was no rival, however remote, in his own field of literary criticism and biography.

Arthur was an eccentric who 'would take up the Differential Calculus' as light reading.[61] He suffered mysterious 'attacks', probably mild epilepsy, and was the only Rossetti without artistic ambition. He wanted to be an electrical engineer. William put up the money for him to train with an engineering company in Salford where the manager, J. Slater Lewis, befriended him, as did his daughter Dora. On 4 August 1901 the Rossetti family was reunited for the first time since November 1897, just before Olive's marriage. She immediately suggested 'we all go off, & get photographed in a family-group – at Lambert's in High St, Camden Town. It seemed a very good suggestion, & we sallied forth. A complete group (of course including Dora) was taken' (fig. 127).[62]

Arthur and Dora married on 14 September 1901 at St Luke's Church, West Norwood. William thought the bride seemed 'painfully pale' as she entered the church but she rallied and radiated sweetness and happiness. As father-in-law, William always loved Dora and carried on an affectionate correspondence with her when she and Arthur lived in Bolton. He often enclosed 'tin' which she was enjoined to keep secret from Arthur so as not to offend his sensibilities. She gave birth to his first grandchild, Geoffrey, in October 1902 whom William found 'an engaging little fellow' when he travelled up to Bolton to see him six weeks later. In a home dominated by daughters, he was amused to participate in a photograph showing three generations of Rossetti males (fig. 128).

At home, he was no longer forced to give or attend the lavish parties or soirées that Lucy had once enjoyed. He preferred his family, his newly adult children, or company on a one-to-one basis. The animated Mrs Allport, who had been a friend of Lucy's and whose son William and Helen stayed with in Sydney in March 1897, was a frequent guest. She stayed for weeks, sometimes months at a time. William was still an attractive man and his daughters considered he could have easily remarried had he wished to do so. He enjoyed new friendships with younger men including William Rothenstein, Bernard Shaw and Dr Alfred Rake, and nurtured old ones with Georgie Burne-Jones

127. The Rossetti family, 4 August 1901, photographed by E.J. Lambert of Elliott and Fry, 56 High Street, Camden Town, London. Left to right, Dora Brandreth Lewis, Arthur, William Michael Rossetti, Mary, Helen (seated on floor), Olive. Private collection.

128. Arthur, Geoffrey and William Michael Rossetti, 16 October 1905, photographed by Lambert. Private collection.

and Marie Stillman, who was always interesting and 'one of my special admirations'.[63] But sometimes he was content, as on Christmas Day 1903, to be 'quite alone; but cheerful none the less'.

Helen's marriage was short-lived, as she herself had foreseen. Her husband was already in perilous health when she married him. The 'final & early catastrophe' William had dreaded took place when Gastone Angeli died on 18 July 1904. Gastone's posthumous daughter, Imogene Lucy, was born in Rome on 15 September. On 8 November William travelled with Mary to Rome where he stayed until early February. He worried about Helen's health, and the baby who had to have a succession of wet-nurses, and as usual when in Italy he suffered gastric problems. However, he accompanied Olive to Christmas Day mass in the church of S. Giovanne Laterano, revisited Shelley's grave, and at a demonstration in the Piazza del Popolo following the insurrection in Russia, called out, twice, 'Abbasso lo Czar'.[64] But at seventy-five, he was beginning to feel more secure at home and he returned with relief to London on 8 February 1905. Helen and the baby eventually decided to live at 3 St Edmund's Terrace. William dedicated his edition of *The Diary of John William Polidori* (1911) to 'my two daughters Helen and Mary who with my little grand-daughter Imogene keep the house of my closing years still in good cheer'.

William did not suffer any real diminution of his physical and mental energies until his early eighties. He was not ill but 'a decided abatement of general strength and elasticity' was apparent, his eyesight weakened and he began to apologize for his 'cranky' handwriting.[65] He told 'Good Kind [Richard] Curle' in 1913 that he had reached a 'very low condition' and was suffering 'general derangement of the natural resources of sleep and bodily functions'.[66] As he had observed to Lucy during his vigorous middle-age almost three decades earlier, 'the decline & the last lees of life are sad affairs'. Extreme old age offers 'neither reprieve nor respite'.[67] Yet in 1914 his old enthusiasms were unabated. 'At the age of 85 I retain unimpaired my love for Walt Whitman…a towering and majestic figure in American and world-wide literature'.[68] And he exulted to 'Dearest Ol' at the end of the Great War, 'What a change these few last days! It really looks as if we had won the war. A wondrous deliverance'.[69]

But it was a rare letter and William's feelings of elation were tempered by an almost constant mood of quiet elegy. He remained true to his lifelong agnosticism and to the lines of a sonnet he had written long ago:

> so man's content to deem
> He knows not what of life & death, as ever:
> Because still, as of old, there is a quiver
> Of joy some moments at his heart.[70]

He had only four months left to live and no longer kept his diary. On 5 February 1919, at 10 a.m., William died quietly at home, of 'old age', as his doctor certified, after an illness of only two or three days.[71] Compared with the drawn-out deathbed vigils of his father, mother, brother, sisters and wife, it was a modest death. Mary and Arthur were with him but Helen, speeding back from Paris, arrived too late. The next morning, on the eighty-eighth Day of the Armistice, the *Daily Express* announced 'W.M. Rossetti Dead – The last of the Famous Pre-Raphaelites'. His work, the paper evaluated 'both as an editor and a writer, was of a high order, and literature owes much to his thoughtful, discriminating criticism.' After cremation, his ashes were buried at Highgate, in the Rossetti family grave at 11.30 a.m. on Saturday, 8 February in the presence of his four children, as well as Edith Holman Hunt, Alice Rothenstein and two representatives from the Italian Embassy.

Of the many obituaries of William Michael Rossetti, perhaps the most discerning came from John Lewis Paton in the *Manchester Guardian*.[72] Paton was High Master at Manchester Grammar School but previously had been headmaster at University College School, not far from William's home, where he had been a welcome visitor. Paton gave a lengthy and accurate account of William's contribution to Pre-Raphaelitism and the landmarks of his literary career, highlighting *Dante Gabriel Rossetti: His Family Letters with a Memoir* as 'the first complete and authoritative biography' of the artist. But the real interest of the obituary lay in its enchanting use of private anecdote, displaying William in symbolic acts of true generosity, personal charm, and independent spirit well into extreme old age. Paton recalled:

What made me realise that I had settled in London somewhere in his neighbourhood was being stopped one day on Primrose Hill by a dark-eyed olive-skinned foreigner, who seemed to speak any language but English, and the burden of whose quest was 'Signoro Rossetti.' It was not by any means the only time I was asked the way to his house. Wherever there was an Italian in London who needed help, whether he was oboe-player in an orchestra, an organ-grinder with a monkey buttoned up under his coat, or a hokey-pokey man in search of the capital to set up his nomad shop on wheels – wherever there was an Italian in distress, he seemed inevitably to find his way to the home of 'Signoro Rossetti,' who was a sort of consul-general for all Italians in London *qui n'avaient pas le sou*.

They could not have come to a more unfailing fountain of generosity. He must have been duped again and again; yet it made no difference. He was always just as generous to the next needy applicant, for his faith in humanity and his patience with the most stupid and degenerate specimens of the species were inexhaustible. 'No, no; you must really go,' I heard him say after he had taken his strange visitor up to his bedroom and rigged him up with a new set of underclothing and a new suit with half-a-crown in the pocket of it. 'You must really go. I can't be teased any more. You have teased me long enough.' Some two hours later, after midnight, the house would be knocked up by the policeman with a drunken man in charge. 'I can't get nothing out of 'im, sir, but his clothes 'as all got marked "Rossetti," and I reckoned they belonged to you, if he didn't.'

In latter years, Paton had encountered William out walking across Primrose Hill. It was his favourite haunt for contemplative exercise. 'Sometimes at night you would find him on the open space at the top looking out over the great black space on the south to the great mass of lights beyond, and listening to the "low sullen roar" of London's life, the still, sad music of London's humanity.'

129. Max Beerbohm, *The Small Hours in the 'Sixties at 16, Cheyne Walk. – Algernon Reading 'Anactoria' to Gabriel and William*, 1916. Pencil and watercolour on paper, 225 × 349 mm. © Tate, London 2003.

In the jazz age following William's death, Max Beerbohm published *Rossetti and his Circle* (1922), a series of brilliant watercolour sketches capturing the quintessence of Pre-Raphaelite life.[73] One caricature showed a lugubrious William, overshadowed by the huge bulk and genius of his brother Gabriel and the mercurial wit of Swinburne, stationed symbolically behind them in his role as loyal recording angel (fig. 129).

However, Beerbohm drew a far more accurate and sympathetic portrait-sketch of William on a manuscript page crowded with Pre-Raphaelite personalities – an affectionate coda to all the many images of William Michael Rossetti (fig. 130).

130. Max Beerbohm, portrait of William Michael Rossetti, possibly after Legros (see fig. 28), from *The Mirror of the Past*, pencil (detail). Robert H. Taylor Collection, Department of Rare Books and Special Collections, Princeton University Library.

ABBREVIATIONS

People

LMB	(Emma) Lucy Madox Brown (until her marriage to WMR, 31 March 1874)
LMBR	(Emma) Lucy Madox Brown Rossetti (after 31 March 1874)
WMR	William Michael Rossetti
CGR	Christina Georgina Rossetti
DGR	Dante Gabriel Rossetti
FMB	Ford Madox Brown
FMLR	Frances Mary Lavinia Rossetti (née Polidori)
HRA	Helen Rossetti Angeli

Collections

Austin	Harry Ransom Humanities Research Center, University of Texas at Austin
Berg	Berg Collection, The New York Public Library
BL	British Library
Bodleian	Bodleian Library, University of Oxford
Fredeman Family Collection	The Fredeman Family Collection, Vancouver, British Columbia, Canada
HLRO	House of Lords Record Office
Pforzheimer	Pforzheimer Collection, The New York Public Library
UBC	University of British Columbia Library, Rare Books and Special Collections, Angeli–Dennis Collection

Works

Agresti	Olivia Rossetti Agresti, *The Anecdotage of an Interpreter* (Columbia University, Rare Books and Manuscript Library, 98-2115-3, unpublished typescripts, 1958).
CGRFL	*Family Letters of Christina Rossetti*, ed. by William Michael Rossetti (London: Brown, Langham, 1908).
Dante: Hell	*The Comedy of Dante Allighieri: Part I, The Hell*, trans. by William Michael Rossetti (London: Macmillan, 1865).
DGRFLM	*Dante Gabriel Rossetti: His Family Letters with a Memoir*, ed. by William Michael Rossetti, 2 vols (London: Ellis and Elvey, 1895).
DS	William Michael Rossetti, *Democratic Sonnets*, 2 vols (London: Alston Rivers, 1907).
Diary	William Michael Rossetti MS Diary, University of British Columbia Library, Rare Books and Special Collections, Angeli–

	Dennis Collection and on microfilm at Bodleian Library, University of Oxford, Modern Papers Reading Room, Department of Western Manuscripts.
D&W	*Letters of Dante Gabriel Rossetti*, ed. by Oswald Doughty and J.R. Wahl, 4 vols (Oxford: Oxford University Press, 1967).
Fine Art	William Michael Rossetti, *Fine Art, Chiefly Contemporary* (London, Macmillan, 1867).
FMBD	*Diary of Ford Madox Brown*, ed. by Virginia Surtees (New Haven and London: Yale University Press , 1981).
Fredeman	*The Correspondence of Dante Gabriel Rossetti*, ed. by William E. Fredeman, 2 vols (Cambridge: D.S. Brewer, 2002).
The *Germ*	*The Germ: The Literary Magazine of the Pre-Raphaelites*, a reprint of the facsimile edition of 1901 (Oxford: Ashmolean Museum, 1992).
Harrison	*The Letters of Christina Rossetti*, ed. by Antony H. Harrison, 3 vols (Charlottesville and London: The University Press of Virginia, 1997–2000).
Jottings	Catherine Madox Brown Hueffer, *Jottings* (Private collection, unpublished MS, August 1922).
Mrs Shelley	Lucy Madox Rossetti, *Mrs Shelley* (London: W.H. Allen, 1890).
Peattie	*Selected Letters of William Michael Rossetti*, ed. by Roger W. Peattie (University Park, Pa: The Pennsylvania State University Press, 1990).
PRB Journal	*The PRB Journal. William Michael Rossetti's Diary of the Pre-Raphaelite Brotherhood 1849-1853*, ed. by William E. Fredeman (Oxford: Clarendon Press, 1975).
Retrospect	Catherine Madox Brown Hueffer, *A Retrospect* (House of Lords Record Office, Stow Hill Papers, STH/BH/2/3-6, undated MS).
Séance Diary	UBC microfilm Diaries of William Michael Rossetti Reel 3, A.1.3, also a copy at the Bodleian on microfilm.
SR	William Michael Rossetti, *Some Reminiscences*, 2 vols (London: Brown, Langham, 1906).
Surtees	Virginia Surtees, *The Paintings and Drawings of Dante Gabriel Rossetti (1828–1882) A Catalogue Raisonné* (Oxford: Clarendon Press, 1971).
1908 Inventory	UBC 18-4, MS 'List of Works of Art framed or otherwise displayed in No. 3 St. Edmund's Terrace with Estimated Value [e]tc/Date 6 Decr. 1908' by William Michael Rossetti.

NOTES

A Certain Tremor

1 *SR*, II, 435.

2 *CGRFL*, p. 159 (CGR to WMR, 5 February 1887).

3 BL: Add. 49525A f 69 (WMR to James Dykes Campbell, 13 February 1887).

4 *SR*, II, 436.

5 Blanchard Jerrold, *The Life and Remains of Douglas Jerrold* (Boston: Ticknor & Fields, 1859), p. 323.

6 *SR*, II, 436.

7 Information from *Il Terremoto del 23 Febbraio 1887 nel Dianese* by G. Abbo and others (Diano Marina: Communitas Diani, 1987).

8 1908 Inventory, Item 146; Fredeman Family Collection (HRA's Inventory 27 May 1948).

9 UBC, 8-15 (FMB to LMBR, 'Sunday after Xmas [18]86').

10 UBC, 9-6 (LMBR to WMR, 17 March 1887).

11 UBC, 9-6 (LMBR to WMR, 29 March 1887).

12 *CGRFL*, pp. 162–3 (CGR to WMR [28 February 1887]).

13 Ibid., p. 163 (CGR to LMBR, 21 March 1887).

14 UBC, 9-1 (LMBR to FMB, 5 March 1887).

15 Alex. Ostrowicz, *Stranger's Guide to San Remo* (Munich: Bruckmann, 1894), p. 53.

16 *SR*, II, 437.

17 UBC, 9-9 (LMBR to WMR, 18/19 August 1892).

Chapter 1: Portraits

1 Reproduced in William Michael Rossetti, *Gabriele Rossetti: A Versified Autobiography*, (London: Sands, 1901) facing p. 130.

2 Susan Sontag, *On Photography* (Harmondsworth: Penguin, 1979), p. 95.

3 *DGRFLM*, II, facing p. 39 (Surtees, 452, pl. 416).

4 Surtees dates it 1846, WMR dates it *c*. 1847 on his handwritten 1908 inventory of art works, and 1848 when he published it in *Dante Gabriel Rossetti: His Family Letters with a Memoir*, 1895.

5 Amy Woolner, *Thomas Woolner, R.A. Sculptor and Poet His Life in Letters* (New York: E.P. Dutton, 1917), pp.45–6.

6 Bateman and Smith had accompanied Woolner on his Australian venture.

7 Helen Rossetti Angeli's notes on her father William Michael Rossetti, typescript quoted with permission from the Fredeman Family Collection.

8 Bodleian, Ms.don.e.76 (WMR to F.G. Stephens, 8 January 1903).

9 T.S. Eliot, *Selected Poems 1909–1962* (London: Faber & Faber, 1963), p. 14 ('The Love Song of J. Alfred Prufrock').

10 A similar snake-headed pin was also worn by DGR in a self-portrait, 20 September 1855 (Surtees 436; Fitzwilliam, Cambridge). In a letter to WMR, 17 May 1854 (D&W 173) Fredeman I, 54.47, he suggests WMR should 'spout' (pawn) both pins 'since tin is absolutely nil'. In his will WMR left his 'breast pin which used to belong to Napoleon I' to his youngest daughter, Mary Rossetti.

11 Raleigh Trevelyan, *A Pre-Raphaelite Circle* (London: Chatto & Windus, 1978), pp. 127–8.

12 UBC, 10-3.

13 *PRB Journal*, p.131 (William M. Rossetti, 'Mrs. Holmes Grey', lines 21–6)

14 Peattie 115–16, WMR to William Bell Scott, 28 April [1861].

15 Harrison, I, 147 (CGR to Mrs Amelia Barnard Heimann, Monday morning [?August 1861]).

16 This photograph is listed in WMR's 1908 Inventory, p. 16, item 234.

17 Amanda Hopkinson, *Julia Margaret Cameron* (London: Virago, 1986), p. 88; Gernsheim Collection, Austin.

18 William Michael Rossetti, 'Mrs Cameron's Photographs', *Chronicle*, 31 Augsut 1867, pp. 546–7.

19 Susan Sontag, *On Photography* (Harmondsworth: Penguin, 1979), p. 15.

20 Amanda Hopkinson, *Julia Margaret Cameron* (London: Virago, 1986), p. 146.

21 UBC, 9-5 (LMBR to WMR, 8 April 1886).

22 *FMBD*, pp. 39–40 (19 and 20 April, 1848).

23 Ibid., p. 65 (1 July, 1849).

24 Ibid., p. 4 (4 September, 1847).

25 Ibid., p. 6 (12 and 13 September, 1847).

26 Ibid., p. 25 (16 January, 1848).

27 Ibid., p. 23 (5 January, 1848).

28 *FMBD*, p. 58 and p. 58 n. 2.

29 Laura Hain Friswell, *In the Sixties and Seventies: Impressions of Literary People and Others* (London: Hutchinson, 1905), pp. 241–3.

30 Nathaniel Hawthorne, *The Marble Faun* (New York: Dell, 1960), p. 68

31 *SR*, I, 136.

32 House of Lords Record Office, STH/BH/2/3-6 (carte-de-visite photograph of Lucy Madox Brown), reproduced in *SR*, II, facing p. 420.

33 UBC, 7-3 (Elizabeth Cooper to LMB, 22 October 1873).

34 Reproduced in Mary Sandars, *Life of Christina Rossetti* (London: Hutchinson, 1930), p.156.

35 *SR*, II, 423.

36 UBC, 13-4 (WMR to Frances Rossetti, 15 August 1874), partly quoted in Peattie, p. 317, n. 1.

37 Diary, 28 February 1877.

38 *SR*, II, 423.

39 Information from Edward G. Wakeling, editor of Lewis Carroll's diaries.

40 Viola Meynell (ed.), *The Best of Friends: Further Letters to Sydney Carlyle Cockerell*, (London: Rupert Hart-Davis, 1956), p. 30 (5 June 1923).

41 *SR*, II, 322.

42 *William Michael Rossetti* by Alphonse Legros. 1908 Inventory, item 31, 'Reproduced in my Reminiscences, and exhibited in Wolverhampton Art Exhibition 1902 – I gave this to my mother, who bequeathed it back to me.' Private Collection.

43 *SR*, II, 323.

44 William Michael Rossetti (ed.), *Poems by the late John Lucas Tupper* (London: Longmans, Green, 1897), pp. 66–9 ('A Quiet Evening', 1850).

45 James H. Coombs et al (eds), *A Pre-Raphaelite Friendship: The Correspondence of William Holman Hunt and John Lucas Tupper* (Ann Arbor: UMI Research Press, 1986), p. 121 (John Lucas Tupper to William Holman Hunt, 24 May 1870)

46 *William Michael Rossetti Seated Reading* by William Bell Scott. WMR's 1908 Inventory, item 485: 'Was given by Miss Boyd to Christina as a reminiscence of Scott, soon after his death in 1889.' On baize door of front bedroom, Probate Inventory, 1919.

47 I am grateful to the late Professor W.E. Fredeman who helped me to identify this portrait.

48 Although dated 17 November 1896, probably for presentation purposes.

49 *SR*, II, 462.

50 During the Olympic Games in 2000, some officials were housed in the original second-class quarters.

51 I am grateful to Roger Neill for information about the Falk Studios.

52 Alexander Gilchrist, *The Life of William Blake*, 2 vols (London: Macmillan, 1863).

53 UBC, 12-13 (WMR to Helen Rossetti Angeli, 18 June 1901).

54 Barry C. Johnson, 'Called at the Rossettis', *The Review of the Pre-Raphaelite Society*, 2 (Spring 1994), pp. 21–6 (quoting Olive Garnett's Diary, 23 February 1902).

55 Diary, 26 July 1902.

56 Diary, 26 January 1909.

57 William Rothenstein, *Men and Memories*, 3

vols (London: Faber & Faber, 1931–9), I, 229–31.

58 Heinz Archive, National Portrait Gallery (HRA to H.M. Hake, 17 February 1931).

Chapter 2: Scenes from Family Life

1 Quoted in *CGRFL*, p. 213.

2 Horace Traubel, *With Walt Whitman in Camden* (Boston, Mass: Small, Maynard 1906), p. 438.

3 Ibid., p. 438; Peattie, p. 462.

4 *Fine Art, Chiefly Contemporary*, 1867; *Family Letters of Christina Rossetti*, 1908.

5 Agresti, p. 12.

6 London Metropolitan Archives, Register of Baptisms for Holy Trinity Church, Marylebone Road, St Marylebone, p. 41, entry 325, microfilm X023/112.

7 *DGRFLM*, I, 41.

8 Ibid., II, 18.

9 *SR*, I, 17.

10 *CGRFL*, p. xlviii.

11 *DGRFLM*, I, 42.

12 *SR*, I, 6–7.

13 *SR*, I, 109.

14 UBC, 13-3 (WMR to FMLR, 20 July 1853).

15 Approximately equivalent to £13,400 today.

16 Diary, 29 October 1890.

17 *SR*, I, 114–15.

18 *SR*, I, 128.

19 Peattie, p. 43 (WMR to FMLR, 10 April [1853]).

20 Peattie, p. 9 (WMR to FMLR, 28 September, 1849).

21 UBC, 7-9, mentioned in WMR to LMBR, 18 February 1881, 3.20.

22 *SR*, I, 291–2.

23 *DGRFLM*, I, 22.

24 Peattie, p. 43 (WMR to FMLR, 10 April [1853]).

25 Harrison, I, 195 (CGR to Amelia Heimann [6 April 1864]).

26 For discussion of WMR's translation see chapter six, pp. 188–93.

27 UBC, 6-14 (FMLR to WMR 25 July 1879).

28 UBC, 13-3 (WMR to FMLR, 20 July 1853).

29 UBC, 13-9 (Maria Rossetti to LMB, [September 1872?]).

30 Renamed 5 Endsleigh Gardens in 1880.

31 *SR*, II, 422.

32 Ibid.

33 UBC, 13-1, Frances Rossetti's account book, entries kept by Christina. Lucy's dress cost £2 7s 0d on 17 January 1884.

34 *DGRFLM*, quoted I, 402.

35 Ibid., I, 24.

36 Austin, W.M. Rossetti Letters I Bound 17503 (WMR to Kate Howell, 6 November 1869).

37 Diary, 31 March–11 April 1886.

38 *SR*, II, 525–6.

39 Ibid., II, 541.

40 Fitzwilliam Museum, Cambridge, W.M. Rossetti, Gen. Ser. Large MS 1700-1977. (Maud Newman's note appended to Dr Gill's notes accompanying WMR's poem 'My Doctor', March 1901.)

41 Charles Churchill Osborne, *Philip Bourke Marston* (London: Times Book Club, 1926), p. 27 (letter from PBM, 17 April 1886).

42 Peattie, p. 243 (WMR to Moncure Conway, 16 December [1869]).

43 Ford M. Hueffer, *Ford Madox Brown* (1896), p. 27.

44 UBC, 12-10 (Elisabeth Bromley's notebook).

45 Lucy Madox Rossetti, 'Ford Madox Brown', *The Magazine of Art*, 13 (1890), 290.

46 Important British Art, sale at Christie's 14 June 2000, lot 12.

47 Melliker was alternatively spelled Milliker and still is today.

48 Lucy Madox Rossetti, 'Ford Madox Brown', *The Magazine of Art*, 13 (1890), 291.

49 Fredeman Family Collection (HRA's typescript notes on Lizzie Siddal, February 1965).

50 Barry C. Johnson (ed.), *Tea and Anarchy! The Bloomsbury Diary of Olive Garnett* (London: Bartletts Press, 1991), pp. 127–8 (Sunday, 23 October 1892).

51 British Art on Paper, sale at Christie's 28 November 2000, included in lot 26. Private collection.

52 Information from Auction Particulars of Milton Lodge in the Parish of Milton, Gravesend, 2 May 1854, by Messrs. W. & C. Pugh, auctioneers, 6 Blackman Street, Southwark.

53 Diary, 18 June 1881.

54 For example in 1877, Helen Bromley visited the Rossettis for twelve days, 3–15 January and again for a week at Christmas 1877. William, Lucy and Olive visited her on 23 September 1877 (WMR's MS Diary).

55 UBC, 26-11 (funeral card of Helen Bromley).

56 *SR*, I, 137.

57 Fredeman Family Collection (HRA's typescript notes on Lizzie Siddal, February 1965).

58 UBC, 5-4 (FMB to LMB, Sunday evening, January 1855).

59 UBC, 5-4 (FMB to LMB, 4 February 1855).

60 House of Lords Record Office, STH/BH/2/3-6 (Catherine Madox Brown Hueffer, *In Retrospect*, unpublished MS reminiscences).

61 UBC, 5-4 (FMB to LMB, 4 February 1855).

62 Ibid. (FMB to LMB, Wednesday night [Summer 1866?]).

63 Ibid. (FMB to LMB, [?1865 September]).

64 Ibid. (FMB to LMB, 13 September 1867).

65 Ibid. (FMB to LMB, 8 September 1869).

66 UBC, 9-14 (LMBR to FMB, 26 February 1887).

67 UBC, 8-17 (Elizabeth Cooper, née Bromley, to LMB, [Summer 1864]).

68 UBC, 9-1 (LMB to Cathy Madox Brown, 22 September 1866).

69 UBC, 8-17 (Elizabeth Cooper, née Bromley, to LMB, 16 January 1867).

70 Ibid. (Elizabeth Cooper, née Bromley, to LMB, 25 May 1867).

71 Ibid. (Elizabeth Cooper, née Bromley, to LMB, 16 [July 1867]).

72 *SR*, II, 426.

73 UBC, 6-14 (Frances Rossetti to LMBR, 13 November 1875).

74 Diary, 15 September 1881.

75 *Jottings.*

76 *FMBD*, p. 107.

77 Obituary of Cathy Madox Brown Hueffer, 'Mrs. Francis Hueffer', *The Times*, 6 June 1927, p. 15.

78 Richard M. Ludwig (ed.), *Letters of Ford Madox Ford* (Princeton: Princeton University Press, 1965) p. 8, (Ford Madox Ford to Edward Garnett [1894?]).

79 UBC, 9-3 (LMBR to WMR, 26 July 1883).

80 UBC, 9-3 (LMBR to WMR, 27 July 1883).

81 Ford Madox Ford and Oliver Hueffer.

82 Juliet Soskice, née Hueffer, known as 'Poppy'.

83 UBC, 12-16 (HRA's unpublished MS Reminiscences).

84 *Jottings.*

85 *FMBD*, p. 164.

86 Berg (WMR to Catherine Madox Brown, 14 August [1872]).

87 *CGRFL*, p. 37; Harrison, I, 404 (CGR to WMR, [5 September 1872]).

88 1908 Inventory, item 235a: 'Helen Angeli (Rossetti) watercolour, *c.*1887 (sitter, second daughter of WMR & Lucy, wd. have been about 8 years old)'.

89 Peattie, p. 524 (WMR to LMBR, 20 January 1889).

90 Berg (WMR to Catherine Madox Brown Hueffer, 25 January 1889).

91 Berg; Peattie, p. 528 (WMR to Catherine Hueffer, 24 January 1889).

92 Peattie, pp. 524–5 (WMR to LMBR, 22 January 1889).

93 Peattie, p. 531 (WMR to LMBR, 6 February 1889).

94 Trinity College Dublin 2075/240 (WMR (in the hand of LMBR) to John Pentland Mahaffy, 1 June 1889).

95 Peattie, p. 552 (WMR to LMBR, 28 April 1892).

96 UBC, 9-9 (LMBR to WMR, 29 April 1892).

97 UBC, 9-9 (LMBR to WMR, 2 May 1892).

98 Berg (WMR to Catherine Hueffer, 19 March 1894).

99 Berg (WMR to Catherine Hueffer, 22 March, 1894, 9 ½ a.m.).

100 UBC, Colbeck Collection, folder 1 (on reverse of LMBR's printed death notice card, WMR's note to 'my dear old Friend').

101 Berg (WMR to Catherine Hueffer, 20 April 1894).

102 1908 Inventory, probably Item 178, 'Lucy Rossetti – Oliver Madox Brown – Chalks *c.* 1872', currently unlocated.

103 1908 Inventory, perhaps item 180, 'Cathy Hueffer – Lucy Rossetti – Chalk *c.*1890', currently unlocated.

104 Possibly FMB's pencil portrait of Lucy dated Dec 5/47 and inscribed later 'To Cathy', see fig. 4.

105 UBC, 21-14 (Catherine Hueffer to WMR, 20 April 1894).

106 Berg (WMR to Catherine Hueffer, 20 April 1894).

107 Berg (WMR to Catherine Hueffer, 6 April 1895).

108 UBC, 21-14 (Catherine Hueffer to WMR, 25 August 1894).

109 UBC, 21-14 (Catherine Hueffer to WMR, 15 December 1896).

110 Harrison, II, 35-6 (CGR to Caroline Gemmer [2 January 1875]).

111 Poet, also known as Gerda Fay.

112 Phillips sale no. 31,053, 30 March 2001, lot 286 (CGR to Amelia Heimann, 8 February 1858).

113 *CGRFL*, p.36; Harrison, I, 395 (CGR to WMR, 10 June 1872).

114 *CGRFL*, p. 38; Harrison, I, 424 (CGR to DGR, 28 April 1873).

115 *CGRFL,* pp. 41–2, (WMR's introductory note to CGR to WMR [5 November 1873]); Harrison, I, 437–8.

116 *CGRFL*, pp. 42–3; Harrison, I, 437–8 (CGR to WMR, [5 November 1873]).

117 *CGRFL*, p. 51; Harrison, II, p. 56 (CGR to DGR [10 September 1875]).

118 *CGRFL*, p. 75; Harrison, II, 166–7 (CGR to LMBR, [?12] June 1878).

119 Harrison, II, 60 (CGR to DGR, 21 [September 1875]).

120 Fitzwilliam Museum, W.M. Rossetti, Gen. Ser. Large MS 1700-1977 (From verse 1 of WMR's poem to Dr Gill, 'My Doctor', copied by Maud Newman, March 1901).

121 *SR*, I, 36.

122 *CGRFL*, p. 57; Harrison, II, 88 (CGR to DGR, 18 [July 1876]).

123 *CGRFL*, p.58; Harrison, II, 90 (CGR to LMBR, [September 1876]).

124 *CGRFL*, pp. 74–5; Harrison, II, 166-7 (CGR to LMBR, [? June 1878]).

125 Harrison, II, 287 (CGR to LMBR, 3 August 1881).

126 *CGRFL*, pp. 103–4 (CGR to LMBR [21 December 1881]).

127 Ibid., p.118 (CGR to LMBR, 17 July [1882]).

128 Ibid., p. 121 (CGR to LMBR [Autumn 1882]).

129 Lucy Madox Brown's copy of *The Musical Library*, vol. 4, 1837, dated by her 'Christmas 1865' (private collection). Discussed by Lucy's grandson Oliver Rossetti in 'The Musical Library 1837', *The Caian* vol. 39, no. 3 (Cambridge: Easter Term, 1931), pp. 78–82.

130 *CGRFL*, p. 137 (CGR to LMBR, 22 August 1883).

131 Ibid., p. 138 (CGR to LMBR, [24 August 1883]).

132 Ibid., p. 149 (CGR to LMBR, 11 [January] 1886).

133 Ibid., p. 151 (CGR to LMBR [1886? January]).

134 Ibid., p. 151-2 (CGR to LMBR [16 February, 1886])

135 Ibid., p. 153 (CGR to LMBR [1886? 5 March]).

136 Ibid., p. 154 (WMR's note).

137 Ibid., p. 154 (CGR to LMBR, 19 April [1886]).

138 Ibid., p. 155 (CGR to LMBR, 21 April 1886).

139 Ibid., p. 157 (CGR to WMR, 20 August 1886).

140 He eventually arrived in San Remo over the weekend of 22/23 January 1887.

141 Ibid., p. 159 (CGR to LMBR, 25 January [1887]).

142 Ibid., pp. 159–60 (CGR to WMR, 5 February 1887).

143 Fitzwilliam Museum, W.M. Rossetti, Gen. Ser. Large MS 1700-1977 (Notes dictated by Dr William Gill to Maud Newman, March 1901).

144 *CGRFL*, p. 164 (CGR to LMBR, [Summer 1887?]).

145 Ibid., p. 165 (CGR to LMBR, [1888 ? June]).

146 UBC, 26-12 (CGR's recipe for a mustard bath).
   At the <u>very outset</u> of a Cold.
   1 Teaspoonful of Cayenne Pepper
   1 Tablespoonful of Mustard,
   Half a Wineglass of Vinegar, –
   Mix all together, & let it stand for a little while covered over. Put it into a basin with hot water enough to cover the feet and ankles, as hot as can be borne. Soak the feet for 5 minutes, & then get into bed without drying them.

147 *CGRFL*, p. 169 (CGR to LMBR, 13 December 1888).

148 Ibid., p. 127 (CGR to WMR, 29 June 1883).

149 Ibid., p. 173 (WMR's note to CGR to LMBR, 1 October 1889).

150 UBC, 9-8 (LMBR to WMR, 30 May 1890).

151 Fredeman Family Collection (Inscribed copy of *Mrs Shelley*).

152 UBC, 9-8 (LMBR to WMR, 3 June 1890).

153 *CGRFL*, p. 195 (CGR to WMR [19 April 1893]).

154 Diary, 29 September 1893; *CGRFL*, p. 218.

155 *CGRFL*, p. 196 (CGR to WMR, 7 October 1893).

156 Ibid., p. 198 (CGR to WMR, 7 October 1893).

157 Ibid., p. 199 (CGR to WMR, 11 October 1893).

158 Ibid., p. 201 (CGR to WMR [29 December 1893]).

159 Ibid., pp. 200-1 (CGR to WMR [24 December 1893]).

160 Ibid., p. 202.

161 Harrison, I, 139 (CGR to WMR 30 November 1860).

162 *CGRFL*, p. 204 (CGR to WMR [18 April 1894]).

163 D&W, III, 1074 (DGR to WMR [25 September 1872]).

164 *SR*, I, 21.

165 Ibid., I, 57.

166 Ibid., I, 20.

167 Ibid., I, 57.

168 Ibid., I, 57.

169 Ibid., I, 27.

170 Ibid., I, 28.

171 UBC, 26-9 (WMR to Gabriele Rossetti, 18 February 1837).

172 *DGRFLM*, I, 43.

173 Peattie, p. 528 (WMR to Catherine Hueffer, 24 January 1889).

174 W. Holman Hunt, *Pre-Raphaelitism and the Pre-Raphaelite Brotherhood*, 2 vols (London: Macmillan, 1905), II, 421.

175 *SR*, I, 33.

176 Ibid., I, 33.

177 Ibid., I, 33–4.

178 For discussion of *Mrs Holmes Grey* see chapter six, pp. 186-7.

179 D&W, I, 66–9 (DGR to WMR [Monday, 8 October 1849]). Fredeman, 49.18.

180 Ibid., I, 92 (DGR to WMR, Tuesday, 3 September 1850). William's review was probably 'The Water-colour Galleries', *Critic*, 15 August 1850, 408–9.

181 D&W, I, 57 (DGR to WMR Monday [24 September] 1849).

182 Ibid., I, 65 (DGR to WMR, [4 October 1894]) and for List of Immortals see W. Holman Hunt, *Pre-Raphaelitism and the Pre-Raphaelite Brotherhood*, 2 vols (London: Macmillan, 1905), I, 159.

183 *SR*, I, 58.

184 D&W, I, 198 (DGR to WMR, 17 May 1854).

185 Ibid., I, 233 (DGR to WMR, 19 November 1854).

186 Ibid., I, 344 (DGR to WMR, 31 December 1858).

187 Frances Horner, *Time Remembered* (London: William Heinemann, 1933), p. 22

188 For further details see Anne Drewery, Julian Moore and Christopher Whittick, 'Re-presenting Fanny Cornforth: The makings of an historical identity', *British Art Journal*, 2 (no. 3, Spring/Summer 2001), 3–15.

189 *DGRFLM*, I, 175.

190 Inscribed copy of *DGRFLM* 'To Mrs. Morris with sincere regard W.M. Rossetti Decr/95' in the collection of Mark Samuels Lasner.

191 UBC, 26-11 (May Morris to WMR, telegram 27 January 1914).

192 *DGRFLM*, I, 174.

193 Ibid., I, 175.

194 D&W, I, 363 (DGR to Mrs Gabriele Rossetti, Friday, 13 April 1860).

195 Ibid., I 364 (DGR to FMB, 22 April 1860).

196 William Michael Rossetti, 'Dante Rossetti and Elizabeth Siddal', *Burlington Magazine*, 1 (no. 3, May 1903), 273–95 (p. 277).

197 D&W, I, 363 (DGR to WMR, 17 April 1860).

198 Peattie, p. 112 (WMR to William Bell Scott, 14 May 1860).

199 From 'Dead Love' by Lizzie Siddal, William Michael Rossetti, *Ruskin: Rossetti: PreRaphaelitism* (London: George Allen, 1899) p. 151.

200 Georgiana Burne-Jones, *Memorials of Edward Burne-Jones*, 2 vols (London: Macmillan, 1904), I, 208.

201 C.L. Cline (ed.), *The Collected Letters of George Meredith*, 3 vols (Oxford: Clarendon Press, 1970), I, 149 (George Meredith to Frederick A. Maxse, 9 June 1862).

202 Diary, 23 October 1866.

203 Diary, 5 October 1866.

204 Austin, Rossetti W misc (WMR to Fanny Hughes [Cornforth], 1 October 1869).

205 Approximately equivalent to £136,000 today.

206 D&W, II, 388–9 (DGR to WMR, 18 January 1861).

207 Bodleian, Ms. Facs.d.269 (List of DGR's books drawn up in 1867 by WMR, and dated by WMR's MS Diary, 15 April 1869).

208 Diary, 4 September 1867.

209 Diary, 7 February 1867.

210 Diary, 4 December 1866.

211 Diary, 13 May 1867.

212 Odette Bornand (ed.), *The Diary of W.M. Rossetti 1870-1873* (Oxford: Oxford University Press, 1977), pp. 206–7 (5 June 1872).

213 For full discussion see William E. Fredeman, 'Prelude to the Last Decade: Dante Gabriel Rossetti in the summer of 1872', *Bulletin of the John Rylands Library*, 53 (No. 1, Autumn, 1970 and No. 2, Spring 1971).

214 Ibid., p. 34.

215 William Michael Rossetti, *Rossetti Papers 1862–1870* (London: Sands, 1903), p. 473 (WMR to DGR, 14 October 1869).

216 *DGRFLM*, I, 307.

217 W. Minto (ed.), *William Bell Scott, Autobiographical Notes of the Life of William Bell Scott*, 2 vols (New York: Harper, 1892), II, 174.

218 *DGRFLM*, I, 320.

219 Bodleian Ms. Don. e. 76 f.177, (WMR to Frederic George Stephens, 10 December 1895).

220 William had become engaged to Lucy Madox Brown on 1 July 1873.

221 Quoted in William E. Fredeman, 'Prelude to the Last Decade: Dante Gabriel Rossetti in the Summer of 1872', *Bulletin of the John Rylands Library*, 53 (no. 1, Autumn, 1970 and no. 2, Spring 1971), 55, n. 1 (William Bell Scott to Alice Boyd, 31 October 1873).

222 Ibid., 60 (William Bell Scott to Alice Boyd, 20 June 1872).

223 D&W, III, 1074 (DGR to WMR [25 September 1872]).

224 Ibid., III, 1077 (DGR to WMR [27 September 1872]).

225 Ibid., III, 1313 (DGR to WMR [2 October 1874]).

226 Diary 26 January, 2 February, 1 March 1880.

227 UBC, 7-9, WMR to LMBR, 15 February 1881.

228 Diary, 2 July 1881.

229 Diary, 19 December 1881.

230 *DGRFLM*, I, 395–401 and Diary, 6–26 April 1882.

231 UBC, 9-1 (note appended by WMR to LMBR to FMB, 12 April 1882).

232 Inscribed lower left 'Dante Gabriel Rossetti Easter Monday 1882' and lower right 'Done in anguish of heart F.J. Shields'.

Chapter 3: The Victorian

1 Although in May 1887, William 'took an affectionate leave of Lyster' who had been a colleague since 1848, 'a very old, attached, & well-loved friend of mine, whom I shall be sorry to lose from the associations of my day-by-day life' (WMR's MS Diary 10 and 12 May 1887). Alfred Chaworth Lyster was William's only intimate friend unconnected with art or literature. Gabriel did a pen and ink likeness of Lyster in 1855, see Surtees 348.

2 Now demolished.

3 Peattie, p. 34 (WMR to Frederic George Stephens [11 November 1852]).

4 Approximately equivalent to £39,200 today.

5 UBC, 9-2 (LMBR to WMR, 5 September 1879).

6 UBC, 7-6 (WMR to LMBR, 21 September 1874).

7 *SR*, II, 411.

8 Ibid., II, 415.

9 'The Taxman and the Aesthete: The Canon according to W.M. Rossetti', paper given by Peter Mandler at the Rossetti Conference, Cambridge, July 2001; Diary, 17 February 1891 and 9 March 1892.

10 For further discussion, see chapter ten.

11 Séance Diary, 11 November 1865, recorded 15 November 1865.

12 Ibid., 17 November 1865.

13 Spencer Boyd was the brother of Bell Scott's mistress, Alice Boyd.

14 William Michael Rossetti (ed.), *The Diary of Dr John William Polidori* (London: Elkin Mathews, 1911), pp. 10–11.

15 Séance Diary, 25 November 1865.

16 Ibid., 25 November 1865, second entry.

17 Ibid., 27 November 1865.

18 Ibid., 4 January 1866.

19 Surtees, no. 405.

20 Surtees, no. 182.

21 George Rae of Birkenhead (1817–1902), banker and collector and a major purchaser of DGR's pictures, commissioned the picture from DGR in 1863 for £300. He took delivery of *The Beloved* on 23 February 1866.

22 Séance Diary, 25 February 1866.

23 Ibid., 12 May 1866.

24 Ibid., 18 October 1866.

25 Ibid., 23 October 1866.

26 Ibid., 1 December 1866.

27 Ibid., 15 December 1866 and note added later, 2 April 1868.

28 Ibid., 1 April 1868.

29 Ibid., 24 April 1868.

30 Ibid., 14 August 1868.

31 Diary, 23 January 1902.

Chapter 4: Pre-Raphaelite

1 *SR*, I, 40–1.

2 *PRB Journal*, p. 6 (23 May 1849).

3 Ibid., p. 6 (24 May 1849).

4 Ibid., p. 7 (27 May 1849).

5 Ibid., p. 7 (29 May 1849).

6 Peattie, p. 4 (WMR to F.G. Stephens, 30 June 1849).

7 *PRB Journal*, p. 12 (24 August 1849).

8 Andrea Rose remembers seeing the pencil sketch in the private collection of one of William's descendants over twenty years ago when she was assured that this was indeed by William. It is certainly signed 'WM Rossetti' (but not in his typical hand) and dated 'Sept. 27. 1846' – in what looks like his more usual hand.

9 Surtees, no. 452, pl. 416.

10 Teresa Newman and Ray Watkinson, *Ford Madox Brown* (London: Chatto & Windus, 1991), Plate 51.

11 *SR*, I, 70.

12 D&W, I, 130, Fredeman I, 53.22 (DGR to Mrs Ford Madox Brown, 9 April [1853]).

13 Fredeman I, 53.29, 256 (DGR to William Bell Scott, 7 May [1853]).

14 D&W, I, 132, Fredeman I, 53.23 (DGR to Thomas Woolner, 16 April 1853).

15 Peattie p. 43 (WMR to FLMR, 10 April [1853]).

16 *Christina Rossetti* by William Michael Rossetti, 22 June 1853, pencil. Private collection (see fig. 60).

17 *Frances Rossetti* by William Michael Rossetti, 22 June 1853, pencil, Christie's sale 'British Art on Paper' 28 November 2000, lot 33. Private collection.

18 Private collection and 1908 Inventory, item 160.

19 Fredeman Family Collection.

20 Page from WMR's sketch-book, pencil, Fredeman Family Collection.

21 Both 1855, pencil sketches, MS Vault Shelves Rossetti, Beinecke Rare Books and Manuscript Library, Yale University.

22 *Ferdinand Lured by Ariel* by J.E. Millais, 1850.

23 WMR to FMLR, 28 September 1849, Peattie, p. 9.

24 *SR* p. 68.

25 Bodleian Ms.Don e 76 f 188; Peattie, p. 598 (WMR to F.G. Stephens, 2 December 1896).

26 Flora Masson, *Victorians All* (London: Chambers, 1931), pp. 18–19.

27 *SR*, I, 89–92.

28 Peattie, p. 17, n. 5 (WMR to LMBR, 1 May 1892).

29 Peattie, p. 288 (WMR to Mrs Charlton Bastian [daughter of Mrs Orme] 15 June [1872]).

30 William E. Fredeman (ed.), 'A Rossetti Cabinet: A Portfolio of Drawings by Dante Gabriel Rossetti', *Journal of Pre-Raphaelite and Aesthetic Studies*, 2 (Fall 1989), figs 48a, 50a.

31 Peattie, p. 47 (WMR to William Bell Scott, 23 October [1853]).

32 The last seven lines of Christina Rossetti's poem 'The Wombat' (dated 1869 by WMR) can be seen showing through Maria's portrait: 'Deh non fuggire/Qual vagabondo,/Non disparire/Forando il mondo:/Pesa davvero/D'un emisfero/Non lieve il pondo', which suggests a date for the drawing close to the composition of the poem.

33 Illustrated in Robert S. Fraser, 'The Rossetti Collection of Janet Camp Troxell: A Survey with some Sidelights' in Robert S. Fraser (ed.), *Essays on the Rossettis*, (Princeton: Princeton University Library Chronicle, 1972), fig. 1, facing p. 150. Troxell Collection of Rossetti Manuscripts, C0189, Box 1, Folder 16, Department of Rare Books and Special Collections, Princeton University Library.

34 William E. Fredeman, 'Prelude to the Last Decade: Dante Gabriel Rossetti in the summer of 1872', *Bulletin of the John Rylands Library*, 53 (no. 1, Autumn 1970 and no. 2, Spring 1971) (William Bell Scott to Alice Boyd, 9 November 1868), p. 26.

35 D&W, II, 675 (DGR to Alice Boyd, 17 November 1868).

36 Odette Bornand (ed.), *The Diary of William Michael Rossetti 1870–1873* (Oxford: Oxford University Press, 1977), p. 79 (23 July 1871).

37 Both Christie's sale British Art on Paper, 28 November 2000, lot 33. Private collection.

38 William Michael Rossetti, *Rossetti Papers 1862–1870* (London: Sands, 1903), p. 237 (18 July 1867).

39 Peattie, p. 231 (WMR to DGR 16 September [1869]).

40 William Michael Rossetti (ed.), *Rossetti Papers 1862–1870* (London: Sands, 1903), p.185 (26 May 1866).

41 *Etchings for the Art Union of London by the Etching Club*, 1857.

42 Exhibited, Fermoy Art Gallery, King's Lynn, Norfolk, England, 1971. Private collection.

43 For example *Yarmouth Jetty* by John Crome (1768–1821) *c.*1808–9, oil on canvas, 44.5 × 57.5 cm. Norwich Castle Museum.

44 *DGRFLM*, I, 127.

45 UBC, 18-8 (undated document by WMR).

46 In French 1876 (at first satirically) *impressionniste*, derived from Monet's picture *Impression: Soleil levant*. WMR would have been aware of the French usage.

47 Approximately equivalent to £3,100 today.

48 *SR*, I, 99

49 For a full list of WMR's contributions to art journalism, see R.W. Peattie's 'William Michael Rossetti's Art Notices in the Periodicals, 1850–1878, An Annotated Checklist', *Victorian Periodicals Newsletter*, 8 (June 1975), 79–92, and for discussion of WMR's art criticism, see Julie L'Enfant, *William Rossetti's Art Criticism: The Search for Truth in Victorian Art*, (Lanham, Md: University Press of America, 1999)

50 Robin Ironside and John Gere, *Pre-Raphaelite Painters* (London: Phaidon Press, 1948), p. 13.

51 Amy Woolner, *Thomas Woolner, R.A.. Sculptor and Poet: His Life in Letters* (New York: E.P. Dutton, 1917), p. 9.

52 *SR*, I, 94.

53 Ibid.

54 Daphne du Maurier (ed.), *The Young George du Maurier, A Selection of his Letters 1860–67* (London, Peter Davies, 1951), p. 207 (George du Maurier to Tom Armstrong [August 1863]).

55 *SR*, I, p. 95.

56 Collection Mark Samuels Lasner (John Ruskin to W.J. Stillman, 15 February 1855).

57 Private collection, by descent from Daisy Brett (John Brett to Rosa Brett, 22 March 1860).

58 Diary, 20 December 1866.

59 *Fine Art*, p. 21.

60 'Verum ego non tam aliis legem ponam quam legem vobis meae propriae mentis exponam: quam qui probaverit teneat, cui non placuerit abjiciat' – But I shall not so much propound a law for others as expound to you a law of my own mind: let him who approves something keep it, and let him who dislikes it throw it away.

61 This phrase was probably first used in France as early as 1804 by Benjamin Constant in his Journal Intime, 11 February 1804 'l'art pour l'art'.

62 *Fine Art*, p. xiv.

63 John L. Sweeney (ed.), Henry James, *The Painter's Eye* (Wisconsin: University of Wisconsin Press, 1989), p. 37, 'An English Critic of French Painting, 1868', originally published (but ironically, unsigned), in the *North American Review*, April 1868.

64 *Fine Art*, p. xi.

65 Ibid., pp. 5–6.
66 Ibid., p. 10.
67 Ibid., p. 37.
68 Ibid., p. 193.
69 Ibid., p. 206.
70 Ibid., p. 207.
71 Ibid., pp. 229–30.
72 Ibid., p. 235.
73 Ibid., pp. 237–8.
74 Ibid., p. 254.
75 Ibid., pp. 262–71.
76 Ibid., pp. 272–6.
77 Of Millais's *The Rescue*, 1855, ibid., p. 217.
78 Of the horse in Millais's *A Dream of the Past, Sir Isumbras at the Ford,* 1857, ibid., p 221.
79 *Fine Art*, p. 205.
80 Ibid., p. 333.
81 Ibid., p. 330.
82 *Chronicle*, 13 July 1867, pp. 377–8.
83 William Michael Rossetti (ed.), *Rossetti Papers 1862–1870* (London: Sands, 1903), p. 351 (John Camden Hotten to WMR, 21 April 1868).
84 Cecil Y. Lang (ed.), *The Letters of Swinburne*, 6 vols (New Haven: Yale University Press, 1959–62), I, 296 [3 May 1868].
85 William Michael Rossetti and Algernon C. Swinburne, *Notes on the Royal Academy Exhibition*, (London: John Camden Hotten, 1868), p. iv.
86 Ibid., p. 25.
87 Ibid., p. 5.
88 Ibid., pp. 6–7.
89 Ibid., p. 9.
90 Ibid., p. 16.
91 Ibid., p. 21.
92 Ibid., p. 19.
93 Ibid., p. 8.
94 Ibid., p. 2.
95 Ibid., p. 20.
96 Ibid., p. 11.
97 Ibid., p. 27.
98 Ibid., p. 23.
99 Ibid., pp. 12–13.
100 William Michael Rossetti (ed.), *Rossetti Papers 1862–1870* (London: Sands, 1903), p. 320 (29 July 1868).
101 *SR*, I, 266.
102 UBC, 21–5 and Jeremy Maas, *Gambart* (London: Barrie & Jenkins, 1975), pp. 94–5 (Ernest Gambart to WMR, 10 July 1857).
103 *SR*, I, 266.
104 *New York Times*, 7 November 1857, p. 2.
105 William Michael Rossetti, *Ruskin: Rossetti: PreRaphaelitism: Papers 1854 to 1862* (London: George Allen, 1899), pp. 187–8 (William J Stillman to WMR, 15 November 1857).
106 'Brief Critique of British Artists Exhibiting in a British Exhibition Touring America 1857–8' by WMR, holograph abstract, William Michael Rossetti Collection, GEN MSS 269, Box 1, folder 18, Beinecke Rare Book and Manuscript Library, Yale University.
107 William Michael Rossetti, 'Art News from England', *Crayon*, August 1856, p. 245.
108 *Pennsylvania Inquirer*, 3 February 1858, p.2.
109 *Philadelphia Sunday Dispatch*, 14 February 1858, p.1.
110 *Crayon,* 4 November 1857, p. 343.
111 William Michael Rossetti, *Ruskin: Rossetti: PreRaphaelitism: Papers 1854 to 1862* (London: George Allen, 1899), p. 182.
112 *New York Times*, 7 November 1857, p. 2.
113 *Christian Register*, 17 April 1858, p. 3.
114 *Atlantic Monthly*, 1 February 1858, p. 503.
115 *New York Times*, 7 November 1857, p. 2.
116 *Philadelphia Sunday Dispatch*, 14 February 1858, p. 1.
117 Susan P. Casteras, *English Pre-Raphaelitism and its Reception in America in the Nineteenth Century* (Rutherford, NJ: Fairleigh Dickinson University Press, 1990), p. 47.
118 *Atlantic Monthly*, 1 February 1858, pp. 505–6.
119 Library of Congress, Washington, Pennell-Whistler Collection, 298, f 4015-7 (WMR's MS 'Memoir of Whistler' November 1906).
120 Review of the Academy Exhibition by William Michael Rossetti, *Fraser's Magazine*, June 1863, p. 793; *Fine Art*, pp. 21–8.
121 *Reader*, 4 April 1863, p. 342; *Fine Art*, p. 273.
122 Linda Merrill, *A Pot of Paint: Aesthetics on Trial in Whistler v. Ruskin* (Washington: Smithsonian Institution Press, 1992), p. 345, n. 37.
123 Two hundred guineas = £210, approximately equivalent to £9,700 today.
124 John Ruskin, 'Letter 79: Life Guards of New Life', *Fors Clavigera*, 7 July 1877.
125 Diary, 5 March 1878.
126 Diary, 28 March 1878.
127 Diary, 22 November 1878.
128 Diary, 1 December 1878.
129 Linda Merrill, *A Pot of Paint: Aesthetics on Trial in Whistler v. Ruskin* (Washington: Smithsonian Institution Press, 1992), pp. 156–7, transcript of the trial reconstructed from contemporary newspaper reports.
130 Approximately equivalent to 5 pence today.
131 William Michael Rossetti, 'Notes on Art', *Academy*, 21 July 1877.
132 William Michael Rossetti, 'Fine Art: The Grosvenor Gallery (First Notice)', *Academy*, 18 May 1878, p. 447.
133 Diary, 17 June 1878.
134 In 1904, William collated his copies of the *Athenaeum* and had them bound up into a score or more volumes, now held at the Book Library of the Courtauld Institute of Art in London. He marked up those articles he had contributed, noting they were 'more numerous between 1878 & 1895 than at other dates.'
135 *SR*, II, 550.
136 Approximately equivalent to £1,000 today.
137 *SR*, II, 551.
138 Odette Bornand (ed.), *The Diary of William Michael Rossetti 1870–1873*, (Oxford: Clarendon

Press, 1977), p. 231 (Tuesday, 21 January 1873).

139 Ibid., p. 248 (17 March 1873).

140 Ibid., p. 250 (26 March 1873).

141 Unpublished transcript by Anne Lee-Michell of the diaries of Olive Garnett, reproduced with permission from Caroline White.

142 1908 Inventory.

143 Henry James, *The Spoils of Poynton* (London: Penguin, 1987), p. 203.

144 Richard Curle, 'Victorian Portrait', *Listener*, 10 February 1944, p. 161.

145 William Michael Rossetti, 'Japanese Exhibition', *Spectator*, 28 January 1854, p. 95.

146 *SR*, I, 278.

147 *Fine Art*, pp. 127–8; first published as 'The Fine Art of the International Exhibition', *Fraser's Magazine*, August 1862, pp. 188–99.

148 *SR*, I, 276–7.

149 Ibid., I, 279.

150 Ibid., II, 561.

151 Susan Sontag, *The Volcano Lover* (London: Jonathan Cape, 1992), p. 367.

Chapter 5: Artist

1 *SR*, II, 423.

2 William M. Hardinge, 'A Reminiscence of Mrs. W.M. Rossetti', *The Magazine of Art*, 18 (1895), 341–6 (p. 343).

3 Probate Inventory drawn up by H. Ley Clark, estate agent and valuer, 3a Wimpole Street, London, February 1919, p. 41c, duplicate copy in the Fredeman Family Collection.

4 Later the novelist Ford Madox Ford.

5 Negotiating with the trustees of the Plint estate – Thomas Plint, who died in 1861 aged 38, had been Madox Brown's major patron.

6 Ford Madox Hueffer, *Ford Madox Brown* (London: Longmans, Green, 1896), p 203.

7 *FMBD*, p. 210, n.25.

8 Austin, Rossetti W.M. Letters I Bound 17503 (WMR to Kate [Howell], 30 June 1867).

9 Teresa Newman and Ray Watkinson, *Ford Madox Brown* (London: Chatto & Windus, 1991), p. 156 and Austin (FMB to Howell 20.8.1867).

10 Christina Rossetti to Amelia Heimann, 22 August 1867, Phillips sale no. 31,053, Books, Maps, Photographs & Manuscripts, 30 March 2001, lot 286.

11 Diary, 21 August 1867.

12 H. Allingham and D. Radford (ed.), William Allingham, *The Diaries*, (London: The Folio Society, 1990), pp. 164–5.

13 Ibid., p. 181.

14 Ellen Clayton, *English Female Artists*, 2 vols (London: Tinsley Brothers, 1876), II, p.117.

15 'British Art on Paper', Christie's, London, 28 November 2000.

16 Obituary of Cathy Madox Brown Hueffer, 'Mrs Francis Hueffer', *The Times*, 6 June 1927, p.15.

17 House of Lords Record Office, Stow Hill Papers, STH/BH/2/3-6 (*Love's Problem*, by Ford Madox Brown, November 1869).

18 Ibid. (*An Understanding*, Sonnet 4, by Ford Madox Brown).

19 Ibid. (*Sonnet to Emma* by Ford Madox Brown).

20 Ibid. (*To D.G. Rossetti: An End* by Ford Madox Brown, 16 January 1870).

21 Details from Olivia Rossetti Agresti, *The Anecdotage of an Interpreter* (Columbia University, Rare Books and Manuscript Library, unpublished typescripts, 1958), p. 41.

22 1908 Inventory, item 186, *Shanklin Chine*, watercolour, Mrs Stillman, '1867 – was I think her first painting, given to Lucy'.

23 Zuzanna Shonfield, *The Precariously Privileged – A Professional Family in Victorian London* based on the diary of Jeannette Marshall (Oxford: Oxford University Press, 1987), p. 86.

24 Obituary of Marie Spartali Stillman, *The Times*, 8 March 1927.

25 Bodleian, Ms.Facs.d.289 (LS [Lisa Stillman?] to Helen Rossetti Angeli n.d.).

26 William Michael Rossetti, 'Arthur Hughes – Windus – Miss Spartali – the Younger Madox Browns', in *English Painters of the Present Day. Essays by J.B. Atkinson and others* (London: Seeley, Jackson & Co., 1871). William, following Hazlitt, used the technical term 'keeping' to refer to the harmonious balance in a picture of such qualities as 'expression, grouping, colour, *couleur-locale*, surface-handling and so on.' *Fine Art*, 1867, p. 30.

27 Ellen Clayton, *English Female Artists*, 2 vols (London: Tinsley Brothers, 1876), II, p. 118.

28 Ford Madox Hueffer, *Ford Madox Brown* (London: Longmans, Green, 1896), p. 250 (FMB to F.G. Shields, 9 February 1869).

29 Ibid., p. 252 (FMB to F.G. Shields, 20 May 1869).

30 Richard Dorment, *Daily Telegraph*, 7 January 1998. The exhibition began in Manchester and then moved on to Birmingham and Southampton.

31 William M. Hardinge, 'A Reminiscence of Mrs W.M. Rossetti', *Magazine of Art*, 18, (1895), 341–6 (p. 342).

32 Now in the William Morris Gallery at Walthamstow.

33 UBC, 5-4 (FMB to LMB [?1865 September]).

34 UBC, 7-1.

35 Exhibited Royal Academy, 1870; 1908 Inventory, item 100. Private collection.

36 Percy H. Bate, *The English Pre-Raphaelite Painters: their Associates and Successors* (London: G. Bell & Sons, 1899), p. 22 and UBC, 18-4 (1908 Inventory, comment on item 100).

37 *Art-Journal*, 9 (1 March 1870), p. 87.

38 See chapter one, pp. 22-24

39 UBC, 26-11 (Helen Bromley jnr to Elizabeth Madox Brown, née Bromley, n.d. [?1844]).

40 *Romeo and Juliet in the Tomb* by Lucy Madox Brown. Provenance: Dudley Gallery, 1871, no. 336, bought by Mr Wilson of Ambleside for £105; WMR's 1908 Inventory, item 94: bequeathed by Lucy to Mr W.M. Harding for his life-time; then to Mary Rossetti (daughter); now at Wightwick Manor, National Trust.

41 Lucy Madox Rossetti, 'Ford Madox Brown', *Magazine of Art*, 13 (1890), 289–96 (p. 295).

42 Ford Madox Hueffer, 'The Younger Madox Browns', *The Artist*, 19 (February 1897), 49–55 (pp. 50–1).

43 Now in Tate Britain, titled *Nocturne: Blue and Silver – Chelsea*.

44 UBC, 5-5 (FMB to LMBR, 12 September 1882, and 18 July 1884).

45 UBC, 8-2 (WMR to LMBR 19 November 1886).

46 Although this is not where Lucy actually copied her *Dancing Faun* as the British Museum probably never exhibited a cast of this piece. I am grateful for information from Dr Ian Jenkins, Department of Greek and Roman Antiquities, the British Museum.

47 Princeton University Library (FMB to F.G.Shields, April [1869]) and Kenneth Bendiner, *The Art of Ford Madox Brown* (University Park, Pa: Pennsylvania State University Press, 1998), p. 174, n. 75.

48 Ellen Clayton, *English Female Artists*, 2 vols (London: Tinsley Brothers, 1876), II, p. 118.

49 UBC, 18-4, WMR's 1908 Inventory, items 73, 75 and 108.

50 Francis Haskell and Nicholas Penny, *Taste and the Antique* (New Haven: Yale University Press, 1981), pp. 205–6, fig. 106.

51 UBC, 17-12 (note dated 1898, appended to thoughts on the poet James Thomson by William Michael Rossetti, 14 July 1888).

52 Unpublished letter Dante Gabriel Rossetti to William Bell Scott, c. 2 September 1871, Troxell Collection, Princeton University Library.

53 Nathaniel Hawthorne, *The Marble Faun* (New York: Dell, 1960), pp. 33–5.

54 John H. Ingram, *Oliver Madox Brown* (London: Elliot Stock, 1883), p. 30 and facing p. 30.

55 Exhibited Dudley Gallery, 1872.

56 William Shakespeare, *The Tempest*, I.ii. 397–9.

57 Ibid., V.i. 172–4.

58 Ibid., V.i. 181–4.

59 See chapter one, p. 37.

60 Approximately equivalent to £4,700 today.

61 Odette Bornand (ed.), *The Diary of W.M. Rossetti 1870–1873* (Oxford: Oxford University Press, 1977), p. 142.

62 J.B. Steane (ed.), Thomas Nashe, *The Unfortunate Traveller and other Works* (London: Penguin, 1985), pp. 288–99.

63 Gérald Schurr and Pierre Cabanne, *Dictionnaire des Petits Maîtres de la Peinture 1820–1920*, 2 vols (Paris: Les éditions de l'amateur, 1996), II, 325–6.

64 D&W, III, 1278 (DGR to FMB, 8 May [1874]).

65 A.L. Rowse (ed.), William Roper, *A Man of Singular Virtue* (London: The Folio Society, 1980), pp. 92–3.

66 A chalk portrait of Oliver Madox Brown by Lucy was recorded in William's 1908 inventory, item 178, but is unfortunately untraced. William refers to Lucy's (unlocated) picture of Cathy with her son Ford in a letter to Lucy, 11 August 1881, UBC, 7-9. A sketch of Cathy Madox Brown by Oliver appeared at the Christie's sale British Art on Paper, part of lot 34, in November 2000, which suggests that the siblings drew each other as studio exercises.

67 Ford Madox Hueffer, *Ancient Lights and Certain New Reflections* (London: Chapman and Hall, 1911), p. 51.

68 Diary, 2 July 1905.

69 *SR*, II, 388.

70 *Madame Roland* by Mathilde Blind, inscribed 'Lucy Rossetti with Mathilde's love 12 Feb 1886'. Private collection.

71 Teresa Newman and Ray Watkinson, *Ford Madox Brown and the Pre-Raphaelite Circle* (London: Chatto & Windus, 1991), p. 148 (William Bell Scott to Alice Boyd, 17 November 1868).

72 Austin, Garnett R (recip) 17508 (WMR to R. Garnett, 22 December 1906).

73 D&W, III, 1234 (DGR to WMR [13 November 1873]).

74 UBC, 13-9 (Maria Francesca Rossetti to LMBR [1874]).

75 1908 Inventory, item 146 and Fredeman Family Collection (HRA's Inventory 27 May 1948).

76 Letter to the author from Mrs Phyllis M. Marshall, 31 May 1997. Unfortunately both these portraits are currently untraced.

77 1908 Inventory, items 476[1] and 486.

78 UBC, 5-4 (FMB to LMBR, 8 July 1879 and undated fragment).

79 *CGRFL*, pp. 161–2 (CGR to WMR, 21 February 1887).

80 *Posthumous Portrait of Michael Rossetti, his Pillows Strewn with Snowdrops* by Lucy Madox Brown Rossetti, 1883, coloured chalks, 12 ¾ × 18", 1908 Inventory, item 135; Wightwick Manor catalogue of pictures, no. 61. Unlocated.

81 UBC, 7-12 (WMR to LMBR, 26 July [18]83, 11 a.m.).

82 Juliet M. Soskice, *Chapters from Childhood* (London: Selwyn & Blount, 1921), pp. 2–4.

83 1908 Inventory, item 445.

84 Lucy went to Broadstairs with her stepmother, Emma Madox Brown, in April 1876. WMR came down for a weekend and on 21 April wrote to Lucy that he was 'greatly pleased' that 'you have begun a sea-view'. UBC, 7-6.

85 William gave two of Lucy's 'watercolour sketches at Biarritz' to a friend, Mrs Allport, on 15 June 1898 (MS Diary).

86 Austin (FMB to Charles Augustus Howell, 9 December 1871).

87 Ellen Clayton, *English Female Artists*, 2 vols (London: Tinsley Brothers, 1876), I, 121.

88 *Mrs Shelley*, pp. 53–4.

89 UBC, 7-8 (WMR to LMBR, 5 July 1878, 8.30 a.m.). WMR's sketch of Charmouth is in this letter.

90 1908 Inventory, item 81.

91 1908 Inventory, item 146, and HRA's Inventory 27 May 1948, Fredeman Family Collection.

92 UBC, 9-5 (LMBR to WMR from San Remo, 22 December 1886).

93 1908 Inventory, item 492.

94 William M. Hardinge, 'A Reminiscence of Mrs. W.M. Rossetti', *Magazine of Art*, 18 (1895), 341–6.

95 HRA's Inventory, 27 May 1948, Fredeman Family Collection.

96 Elsa Honig Fine, *Women and Art*, (Prior Montclair, N.J./London: Allanheld & Schram, 1978), p. 82, fig. 4-14.

97 18 June 1998.

98 Diary, 30 January 1909.

Chapter 6: Man of Letters

1 Heinz Archive, National Portrait Gallery (HRA to H.M. Hake, director of the National Portrait Gallery, London, 20 December 1930).

2 Peattie, p. 643 (22 October 1904).

3 Heinz Archive, National Portrait Gallery (HRA to H.M. Hake, director of the National Portrait Gallery, London, 20 December 1930).

4 Merlin Holland and Rupert Hart-Davis (eds), *The Complete Letters of Oscar Wilde* (London: Fourth Estate, 2000) (Oscar Wilde to WMR [14 July 1877]).

5 BL: Add.49525A f.65-66 (WMR to James Dykes Campbell, 5 July 1886).

6 W. Holman Hunt, *Pre-Raphaelitism and the Pre-Raphaelite Brotherhood*, 2 vols (London: Macmillan, 1905), I, 140.

7 *DGRFLM*, I, 135.

8 Sondra J. Stang and Karen Cochran (eds), *The Correspondence of Ford Madox Ford and Stella Bowen* (Bloomington: Indiana University Press, 1992), p. 441.

9 *PRB Journal*, p. xxv.

10 *PRB Journal*, pp. 7–8.

11 *Some Pre-Raphaelite and later pictures that WMR modelled for:*

   A William Holman Hunt, *Rienzi Swearing Revenge for his Brother's Death*, 1849, oil on canvas, 86.3 × 122. Private collection. WMR says he sat for 'the young Colonna', Hunt says he sat for Adrian di Castello, the figure on extreme left of the picture.

   B Dante Gabriel Rossetti, *Ecce Ancilla Domini!* 1849–50, oil on canvas, 72.6 × 41.9. Tate Britain. WMR modelled for the figure of the angel.

   C John Everett Millais, *Lorenzo and Isabella*, 1848–9, oil on canvas, 102.9 × 142.9. Walker, Liverpool. WMR sat for the head of Lorenzo.

   D William Holman Hunt, *A Converted British Family Sheltering a Christian Missionary from Persecution from the Druids*, 1849–50, oil on canvas, 111 × 141. Ashmolean, Oxford. WMR posed for the head of the Christian missionary, 7 April 1850.

   E Ford Madox Brown, *Geoffrey Chaucer Reading the 'Legend of Custance' to Edward III and his Court*, 1851 and 1867–8, oil on canvas, 123.2 × 99. Tate Britain. WMR modelled for the Provençal troubadour.

   F Ford Madox Brown, *Jesus Washing Peter's Feet*, 1851–6, oil on canvas, 117 × 133.5. Tate Britain. WMR sat for the second apostle from the left.

   G Dante Gabriel Rossetti, an early study for the farmer's head in *Found*, begun 1854, oil, 91.4 × 80 (See fig.51).

   H John Everett Millais, *The Order of Release*, 1852–3, oil on canvas, 102.9 × 73.7. Tate Britain. WMR modelled for the male hands.

   I Dante Gabriel Rossetti, *The First Anniversary of the Death of Beatrice*, 1853–4 watercolour, 42 × 61. Ashmolean, Oxford. WMR posed for the figure of Dante.

   J William Bell Scott, *Palace of Venus*, 1867. WMR modelled for a head of a courtier of Venus 'which is now, I think, quite recognizably like me'. (*Rossetti Papers 1862–1870*, p.237). Scott executed a series of murals at Penkill Castle, Ayrshire, in illustration of *The Kingis Quair*, a long poem by James I of Scotland, written in the early fifteenth century while he was imprisoned in England.

   K Lucy Madox Brown, *Ferdinand and Miranda Playing Chess*. WMR posed for the figure of Prospero (see fig. 87).

12 W. Minto (ed.), William Bell Scott, *Autobiographical Notes*, 2 vols (New York: Harper, 1892), I, 324–5.

13 Odette Bornand (ed.), *The Diary of W.M. Rossetti 1870–1873* (Oxford: Oxford University Press, 1977), pp. xix–xx.

14 The *Germ* (no. 1, January 1850), pp. 34–46

15 Rupert Christiansen, *The Voice of Victorian Sex: Arthur H. Clough 1819–1861,* (London: Short Books, 2001), p. 57.

16 The *Germ* (no. 1, January 1850), p. 35.

17 Shirley Chew (ed.), *Arthur Hugh Clough Selected Poems* (Manchester: Carcanet for Fyfield Books, 1987), pp. 77–8 ('The Bothie of Tober-na-vuolich').

18 The *Germ* (no. 1, January 1850), p. 44.

19 Arthur Hugh Clough to Professor Adolf Heimann, 24 January 1850. Quoted by Roger W. Peattie in his letter to the *Times Literary*

Supplement, 'William Michael Rossetti', 30 July 1964, p. 665, UBC 20–1.

20 The *Germ* (no. 2, February 1850), pp. 84–96.

21 BL: Add.49525A f 65-66 (WMR to James Dykes Campbell, 5 July 1886).

22 The *Germ* (no. 4, May 1850), pp. 187–92.

23 The *Guardian,* 20 August 1850 (*The Germ – A Facsimile Reprint* introduced by William Michael Rossetti, 1901), 13–14.

24 *SR,* I, 81.

25 *DGRFLM,* II, 63.

26 *PRB Journal,* Appendix 7, pp. 131–54 (*Mrs Holmes Grey* by William M. Rossetti, lines 398–406, 612–17).

27 William M. Rossetti, 'Mrs Holmes Grey', *The Broadway Annual* (London: Routledge, 1868), pp. 449–59.

28 Cecil Y. Lang (ed.), *The Letters of Swinburne,* 6 vols (New Haven: Yale University Press, 1959–62), I, 284 (New Year's Day [1868]).

29 Ibid., I, 288–9 (1 February [1868]).

30 Algernon Charles Swinburne, *William Blake: A Critical Essay* (London: John Camden Hotten, 1866), p. v.

31 J. Dover Wilson (ed.), Matthew Arnold, *Culture and Anarchy,* (Cambridge: Cambridge University Press, 1966), p. 70.

32 *DGRFLM,* I, p. 64.

33 BL: Ashley 1446; Peattie, p. 388 (WMR to A.C. Swinburne, 13 December [1880]).

34 Approximately equivalent to £2,500 today.

35 Both in Mark Samuels Lasner Collection.

36 Bodleian: Ms. Eng. Lett. c. 35 f 285 (John Ruskin to WMR, 4 May 1865).

37 *Dante: Hell,* p. iv.

38 *Dante: The Divine Comedy: Vol.1: Inferno,* trans. by Mark Musa (London: Penguin, 1984), p. 42.

39 Ibid., p. 36.

40 Ibid., p. 36.

41 *Dante: Hell,* p. i.

42 Bodleian: Ms.Eng.poet.e.96 f 1–3 (WMR to Dr Edwards 9 January 1900 and 8 May 1904).

43 'The Comedy of Dante Allighieri. Part I – *The Hell.* Translated into Blank Verse by W.M. Rossetti', *The Athenaeum,* no. 1953, 1 April 1865, pp. 452–3.

44 *Dante: Hell,* p. iv.

45 Aleksandr Pushkin, *Eugene Onegin,* trans. by Vladimir Nabokov (New York: Bollingen Foundation, 1964).

46 *Dante: The Divine Comedy: Vol I: Inferno,* trans. by Mark Musa (London: Penguin, 1984), p. 67.

47 *Dante: Hell,* p. 1.

48 *Dante: The Divine Comedy: Vol.1: Inferno,* trans. by Mark Musa (London: Penguin, 1984), p. 60.

49 *Dante: Hell,* pp. iii–v.

50 John Keats, 'Ode to a Nightingale' (May 1819), stanza vi.

51 Matthew Arnold, 'Dover Beach', (1867), l. 35.

52 *Dante: Hell,* p. 37.

53 'Dante and his Latest English Translators', *North American Review,* 102 (April 1866), 163.

54 Vladimir Nabokov, *Speak, Memory* (Harmondsworth: Penguin, 1982; originally published as *Conclusive Evidence,* New York: Harper & Bros, 1951).

55 Georgiana Burne-Jones, *Memorials of Edward Burne-Jones,* 2 vols (London: Macmillan, 1904), I, pp. 291–2.

56 William Michael Rossetti, *Swinburne's Poems and Ballads. A Criticism* (London: John Camden Hotten, 1866), p. 20.

57 Ibid., p. 16.

58 Ibid., p. 21.

59 Ibid., p. 24.

60 Ibid., p. 36.

61 Ibid., p. 45.

62 Ibid., pp. 65–7.

63 Ibid., p. 70.

64 *Chronicle,* 1 (6 July 1867), 352–4.

65 Austin (WMR to Thomas Dixon, 12 January [1866?]).

66 All WMR's quotations in these two paragraphs from the *Chronicle,* 1 (6 July 1867), 352–4.

67 BL: Ashley 1446, Peattie p. 177 (WMR to A.C. Swinburne, 22 September [1867]).

68 BL: Ashley 1446, Peattie pp. 177–8 (WMR to A.C. Swinburne, 22 September [1867]).

69 In the Pierpont Morgan Library, New York.

70 William Michael Rossetti (ed.), *Poems of Walt Whitman,* (London: John Camden Hotten, 1868), pp. 1–27 (Prefatory Notice).

71 Peattie, p. 459; Trinity College, Dublin, 3147-54/411 536 (WMR to Edward Dowden, 17 January 1884).

72 She brought out *The Life of William Blake,* 2 vols, by her late husband Alexander Gilchrist with the help of William and Dante Gabriel Rossetti (London: Macmillan, 1863).

73 Herbert Harlakenden Gilchrist (ed.), *Anne Gilchrist: her Life and Writings,* (London: T. Fisher Unwin, 1887), p. 177.

74 Horace Traubel, *With Walt Whitman in Camden,* 4 vols (Boston, Mass: Small, Maynard, 1906), I, 281.

75 Clarence Gohdes and Paull Franklin Baum (eds), *Letters of William Michael Rossetti to Anne Gilchrist* (Durham, NC: Duke University Press, 1934), pp. 181–3 (WMR to [Grover Cleveland], President of the United States, 13 June 1885) (Library of Congress, Grover Cleveland Papers, Reel 14, Series 2).

76 Diary, 16 November 1867.

77 Horace Traubel, *With Walt Whitman in Camden,* 4 vols (Boston, Mass: Small, Maynard, 1906), I, 282.

78 William Michael Rossetti (ed.), *The Poetical Works of Henry W. Longfellow* (London: Moxon, 1870) 2nd ed. (London: Ward, Lock, 1882), p. xvi, (Prefatory Notice).

79 Diary, 21 May 1887.

80 Agresti, p. 43.

81 William Michael Rossetti (ed.), *Swinburne's Poems and Ballads. A Criticism* (London: John

Camden Hotten, 1866), p. 45 and b) *SR*, II, p. 501.

82 Diary, 23 December 1880, on death of George Eliot.

83 *SR*, I, p. 87.

84 William Michael Rossetti, *A Memoir of Shelley* (London: Richard Clay for the Shelley Society, 1886), p. 22.

85 *SR*, I, p. 125.

86 Pforzheimer, S.ana 735-736 (WMR to 'My dear Sir', 21 June [1870?]).

87 Peattie p. 212; BL: Ashley A 1444 (WMR to A.C. Swinburne, 25 May [1869]).

88 Mathew Arnold, *Essays in Criticism,* 2nd series (London: Macmillan, 1888, reprinted 1905), p. 252.

89 William Michael Rossetti, *A Memoir of Shelley* (London: Richard Clay for the Shelley Society, 1886), p. 28, n.1.

90 William Michael Rossetti (ed.), *Ruskin: Rossetti: Preraphaelitism: Papers 1854 to 1862* (London: George Allen, 1899), p. viii.

91 UBC, 17-17 (MS of WMR's 1875 lecture on Shelley's Life and Poetry, first delivered at Birmingham).

92 Item 115 on WMR's 1908 Inventory of art works: 'P.B. Shelley – Heron's Oak Windsor, sketch of Mr. Roberts [e]tc at back – water-colour – c. 1812…Mr. Roberts was a noted character at Eton, brother of a then Provost.' WMR valued it at £65.

93 Pforzheimer, Rossetti 6-11 (WMR to the Rev. F. Fleay, 17 October [1870?]).

94 Pforzheimer (WMR's *Preface* to the 3 volume proof copy of his 1870 *Shelley* with a *Memoir*).

95 *SR*, II, 359–61.

96 Eventually sold on 19 April 1926 to Carl H. Pforzheimer.

97 Pforzheimer, bookseller's note.

98 William Benzie, *Dr. F.J. Furnivall* (Norman, Oklahoma: Pilgrim Books, 1983), pp. 243–4.

99 Approximately equivalent to £7,595 today.

100 Charles Churchill Osborne, *Philip Bourke Marston* (London: Times Book Club, 1926), p. 26 (letter from PBM, 17 April 1886).

101 BL: Ashley 1449; Peattie, 503 (WMR to Frederick James Furnivall, 8 March 1887).

102 Diary, 11 March 1887.

103 BL: Ashley 1449; Peattie, 504 (WMR to Frederick James Furnivall, 8 March 1887).

104 BL: Add 50511 f. 355 (WMR to George Bernard Shaw, 10 November 1887).

105 UBC, 17-18 (William Michael Rossetti, 'Shelley and the Element of Water').

106 Fredeman Family Collection (HRA's type-script notes, in response to Jerome Thale, 'The Third Rossetti', University of Utah, Western Humanities Review X, Summer 1956, 277–84).

107 *SR*, II, pp. 399–400.

108 Ibid., II, pp. 301–2.

109 William Michael Rossetti, 'Leopardi', in *Studies in European Literature being the Taylorian*

Lectures 1889–1899, (Oxford: Clarendon Press, 1900), pp. 55–91.

110 *The Quarterly Review,* 172 (March 1850), 295–336.

111 William Michael Rossetti, 'Leopardi', in *Studies in European Literature being the Taylorian Lectures 1889–1899,* (Oxford: Clarendon Press, 1900), pp. 55–91.

112 D & W, IV, 1906 (DGR to WMR, 25 March 1878).

113 Diary, 10 February 1880.

114 Bodleian, Ms. Facs. d. 280; Harrison, III, 51(CGR to WMR, 26 July 1882) and 218 (CGR to WMR, 4 October 1884).

115 Edmund Gosse, *Sunday Times*, 6 May 1928, p. 8.

116 UBC, 5-7 (FMB to LMBR, 7 August 1887)

117 William Michael Rossetti, *Life of John Keats* (London: Walter Scott, 1887), p.12.

118 WMR to Ford Madox Brown, 30 October 1887, the National Art Library, Victoria and Albert Museum, MSL/1995/14/91.

119 John Wyse Jackson (ed.), *Aristotle at Afternoon Tea: the Rare Oscar Wilde,* (London: Fourth Estate, 1991), pp. 100–3 (reprints 'Two Biographies of Keats' by Oscar Wilde, *Pall Mall Gazette,* 27 September 1887).

120 *DGRFLM*, I, p. xii.

121 Ibid., I, p. 241.

122 Ibid., I, p. 331.

123 Ibid., I, p. 359.

124 Ibid., I, p. 407.

125 Ibid., I, pp. 233 and 278.

126 Ibid., I, p. 423.

127 Diary, 10 April 1895.

128 Merlin Holland and Rupert Hart-Davis (eds), *The Complete Letters of Oscar Wilde,* (London: Fourth Estate, 2000), p. 789.

129 Geoffrey Grigson, *Times Literary Supplement,* 11 April 1980, p. 409.

130 Diary, 28 July 1898.

131 Janet Camp Troxell (ed.), *Three Rossettis: Unpublished Letters to and from Dante Gabriel, Christina, William* (Cambridge: Harvard University Press, 1937) p. 206.

132 *DGRFLM*, I, 128.

133 Ibid., I, p. xii.

134 Joseph Conrad, *Some Reminiscences*, first published in the *English Review*, December 1908–June 1909 and in book form in 1912, later re-titled as *A Personal Record*.

135 William Rossetti at Holman Hunt's funeral. National Library of Scotland, Edinburgh, MS 2922, f.10.

136 National Library of Scotland, Edinburgh, MS 2919.

137 Diary, 8 & 12 September 1910.

Chapter 7: Marriage

1 UBC, 7-6 (WMR to LMBR, 18 September 1874).

2 UBC, 9-2 (LMBR to WMR, 19 September 1876).

3 Delivered at the Taylor Institution, Oxford, published in *Studies in European Literature, Being the Taylorian Lectures 1889–1899* (Oxford: Clarendon Press, 1900), pp. 55–91.

4 *DGRFLM*, I, p. 212.

5 *SR*, I, p. 99.

6 Surtees, no. 54.

7 For this reason Virginia Surtees dates the drawing 1856–8.

8 UBC, 13-3 (WMR to FMLR, 24 July 1855).

9 Harrison, III, 23 (CGR to John H. Ingram, 13 March [1882]).

10 Neither side of the WMR–Henrietta Rintoul correspondence appears to have survived.

11 UBC, 13-3 (WMR to FMLR, 14 August 1858).

12 UBC, 13-3 (WMR to FMLR, 31 July [1856]).

13 *FMBD*, p. 181 (6 July 1856).

14 UBC, 13-3 (WMR to FMLR, 14 August 1858).

15 Harrison, I, 138–9 (CGR to WMR, 30 November 1860).

16 UBC, 13-3 (WMR to FMLR, 27 September [1862]).

17 Harrison, I, 216 (CGR to WMR, 2 [January] 1865).

18 Ibid., I, 219 (CGR to WMR, 15 [January] 1865).

19 'In and about 1855 a friend, Miss (Henrietta) Rintoul, daughter of the then editor of *The Spectator*, took up photography as a diversion, and she made some photographs of Christina, which seem to be the earliest sun-pictures ever taken of her. Two of these photographs remain. In both Christina is seated in a little balcony abutting on the leads of the house; alone in one instance – in the other along with myself. Both of these are very good likenesses of my sister; unfortunately, they have faded to a great extent.' WMR's *Memoir* (pp. lxii–lxiii) prefacing *The Poetical Works of Christina Georgina Rossetti*, 1904. Unfortunately, these photographs may not have survived but see fig. 48.

20 'Mrs. B looks as if she was hiding behind her long pretty black locks, like a King Charles's spaniel behind its hanging ears, & peering out with something between shamefacedness & a leer', WMR to William Allingham, 6 March 1859 (UBC, 26-9). Reproduced in *Some Reminiscences*, I, facing p. 244.

21 Fredeman Family Collection (HRA's notes on William Michael Rossetti).

22 Diary, 25 November, 1904.

23 Diary, 22 March, 1905.

24 Thomas Wright, *Life of John Payne* (London: T. Fisher Unwin, 1919), p. 25.

25 Virginia Surtees (ed.), *The Diaries of George Price Boyce* (Norwich: Real World Publishers, 1980), p. 54.

26 *SR*, II, 424.

27 *DGRFLM*, I, 359

28 Zuzanna Shonfield, *The Precariously Privileged: A Professional Family in Victorian London* (Oxford: Oxford University Press, 1987), p. 86.

29 Fredeman Family Collection (HRA's notes on Charlotte Kirby).

30 Justin McCarthy, *Reminiscences*, 2 vols (London: Chatto & Windus, 1899), pp. 314–18.

31 *SR*, II, 420.

32 UBC, 7-1.

33 Ibid.

34 Thomas Wright, *Life of John Payne* (London: T. Fisher Unwin, 1919), pp. 51, 213.

35 William E. Fredeman, 'Prelude to the Last Decade: Dante Gabriel Rossetti in the summer of 1872', *Bulletin of the John Rylands Library*, 53 (no. 1, autumn, 1970 and no. 2, spring 1971), p. 87 (Dr Hake to W.B. Scott, 23 August 1872).

36 UBC, 13-4 (WMR to FMLR, 15 May 1873).

37 UBC, 7-6 (WMR to LMB, 22 May 1873).

38 William Bell Scott's passport and note of the route in 1873, with thanks to the Fredeman Family Collection.

39 UBC, 13-4 (WMR to FMLR, 10 June 1873).

40 Peattie, p. 308 (WMR to FMLR, 9 July [1873])

41 UBC, 5-4 (FMB to LMB, 7 July 1873).

42 UBC, 5-4 (FMB to LMB, 8 July 1873).

43 Peattie, pp. 308–9 (WMR to FMLR, 9 July [1873]).

44 Princeton, BL RP 5907 (WMR to Mrs Heimann, 6 March [1874]).

45 *DGRFLM*, I, 32.

46 UBC, 12-16 (HRA's handwritten Reminiscences); *SR*, I, 6.

47 UBC, 6-14 (FMLR to Eliza Polidori, 10 July 1873).

48 William E. Fredeman, 'The Letters of Pictor Ignotus: William Bell Scott's Correspondence with Alice Boyd, 1859–1884: II', *John Rylands Library Bulletin*, 58 (1975–6), 306–52 (p. 307).

49 Ibid., p. 308.

50 UBC, 7-2 (Cathy Madox Brown Hueffer to LMB [?July 1873]).

51 UBC, 7-3 (Lizzie Cooper to LMB, August [1873?]).

52 University of Leeds, Brotherton Library, Gosse Papers (William Bell Scott to Edmund Gosse, n.d. [1873]):

> My name begins with W,
> And hers begins with L., –
> She's not without her merits,
> And I like her pretty well.

also reported by Julian Osgood Field, *Things I Shouldn't Tell* (London: E. Nash & Grayson, 1924), p. 77, and similarly in Kerrison Preston (ed.), *Letters from Graham Robertson* (London: Hamish Hamilton, 1953), p. 268 (15 April 1932).

53 D&W, III, 1187–8 (DGR to WMR, 10 July 1873).
54 Harrison, I, 433 (CGR to WMR, 10 July 1873); *CGRFL*, p. 40.
55 Harrison, I, 434 (CGR to LMB, 10 July 1873); *CGRFL*, p. 39.
56 Teresa Newman & Ray Watkinson, *Ford Madox Brown* (London: Chatto & Windus, 1991), p. 168.
57 Virginia Surtees (ed.), *Diaries of George Price Boyce*, (Norwich: Real World Publishers, 1980), p. 60 (30 March 1874).
58 D&W, III, 1268 (DGR to WMR [13 March 1874]); *DGRFLM*, p. 306.
59 Norman Kelvin (ed.), *Collected Letters of William Morris* (Princeton: Princeton University Press, 1984–96), III, 264n (William Morris to Louisa Baldwin, 26 March 1874).
60 UBC, 9-1, (LMB to FMB, 19 July 1869).
61 *SR*, I, 217.
62 Ibid., I, 214–15.
63 Virginia Surtees (ed.), *The Diaries of George Price Boyce* (Norwich: Real World Publishers, 1980), p. 60 (26 March 1874).
64 UBC, 7-2.
65 UBC, 18-4 (1908 Inventory, item 401).
66 Ibid., item 327.
67 Ibid., item 496.
68 Diary, 3 March 1880, notes when the dish was stolen.
69 UBC, 7-5 (Augusta Webster to LMB, 14 March 1874).
70 UBC, 7-2 (Edmund Gosse to LMB, 27 March 1874).
71 Peattie, p. 312, n.1.
72 Private collection.
73 *SR*, II, 421.
74 UBC, 13-4 (WMR to FMLR, 1 April 1874).
75 UBC, 17-1 (WMR's Travel Diary 1874).
76 UBC, 18-4 (1908 Inventory, item 397).
77 UBC, 12-6 (WMR to Oliver Madox Brown, 4 April 1874).
78 UBC, 13-4 (WMR to FMLR, 25 April 1874).
79 D&W, III, 1279 (DGR to FMB, 8 May [1874]).
80 Ibid., III, 1280–1 (DGR to FMLR, 17 May 1874).
81 Ibid., III, 1292 (DGR to Thomas Gordon Hake, 9 June 1874).
82 Agresti, p. 12.
83 Approximately equivalent to £5,700 today.
84 Now no longer standing.
85 UBC, 12-16 (unpublished reminiscences by HRA).
86 I am grateful to Robert Wright Books, Ontario, Canada, for generously providing me with a copy of the original lease. It was signed by WMR and the lessor B.B. Williams in the presence of the clerk to WMR's solicitor, J. Anderson Rose.
87 UBC, 12-16 (unpublished reminiscences by Helen Rossetti Angeli, pp. 16–19).
88 Jan Marsh, *Dante Gabriel Rossetti: painter and poet* (London: Weidenfeld & Nicolson, 1999), p. 481.
89 *SR*, II, 422.
90 Bryn Mawr College Archives, Maser Collection (CGR to 'My dear Friend', probably Caroline Gemmer, 3 January 1888).
91 Bryn Mawr College Archives, Maser Collection (CGR to Caroline Gemmer, Saturday evening. [2 January 1875]) and Harrison, II, 35–6.
92 William M. Hardinge, 'A Reminiscence of Mrs W.M. Rossetti', *Magazine of Art*, 18 (1895)), 341–6 (p. 345).
93 *SR*, II, 422–3.
94 Ibid., II, 432–3.
95 UBC, 9-2 (LMBR to WMR, 4 January 1876).
96 UBC, 7-6 (WMR to LMBR, 5 January 1876).
97 UBC, 7-6 (WMR to LMBR, 7 January 1876).
98 UBC, 7-6 (WMR to LMBR, 18 April 1876).
99 Harrison, III, 154 (CGR to WMR, 23 August 1883).
100 UBC, 9-2 (LMBR to WMR, 23 August 1878).
101 BL: Ashley 1446; Peattie, p. 327 (WMR to A.C. Swinburne, 15 October [1875]).
102 *The Athenaeum*, no. 2521, 19 February 1876, pp. 263–4.
103 BL: Ashley 1446; Peattie, p. 329 (WMR to A.C. Swinburne, 2 November [1875]).
104 Diary, 12 to 25 April 1881.
105 UBC, 9-2 (LMBR to WMR [12 September 1876]).
106 UBC, 9-2 (LMBR to WMR [15 September 1876]).
107 Agresti, p. 27.
108 Peattie, p. 354, n. 6 (WMR to LMBR, 17 January 1887).
109 UBC, 7-6 (WMR to LMBR, 16 September [1876]).
110 UBC, 9-2 (LMBR to WMR, 24 April 1876).
111 UBC, 9-2 (LMBR to WMR, 20 April 1876).
112 UBC, 7-6 (WMR to LMBR, 20 April 1876).
113 UBC, 9-2 (LMBR to WMR, 21 April 1876).
114 UBC, 9-2 (LMBR to WMR, 23 April 1876).
115 I am grateful to Jonathon Green for this information and Jonathon Green, *Cassell's Dictionary of Slang* (London: Cassell, 1998) p. 110.
116 UBC, 7-8 (WMR to LMBR, 13 August 1878).
117 UBC, 9-2 (LMBR to WMR, 10 September 1876).
118 UBC, 9-2 (LMBR to WMR, 17 September 1876).
119 UBC, 9-3 (LMBR to WMR, 1 October 1884).
120 UBC, 12-14 (WMR to HRA, 9 April 1905).
121 UBC, 9-2 (LMBR to WMR, 26 April 1876).
122 UBC, 9-2 (LMBR to WMR, 21 September 1876).
123 UBC, 9-2 (LMBR to WMR, 19 September 1876).
124 UBC, 9-2 (LMBR to WMR, 23 August 1878).

125 UBC, 9-2 (LMBR to WMR, 28 August 1878).
126 UBC, 9-2 (LMBR to WMR, 31 August 1878).
127 UBC, 9-2 (LMBR to WMR, 2 September 1878).
128 Zuzanna Shonfield, *A Professional Family in Victorian London* (Oxford: Oxford University Press, 1987), pp. 88–9.
129 UBC, 9-2 (LMBR to WMR, 7 August 1880).
130 D&W, III, 1274 (DGR to FMLR, 23 April 1874).
131 UBC, 7-6 (WMR to LMBR, 6 January 1876).
132 UBC, 17-5.
133 Peattie, p. 407 (WMR to LMBR, 3 April [1882] 11.15); Peattie, p. 410 (6 April [1882] 9 ½ p.m.); Peattie, p. 413 (8 April [1882]); Peattie, p. 426 (23 June [1882] 10 ¼ a.m.)
134 Peattie, pp. 426–7 (WMR to LMBR, 23 June [1882] 10 ¼ a.m.).
135 UBC, 7-10, WMR to LMBR, 21 June 1882.
136 UBC, 7-10, WMR to LMBR, 27 June 1882.
137 Diary, Saturday, 1 March 1879.
138 Diary, 20 March 1880.
139 Peattie, p. 434 (WMR to LMBR, 17 August 1882, noon).
140 Fredeman Family Collection (HRA, 'WMR – Swinburne – Whitman', undated MS).
141 Diary, 19 April 1880.
142 Diary, 8 January 1881.
143 Later Sir Algernon Edward West, KCB, Chairman of the Board of Inland Revenue, November 1881–May 1892.
144 UBC, 9-1 (LMBR to FMB, 7 November 1883).
145 Diary, 21 June 1887.
146 William E. Fredeman, 'The Letters of Pictor Ignotus: William Bell Scott's Correspondence with Alice Boyd, 1859–1884: II', *John Rylands Library Bulletin*, 58 (1975-76), 306–52 (p.322).
147 UBC, 7-1 (Ms. List by LMBR).
148 The author Vernon Lee who had published her successful *Studies of the Eighteenth Century in Italy* in 1880.
149 Diary, 22 June 1881.
150 I.C. Willis (ed.), *The Letters of Vernon Lee* (privately printed, 1937), p. 63–4 (VL to her mother, 16 June 1882).
151 Ibid., p. 87 (VL to her mother, 22 June 1881).
152 Ford Madox Hueffer, 'The Younger Madox Browns', *Artist*, 19 (February 1897), 49–55 (p. 49).
153 UBC, 13-14 (WMR to Mary Rossetti, 8 August 1885 and 27 September 1885).
154 Juliet M. Soskice, *Chapters from Childhood* (London: Selwyn & Blount, 1921), p. 5 and pp. 20–1.
155 Agresti, p. 22.
156 UBC, 12-16 (unpublished reminiscences by HRA).
157 Diary, 16 September 1880.
158 Arthur, Helen and Mary Rossetti and Juliet Hueffer, later Soskice, Lucy's niece and Cathy's daughter.
159 UBC, 9-1 (LMBR to FMB, 3 March 1884).
160 Juliet M. Soskice, *Chapters from Childhood* (London: Selwyn & Blount, 1921), p.7.
161 Transcript of BBC Radio interview with Helen Rossetti Angeli *c.* 1963. Private collection.
162 UBC, 13-14 (WMR to Mary Rossetti, 2 May 1892).
163 Prince Peter Kropotkin (1842–1921), Russian anarchist and émigré, author of *Memoirs of a Revolutionist*, 1899.
164 Clemence Louise Michel (1830-1905), French Communist and anarchist, associated with Kropotkin.
165 Transcript of BBC Radio interview with Helen Rossetti Angeli *c.* 1963. Private collection.
166 UBC, 12-16 (unpublished reminiscences by HRA, p. 20).
167 Austin, Swinburne A Misc. 17600 (LMBR to Algernon Swinburne, n.d. [Jan/Feb 1883]).
168 UBC, 7-5 (Marie Spartali Stillman to LMBR, 4 December 1883).
169 UBC, 12-16 (unpublished reminiscences by HRA, pp. 21–2).
170 UBC, 8-2 (WMR to LMBR, 31 March 1886).
171 UBC, 9-7 (LMBR to WMR, 17 January 1888).
172 Diary, 17 January 1888.
173 Diary, 17 September 1890.
174 UBC, 12-16 (unpublished reminiscences by HRA); Olive Garnett's unpublished diary, with thanks to Barry Johnson and Caroline White.
175 Hardinge's dates, with thanks to Balliol College Library, Oxford.
176 Billie Andrew Inman, 'Estrangement and Connection: Walter Pater, Benjamin Jowett, and William M. Hardinge', in Laurel Brake and Ian Small (eds), *Pater in the 1990s* (Greensboro, NC: ELT Press, 1991).
177 William Money Hardinge, *Troy* (Oxford: T. Shrimpton, 1876), p.6.
178 Marion Mainwaring, *Mysteries of Paris: The Quest for Morton Fullerton*, (Hanover and London: University Press of New England, 2001), p. 41.
179 Tom Stoppard, *The Invention of Love* (London and Boston: Faber and Faber, 1997), pp. 9 and 46.
180 William M. Hardinge, 'Note on the Louvre Sonnets of Rossetti', *Temple Bar*, 91 (March 1891), 433–43.
181 *SR*, II, 494.
182 UBC, 17-12 (note dated 1898, appended to thoughts on the poet James Thomson by William Michael Rossetti, 14 July 1888).
183 UBC, 7-5 (Marie Spartali Stillman to LMBR, 27 December [1883?]).
184 Barry C. Johnson (ed.), *Tea and Anarchy! The Bloomsbury Diary of Olive Garnett 1890-1893*

(London: Bartletts Press, 1989) p. 139 (22 December 1892).

185 William M. Hardinge, 'A Reminiscence of Mrs. W.M. Rossetti', *Magazine of Art*, 18 (1895), 341–6.

186 Ibid., p. 342.

187 Diary, 2 March 1893.

188 Henry James, 'Ibsen's New Play', *Pall Mall Gazette*, 17 February 1893, quoted by Philip Horne, *Henry James: A Life in Letters* (Harmondsworth: Allen Lane, 1999), p. 256.

189 Diary, 'M.March 6 to S.June 17' 1893.

190 UBC, 7-2 (MS note by HRA, Woodstock, May 1964, attached to an office copy of Lucy's will).

191 Peattie, p. 573 (WMR to CGR, 18 April 1894).

192 Approximately equivalent to £190,340 today.

193 UBC, 22-2 (W. Holman Hunt to WMR, 15 April 1894).

Chapter 8: Radicals

1 W.J. Stillman, *Autobiography of a Journalist* (London: Grant Richards, 1901), p. 192.

2 W. Holman Hunt, *Pre-Raphaelitism and the Pre-Raphaelite Brotherhood*, 2 vols (London, Macmillan, 1905), I, 154–5.

3 Agresti, p. 9. Unlike his father, William was not a Freemason.

4 T. Gordon Hake, *Memoirs of Eighty Years* (London: Richard Bentley, 1892), p. 230.

5 Agresti, p. 20 and quoted by Felicita Jurlaro, *Christina Georgina Rossetti* (London: Excalibur Press, 1990), p. 75.

6 Jan Marsh, *Dante Gabriel Rossetti: Painter and Poet* (London: Weidenfeld & Nicolson, 1999), p. 65.

7 *DGRFLM*, I, 71.

8 Ibid., I, 158.

9 Ibid., I, 408.

10 *SR*, I, 122.

11 Peattie, p. 286 (WMR to Walt Whitman, 31 March 1872).

12 For details of pictures William modelled for, see chapter six, note 11.

13 UBC, 7-6 (WMR to LMBR, 12 September [18]76).

14 Peattie, p. 286 (WMR to Walt Whitman, 31 March 1872).

15 Peattie, p. 669 (WMR to Marchese Antonio di San Giuliano, 12 September 1909).

16 Diary, 9 February 1881.

17 UBC, 7-9 (WMR to LMBR, 14 February 1881).

18 UBC, 7-9 (WMR to LMBR, 15 February 1881).

19 D&W, IV, 1865 (DGR to LMBR [12 April 1881]).

20 Peattie, pp. 396–7 (WMR to DGR, 13 April [1881]).

21 D&W, IV, 1870 (DGR to WMR [14 April 1881]).

22 *DS*, I, xix.

23 Peattie, p. 186 (WMR to Walt Whitman, 8 December 1867).

24 William Michael Rossetti, 'English Opinion on the American War', *Atlantic Monthly*, 17 February 1866, pp. 129–30.

25 Diary, 2 November 1866.

26 *DS*, I, xxvii.

27 Ibid., I, xxxiv.

28 Ibid., II, xviii.

29 Ibid., II, xxiii.

30 Ibid., II, xxviii.

31 Lucy Madox Rossetti, *Mrs Shelley* (London: Allen Lane, 1890).

32 UBC, 8-16 (FMB to LMBR, 2 June 1887).

33 UBC, 22-4 (John Ingram to WMR, 11 January 1886).

34 Approximately equivalent to £3,300 today.

35 UBC, 22-4 (WMR to John Ingram, 2 February 1886).

36 *Mrs Shelley*, p. 19.

37 Ibid., p. 23.

38 Ibid., p. 27.

39 Ibid., p. 2.

40 Ibid., pp. 7–8.

41 In the 'Art and Music' section of signatories. Information from the Fawcett Library, London.

42 *Mrs Shelley*, p. 8.

43 Diary, 29 January 1879.

44 *Mrs Shelley*, p. 3.

45 Ibid., pp. 77, 115.

46 UBC, 9-6 (LMBR to WMR, 8 May 1887).

47 *Mrs Shelley*, p. 124.

48 Ibid., p. 88.

49 Ibid., p. 132.

50 Ibid., p. 116.

51 Ibid., p. 130.

52 Ibid., p. 125.

53 William Michael Rossetti, 'The Wives of the Poets', *Atlantic Monthly*, 47 (April 1881), 518–25 (p. 522).

54 UBC, 24-5 (Gertrude Stewart, Secretary of the Central National Society for Women's Suffrage, to WMR, 24 January 1894).

55 *SR*, II, 433.

56 Diary, 1 September 1887.

57 Diary, 22 November 1887.

58 James H. Coombs et al (eds), *A Pre-Raphaelite Friendship: The Correspondence of William Holman Hunt and John Lucas Tupper* (Ann Arbor: UMI Research Press, 1986), p. 106 (Tupper to Hunt, 3 February 1870).

59 Diary, 1 November 1887.

60 Bodleian, Ms.Eng.lett.e.32 (LMBR to John Cordy Jeaffreson, 12 December 1887).

61 'The Life and Letters of Mary Wollstonecraft Shelley. By Mrs. Julian Marshall. 2 vols (Bentley & Son)', unsigned review by W. M. Rossetti, *Athenaeum*, 23 November 1889, vol. 3239, pp. 699–701.

62 Mrs Julian Marshall, *The Life and Letters of Mary Wollstonecraft Shelley*, 2 vols (London: Bentley & Son, 1889), II, 322.

63 Bodleian Ms.Eng.lett.e.32 (LMBR to John Cordy Jeaffreson, 17 April 1890).
64 UBC, 9-8 (LMBR to WMR, 2 June 1890).
65 UBC, 9-8 (LMBR to WMR, 5 May 1890).
66 UBC, 9-6 (LMBR to WMR, 2 June 1890).
67 *Mrs Shelley*, p. 9.
68 Ibid., p. 91.
69 Ibid., p. 53.
70 Ibid., p. 2.
71 Ibid., p. 3.
72 Ibid., p. 15.
73 Ibid., p. 38.
74 Ibid., p. 40.
75 Ibid., p. 116.
76 Ibid., p. 223.
77 Ibid., p. 229.
78 Ibid., p. 84.
79 Ibid., pp. 229–30.
80 Ibid., p. 218.
81 Ibid., p. 216.
82 Ibid., p. 97.
83 Ibid., p. 169.
84 Ibid., p. 130.
85 Ibid., p. 186.
86 UBC, 5-7 (FMB to LMBR, Sunday n.d. [Autumn 1887?]).
87 *Mrs Shelley*, p. 102.
88 Ibid., p. 109.
89 Ibid., pp. 109–10.
90 Ibid., p. 104.
91 Ibid., p. 106.
92 Ibid., p. 153.
93 Ibid., p. 203.
94 Ibid., p. 186.
95 Ibid., p. 207

Chapter 9: The Patient

1 Information from Dr Angelo Bloise, Dirigente: Settore demografico, Sanremo, 18 March 1999.
2 UBC, 9-7 (LMBR to WMR, 24 January 1889).
3 *The Odes of Horace*, trans. by James Michie (London: Hart-Davis, 1964), Book I, no. xxiii.
4 *SR*, II, 444.
5 Information from Mary Rossetti Rutterford, 21 August 2000.
6 Barry C. Johnson (ed.), *Tea and Anarchy! The Bloomsbury Diary of Olive Garnett 1890-1893* (London: Bartletts Press, 1989), pp. 127–8.
7 Information from R.J. Donaldson and L.J. Donaldson, *Essential Public Health Medicine* (Dordrecht and London: Kluwer, 1993) and Walter Pagel and others, *Pulmonary Tuberculosis*, 4th ed. (London: Oxford University Press, 1964), and with thanks to Dr Elspeth Macdonald.
8 *FMBD*, p. 65 (1 July 1849).
9 *Retrospect.*
10 UBC, 13-4 (WMR to FMLR, 27 September [1862?]).
11 UBC, 6-14 (FMLR to WMR, 16 June 1873).
12 Peattie, p. 317 (3 October [1874]).
13 *CGRFL*, p. 47 (CGR to DGR, 28 [September 1874]).
14 *Alphonse Daudet in the Land of Pain*, ed. and trans. by Julian Barnes (London: Jonathan Cape, 2002), pp. 8, 19.
15 D&W, III, 1320 (DGR to Charlotte Polidori, 13 November 1874).
16 Ibid., III, 1326 (DGR to Thomas Hake, 20 December 1874).
17 Diary, 16 May 1877.
18 Diary, 5 January 1878.
19 UBC, 18-1 (William Michael Rossetti's brown silk notebook).
20 Diary, 28 February 1882 and 24 March 1882.
21 Fitzwilliam Museum, Gen Ser large MS 1700-1977 (Dr William Gill's notes appended to WMR's verses 'My Doctor', March 1901).
22 UBC, 7-10 (WMR to LMBR, 2 July 1882).
23 *CGRFL*, p. 228.
24 Peattie, p. 446 (WMR to FMB, 14 April 1883).
25 *Posthumous Portrait of Michael Rossetti, his Pillows Strewn with Snowdrops* by Lucy Madox Brown Rossetti, 1883, coloured chalks, 12 ¼ × 18", 1908 Inventory, item 135; Wightwick Manor catalogue of pictures, no. 61. Unlocated.
26 Bodleian, Ms.Facs.c. 96 (Diary of Frances Rossetti, 12 February 1883).
27 UBC, 9-3 (LMBR to WMR, 30 August 1884 and 1 September 1884).
28 *SR*, II, 434.
29 Arthur Hill Hassall, *The Narrative of a Busy Life: An Autobiography* (London: Longmans, Green, 1893), p. 99.
30 Diary, 26 July 1886.
31 UBC, 9-1 (LMBR to FMB, 13 November 1886).
32 UBC, 9-5 (LMBR to WMR, 18 November 1886).
33 UBC, 9-5 (LMBR to WMR, 2 December 1886).
34 UBC, 9-5 (LMBR to WMR, 17 December 1886).
35 UBC, 9-5 (LMBR to WMR, 25 December 1886).
36 Nathaniel Hawthorne, *The Marble Faun* (New York: Dell, 1960), p. 83.
37 Duncan Fallowell, *To Noto or London to Sicily in a Ford* (London: Dent, 1989), p. 102.
38 Augustus Hare, *The Rivieras* (London: George Allen, 1897), chapter four.
39 Alex. Ostrowicz, *A Stranger's Guide to San Remo* (Munich: Bruckmann, 1894), p. 5.
40 Edward Isaac Sparks, *The Riviera: Sketches of the Health Resorts of the North Mediterranean Coasts of France and Italy* (London: J. & A. Churchill, 1879), p. 332.
41 Arthur Hill Hassall, *San Remo and the Western*

Riviera (London: Longmans, Green, 1879), p. 136.

42 Leon Edel (ed.), *Letters of Henry James*, 4 vols (Cambridge, Mass: Belknap Press of Harvard University Press, 1974–84), II, 348.

43 Emanuele Kanceff (ed.), *Immagini di San Remo nel mondo* (San Remo: Centro Interuniversitario di Ricerche sul Viaggio in Italia, 1998), p. 47.

44 The Rev. Hugh Macmillan, *The Riviera*, 2nd ed. (London: J.S.Virtue, 1892), p. 213.

45 Arthur Hill Hassall, *San Remo and the Western Riviera* (London: Longmans, Green, 1879), p. 33.

46 Alex. Ostrowicz, *A Stranger's Guide to San Remo* (Munich: Bruckmann, 1894), p. 33.

47 Giovanni Ruffini, *Doctor Antonio* (Edinburgh & London: Constable, 1855), p. 120.

48 Ibid., p. 120.

49 *SR*, II, 436.

50 UBC, 9-6 (LMBR to WMR, 7 March 1887).

51 UBC, 9-6 (LMBR to WMR, 18 March 1887).

52 *SR*, I, 394 and Diary, 6 July 1887.

53 I.C. Willis (ed.), *The Letters of Vernon Lee*, (privately printed, 1937), pp. 254–5 (VL to her mother, 8 July 1887).

54 *DGRFLM*, p. 403.

55 UBC, 5-6 (FMB to LMBR, 1 December 1885).

56 WMR to FMB, 22 September 1887, the National Art Library, Victoria and Albert Museum, MSL/1995/14/91.

57 UBC, 7-3.

58 UBC, 9-1 (LMBR to FMB, June 1888?).

59 *SR,* II, 488.

60 UBC, 8-5.

61 Diary, 8 November 1888.

62 Michel Fabré, *Pau pas à pas* (Rohan: Horvath, 1985) and information from Christine Juliat, Archives Municipales de Pau.

63 Dr Alexander Taylor, *Climates for Invalids*, 3rd ed. (London, 1861).

64 Joseph Duloum, *Les Anglais dans Les Pyrénées et les débuts du tourisme européen 1739–1896* (Tarbes: Amis du musée pyrénéen de Lourdes, 1970).

65 UBC, 9-7 (LMBR to WMR, 11 November 1888).

66 *SR*, II, 438.

67 UBC, 9-7 (LMBR to WMR, 11 November 1888).

68 Bodleian Ms Don e.76 f 155 (WMR to F.G. Stephens, 13 November 1888).

69 UBC, 8-5 (WMR to LMBR, 24 November 1888).

70 UBC, 8-5 (WMR to LMBR, 13 November 1888).

71 UBC, 8-5 (WMR to LMBR, 17 November 1888).

72 UBC, 8-5 (WMR to LMBR, 25 November 1888).

73 UBC, 8-5 (WMR to LMBR, 16 November 1888, 11 a.m.).

74 UBC, 8-5 (WMR to LMBR, 29 December 1888, 11 $\frac{1}{2}$).

75 UBC, 8-5 (WMR to LMBR, 31st December 1988, 1 p.m.).

76 UBC, 9-7.

77 UBC, 8-6.

78 *SR*, II, 438.

79 UBC, 8-6 (WMR to LMBR, 11 January 1889, 1 $\frac{1}{4}$).

80 *SR*, II, 438–9.

81 '3 Studies of Sea & Sky, watercolour, at Biarritz' and 'Sketch at Biarritz, watercolour' by Lucy Madox Brown Rossetti, 1908 Inventory, items 106 and 476[2]. After her death William gave two of Lucy's Biarritz sketches to their family friend, Mrs Allport, who had admired them. (WMR's MS Diary, 15 June 1898).

82 Information from Mrs Phyllis M. Marshall, The Stone Gallery, Burford, 31 May 1997, picture now unlocated.

83 UBC, 9-1 (LMBR to WMR, 21 January 1889).

84 UBC, 9-1 (LMBR to WMR, 21 January 1889).

85 UBC, 8-6 (WMR to LMBR, 17 January 1889, 4 $\frac{3}{4}$).

86 UBC, 8-6 (WMR to LMBR, 19 January 1889, 4 p.m.).

87 UBC, 8-6 (WMR to LMBR, 20 January 1889, 12 $\frac{3}{4}$).

88 UBC, 8-6, Peattie, pp. 523–4 (WMR to LMBR, 20 January 1889, 4 $\frac{1}{4}$).

89 UBC, 8-6 (WMR to LMBR, 26 February 1889, 12 $\frac{1}{4}$).

90 UBC, 8-6; Peattie, p. 524 (WMR to LMBR, 22 January 1889, 11 $\frac{1}{2}$ a.m.).

91 UBC, 8-6 (WMR to LMBR, 10 March 1889, 12 $\frac{1}{4}$).

92 UBC, 5-7 (FMB to LMBR, 29 January 1889).

93 Approximately equivalent to £20,000 today.

94 Diary, 3 February 1889; Peattie, p. 529, n.3.

95 UBC, 8-6 (WMR to LMBR, 26 January 1889, 11 $\frac{3}{4}$).

96 UBC, 5-7 (FMB to LMBR, 29 January 1889).

97 UBC, 8-6 (WMR to LMBR, 28 January 1889, noon).

98 UBC, 9-7 (LMBR to WMR, 24 January 1889).

99 I.C. Willis (ed.), *The Letters of Vernon Lee* (privately printed, 1937), p. 75.

100 UBC, 12-16 (Helen Rossetti Angeli, unpublished autobiographical notes).

101 UBC, 8-6 (WMR to LMBR, 25 January 1889, noon).

102 Ford Madox Hueffer, *Ancient Lights and Certain New Reflections* (London: Chapman and Hall, 1911), p. 104.

103 Peattie, p.526 (WMR to LMBR, 23 January 1889, 10 ¼ a.m.).

104 Diary, 26 November 1881.

105 Diary, 4 March 1889; Peattie, p. 532, n.1; UBC, 8-6 (WMR to LMBR, 10 March 1889, 12 ¼).

106 UBC, 8-6 (WMR to LMBR, 30 January 1889, 12 ¾).

107 William Michael Rossetti, *Dante Gabriel Rossetti as Designer and Writer* (London: Cassell, 1889).

108 UBC, 8-6 (WMR to LMBR, 7 March 1889, 11 ¼).

109 BL: Ashley 1448; Peattie, p. 533 (WMR to T.J. Wise, 11 March 1889).

110 *SR*, II, 439.

111 UBC, 8-6 (WMR to LMBR, 10 March 1889, 12 ¼).

112 UBC, 5-7 (FMB to LMBR, 17 March 1889).

113 UBC, 8-6 (WMR to LMBR, 23 April 1889, 9 ¼ p.m.).

114 UBC, 8-6 (WMR to LMBR, 30 April 1889, 7 ½).

115 Diary, 13, 24, 25 August 1890.

116 UBC, 9-8 (LMBR to WMR, 24 August 1891).

117 Peattie, p. 560 (WMR to Frederic George Stephens, 6 July 1892).

118 Barry C. Johnson (ed.), *Tea and Anarchy! The Bloomsbury Diary of Olive Garnett 1890 – 1893* (London: Bartletts Press, 1989), p. 139.

119 Ibid., pp. 144–7.

120 Ibid., p. 176.

121 UBC, 9-3 (LMBR to WMR, 25 July 1883).

122 For discussion of Lucy's will see chapter seven, pp. 249-52.

123 Barry C. Johnson (ed.), *Tea and Anarchy! The Bloomsbury Diary of Olive Garnett 1890 – 1893* (London: Bartletts Press, 1989), pp. 180–1.

124 Peattie, p. 563 (WMR to Thomas Wise, 19 June 1893).

125 *Alphonse Daudet in the Land of Pain*, ed. and transl. by Julian Barnes (London: Jonathan Cape, 2002), pp. 19 and 76.

126 Barry C. Johnson (ed.), *Tea and Anarchy! The Bloomsbury Diary of Olive Garnett 1890 – 1893* (London: Bartletts Press, 1989), pp. 196–7, 202.

127 W.E. Fredeman, 'A Pre-Raphaelite Gazette: The Penkill Letters of Arthur Hughes to W.B. Scott and Alice Boyd', *Bulletin of the John Rylands Library,* 50 (Autumn 1967), 55.

128 Diary, 25 July 1893.

129 HLRO, Stow Hill Papers, STH/BH/2/3-6 (Ford Madox Brown, *To Italy in* [47?]).

130 Barry C. Johnson (ed.), *Tea and Anarchy! The Bloomsbury Diary of Olive Garnett 1890 – 1893* (London: Bartletts Press, 1989), pp. 184–5.

131 UBC, 9-10 (LMBR to WMR, 10 October 1893).

132 Thomas Dormandy, *The White Death: A History of Tuberculosis* (London: Hambledon, 1999), p. 194.

133 UBC, 9-10 (LMBR to WMR, 24/25 October 1893).

134 UBC, 9-10 (LMBR to WMR, 10 November 1893).

135 UBC, 9-10 (LMBR to WMR, 31 December 1893).

136 UBC, 9-10 (LMBR to WMR, 18 February 1894).

137 Francesco De Nicola (ed.), Giovanni Ruffini, *Ritorno a Sanremo/Sanremo revisited* (Genoa: De Ferrari Editore, 1998), p. 56, first published in *Carlino and other Stories* (Leipzig: Tauchnitz, 1872).

138 Gastone Lombardi, *Sanremo ai tempi del Liberty* (Sanremo: Editore Colombo, 2001), p. 199, translation supplied by Valerie Falchi.

139 Helen Rossetti Angeli to the editor of the *Times Literary Supplement*, 2 July 1964, p. 571.

140 Berg (WMR to Cathy Hueffer, 22 March 1894, 9 ½ a.m.).

141 Susan Sontag, *Illness as Metaphor* (Harmondsworth: Penguin, 1983), p. 18.

142 UBC, 18-1 (WMR's notebook).

143 Peattie, p. 574 (WMR to CGR, 18 April 1894).

144 UBC, 9-4 (LMBR to WMR, 8 January 1887).

145 In fact *The Duet* was first exhibited at the Royal Academy in 1870 and later shown at the Dudley Gallery 1877.

Chapter 10: Coda

1 *SR*, II, 528.

2 'Ford Madox Brown: Characteristics' by William Michael Rossetti, Century Guild *Hobby Horse*, vol. I (1886), 48–54.

3 Ford Madox Hueffer, *Ancient Lights and Certain New Reflections* (London: Chapman and Hall, 1911), pp. 224–5.

4 See MS Diary, 13 March 1878, 'Hunt I regard as on the whole my dearest friend, next only to Brown.'

5 Diary, 10 April 1895.

6 *SR*, II, 553.

7 Peattie, p. 443; BL: Ashley B. 3864 (WMR to Algernon Charles Swinburne, 13 February 1883).

8 Quoted by John Collins, *The Two Forgers* (Aldershot: Scolar Press, 1992), p. 193 (Harry Buxton Forman to WMR, 21 January 1904).

9 *SR*, II, 553.

10 William's will, made in 1909, left bequests according to Christina's instructions: £1,000 to the Society for the Propagation of the Gospel in Foreign Parts, £500 to All Saints Sisterhood, Margaret Street (where Maria Rossetti had been a nun), and £500 to the Rev. Charles Gutch of St Cyprian's Church, Dorset Square, for distribution to charities in his parish.

11 Richard M. Ludwig (ed.), *Letters of Ford Madox Ford* (Princeton: Princeton University Press, 1965), p. 7 (Ford Madox Ford to Edward Garnett [1894?]).

12 Ford Madox Hueffer, *Ancient Lights and Certain New Reflections* (London: Chapman and Hall, 1911), p. 225.
13 *SR*, II, 532–3.
14 BL: Ashley 1451; Cecil Y. Lang (ed.), *The Letters of Swinburne*, 6 vols (New Haven: Yale University Press, 1959–62), VI, 176 (A.C. Swinburne to WMR, 25 January 1904).
15 Diary, 4 and 9 November 1894.
16 Diary, 29 December 1894.
17 A hard cancer.
18 Diary, 30 December 1894.
19 Diary, 31 December 1894.
20 Diary, 2 January 1895.
21 *SR*, II, 542.
22 Peattie, p. 443; BL: Ashley B. 3864 (WMR to Algernon Charles Swinburne, 13 February 1883).
23 Housekeeper.
24 Diary, 1 April 1895.
25 Diary, 28 May 1902.
26 Peattie, p. 408 (WMR to LMBR, 5 April [1882]). *Paradiso*, 17:24, translated by Laurence Binyon.
27 Diary, 3–9 July 1895.
28 Diary, 11 January 1895.
29 Diary, 1 August 1896.
30 Diary, 12 March 1903.
31 Bodleian, Ms. Don e 76 f 167 (WMR to F.G. Stephens, 30 August 1894).
32 Diary, 25 May 1895.
33 Diary, 16 January 1903.
34 Diary, 20 March 1903.
35 Diary, 17 September 1895.
36 *SR*, I, 6–7.
37 Diary, 30 September 1898. The house was demolished in 1964, although Polidoris Lane and Rossetti Place in the village still record the connection. Another cottage also called Polidori's Cottage stands today in front of the site of the original house. The pond may still be seen.
38 William Michael Rossetti (ed.), *Bibliography of the Works of Dante Gabriel Rossetti* (London: Ellis, 1905). Previous versions published in 'The Bibliographer', New York, December 1902, January 1903, April 1903.
39 Augusta Webster, *Mother and Daughter: An Uncompleted Sonnet Sequence* (London: Macmillan, 1895) with introduction by WMR.
40 Diary, 14 February 1895.
41 Fitzwilliam Museum, Gen. Ser. Large MS. 1700-1977 (Three of six verses 'My Doctor' presented to Dr Gill by WMR together with a copy of *Preraphaelite Diaries and Letters*, 'To William Gill with affectionate regards, W.M. Rossetti Oct 1900').
42 Dr Gill's note to this verse, March 1901.
43 Diary, 17 September 1901.
44 Diary, 29 December 1903.
45 Diary, 17 May 1904.
46 Bodleian, Ms. Don e 76 f. 222 (WMR to F.G. Stephens, 23 April 1901).
47 UBC, 21-15 (Ford Madox [Ford] Hueffer to WMR, 13 January 1904, 25 February 1905, 19 January 1909); Diary, 14 and 15 January 1904 and 3 October 1904.
48 Peattie, p. 644 (WMR to Ford Madox Hueffer, 28 October 1904).
49 Diary, 13 August 1896.
50 Diary, 23 May 1895.
51 Diary, 3 October 1896.
52 Library of Congress: Whistler-Pennell 298 f 4042-3 (WMR to Joseph Pennell, 13 December 1911).
53 Peattie, p. 99 (WMR to FMLR, 1 September [1858]).
54 University of British Columbia Library, Rare Books and Special Collections, Colbeck MS. Collection, f. 1 (WMR to 'Dear Sir' [Everard Meynell?], 24 October 1912).
55 From Everard Meynell's collection of drafts and material for his article on Simeon Solomon for the *Dictionary of National Biography* for sale on the internet, 3 August 2000, abebooks.com. Now private collection.
56 Peattie, p. 99 (WMR to FMLR, 1 September [1858]).
57 Sondra J. Stang (ed.), *The Ford Madox Ford Reader* (Manchester: Carcanet, 1986), p. 138.
58 Fitzwilliam Museum, Gen. Ser. Large MS. 1700-1977 (notes by Dr Gill dictated to Maud Newman, March 1901, and appended to WMR's poem 'My Doctor').
59 Bodleian, Ms. Don e. 76 (WMR to F.G. Stephens, 14 November 1903).
60 Diary, 7 May 1902.
61 *SR*, II, 454.
62 Diary, 4 August 1901.
63 Library of Congress; Whistler-Pennell 298 f. 4039 (WMR to Joseph Pennell, 16 November 1906).
64 'Down with the Czar'. Diary, 29 January 1905.
65 Peattie, p. 671 (WMR to Sydney Carlyle Cockerell, 7 December 1911)
66 Peattie, p. 671 (WMR to Richard Curle, 20 June 1913).
67 UBC, 8-2 (WMR to LMBR, 18 March 1886).
68 Peattie, pp. 671-2 (WMR to Charles Nathan Elliot, 15 November 1914).
69 Peattie, p. 672 (WMR to Olivia Rossetti Agresti, 13 October 1918).
70 Bodleian, Ms. Don. e. 76 ('The Dogmatist', undated sonnet by WMR).
71 WMR's death certificate, 6 February 1919, signed by his doctor, W.G. Blackstone M.R.C.S., St Marylebone Registration District.
72 J.L. Paton, 'William Michael Rossetti', *Manchester Guardian*, 7 February 1919.
73 Tate Britain, Max Beerbohm's twenty-three drawings of the PRB, 1916–17, exhibited at

the Leicester Galleries September 1921 as 'Rossetti and his Friends'. Max Beerbohm, *Rossetti and his Circle* (New Haven and London: Yale University Press, 1987, reprint of first ed. 1922), pl. 11.

BIBLIOGRAPHY

The bibliography is arranged in three sections: first, principal publications by William and Lucy; secondly, a list of works cited in the text; and thirdly, some of those works which have helped me to imaginatively enter the Victorian age in which they both lived and the early twentieth century into which William, the last of the Pre-Raphaelites, survived. On the whole, but not invariably, it is a list of books rather than articles.

Part 1a
Publications by Lucy Madox Brown Rossetti

Rossetti, Lucy Madox, *Mrs. Shelley*, (London: W. H. Allen, 1890).

Rossetti, Lucy Madox, 'Ford Madox Brown', *The Magazine of Art*, 13 (1890), 289–96.

Part 1b
Principal Publications by William Michael Rossetti

Rossetti, William Michael, ed., *The Germ: Thoughts towards Nature in Poetry, Literature, and Art*, 4 issues (London: Aylott & Jones, January–April 1850).

Rossetti, William Michael, trans., *The Comedy of Dante Allighieri, Part I, The Hell* (London: Macmillan, 1865).

Rossetti, William Michael, *Swinburne's Poems and Ballads. A Criticism* (London: John Camden Hotten, 1866).

Rossetti, William Michael, 'The Stacyons of Rome', in *Political, Religious and Love Poems from the Archbishop of Canterbury's Lambeth MS., Number 306 and other Sources*, Early English Text Society, 1866.

Rossetti, William Michael, *Fine Art, Chiefly Contemporary* (London: Macmillan, 1867).

Rossetti, William Michael, and Algernon C. Swinburne, *Notes on the Royal Academy Exhibition* (London: John Camden Hotten, 1868).

Rossetti, William Michael, ed., *Poems of Walt Whitman* (London: John Camden Hotten, 1868).

Rossetti, William Michael, 'Mrs. Holmes Grey', *The Broadway Annual*, 1868, pp. 449–59.

Rossetti, William Michael, 'Italian Courtesy-Books', in *Queene Elizabethes Achademy, by Sir Humphrey Gilbert, a Booke of Precedence*, Early English Text Society, vol. 8, 1869.

Rossetti, William Michael, ed., *The Poetical Works of Henry Wadsworth Longfellow* (London: E. Moxon, 1870).

Rossetti, William Michael, ed., *The Poetical Works of Lord Byron* (London: E. Moxon, 1870).

Rossetti, William Michael, ed., *The Poetical Works of Sir Walter Scott* (London: E. Moxon, 1870).

Rossetti, William Michael, ed., *The Poetical Works of Percy Bysshe Shelley* unannotated (London: E. Moxon, 1870).

Rossetti, William Michael, ed., *The Poetical Works of Percy Bysshe Shelley*, 2 vols with notes and a memoir (London: E. Moxon, 1870).

Rossetti, William Michael, ed., *The Poetical Works of Thomas Hood* (London: E. Moxon, 1871).

Rossetti, William Michael, ed., *The Poetical Works of Robert Burns* (London: E. Moxon, 1871).

Rossetti, William Michael, ed., *The Poetical Works of John Milton* (London: E. Moxon, 1871).

Rossetti, William Michael, ed., *The Poetical Works of Thomas Campbell* (London: E. Moxon, 1871).

Rossetti, William Michael, ed., *The Poetical Works of William Wordsworth* (London: E. Moxon, 1871).

Rossetti, William Michael, ed., *American Poems* (London: E. Moxon, 1872).

Rossetti, William Michael, ed., *Humorous Poems* (London: E. Moxon, 1872).

Rossetti, William Michael, ed., *The Poetical Works of John Keats* (London: E. Moxon, 1872).

Rossetti, William Michael, ed., *The Poetical Works of Samuel T. Coleridge* (London: E. Moxon, 1872).

Rossetti, William Michael, ed., *The Poetical Works of Thomas Moore* (London: E. Moxon, 1872).

Rossetti, William Michael, ed., *The Poetical Works of William Cowper* (London: E. Moxon, 1872).

Rossetti, William Michael, ed., *The Poetical Works of Mrs. Felicia Hemans* (London: E. Moxon, 1873).

Rossetti, William Michael, ed., *The Poetical Works of Alexander Pope* (London: E. Moxon, 1873).

Rossetti, William Michael, ed., *The Poetical Works of William Blake* (London: G.Bell & Sons, Aldine Poets, 1874).

Rossetti, William Michael with F. Hueffer, eds, *The Dwale Bluth, Hebditch's Legacy, and other Literary Remains of O.M. Brown* (London: Tinsley Bros, 1876).

Rossetti, William Michael, *Lives of Famous Poets* (London: E. Moxon, 1878).

Rossetti, William Michael, ed., *The Poetical Works of Percy Bysshe Shelley*, 3 vols (London: E. Moxon, 1878).

Rossetti, William Michael, ed., *The Complete Works of Shakespeare* (London: E. Moxon, 1879).

Rossetti, William Michael, ed., *The Poetical Works of John Greenleaf Whittier* (London: E. Moxon, 1879).

Rossetti, William Michael, *Shelley's Prometheus Unbound: A Study of its meaning and personages* (London: privately printed, 1886).

Rossetti, William Michael, ed., *The Collected Works of Dante Gabriel Rossetti*, 2 vols (London: Ellis and Scrutton, 1886).

Rossetti, William Michael, ed., *The Collected Works of Dante Gabriel Rossetti* (London: Ellis and Elvey, 1886) and subsequent editions in 1891, 1898, 1900, 1904, 1908, 1911.

Rossetti, William Michael, *Life of John Keats* (London: Walter Scott, 1887).

Rossetti, William Michael, *A Memoir of Shelley*, 2nd edn (London: Richard Clay for the Shelley Society, 1886) (first published, 1870).

Rossetti, William Michael, *Dante Gabriel Rossetti as Designer and Writer* (London: Cassell, 1889).

Rossetti, William Michael, ed., *The Adonais of Shelley* (Oxford: Clarendon Press, 1891).

Rossetti, William Michael, ed., *Dante Gabriel Rossetti: His Family Letters with a Memoir*, 2 vols (London: Ellis and Elvey, 1895).

Rossetti, William Michael, ed., *The Poetical Works of James Russell Lowell* (London: E. Moxon for Ward, Lock & Bowden, 1895).

Rossetti, William Michael, ed., *New Poems by Christina Rossetti* (London: Macmillan, 1896).

Rossetti, William Michael, 'A Pre-Raphaelite Collection', *The Art Journal* (May 1896) pp. 129–34.

Rossetti, William Michael, ed., *Poems by the Late John Lucas Tupper* (London: Longmans Green, 1897).

Rossetti, William Michael, ed., *Ruskin: Rossetti: PreRaphaelitism: Papers 1854 to 1862* (London: George Allen, 1899).

Rossetti, William Michael, 'Leopardi', in *Studies in European Literature being the Taylorian Lectures 1889–1899*, (Oxford: Clarendon Press, 1900), pp. 55–91.

Rossetti, William Michael, ed., *Præraphaelite Diaries and Letters* (London: Hurst and Blackett, 1900).

Rossetti, William Michael, *Gabriele Rossetti: A Versified Autobiography* (London: Sands, 1901).

Rossetti, William Michael, ed., *The Germ…Being a Facsimile Reprint of the Literary Organ of the Pre-Raphaelite Brotherhood, Published in 1850: With an Introduction* (London: Stock, 1901).

Rossetti, William Michael, ed., *Rossetti Papers 1862–1870* (London: Sands, 1903).

Rossetti, William Michael, 'Dante Rossetti and Elizabeth Siddal', *The Burlington Magazine*, I (May 1903), 273–95.

Rossetti, William Michael and A.O. Prickard, eds, *The Adonais of Shelley* (Oxford: Clarendon Press, 1903).

Rossetti, William Michael, ed., *Poems of Christina Rossetti*, (London: Macmillan, 1904).

Rossetti, William Michael, *Bibliography of the Works of Dante Gabriel Rossetti* (London: Ellis, 1905).

Rossetti, William Michael, *Some Reminiscences*, 2 vols (London: Brown, Langham, 1906).

Rossetti, William Michael, *Democratic Sonnets*, 2 vols (London: Alston Rivers, 1907).

Rossetti, William Michael, ed., *Family Letters of Christina Rossetti* (London: Brown, Langham, 1908).

Rossetti, William Michael, *Dante and his Convito* (London: Elkin Mathews, 1910).

Rossetti, William Michael, ed., *Diary of Dr. John William Polidori 1816* (London: Elkin Mathews, 1911).

Rossetti, William Michael, unpublished *MS Diaries*; regular diaries, various years 1865–1913; travel diaries, various years 1855–96; séance diaries, 1865–8, (University of British Columbia, Rare Books and Special Collections, Angeli-Dennis Collection, also on microfilm at the Bodleian).

For William Michael Rossetti's hundreds of art reviews in the periodical press, see Roger W. Peattie's 'William Michael Rossetti's Art Notices in the periodicals, 1850–1878: An Annotated Checklist', *Victorian Periodicals Newsletter*, 8 (June 1975), 79–92. There is currently no complete list of his literary articles.

PART 2
Other Works Cited in the Text

Abbo, G., and others, *Il Terremoto del 23 Febbraio 1887 nel Dianese* (Diano Marina: Communitas Diani, 1987).

Agresti, Olivia Rossetti, *The Anecdotage of an Interpreter* (Columbia University, Rare Book and Manuscript Library, 98-2115-3, unpublished typescripts, 1958).

Allingham, William, *The Diaries*, ed. by H. Allingham and D. Radford (London: The Folio Society, 1990).

Arnold, Matthew, *Culture and Anarchy*, ed. by J. Dover Wilson (Cambridge: Cambridge University Press, 1966).

Arnold, Matthew, *Essays in Criticism*, 2nd series (London: Macmillan, 1888, reprinted 1905).

Barnes, Julian, ed. and trans., *Alphonse Daudet in the Land of Pain* (London: Jonathan Cape, 2002).

Bate, Percy H., *The English Pre-Raphaelite Painters: Their Associates and Successors* (London: G. Bell & Sons, 1899).

Beerbohm, Max, *Rossetti and his Circle* (New Haven and London: Yale University Press, 1987, reprint of first edn, 1922).

Bendiner, Kenneth, *The Art of Ford Madox Brown* (University Park, Pa.: Pennsylvania State University Press, 1998).

Benzie, William, *Dr. F.J. Furnivall* (Norman, Oklahoma: Pilgrim, 1983).

Bornand, Odette, ed., *The Diary of W.M. Rossetti 1870–1873* (Oxford: Clarendon Press, 1977).

Brake, Laurel, & Ian Small, eds, *Pater in the 1990s* (Greensboro, NC: ELT Press, 1991).

Buchanan, R.W. [Thomas Maitland], 'The Fleshly School of Poetry', *Contemporary Review*, October 1871.

Burne-Jones, Georgiana, *Memorials of Edward Burne-Jones*, 2 vols (London: Macmillan, 1904).

Chew, Shirley, ed., *Arthur Hugh Clough Selected Poems* (Manchester: Carcanet, 1987).

Clayton, Ellen, *English Female Artists*, 2 vols (London: Tinsley Brothers, 1876).

Cline, C.L., ed., *The Collected Letters of George Meredith*, 3 vols (Oxford: Clarendon Press, 1970).

Collins, John, *The Two Forgers* (Aldershot: Scolar, 1992).

Conrad, Joseph, *A Personal Record*, ed. by Zdzislaw Najder (Oxford: Oxford University Press, 1988) (first published as *Some Reminiscences*, English Review, 1908–9).

Coombs, James H., and others, eds, *A Pre-Raphaelite Friendship: The Correspondence of William Holman Hunt and John Lucas Tupper* (Ann Arbor, Mich.: UMI Research Press, 1986).

Donaldson, R.J., and L.J. Donaldson, *Essential Public Health Medicine* (Dordrecht and London: Kluwer, 1993).

Dormandy, Thomas, *The White Death: A History of Tuberculosis* (London: Hambledon, 1999).

Doughty, Oswald, and J.R. Wahl, eds, *Letters of Dante Gabriel Rossetti*, 4 vols (Oxford: Oxford University Press, 1967).

du Maurier, Daphne, ed., *The Young George du Maurier: A Selection of his Letters 1860-67* (London: Peter Davies, 1951).

Duloum, Joseph, *Les Anglais dans Les Pyrénées et les débuts du tourisme européen (1739–1896)* (Tarbes: Amis du musée pyrénéen de Lourdes, 1970).

EDEL, Leon, ed., *Letters of Henry James*, 4 vols (Cambridge, Mass.: Belknap Press of Harvard University Press, 1974–84).

FABRÉ, Michel, *Pau pas à pas* (Rohan: Horvath, 1985).

FALLOWELL, Duncan, *To Noto or London to Sicily in a Ford* (London: Dent, 1989).

FIELD, J. Osgood, *Things I shouldn't tell* (London: E. Nash & Grayson, 1924).

FINE, Elsa Honig, *Women and Art* (Prior Montclair, NJ: Allanheld & Schram, 1978).

FRASER, Robert S., ed., *Essays on the Rossettis* (Princeton: Princeton University Library Chronicle, 1972).

FREDEMAN, William E., *A Pre-Raphaelite Gazette: The Penkill Letters of Arthur Hughes to William Bell Scott and Alice Boyd, 1886–97* (Bulletin of the John Rylands Library, Manchester, vol. 49, no. 2 and vol. 50, no. 1, 1967).

FREDEMAN, William E., ed., *Correspondence of Dante Gabriel Rossetti*, 2 vols (Cambridge: D.S. Brewer, 2002).

FREDEMAN, William E., ed., *The PRB Journal. William Michael Rossetti's Diary of the Pre-Raphaelite Brotherhood 1849–1853* (Oxford: Clarendon Press, 1975).

FREDEMAN, William E., *Prelude to the Last Decade: Dante Gabriel Rossetti in the Summer of 1872* (Bulletin of the John Rylands Library, Manchester, vol. 53, nos 1 and 2, 1970 and 1971).

FREDEMAN, William E., *The Letters of Pictor Ignotus: William Bell Scott's Correspondence with Alice Boyd, 1859–1884* (Bulletin of the John Rylands Library, Manchester, vol. 58, 1975–6).

FREDEMAN, William E., *A Rossetti Cabinet* (Vancouver: The Journal of Pre-Raphaelite and Aesthetic Studies, II:2 Fall 1989; 1991, special issue).

FRISWELL, Laura Hain, *In the Sixties and Seventies: Impressions of Literary People and Others* (London: Hutchinson, 1905).

GILCHRIST, Alexander, *The Life of William Blake*, 2 vols, including 'Annotated Lists of Blake's Paintings and Drawings' by W.M. Rossetti (London: Macmillan, 1863).

GILCHRIST, Herbert Harlakenden, ed., *Anne Gilchrist: her Life and Writings* with Prefatory Notice by W.M. Rossetti (London: T. Fisher Unwin, 1887).

GOHDES, Clarence and Paull Franklin Baum, eds, *Letters of William Michael Rossetti to Anne Gilchrist* (Durham, NC: Duke University Press, 1934).

HAKE, T. Gordon, *Memoirs of Eighty Years* (London: Richard Bentley, 1892).

HARDINGE, William Money, *Troy* (Oxford: T. Shrimpton, 1876).

HARDINGE, William Money, 'A Reminiscence of Mrs. W.M. Rossetti', *The Magazine of Art*, 18, (1895), 341–6.

HARE, Augustus, *The Rivieras*, (London: George Allen, 1897).

HARRISON, Antony H., *The Letters of Christina Rossetti*, 3 vols (Charlottesville and London: University Press of Virginia, 1997, 1999 and 2000).

HASKELL, Francis and Nicholas Penny, *Taste and the Antique* (New Haven and London: Yale University Press, 1981).

HASSALL, Arthur Hill, *San Remo and the Western Riviera* (London: Longmans, Green, 1879).

HASSALL, Arthur Hill, *The Narrative of a Busy Life: An Autobiography* (London: Longmans, Green, 1893).

HAWTHORNE, Nathaniel, *The Marble Faun* (New York: Dell, 1960) (first published in the UK as *Transformation*, 1859, and as *The Marble Faun* in the USA, 1860).

HOLLAND, Merlin and Rupert Hart-Davis, eds, *The Complete Letters of Oscar Wilde* (London: Fourth Estate, 2000).

HOPKINSON, Amanda, *Julia Margaret Cameron* (London: Virago, 1986).

HORNE, Philip, *Henry James: A Life in Letters* (Harmondsworth: Allen Lane, 1999).

HORNER, Frances, *Time Remembered* (London: William Heinemann, 1933).

HUEFFER, Catherine Madox Brown, *A Retrospect* (House of Lords Record Office, Stow Hill Papers, STH/BH/2/3-6, unpublished, undated MS).

HUEFFER, Catherine Madox Brown, *Jottings* (Private collection, unpublished MS, August 1922).

HUEFFER, Ford Madox, *Ancient Lights and Certain New Reflections* (London: Chapman and Hall, 1911).

HUEFFER, Ford Madox, *Ford Madox Brown* (London: Longmans, Green, 1896).

HUEFFER, Ford Madox, 'The Younger Madox Browns: Lucy, Catherine, Oliver', *The Artist*, 19 (February 1897), 49–56.

HUNT, W. Holman, *Pre-Raphaelitism and the Pre-Raphaelite Brotherhood*, 2 vols (London: Macmillan, 1905), 2nd ed. 1913.

INGRAM, John H., *Oliver Madox Brown* (London: Elliot Stock, 1883).

IRONSIDE, Robin and John Gere, *Pre-Raphaelite Painters* (London: Phaidon, 1948).

JACKSON, John Wyse, ed., *Aristotle at Afternoon Tea: The Rare Oscar Wilde* (London: Fourth Estate, 1991).

JAMES, Henry, *The Painter's Eye*, ed. by John L. Sweeney (Wisconsin: University of Wisconsin Press, 1989).

JAMES, Henry, *The Spoils of Poynton*, ed. by David Lodge (Harmondsworth: Penguin, 1987) (first published 1897).

JERROLD, Blanchard, *The Life and Remains of Douglas Jerrold* (Boston, Mass.: Ticknor & Fields, 1859).

JOHNSON, Barry, ed., *Tea and Anarchy! The Bloomsbury Diary of Olive Garnett 1890–1893* (London: Bartletts Press, 1989).

JURLARO, Felicita, *Christina Georgina Rossetti* (London: Excalibur, 1990).

KANCEFF, Emanuele, ed., *Immagini del San Remo nel mondo* (Sanremo: Centro Interuniversitario di Ricerche sul Viaggio in Italia, 1998).

KELVIN, Norman, ed., *Collected Letters of William Morris*, 4 vols (Princeton: Princeton University Press, 1984–96).

L'ENFANT, Julie, *William Rossetti's Art Criticism: the Search for Truth in Victorian Art* (Lanham, Md: University Press of America, 1999).

LANG, Cecil Y., ed., *The Letters of Swinburne*, 6 vols (New Haven: Yale University Press, 1959–62).

LOMBARDI, Gastone, *Sanremo ai tempi del Liberty* (Sanremo: Editore Colombo, 2001).

LUDWIG, Richard M., ed., *Letters of Ford Madox Ford* (Princeton: Princeton University Press, 1965).

MACMILLAN, The Revd. Hugh, *The Riviera*, 2nd edn (London: J.S. Virtue, 1892).

MAINWARING, Marion, *Mysteries of Paris: The Quest for Morton Fullerton* (Hanover, NH: University Press of New England, 2001).

MARSH, Jan, *Dante Gabriel Rossetti: Painter and Poet* (London: Weidenfeld & Nicolson, 1999).

MARSH, Jan and Pamela Gerrish Nunn, *Pre-Raphaelite Women Artists* (London: Thames and Hudson, 1998).

MARSHALL, Mrs. Julian, *The Life and Letters of Mary Wollstonecraft Shelley*, 2 vols (London: Bentley & Son, 1889).

MASSON, Flora, *Victorians All* (London: Chambers, 1931).

MCCARTHY, Justin, *Reminiscences*, 2 vols (London: Chatto & Windus, 1899).

MERRILL, Linda, *A Pot of Paint: Aesthetics on Trial in Whistler v. Ruskin* (Washington: Smithsonian Institution Press, 1992).

MEYNELL, Viola, ed., *The Best of Friends: Further Letters to Sydney Carlyle Cockerell* (London: Rupert Hart-Davis, 1956).

MICHIE, James, trans., *The Odes of Horace* (London: Hart-Davis, 1964).

MUSA, Mark, trans., *Dante: The Divine Comedy: Vol. I: Inferno* (Harmondsworth: Penguin, 1984) (first published Indiana University Press, 1971).

NABOKOV, Vladimir, *Speak Memory* (Harmondsworth: Penguin, 1982) (first published as *Exclusive Evidence*, 1951).

NASHE, Thomas, *The Unfortunate Traveller and other works*, ed. by J.B. Steane (London: Penguin, 1985) (first published 1594).

NEWMAN, Teresa and Ray Watkinson, *Ford Madox Brown and the Pre-Raphaelite Circle* (London: Chatto & Windus, 1991).

OSBORNE, Charles Churchill, *Philip Bourke Marston* (London: Times Book Club, 1926).

OSTROWICZ, Alex., *Stranger's Guide to San Remo* (Munich: Bruckmann, 1894).

PAGEL, Walter and others, *Pulmonary Tuberculosis*, 4th edn (London: Oxford University Press, 1964).

PEATTIE, Roger W., ed., *Selected Letters of William Michael Rossetti* (University Park, Pa: Pennsylvania State University Press, 1990).

PRESTON, Kerrison, ed., *Letters from Graham Robertson* (London: Hamish Hamilton, 1953).

PUSHKIN, Alexandr, *Eugene Onegin*, trans. by Vladimir Nabokov, 4 vols (New York: Bollingen Foundation, 1964).

ROPER, William, *A Man of Singular Virtue*, ed. by A.L. Rowse (London: The Folio Society, 1980).

ROSE, Andrea, *Pre-Raphaelite Portraits* (Yeovil: Oxford Illustrated Press, 1981).

ROSSETTI, Olivia, Helen Rossetti and Arthur Rossetti, eds, *Torch; a Journal of International Socialism* (London: 1891–5) later *The Torch: A Revolutionary Journal of Anarchist-Communism* (London: F. Macdonald, 1894–5).

ROTHENSTEIN, William, *Men and Memories*, 3 vols (London: Faber & Faber, 1931–9).

RUFFINI, Giovanni, *Doctor Antonio* (Edinburgh and London: Constable, 1855).

RUFFINI, Giovanni, *Ritorno a Sanremo*, ed. by Francesco De Nicola (Genoa: De Ferrari, 1998).

SANDARS, Mary, *Life of Christina Rossetti* (London: Hutchinson, 1930).

SCHURR, Gérald and Pierre Cabanne, *Dictionnaire des Petits Maîtres de la Peinture 1820–1920* (Paris: Les éditions de l'amateur, 1996).

SCOTT, William Bell, *Autobiographical Notes*, ed. by W. Minto, 2 vols (London: Osgood, McIlvaine, 1892).

SHONFIELD, Zuzanna, *The Precariously Privileged – A Professional Family in Victorian London* (Oxford: Oxford University Press, 1987).

SONTAG, Susan, *Illness as Metaphor* (Harmondsworth: Penguin, 1983).

SONTAG, Susan, *On Photography* (Harmondsworth: Penguin, 1979).

SONTAG, Susan, *The Volcano Lover* (London: Jonathan Cape, 1992).

SOSKICE, Juliet M., *Chapters from Childhood* (London: Selwyn & Blount, 1921).

SPARKS, Edward Isaac, *The Riviera: Sketches of the Health Resorts of the North Mediterranean Coasts of France and Italy* (London: J. & A. Churchill, 1879).

STANG, Sondra J., ed., *The Ford Madox Ford Reader* (Manchester: Carcanet, 1986).

STILLMAN, W.J., *Autobiography of a Journalist* (London: Grant Richards, 1901).

STOPPARD, Tom, *The Invention of Love* (London and Boston: Faber and Faber, 1997).

SURTEES, Virginia, ed., *Diary of Ford Madox Brown* (New Haven and London: Yale University Press, 1981).

SURTEES, Virginia, ed., *The Diaries of George Price Boyce* (Norwich: Real World Publishers, 1980).

SURTEES, Virginia, *The Paintings and Drawings of Dante Gabriel Rossetti (1828–1882) A Catalogue Raisonné* (Oxford: Clarendon Press, 1971).

TAYLOR, Dr Sir Alexander, *Climates for Invalids*, 3rd edn. (London: John Churchill, 1861).

TRAUBEL, Horace, *With Walt Whitman in Camden*, 4 vols (Boston, Mass: Small, Maynard, 1906).

TREVELYAN, Raleigh, *A Pre-Raphaelite Circle* (London: Chatto & Windus, 1978).

TROXELL, Janet Camp, ed., *Three Rossettis* (Cambridge, Mass: Harvard University Press, 1937).

WEBSTER, Augusta, *Mother and Daughter: An Uncompleted Sonnet Sequence* with an introductory note by W. M. Rossetti (London: Macmillan, 1895).

WILLIS, I.C., ed., *The Letters of Vernon Lee* (privately printed, 1937).

WOOLNER, Amy, *Thomas Woolner, R.A. Sculptor and Poet His Life in Letters* (New York: E.P. Dutton, 1917).

WRIGHT, Thomas, *Life of John Payne* (London: T. Fisher Unwin, 1919).

PART 3
A Selection of Other Works Consulted

ADAMS, Francis, *Tiberius* (London: T. Fisher Unwin, 1894).

ALLEN, Vivien, *Dear Mr. Rossetti: The letters of Dante Gabriel Rossetti and Hall Caine 1878–1881* (Sheffield: Sheffield Academic Press, 2000).

ALLEN, Vivien, *Hall Caine: Portrait of a Victorian Romancer* (Sheffield: Sheffield Academic Press, 1997.

ALLOTT, Miriam, ed., *Essays on Shelley* (Liverpool: Liverpool University Press, 1982).

ALLOWAY, Lawrence, *The Venice Biennale 1895–1968* (Greenwich, Conn.: New York Graphic Society, 1968).

ANDERSON, Ronald and Anne Koval, *James McNeill Whistler: Beyond the Myth* (New York: Carroll & Graf, 1995).

ANGELI, Helen Rossetti, *Dante Gabriel Rossetti: His Friends and Enemies* (London: Hamish Hamilton, 1949).

ANGELI, Helen Rossetti, *Pre-Raphaelite Twilight: the story of Charles A. Howell* (London: Richards Press, 1954).

ANSTRUTHER, Ian, *Coventry Patmore's Angel* (London: Haggerston Press, 1992).

ARSENAU, Mary, Antony H. Harrison and Lorraine Janzen Kooistra, eds, *The Culture of Christina Rossetti* (Athens, Ohio: Ohio University Press, 1999).

ATKINSON, J.B., and others, *English Painters of the Present Day* (London: Seeley, Jackson & Co., 1871).

BARTRAM, Michael, *The Pre-Raphaelite Camera* (London: Weidenfeld & Nicolson, 1985).

BATTISCOMBE, Georgina, *Christina Rossetti: A Divided Life* (New York: Holt, Rhinehart and Winston, 1981).

BECKSON, Karl, *London in the 1890s* (New York: W.W. Norton, 1992).

BELL, Mackenzie, *Christina Rossetti* (London: Hurst and Blackett, 1898).

BENNETT, Mary, *Artists of the Pre-Raphaelite Circle, The First Generation* (London: Lund Humphries, for the National Museums and Galleries on Merseyside, 1988).

BENSON, A.C., *Memories and Friends* (London: John Murray, 1924).

BENSON, A.C., *Rossetti* (London: Macmillan, 1926) (first published 1904).

BISHOP, Franklin, *Polidori: a life of Dr. John Polidori* (Chislehurst: Gothic Society, 1991).

BLIND, Mathilde, *George Eliot* (London: W.H. Allen, 1883).

BLIND, Mathilde, *Madame Roland* (Boston, Mass: Roberts Brothers, 1886).

BLIND, Mathilde, trans., *The Journal of Marie Bashkirtseff* (London: Virago, 1985).

BRIGGS, Asa, *Victorian Things* (Harmondsworth: Penguin, 1990).

BROUGHTON, Trev Lynn, *Men of Letters, Writing Lives* (London: Routledge, 1999).

BRYDEN, Inge, *The Pre-Raphaelites: Writings & Sources*, 4 vols (London: Routledge, 1998).

BRYSON, John, in association with Janet Camp Troxell, eds, *D.G. Rossetti and Jane Morris, Their Correspondence* (Oxford: Clarendon Press, 1976).

CAINE, Hall, *My Story* (London: William Heinemann, 1908).

CAINE, Hall, *Recollections of Rossetti* (London: Cassell, 1928).

CALLEN, Anthea, *Angel in the Studio: Women in the arts and crafts movement, 1870–1914* (London: Astragal, 1979).

CASTERAS, Susan P., and Linda H. Peterson, *A Struggle for Fame: Victorian Women Artists and Authors* (New Haven: Yale Center for British Art, 1994).

CASTERAS, Susan P., *English Pre-Raphaelitism and its Reception in America in the Nineteenth Century* (Rutherford, NJ: Fairleigh Dickinson University Press, 1990).

CASTERAS, Susan, and Colleen Denney, *The Grosvenor Gallery – A Palace of Art in Victorian England* (New Haven: Yale University Press, 1996).

CHADWICK, Whitney, *Women, Art, and Society* (London: Thames & Hudson, 1990).

CHAMPNEYS, Basil, *Memoirs and Correspondence of Coventry Patmore*, 2 vols (London: George Bell, 1900).

CHERRY, Deborah, *Painting Women: Victorian Women Artists* (Rochdale: Rochdale Art Gallery, 1987).

CHESSMAN, Harriet Scott, *Lydia Cassatt Reading the Morning Paper* (New York: The Permanent Press/Seven Stories Press, 2001).

CHRISTENSEN, Allen Conrad, *A European Version of Victorian Fiction: The Novels of Giovanni Ruffini* (Atlanta, Ga: Rodopi Amsterdam, 1996).

CHRISTIANSEN, Rupert, *The Voice of Victorian Sex: Arthur H Clough 1819–1861* (London: Short Books, 2001).

CLIFFORD, David and Laurence Roussillon, eds, *Outsiders Looking In: The Rossettis, Then and Now* (London: Anthem Press, 2003).

CLINE, C.L., ed., *The Owl and the Rossettis* (University Park, Pa: Pennsylvania State University Press, 1978).

CONWAY, Moncure Daniel, *Travels in South Kensington* (New York: Harper & Brothers, 1882).

COX, Julian and Colin Ford, *Julia Margaret Cameron: the complete photographs* (London: Thames & Hudson, 2003).

CRANE, David, *Lord Byron's Jackal: A Life of Edward John Trelawny* (London: Harper Collins, 1998).

DAKERS, Caroline, *The Holland Park Circle* (New Haven and London: Yale University Press, 1999).

DALZIEL, George, and Edward Dalziel, *The Brothers Dalziel* (London: Methuen, 1901).

DICKASON, David Howard, *The Daring Young Men* (Bloomington, Ind: Indiana University Press, 1953).

DOBBS, Brian, and Judy Dobbs, *Dante Gabriel Rossetti: An Alien Victorian* (London: MacDonald and Jane's, 1977).

DORFMAN, Deborah, *Blake in the Nineteenth Century* (New Haven: Yale University Press, 1969).

DOUGHTY, Oswald, *A Victorian Romantic* (Oxford: Oxford University Press, 1968, reprint of the 2nd edn, 1960, first published 1949).

DOUGLAS, James, *Theodore Watts-Dunton: Poet, Novelist, Critic* (London: Hodder & Stoughton, 1904).

DUNBAR, Clement, *A Bibliography for Shelley Studies 1823–1950* (Folkestone: Dawson, 1976).

DUNN, Henry Treffry, *Recollections of Dante Gabriel Rossetti and His Circle* (London: Elkin Matthews, 1904).

ELLIOTT, David B., *Charles Fairfax Murray* (Lewes: The Book Guild, 2000).

ELZEA, Betty, *Frederick Sandys: A Catalogue Raisonné* (Woodbridge: Antique Collectors' Club, in association with Norfolk Museums Archaeology Service, 2001).

ELZEA, Rowland, ed., *The Correspondence Between Samuel Bancroft, Jr. and Charles Fairfax Murray 1892–1916*, Delaware Art Museum Occasional Paper Number 2 (February 1980).

FALCHI, Rodolfo and Valerie Wadsworth, *Arti Figurativi tra l'800 e il '900 nel Ponente Ligure* (Poggibonsi: Lalli Editore, in association with the Comune di Sanremo, 2000).

FAXON, Alicia Craig, *Dante Gabriel Rossetti* (London: Phaidon, 1994) (first published 1989).

FAWCETT, Trevor, and Clive Phillpot, *The Art Press: Two Centuries of Art Magazines* (London: Victoria & Albert Museum, 1976).

FERBER, Linda S., and William H. Gerdts, *The New Path: Ruskin and the American Pre-Raphaelites* (New York: Brooklyn Museum, 1985).

FITZGERALD, Penelope, *Edward Burne-Jones* (London: Michael Joseph, 1975).

FLANDERS, Judith, *A Circle of Sisters* (London: Viking, 2001).

FLEMING, G.H., *James Abbott McNeil Whistler: A Life* (Moreton-in-Marsh: Windrush, 1991).

FLEMING, G.H., *John Everett Millais* (London: Constable, 1998).

FLEMING, G.H., *Rossetti & the Pre-Raphaelite Brotherhood* (London: Hart-Davis, 1967).

FOLEY, Jean Duncan, *In Quarantine: A History of Sydney's Quarantine Station 1828-1984* (Kenthurst, NSW: Kangaroo Press, 1995).

FREDEMAN, William E., *Pre-Raphaelitism: A Bibliocritical Study* (Cambridge, Mass: Harvard University Press, 1965).

FREEMAN, Michael, *Railways and the Victorian Imagination* (New Haven and London: Yale University Press, 1999).

FUNNELL, Peter and others, *Millais: Portraits* (London: National Portrait Gallery, 1999).

GARNETT, R.S., *Letters about Shelley* (London: Hodder and Stoughton, 1917).

GERE, Charlotte, and Geoffrey C. Munn, *Pre-Raphaelite to Arts and Crafts Jewellery* (Woodbridge: The Antique Collectors' Club, 1996).

GERE, Charlotte, with Lesley Hoskins, *The House Beautiful: Oscar Wilde and the Aesthetic Interior* (London: Lund Humphries, in association with the Geffrye Museum, 2000).

GERE, J.A., *Pre-Raphaelite Drawings in the British Museum* (London: British Museum Press, 1994).

Goldman, Emma, *Anarchism and other essays* (New York: Dover, 1969).

GOLDMAN, Paul, *Victorian Illustration* (Aldershot: Scolar, 1996).

GOLDRING, Douglas, *South Lodge* (London: Constable, 1943).

GOLDRING, Douglas, *The Last Pre-Raphaelite* (London: Macdonald, 1948).

GOODWIN, Albert, *The Diary of Albert Goodwin* (privately printed, 1934).

GROSS, John, *The Rise and Fall of the Man of Letters* (Harmondsworth: Penguin, 1991).

GRYLLS, Rosalie Glynn, *Portrait of Rossetti* (Carbondale, Ill: Southern Illinois University Press, 1964).

HAKE, Thomas, and Arthur Compton-Rickett, eds, *The Life and Letters of Theodore Watts-Dunton* (London: T.C. & E.C. Jack, 1916).

HAMERTON, Philip Gilbert, *An Autobiography 1834–1858, and a Memoir by his wife 1858–1894* (London: Seeley, 1897).

HAMILTON, Walter, *The Aesthetic Movement in England* (London: Beeves & Turner, 1882).

HARDING, Ellen, ed., *Re-framing the Pre-Raphaelites* (Aldershot: Scolar, 1996).

HARDWICK, Joan, *An Immodest Violet* (London: André Deutsch, 1990).

HARES-STRYKER, Carolyn, *An Anthology of Pre-Raphaelite Writings* (Sheffield: Sheffield Academic Press, 1997).

HEARNSHAW, F.J.C., *The Centenary History of King's College, London* (London: Harrap, 1929).

HEILBRUN, Carolyn G., *The Garnett Family* (London: George Allen & Unwin, 1961).

HENDERSON, Philip, *Swinburne: Portrait of a Poet* (New York: Macmillan, 1974).

HEWISON, Robert, Ian Warrell and Stephen Wildman, *Ruskin, Turner and the Pre-Raphaelites* (London: Tate Gallery, 2000).

HILTON, Tim, *John Ruskin: The Early Years* (New Haven and London: Yale University Press, 1985).

HILTON, Tim, *John Ruskin: The Later Years* (New Haven and London: Yale University Press, 2000).

HIRSCH, Pam, *Barbara Leigh Smith Bodichon* (London: Chatto & Windus, 1998).

HOLMAN-HUNT, Diana, *My Grandfather, His Wives and Loves* (London: Hamish Hamilton, 1969).

HOLMAN-HUNT, Diana, *My Grandmothers and I* (London: Hamish Hamilton, 1960).

HOLMES, Richard, *Shelley: The Pursuit* (Harmondsworth: Penguin, 1987).

HOWITT, Mary, *An Autobiography*, ed. by Margaret Howitt (London: Isbister, 1891).

HUEFFER, Ford Madox, *The Benefactor: A Tale of a small circle* (London: Brown, Langham, 1905).

HUNT, John Dixon, *The Wider Sea: A Life of John Ruskin* (New York: Viking, 1982).

IONIDES, Luke, *Memories* (Ludlow: Dog Rose Press, 1996, facsimile reprint).

JOHNSON, Barry C., ed., *Olive & Stepniak: The Bloomsbury Diary of Olive Garnett 1893-1895* (Birmingham: Bartletts Press, 1993).

JONES, Kathleen, *Learning not to be first: The life of Christina Rossetti* (Oxford: Oxford University Press, 1992).

JONES, Mervyn, *The Amazing Victorian – A life of George Meredith* (London: Constable, 1999).

JOPLING, Louise, *Twenty Years of my Life 1867–1889* (London: John Lane, 1925).

JUDD, Alan, *Ford Madox Ford* (Cambridge, Mass.: Harvard University Press, 1991).

KIELL, Norman, ed., *Blood Brothers* (New York: International Universities Press, 1983).

KITCHEN, Paddy, *The Golden Veil* (London: Hamish Hamilton, 1981).

KNIGHT, Joseph, *Life of Dante Gabriel Rossetti* (London: Walter Scott, 1887).

LAMBOURNE, Lionel, *The Aesthetic Movement* (London: Phaidon, 1996).

LARG, David, *Trial by Virgins* (London: Peter Davies, 1933).

LAVER, James, *Whistler* (London: Faber & Faber, 1930).

LEONARD, Tom, *Places of the Mind* (London: Jonathan Cape, 1993).

LUKITSH, Joanne, *Julia Margaret Cameron* (Paris: Phaidon, 2001).

MAAS, Jeremy, *Gambart* (London: Barrie & Jenkins, 1975).

MAAS, Jeremy, *Victorian Painters* (London: Barrie & Jenkins, 1970).

MAAS, Jeremy, *The Victorian Art World in Photographs* (London: Barrie & Jenkins, 1984).

MACCARTHY, Fiona, *William Morris: a life for our time* (London: Faber and Faber, 1994).

MACHT, David I. and Nellie L. Gessford, 'The unfortunate drug experiences of Dante Gabriel Rossetti', *The Bulletin of the Institute of the History of Medicine* (1938), 34–60.

MACLEOD, Dianne Sachko, *Art and the Victorian Middle-Class – Money and the making of cultural identity* (Cambridge: Cambridge University Press, 1996).

MARILLIER, Henry Currie, *Dante Gabriel Rossetti: An Illustrated Memorial of his Art and Life* (London: George Bell, 1899).

MARQUESS, William Henry, *Lives of the Poet – John Keats* (University Park, Pa: The Pennsylvania State University Press, 1985).

MARSDEN, Gordon, ed., *Victorian Values*, 2nd edn (London: Longman, 1998).

MARSH, Jan and Pamela Gerrish Nunn, *Women Artists and the Pre-Raphaelite Movement* (London: Virago, 1989).

MARSH, Jan, *Christina Rossetti* (London: Jonathan Cape, 1994).

MARSH, Jan, *Pre-Raphaelite Sisterhood* (London: Quartet, 1992).

MASON, Michael, *The Making of Victorian Sexuality* (Oxford: Oxford University Press, 1994).

MAYNARD, Mary and June Purvis, eds, *Researching Women's Lives from a Feminist Perspective* (London: Taylor & Francis, 1994).

McGANN, Jerome, *Rossetti and the Game that must be Lost* (New Haven and London: Yale University Press, 2000).

MEREDITH, Isabel (pseudonym of Olive and Helen Rossetti), *A Girl Among the Anarchists* (Lincoln, Neb.: University of Nebraska Press, 1992), (first published, London: Duckworth, 1903).

MILES, Frank and Graeme Cranch, *History of King's College School*, (London: the school, 1979).

MILLAIS, J.G., *The Life and Letters of Sir John Everett Millais*, 2 vols (London: Methuen, 1899).

MILLS, Ernestine, *The Life and Letters of Frederic Shields* (London: Longmans, Green, 1912).

MIZENER, Arthur, *The Saddest Story: A Biography of Ford Madox Ford* (New York: Carroll & Graf, 1985).

NEAD, Lynda, *Victorian Babylon* (New Haven and London: Yale University Press, 2000).

NELSON, Michael, *Queen Victoria and the Discovery of the Riviera* (London: I.B. Tauris, 2001).

NOAKES, Vivien, ed., *Edward Lear, Selected Letters* (Oxford: Clarendon Press, 1988).

NOAKES, Vivien, *Edward Lear: The life of a Wanderer* (London: Collins, 1968).

NOWELL-SMITH, Simon, ed., *Letters to Macmillan* (London: Macmillan, 1967).

NUNN, Pamela Gerrish, *Victorian Women Artists* (London: Women's Press, 1987).

OLIVA, Gianni, *I Rossetti tra Italia e Inghilterra* (Rome: Bulzoni, 1984).

OLIVER, H., *The International Anarchist Movement in Late Victorian London* (London: Croom Helm, 1983).

OPPENHEIM, Janet, *The Other World, spiritualism and psychical research in England, 1850–1914* (Cambridge: Cambridge University Press, 1985).

OPPENHEIM, Janet, *"Shattered Nerves": Doctors, Patients and Depression in Victorian England* (New York and Oxford: Oxford University Press, 1991).

ORIGO, Iris, *A Need to Testify* (New York: Books & Co./Helen Marx Books, 2001, first published 1984).

ORMOND, Leonée, *George du Maurier* (London: Routledge, 1969).

ORMOND, Richard, 'Portraits to Australia: a group of Pre-Raphaelite drawings', *Apollo*, vol 85 (January 1967), 25–7.

ORR, Clarissa Campbell, ed., *Women in the Victorian Art World* (Manchester: Manchester University Press, 1995).

OVENDEN, Graham, *Pre-Raphaelite Photography* (London: Academy Editions, 1972).

PACKER, Lona Mosk, *Christina Rossetti* (Cambridge: Cambridge University Press, 1963).

PACKER, Lona Mosk, ed., *The Rossetti-Macmillan Letters* (Berkeley, Ca.: University of California Press, 1963).

PANTER-DOWNES, Mollie, *At the Pines* (London: Hamish Hamilton, 1971).

PARRIS, Leslie, ed., *Pre-Raphaelite Papers* (London: Tate Gallery, 1984).

PARRIS, Leslie, ed., *The Pre-Raphaelites* (London: Tate Gallery, 1984).

PEARCE, Lynn, *Woman/ Image/ Text* (Toronto: University of Toronto Press, 1991).

PEATTIE, Roger W., *William Michael Rossetti as Critic and Editor* (unpublished doctoral thesis, University College, London, 1966).

PEDRICK, Gale, *No Peacocks Allowed* (Carbondale, Ill: Southern Illinois University Press, 1970).

PEMBLE, John, *The Mediterranean Passion* (Oxford: Oxford University Press, 1987).

PERRY, Gill and Colin Cunningham, eds, *Academies, Museums and Canons of Art* (New Haven and London: Yale University Press, in association with the Open University, 1999).

POINTON, Marcia, ed., *Pre-Raphaelites re-viewed* (Manchester: Manchester University Press, 1989).

PROCTOR, Ellen A., *A Brief Memoir of Christina Rossetti* with a preface by W.M. Rossetti (London: S.P.C.K., 1895).

PROPAS, Sharon Weiss, *William Michael Rossetti and the Pre-Raphaelite Brotherhood* (unpublished doctoral dissertation, University of California, Los Angeles, 1982).

RAWLINGS, Peter, ed., *Henry James: Essays on Art and Drama* (Aldershot: Scolar, 1996).

READ, Benedict and Joanna Barnes, eds, *Pre-Raphaelite Sculpture* (London: Lund Humphries, in association with The Henry Moore Foundation, 1991).

READ, Benedict, *Victorian Sculpture* (New Haven and London: Yale University Press, 1982).

REID, Forrest, *Illustrators of the Sixties* (London: Faber & Gwyer, 1928).

ROBERTS, Leonard, *Arthur Hughes: A Catalogue Raisonné* (Woodbridge: Antique Collectors' Club, 1997).

ROBERTSON, W. Graham, *Time Was* (London: Hamish Hamilton, 1931).

ROSE, Andrea, *The Pre-Raphaelites* (London: Phaidon, 1997) (first published 1977).

ROSE, Andrea, ed., *The Germ: The Literary Magazine of the Pre-Raphaelites* (Oxford: Ashmolean Museum, 1992, reprint of the facsimile edition of 1901 which reproduced first edition of 1850).

ROSSETTI, Maria Francesca, *A Shadow of Dante* (London: Rivingtons, 1871).

ROTA, Bertram, *Books from the Libraries of Christina, Dante Gabriel and William Michael Rossetti*, Catalogue No. 180 (London: Bertram Rota, 1973).

ROTHMAN, Sheila M., *Living in the Shadow of Death* (New York: Basic Books, 1994).

ROWLEY, Charles, *Fifty Years of Work without Wages* (London: Hodder & Stoughton, 1912).

RUBINSTEIN, David, *Before the Suffragettes: Women's Emancipation in the 1890s*, (Brighton: Harvester, 1986).

RUSKIN, John, *The Lamp of Beauty*, ed. by Joan Evans (Oxford: Phaidon, 1959).

SALQUAIN, Philippe, *Autrefois Biarritz* (Biarritz: Atlantica, 2000).

SALT, H.S., *The Life of James Thomson* (New York: Kennikat, 1972).

SAUNDERS, Max, *Ford Madox Ford: A Dual Life*, 2 vols (Oxford: Oxford University Press, 1996).

SCOTT, William Bell, *A Poet's Harvest Home*, 2nd edn (London: Elkin Mathews and John Lane, 1893).

SEYMOUR, Miranda, *Mary Shelley* (London: John Murray, 2000).

SHARP, William, *Dante Gabriel Rossetti* (London: Macmillan, 1882).

SHERRY, Norman, *Conrad's Western World* (Cambridge: Cambridge University Press, 1971).

SITWELL, Edith, *English Women* (London: William Collins, 1932).

SMITH, Alison, ed., *Exposed: The Victorian Nude* (London: Tate Publishing, 2001).

SPILLANE, J., *Medical Travellers* (Oxford: Oxford University Press, 1984).

STALEY, Allen, *The Pre-Raphaelite Landscape* (New Haven and London: Yale University Press, 2001).

STORR, Anthony, *The Dynamics of Creation* (Harmondsworth: Penguin, 1972).

STRATTON, Mary Chenoweth, ed., *The Rossettis: Brothers and Brotherhood* (Lewisbury, Pa.: Press of Appletree Alley, 1996).

STURGIS, Matthew, *Passionate Attitudes* (London: Macmillan, 1995).

SURIANO, Gregory R., *The Pre-Raphaelite Illustrators* (New Castle, Del: Oak Knoll Press; London: The British Library, 2000).

SURTEES, Virginia, ed., *Sublime & Instructive* (London: Michael Joseph, 1972).

SURTEES, Virginia, ed., *Reflections of a Friendship* (London: George, Allen & Unwin, 1979).

SURTEES, Virginia, *Rossetti's Portraits of Elizabeth Siddal* (Oxford: Ashmolean Museum, University of Oxford, 1991).

SYMONS, Arthur, ed., *The Poetical Works of Mathilde Blind* (London: T. Fisher Unwin, 1900).

TASKER, Meg, *Struggle and Storm: The Life and Death of Francis Adams* (Carlton South: Melbourne University Press, 2001).

TAYLOR, Ina, *Victorian Sisters* (London: Weidenfeld & Nicolson, 1987).

THALE, Jerome, 'The Third Rossetti', *Western Humanities Review*, 10 (Summer 1956), 277–84.

THIRLWELL, Angela, ed., *The Pre-Raphaelites and their World* (London: The Folio Society, 1995).

THOMAS, Frances, *Christina Rossetti* (London: Virago, 1994).

TINDALL, Gillian, *The Fields Beneath* (London: Maurice Temple Smith, 1977).

TODD, William B., ed., *Thomas J. Wise – Centenary Studies* (Austin: University of Texas Press, 1959).

TREUHERZ, Julian, *Victorian Painting* (London: Thames and Hudson, 1993).

TROLLOPE, Anthony, *The Three Clerks* (London: Oxford University Press, 1959) (first published 1858).

TROXELL, Janet Camp, *Three Rossettis* (Cambridge, Mass.: Harvard University Press, 1937).

TRYPHONOPOULOS, Demetres P., and Leon Surette, *"I Cease Not to Yowl", Ezra Pound's Letters to Olivia Rossetti Agresti* (Urbana, Ill.: University of Illinois Press, 1998).

TUCOO-CHALA, Pierre, *Pau Ville Anglaise* (Pau: Librairie des Pyrénées et de Gascogne, 1999).

TYNAN, Katherine, *Twenty-five Years Reminiscences* (London: Smith, Elder, 1913).

TYNDALE, Walter, *An Artist in the Riviera* (London: Hutchinson, 1916).

VASSALLO, Peter, ed., *Journal of Anglo-Italian Studies*, Volume 6 (Malta: Institute of Anglo-Italian Studies, 2001).

VICINUS, Martha, ed., *Suffer and Be Still* (Bloomington, Ind.: Indiana University Press, 1973).

VINCENT, E. R., *Gabriele Rossetti in England* (Oxford: Clarendon Press, 1932).

VRETTOS, Athena, *Somatic Fictions: Imagining Illness in Victorian Culture* (Stanford: Stanford University Press, 1995).

WALLER, R.D., *The Rossetti Family 1824–1854* (Manchester: Manchester University Press, 1932).

WARNER, Malcolm, *The Victorians: British Painting 1837–1901* (Washington: National Gallery of Art, 1997).

WATKINSON, Raymond, *Pre-Raphaelite Art and Design* (London: Trefoil, 1970).

WATKINSON, Ray, 'A Meeting with Mr. Rossetti', *Journal of Pre-Raphaelite Studies*, vol. 4, no. 1 (November 1983), 136–9.

WATTS, M.S., *George Frederic Watts: the annals of an artist's life*, 2 vols (London, Macmillan, 1912).

WATSON, Margaretta Frederick, *Collecting the Pre-Raphaelites: the Anglo-American Enchantment* (Aldershot: Ashgate, 1997).

WATTS-DUNTON, Clara, *The Home Life of Swinburne* (London: A.M. Philpot, 1922).

WATTS-DUNTON, Theodore, *Old Familiar Faces* (London: Herbert Jenkins, 1916).

WAUGH, Evelyn, *Rossetti* (London: Methuen, 1991) (first published 1928).

WEINTRAUB, Stanley, *Four Rossettis* (London: W.H. Allen, 1978).

WELLAND, D.S.R., *The Pre-Raphaelites in Literature and Art* (London: George G. Harrap, 1953).

WICHMANN, Siegfried, *Japonisme: The Japanese influence on Western Art since 1858* (London: Thames & Hudson, 1981).

WILDMAN, Stephen, *Visions of Love and Life* (Alexandria, Va: Art Services International, 1995).

WILSON, A.N., *The Victorians* (London: Hutchinson, 2002).

WILTON, Andrew and Robert Upstone, *The Age of Rossetti, Burne-Jones and Watts* (London: Tate Gallery, 1997).

WINWAR, Frances, *Poor Splendid Wings* (Boston, Mass: Little, Brown, 1933).

WOOD, Christopher, *The Pre-Raphaelites* (London: Weidenfeld & Nicolson, 1981).

WOOD, Esther, *Dante Gabriel Rossetti and the Pre-Raphaelite Movement* (London: Sampson Low, Marston, 1894).

YELDHAM, Charlotte, *Women Artists in the Nineteenth Century* (New York: Garland, 1984).

PHOTOGRAPHIC ACKNOWLEDGEMENTS

While every effort has been made to trace copyright holders of visual material, any further information would be welcomed. In most cases the illustrations have been made from photographs or transparencies provided by the owners or custodians of the works. Those for which further credit is due are:

Cliff Guttridge: p. ii, 8, 9, 11, 15, 19, 20, 29, 30, 31, 34, 37, 40, 41, 44, 45, 46, 47, 50, 52, 63, 64, 66, 71, 76, 77, 78, 82, 85, 88, 89, 90, 98, 99, 100, 106, 108, 111, 112, 113, 115, 117; Rodolfo Falchi: 1, 118, 121, 122; Leonard Roberts: 10, 38, 48, 49, 53, 79, 105; Prudence Cuming Associates: 18, 22, 23, 28, 74, 75, 80, 87, 107, 116; David Tatnall: 55; Anna de Soissons: 58, 59, 60, 61, 93, 94; Photographic Survey, Courtauld Institute of Art: 70; Jean Christophe Poumeyrol: 120; Estate of Max Beerbohm; reprinted by permission of London Management: 129, 130.